CW01080645

Keystone Environmental Problems

Complete dependency of resulting environmental problems on causative environmental problem

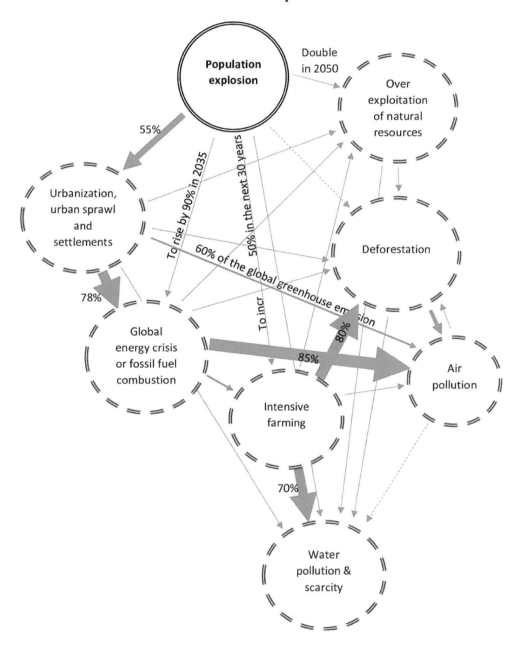

S. Sivaramanan

i

Title	: Keystone Environmental Problems
ISBN	: 9798363021718
First edition	: 2022
Author	: Dr. Sivakumaran Sivaramanan
Contact	: sivaramanansr@gmail.com
Web site	: envo.yolasite.com

Keystone Environmental Problems

Complete dependency of result-environmental-problems on cause-environmental problem

Sivakumaran Sivaramanan

Contents

viii

x

List of Figures

Prolusion

It has been showed that all manmade environmental problems are interconnected as cause and effect in 'The Nexus of Environmental Problems' (previously published book by the author). And, here the keystone environmental problems are identified based on the following criteria, *when mitigating a man-made environmental problem, if it results in the permanent disappearance of one or more man-made environmental problems, then that mitigated problem can be considered as keystone environmental problem.* For instance, Air pollution causes acid rain, and acid rain is caused only by air pollution, in this case air pollution is a keystone environmental problem because when SO_x and NO_x air pollution is mitigated, then the acid rain problem gets disappear. However, if more than one environmental problem causes an environmental problem, then **none** of the causative environmental problems can be considered the keystone. For instance, biodiversity loss is caused by land degradation and competition with invasive species. Here, land degradation is not a keystone environmental problem because even if land degradation is mitigated, competition impact from invasive species continues to fuel biodiversity loss.

Based on the aforesaid scenario eight keystone environmental problems were identified such as population explosion, air pollution, deforestation, overexploitation of natural resources, global energy crisis, intensive farming, water pollution-water scarcity, and urbanization (industrialization)-urban sprawl.

The study was conducted on 40 identified environmental problems, among which above given eight issues were isolated based on the aforesaid criteria. At the climax, the path way of the keystone issues was drawn based on percentile values. *Qualitative content analysis methodology* was used in the study. Among 258 links between 40 environmental issues (as cause-effect), links establishing keystone issue were extracted and depicted as concept flowcharts. Finally, solutions for the keystone environmental problems were given from sustainable to regenerative solutions. In addition, unsustainable solutions also provided with valid reasons.

To sum up, the study found eight keystone environmental problems. When designing solutions most relevant or suitable methods should be followed, otherwise, they would end up in a disaster or lead to succession of environmental problems. The final chapter also showed how the environmental conflicts or wars originated from keystone environmental issues with the support of flowcharts. Authors believe the findings in this book will establish a solid idea on handling environmental issues in a most aristocratic manner.

Acknowledgement

I dedicate this book to my parents and my sister who share lot of my responsibilities at home. Their patients and forbearance have been instrumental and invaluable in my years of research work and career.

Similar to my previous book "Nexus of Environmental problems," which is first part of my PhD thesis, this one is the second part of that. As such, I would like to thank my supervisor, Sarath Kotagama, to whom I owe a great debt of gratitude for his patience and 'wise stewardship'. In particular I wish to thank him for his excellent supervision sessions. I also thank all my colleagues at Environmental Impact Assessment Unit of Central Environmental Authority, Battaramulla, Sri Lanka for their support.

1. Identifying key environmental problems

1.1 Background

All man-made environmental problems are interconnected as cause-and-effect in a hypothetical situation, where human adaptability factors such as economic, social, political, health, genetics, evolution, and behavioural factors are absent.

Keystone environmental problems were identified from the concept map (figure 1.1) based on the criteria given by the following approach. *When mitigating a man-made environmental problem, if it results in the permanent disappearance of one or more man-made environmental problems, then that mitigated problem can be considered as keystone environmental problem.*

E.g., 1: Air pollution causes global warming, ocean acidification, acid rain, ozone depletion, respiratory diseases, etc. Mitigating air pollution would stop all the resulted environmental issues. Thus, air pollution is a keystone environmental problem.

E.g., 2: Water pollution (by agrochemicals and urban or industrial effluents with nitrate and phosphate) causes cultural eutrophication. Mitigation of water pollution (by nutrient loading) would stop cultural eutrophication. Thus, water pollution is a keystone environmental problem.

However, when an environmental problem is caused by more than one man-made environmental problem then their causative environmental problems **cannot** be considered as the keystone links.

E.g.: Biodiversity loss is caused by land degradation and competition with invasive species. Here, land degradation is not a keystone environmental problem because even if land degradation is mitigated, competition impact from invasive species continues to fuel biodiversity loss.

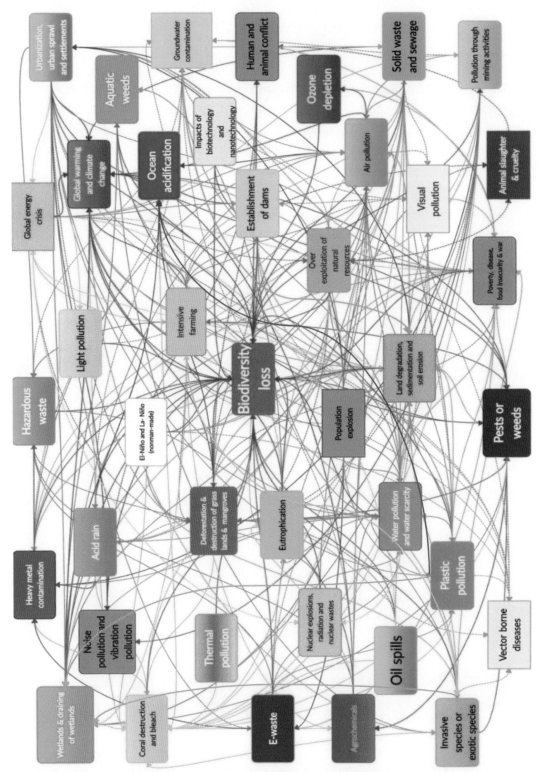

Figure 1.1 Concept map of 40 environmental problems with 258 links

The study was conducted using *qualitative content analysis methodology* (figure 1.2).

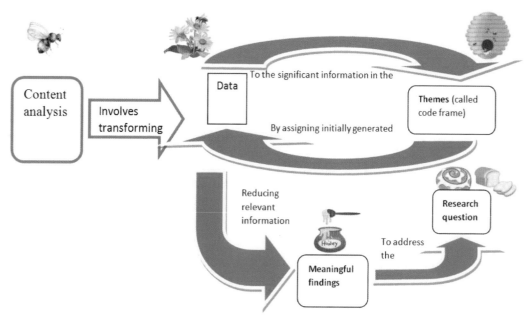

Figure 1.2 Qualitative content analysis methodology

Adapted from (Adu, 2017)

Study identified eight keystone *man-made environmental issues* (highlighted) from our funnelled and selected environmental issues such as solving air pollution and deforestation could lead to the end of several resulted environmental issues. **Air pollution** directly causes climate change & global warming, ocean acidification, acid rain, ozone depletion, respiratory diseases, biodiversity loss, deforestation (low-level ozone affects the trees and acid rain), and visual pollution (smog). Also, through climate change and global warming (direct effect) it indirectly causes draining of wetlands, coral destruction, desertification, sedimentation and land degradation, vector-borne diseases, invasive or exotic species, and water pollution-water scarcity, via water pollution it causes eutrophication, via eutrophication it causes aquatic weeds. Furthermore, via diseases and poverty it indirectly causes overexploitation of natural resources, animal slaughtering, and cruelty and intensive farming, via overexploitation of natural resources it causes groundwater contamination and pollution through mining activities, via pollution through mining activities it causes noise and vibration pollution, via intensive farming it causes solid waste and sewage, agrochemicals, the establishment of dams, and hazardous waste, via solid waste and sewage it causes heavy metal contamination. In addition to deforestation, it indirectly causes human-animal conflict.

Similarly, **deforestation** is linked to biodiversity loss, human & animal conflict, desertification global warming & climate change, ocean acidification, and coral destruction (loss of mangroves affect the corals). The removal of all kinds of air pollution puts an end to man-made global warming (almost), ocean acidification (almost), acid rain (totally), ozone depletion (totally), visual pollution (totally end the smog), and respiratory illness (almost). Similarly, removal of deforestation puts an end to the human and animal conflict, global warming and climate change (almost), ocean acidification (almost), desertification (to an extent), and biodiversity loss (to an extent). Thus, Air pollution and deforestation are keystone links. In addition, **the population explosion** is the precursor and a keystone link. Solutions to more than half of the environmental problems could be found when the human population is reduced. The increasing population causes overexploitation of natural resources, deforestation, urbanization-urban sprawl-settlements, solid waste and sewage, the establishment of dams, intensive farming, global energy crisis, and burning of fossil fuels, plastic waste, e-waste, and animal slaughter and cruelty. When the human population is reduced, natural resources is sustained, and problems related to deforestation, urban sprawl, solid waste, dams, intensive farming, energy crisis and fossil fuel burning, plastic and e-waste generation, animal slaughtering, and cruelty all come to an end, along with, indirectly linked problems such as biodiversity loss due to intensive farming and deforestation is also reduced to a great extent.

Similarly, **overexploitation of natural resources** is a keystone link, because it causes biodiversity loss (to a great extent), deforestation, land degradation, coral destruction, wetlands or draining of wetlands, animal slaughter & cruelty, groundwater contamination, water pollution, and scarcity, pollution through mining activities. And the problem varies based on the type of resource being exploited. When the resource depletion comes to an end, problems such as biodiversity loss (almost) come to an end. Similarly, deforestation, land degradation, coral destruction, wetlands or draining of wetlands, animal slaughtering & cruelty, groundwater contamination, water pollution and scarcity, pollution through mining activities will all get disappear. Furthermore, **the global energy crisis and burning of fossil fuel** causes overexploitation of coal and other resources, pollution through mining activities

4

including fracking, intensive farming of oil palm also cause deforestation, air pollution, the establishment of dams for hydropower generation, etc. Solving the global energy crisis puts an end to several of the above-mentioned problems such as pollution through mining activities, air pollution, and to certain extent deforestation and intensive oil palm cultivation. It also solves indirect links such as groundwater contamination by pollution through mining activities such as fracking and biodiversity loss due to deforestation, etc. In addition, **intensive farming** causes overexploitation of natural resources, desertification, deforestation, biodiversity loss, animal slaughtering & cruelty, agrochemicals, solid waste and sewage, eutrophication, groundwater contamination, the establishment of dams, water pollution & water scarcity, wetlands or draining of wetland and hazardous waste from toxic pesticide chemicals. If intensive farming comes to an end, problems such as resource depletion, desertification, deforestation, animal slaughtering and cruelty, agrochemicals, eutrophication, groundwater contamination, wetlands, and biodiversity loss (to a certain extent) come to an end. In addition, **urbanization-urban sprawl-settlements** causes solid waste and sewage, air pollution, water pollution & scarcity, visual pollution, deforestation, light pollution, noise and vibration pollution, global energy crisis, draining of wetland, and biodiversity loss. If it is possible to find a clear solution for urbanization-urban sprawl-settlements most of the environmental problems such as solid waste and sewage, air pollution, water pollution and scarcity, visual pollution (by man-made structures), light pollution, noise and vibration pollution, global energy crisis, draining of wetlands, deforestation (almost) and biodiversity loss (to a certain extent) would get solved. In addition, indirect links such as climate change and global warming will also get reduced.

Also, **water pollution-water scarcity** causes diseases, vector borne diseases (e.g., mosquito), eutrophication and biodiversity loss. When water pollution and scarcity problem get solved, it is possible to find solution to most of the diseases, which are water borne, eutrophication and subsequent biodiversity loss also can be mitigated. In addition, indirect links such as sedimentation, coral destruction and pests or weeds also get solved.

Above eight (8) highlighted man-made environmental issues are keystone links. Removing such links could bring many directly and indirectly linked environmental problems to an end. But human adaptability factors prevent such solutions. Thus, instead of cutting links, shortcuts are established to solve the problem by regenerative means. However, this is not the case for all man-made environmental problems.

Certain man-made environmental problems can be solved by either sustainable or regenerative or by both means.

However, removing keystone links is not possible due to the presence of human adaptability factors such as economic, social, cultural, historic, health, and political factors.

E.g.,1: removing deforestation is not possible due to economic needs. And some government policies can influence severe deforestation (politics).

E.g.,2: farmers cannot completely switch to organic farming because organically grown vegetables are small and lower in yield, thus, farmers cannot get enough profit (economics).

1.2 Evidence for keystone environmental problems

When solving a man-made environmental problem, if it results in the permanent disappearance of one or more man-made environmental problems, then that mitigated problem can be considered as a keystone environmental problem.

Based on the above given definition, when mitigation of a man-made environmental problem solves one or more resulted-man-made environmental problems, then that mitigated problem is a keystone environmental problem. Accordingly, air pollution can be considered as a keystone problem because if air pollution gets solved, the resulting acid rain and ozone depletion can also come to a halt. However, when an environmental problem is caused by more than one man-made environmental problem then their causative environmental problems **cannot** be considered as the keystone links, for instance, biodiversity loss is caused by land degradation and competition with invasive species. Here, land degradation is not a keystone environmental problem because even if land degradation is mitigated, competition impact from invasive species continues to fuel biodiversity loss. Thus, complete dependency of an emerging environmental problem on its parent environmental problem enables parent problem to be considered as keystone environmental problem.

1.3 Establishing Regenerative vs. Sustainable solutions

Regenerative solutions are less expensive due to low energy and high systemic vitality (figure 1.3). It can also co-evolve (adapt) with nature. It also shows very high resilience to the changes in the environmental factors. "Regeneration is a process co-creating the condition conducive to life to continue. And it is an instrument for co-evolution and process by which human, institutions and materials evolve the capacity to fulfil their inherent potential in a world that is constantly changing around them" –Daniel C. Wahl.

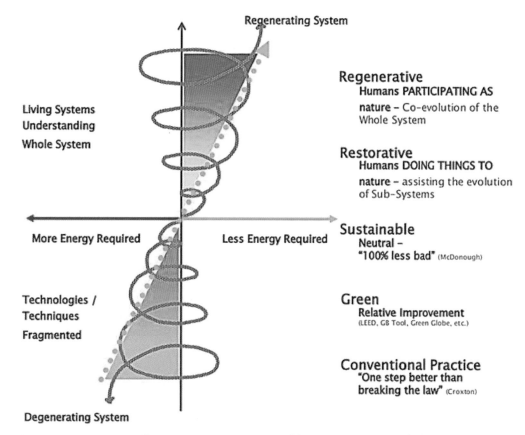

Figure 1.3 Regenerative solution vs. Sustainable Solution
(With permission from Bill Reed)

1.4 Types of Environmental Solutions based on their required energy levels

Based on the energy requirement and resilience or systemic vitality developmental design may vary from degenerating systems to regenerating systems (figure 1.4).

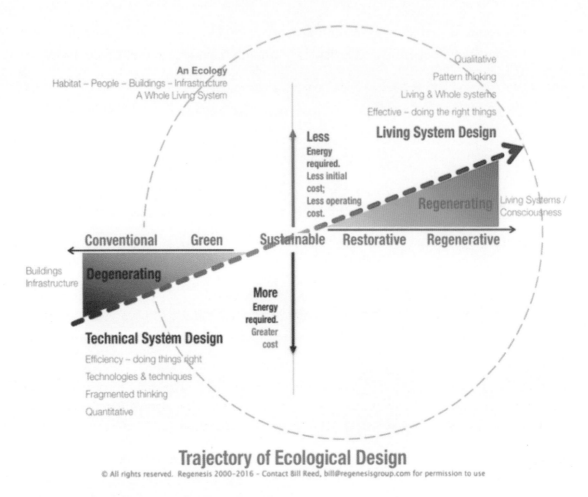

Within the figure:

An Ecology
Habitat – People – Buildings – Infrastructure
A Whole Living System

Qualitative
Pattern thinking
Living & Whole systems
Effective – doing the right things

Living System Design

Less
Energy
required.
Less initial
cost;
Less operating
cost.

Regenerating

Living Systems /
Consciousness

Conventional   Green   Sustainable   Restorative   Regenerative

Buildings
Infrastructure

Degenerating

More
Energy
required.
Greater
cost

Technical System Design

Efficiency – doing things right
Technologies & techniques
Fragmented thinking
Quantitative

Trajectory of Ecological Design

Figure 1.4 Environmental Solution designs

With permission from Bill Reed

A. Conventional solutions

According to Bill Reed, Conventional practices are one step better than breaking the law. For instance, e.g., in case of ozone depletion hydrofluorocarbon (HFC) is an alternative to chlorofluorocarbon (CFC). Here, HFC is ozone friendly gas, but HFC is stronger greenhouse gas than CO_2, thus, conventional mitigation designs are highly expensive, this is due to their high energy requirements, for instance, replacement of refrigerator system with HFC require highest environmental cost as HFC is 1380 times more potent greenhouse gas than CFC (Gerretsen, 2020). Yet usually, conventional practices are the first and immediate solutions because they are less intelligent means to implement to the system. solutions require very high energy for its implementation; thus, they are relatively more expensive. Since they are requiring *extremely high*

8

energy (or high environmental cost), they are *extremely less resilience* and depicts *extremely low systemic vitality*. Just better than breaking the law (just better than CFC, the gas that cause the entry of skin cancer-causing UV radiation by depleting the protective stratospheric ozone layer).

B. Greener solutions

Greener practices are relatively improved solutions than conventional solution, but it is still having malefic (negative) components at *any part* of their lifecycle. For instance, photovoltaic panels are greener solution to energy crisis, but at the end of their lifecycle they produce hazardous heavy metal containing waste, since solar panels (photovoltaic) consist heavy metals such as silver, lead, arsenic and cadmium. Similarly, in case of ozone depletion, cascade system with ammonia and CO_2 in the refrigerator is ozone friendly solution, yet this is not a sustainable solution (net zero impact) because CO_2 is a greenhouse gas and ammonia is unsafe to breath. Thus, in greener solutions minimal harm for the nature (environment and sentient beings) exists, but not as harm as conventional solution. Greener solutions require very high energy for its implementation; thus, they are relatively more expensive. Since they are requiring *very high energy*, they are *very less resilience* and depicts *very low systemic vitality*.

C. Sustainable solutions

According to the definition given by the United Nations Brundtland commission in 1987, "meeting the needs of the present without compromising the ability of future generations to meet their own needs" is called sustainable development (WCED, 1987). According to Bill Reed, sustainable solutions are neither benefit nor harmful to the environment. For instance, in case of ozone depletion, CFC ban by the Montreal protocol in September 16th of 1987 is a sustainable solution because CFC ban does not cause any other harm to the environment such as greenhouse gas emission and unlike reforestation and afforestation; it does not provide any benefit to the ecology and other sentient beings. Similarly, in case of energy crisis, fossil fuel ban is a sustainable solution (net zero: neither addition nor degradation to the nature (ecology and sentient beings). Sustainable solutions require moderately high energy for its implementation; thus, they are relatively expensive. Since they are requiring *(moderately) high energy*, they are *less resilience* and depicts *low systemic vitality*.

D. Restorative solutions

Restorative development is human doing things (addition) to nature (environment and sentient beings). This is a step ahead (better) of net zero or sustainable solution, and there is no harm to the nature. However, human dominance or control over nature still prevails. For instance, in case of human elephant conflict, afforestation or reforestation such as establishing saltlicks and plantation for elephants are additions to nature and controlled or maintained by humans (human dominance), and unlike regenerative systems, restorative systems cannot adapt or self-maintained. For instance, in case of reforestation or afforestation, the newly planted saplings have to be maintained such as protecting from grazing animals, watering, protection from pathogens and pests, fertilizer application, etc. Restorative solutions require *low energy* solutions with *high systemic vitality or resilience*.

E. Reconciliatory solutions

Reconciliatory development is usually traditional or cultural practices that reintegrate humans as integral parts of nature. Here, human dominance is relatively less pronounced. And human do more things (addition) to the nature (environment and sentient beings). For instance, in case of plastic pollution, replacing the plastic products traditional (cultural) or aboriginal product alternatives is a reconciliatory solution such as replacing plastic broom stick with environmentally friendly (biodegradable) coconut fibre broom stick, which has been used traditionally since ancient times. Similarly, in case of human elephant conflict, control wild elephant using trained elephant is a traditional practice. Reconciliatory solutions require *very low energy* and assure *higher systemic vitality or resilience*.

F. Regenerative solutions

According to Wahl (2016), regenerative cultures are healthy, resilient and *adaptable*. They establish the system conducive to life and they require *extremely low energy* and solutions with the *highest systemic vitality or resilience*, which are fathomable ailment for the environmental crisis with less change in the natural environment. Thus, they are least expensive solutions.

For instance, in case of eutrophication, floating wetlands provide adaptable regenerative systems with highest resilience because when there is continuous supply of agrochemical (nitrate and phosphate fertilizer) leaching form the nearby farm, banning chemical fertilizer could be the sustainable but expensive solution. E.g., Sri Lanka's economic crisis of 2022 was primarily due to the agrochemical import ban implemented by the government in April 2021, which later brought a huge economic crisis that led to the change in the leadership through public protest. By considering the Sri Lankan situation it is clear that sustainable solutions are relatively high energy and low resilient solutions. Yet in case of regenerative solutions such as establishing

10

floating wetlands, the wetland plants grow in surplus in seasons where the nutrient flow (chemical fertilizer) is high in the waters and the wetland plants absorb the excess nutrients to maintain the nutrient balance in the aquatic ecosystem thereby preventing the algal blooms and eutrophication. This phenomenon is known as adaptability and this feature is not available in the sustainable developmental designs. Thus, it also can be considered as smart or wise solutions rather going for expensive solutions that create various other problems in terms of country's economy, culture and sociology.

2. Deforestation

2.1 Introduction

Increasing human population and needs cause increases in exploitation of natural resources mainly the forest. Changing patterns of consumption and techno machinery further fuel this issue. World's annual deforestation is estimated as 13.7 million hectares, equal to the area of Greece, if this continues in the same rate the total forest cover may get completely vanished in next hundred years. However, still 30 per cent of the land cover is occupied by forests (figure 2.1). According to DCCEE (Department of Climate Change and Energy Efficiency) 2012 report estimated current average net CO_2 emission is 27 Mt-e and it is projected to be 43 Mt-e in 2020. We are inevitably committed to involve in reconstruction of socio, economic and environmental factors to promote inclusive developmental strategy to ensure the sustainability of forest ecosystem as it leads to firm existence of life in our planet. Man has started clearing forests several thousand years ago, this was mainly for agriculture and ranching purposes. In the nineteenth century transformation of Modern man in terms of industrialism, urbanism, liberal democracy and capitalism he overexploited the nature mainly the nature's forest resource, this causes various negative impacts in the entire ecosystem such as changes in weather patterns, global warming, outbreak of epidemics, droughts, desertification, behaviour, existence and distributional changes in entire biota and its diversity. However, in today's postmodern era man has well understood the importance to conserve nature and becoming eco-centric. "What we are doing to the forest of the world is but a mirror reflection of what we are doing to our self and to one another"- Mahatma Gandhi.

Annual deforestation

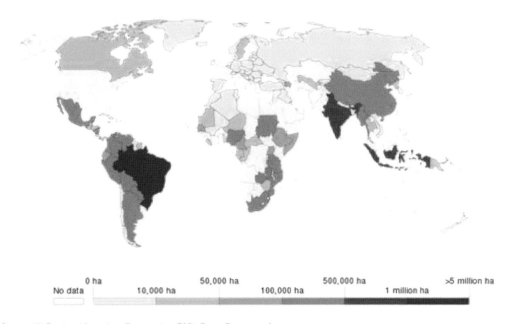

| | 0 ha | | 50,000 ha | | 500,000 ha | | >5 million ha |
| No data | | 10,000 ha | | 100,000 ha | | 1 million ha | |

Figure 2.1 Annual Deforestation
Source: UN Food and Agriculture Organization (Ritchie & Roser, 2021) License: CC BY-SA 4.0

2.2 Importance of forest ecosystem

Forest ecosystem is essential for the existence of our planet, almost 20 per cent of worlds oxygen is produced in Amazon forest as the forest maintains the balance between Oxygen and carbon dioxide, maintains rainfall and gives significant contribution in water cycle, nutrient and mineral cycles are maintained, maintaining weather pattern and reduces the effect of global warming, prevent soil erosion, maintaining soil fertility, prevent the spreading of disease and pests, trapping the pollutants of air and water, sink for various mineral elements, for its services such as source biodiversity, source of gene pool, reservoir of carbon, source for shelter, food(bush meet, fruits, oils & nuts), for medicinal needs, natural fertilizer, natural pesticides, valuable timber, lumber, pulp, gum and fibres, in addition it also known for its educational, recreational, aesthetic value, and refreshing the mind and soul.

13

2.3 Effects of Deforestation

Deforestation causes decline in rainfall all over the world, unusual weather pattern alters the distribution of species as it increases the effect of global warming which causes the loss of habitants of animals such as polar bear and penguins due to melting of glaciers, increase in occurrence of landslides, forest fires and flooding. Oppression and conflicts rise in the society due to poverty, the hardships of sudden weather change, desperately poor resort and increase sex slavery (Figure 2.2).

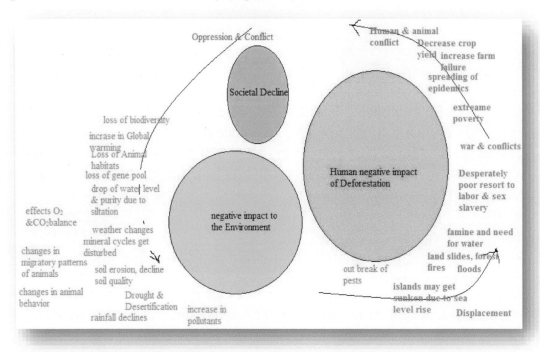

Figure 2.2 Effects of Deforestation
Adapted from ("giornalettismo.com", n.d.)

- **Loss of Biodiversity**

destruction of forest threatens both fauna and flora, indeed it leads to severe extinction of entire biota, there are several species completely become extinct due to anthropogenic means such as Tasmanian wolf, Moa, Woolly mammoth, Cape lion, Atlas bear and several wild plants, there are many other species red listed as Critically Endangered and plenty of species become vulnerable.

- **Increase in Greenhouse gases**

Forest trees absorb carbon dioxide and release oxygen, reduction in forest and increased anthropogenic carbon dioxide emission together amplifies the effect of global warming.

Effects of the warming are loss of habitants of polar bear and penguins due to the melting of glassier, rising sea level also causes small islands to be sunken permanently such as Maldivians questioned their existence in near future (a span of several hundred years). According to Australia's Emission Projections report (2012), emission from deforestation activities is 44 Mt-e and removal from reforestation activities is 26 Mt-e, resulting net emission during the Kyoto period (2008-2012) is 26 Mt-e, and this net value of emission is projected to be 43 Mt-e in 2020 where as projected deforestation emission to be 47 Mt-e.

- **Change in weather pattern**

Forests can withstand severe weather changes due to its high resilience. Increase in temperature and effect of cyclones are minimized in forest covered areas than bare land. It further amplifies the effect of natural drought, which is more severe during ENSO events.

- **Desertification and soil erosion**

Destruction of forest in a huge range eventually causes degradation of soil fertility and water holding capacity. This is amplified during the slash and burn harvesting as the nutrient loss is high. Burned ash do not support for cultivation at all. Many of the today's desert lands were forest lands several million years ago, as the carbon in pre-historic trees now available in the form of fossil fuel. Deforestation directly facilitates soil erosion as open soil is easily taken by wind and flowing water this also leads to siltation of dams that reduces the water holding capacity. An estimated loss of over 100 tons per ha. have been reported in several parts of India, China, Yemen, El Salvador, the Dominican Republic, Kenya, Madagascar and Ethiopia (Paul , 1993).

- **Floods and Landslides**

Flooding and land slide events are rare in the forest regions which is extremely high in urban lands. However, deforestation caused several landslide events around the world resulting loss of live hood and properties. Chances of landslides are extremely high when deforestation occurs at mountain forest.

- **Spread of diseases**

Forest provides natural boundary between colonies of human population. This prevents the direct access between communities thus reduced the chances of epidemics and also filter the air and water for infectious agents. Diseases such as swine flu, Dengue, Ebola can be sealed from spreading to other regions.

- **Increase in pollutants**

Forest traps the pollutants and increases the chances of biodegradation, deforestation declines this natural process and this increases particle pollution and effects of toxic gases. Particles smaller than 10 micrometres in diameter because the greatest threat, when inhaled it may even reach the blood stream, some of such particles and droplets are possibly human carcinogens, e.g. Great smog of London in 1952.

- **Habitat loss**

According to WWF, orangutan, elephants, tigers, rhinos and many other species lose their habitats in the tropical regions such as Africa, Latin America, and Asia, this also increases human animal conflict. Deforestation leads to habitat fragmentation which minimizes the chances of meeting among a group of population or between communities, it severely affects the natural balance, interrelationships and access to food and other ecological spots or resources, alter the seasonal migratory pattern and ultimately increases the stress or changes in animal behavioural patterns.

- **Human animal conflicts**

Increasing human population increases their needs, constructions such as roads, highways and irrigation schemes, dams, etc. This causes habitat fragmentation which increases the chances of meetings between animals and man, several road accidents with wild animals are recorded in many parts. Elephants and monkeys cause many conflict events. Elephant cause destruction of houses and agricultural farm lands even injure the ranching herds, this is very common in south Asia. Similarly, Territorial behaviour of Rhinos often results in conflicts with human and other animals commonly seen in Africa and some parts of India.

2.4 History

There is evidence of clearance of rain forest at least 3000 years ago in Africa, 7000 years ago in south and Central America and possibly 9000 years ago in India and New Guinea. Also evidences of slash and burn technique was retrieved in Northern South America, South East Asia and Central Africa 12,000 years ago. Land hunger, increased economic needs for resources cause the destruction. Historically, English and Dutch migrants lured by a gold rush, collecting spices and mono culture plantations such as tea and rubber are the pioneer reasons for the destruction of forest cover in Brazilian Amazon, North America and South Asian regions. When considering tropical rainforests, in Bangladesh, Haiti, India and Sri Lanka almost all rainforests lost by 1988, China 50% loss in Xishuangbana province, by 1960-85 Philippines and Thailand loss 55 and 45 per cent of rain forest respectively (Chris C. , 1992). In the year between1990 and 2000 the world is estimated to have suffered a net loss of 8.9 million hectares of forest each year, but in the period 2000-2005 this was declined to an estimated 12.9 million hectares per year, recent deforestation rate is annually 7.3 million ha.(Parry, Canziani, Palutikof, & van der Linden, 2007). Overall, world lost about 3 per cent of its forests in the period 1990 to 2005, at present we are losing about 200 square kilometres of forest each day.

2.5 Types of deforestation

1. Land clearing for the grazing of dairy cattle and other life stock
2. To obtain and expand agricultural lands, mono culture such as tea, wheat, paddy, oil palm and vegetables.
3. Subsistence farming through slash and burn forest cuttings including unplanned 'Chena'.
4. Logging for commercial needs such as pulp, rubber, resins, timber harvest, charcoal and fire wood.
5. Development for expanding civilization, industrialization, irrigation, mineral mining, energy, transport and Tourism.
6. Natural catastrophic events such as hurricanes, volcanic eruptions, forest fires or El Nino and other sudden climatic change.
7. Manmade environmental problems
8. War and civil unrest.

Adopted from (Hogan, 2014).

2.6 Underlying causes of Deforestation

Development and over consumption

Massive development programmes such as road or high way constructions, rail ways, water reservoirs, dams, grounds for athletic and sports development, air ports and industrial zones, harbours, mineral mining projects, power plants, military expansion programmes, scientific research programmes and housing and services development activities.

Colonialism

During colonial times forest trees logging was carried for establishing rail ways mainly for sleeper bars and for building naval boats, massive mono culture programmes such as coffee, tea, rubber and spices were carried out in Sri Lanka, Kenya, Togo, and India (Assam and Kumeon). Similarly, Araucaria Zone of southern Brazil, Sahelien Africa and Thailand are badly affected by colonial deforestation.

In Sri Lanka 162,700 acres of forest area was cleared for Coffee cultivation by 1867 ("srilankacoffee.com", n.d.) in Madagascar up to 7 million ha of forest were cleared in the first three decades of the colonial period (Perrier de la Bâthie, 1921) as cited in (Claudia, 2010). The Transmigration program, commenced 1974, caused an average annual loss of 200,000 ha. in Indonesia (Colchester & Lohmann , 1993) as cited in ("rainforestinfo.org.au", n.d.).

Debt Burden and Exploitation by developed countries

Developing nations of South and South East Asian countries uses money of developed nations for their infrastructural development and they pay the loan with their natural resources including timber countries such as Japan utilizes their forest resources and granting loans for various development schemes (Colchester & Lohmann , 1993) as cited in ("rainforestinfo.org.au", n.d.).

In both least developed and developing countries factors such as cheap labour, reduction in tax or land price or subsidies by government, increase in the demand of timber or agricultural land or other forest commodities, high mineral value and debt burden have accelerated the effects and changed the pattern of international trade.

Role of Poverty and Overpopulation

Increasing population increases the land needs for shelters, agriculture, industrial and other developmental needs. Poverty severely effects least developed countries as well as developing countries this increases the over consumption of forest resources without any impact assessment or analysis. Adopted from ("rainforestinfo.org.au", n.d.).

2.7 Causes of deforestation

1. Land clearing for the grazing of dairy cattle and other life stock

2. To obtain and expand Agricultural lands, mono culture such as tea, wheat, paddy, oil palm and vegetables.

3. Subsistence farming through slash and burn forest cuttings including unplanned 'chena'

4. Logging for commercial needs such as pulp, rubber, resins, timber harvest, charcoal and fire wood.

5. Development for expanding civilization, industrialization, irrigation, mineral mining, energy, transport, job creation and tourism.

6. Natural catastrophic events such as hurricanes, earthquakes, volcanic eruptions, acid

18

rain, forest fires or El Nino and other climatic changes.

7. Manmade environmental problems

8. War and civil unrest.

2.8 Afforestation and Reforestation

Planting a tree is generally for establishing wind breaks, shelter belts, timber, fuel wood, flowers, nuts, vegetables, medicinal plants and wildlife. Maintaining or protection against forest degradation can be successful by planting, site preparation, tree improvement, fertilization, uneven aged stand management, thinning, pruning, weeding, cleaning, liberation cutting or other appropriate silviculture techniques, maintaining or increasing the landscape level carbon density using forest conservation strategies, longer forest rotations, fire management and protecting against insect pests (IPCC, 2007).

2.9 Ethno biology (Indigenous knowledge)

It is essential to get access to indigenous community in every forest management programmes as they are considered as part of the forest ecosystem. They are well aware of native plant species, plant animal relationships, and locations of species richness, animal behaviours and exploitable resources such as medicinal plants, structural stratification of the area, soil type, weather pattern, etc. Indigenous people also know the traditional methods of conservation of forest. Agroforestry has been managed by American Indian people for thousands of years, they utilized natural animal behaviours for their own benefits e.g., American Indians cultivate nectar flowers in order to attract predatory ants as it gives protection and techniques for culturing honey bees and otters are used in fishing by Bangladeshi traditional fishermen.

2.10   Silviculture techniques

Silviculture techniques are not so innovative in modern science instead there are adapted or ameliorated practices and methods of our ancient cultivars. However, using advanced techniques not always result in best result it also require proper analysis and assessments prior to the implementation and it is also important to select the right species at the right habitat for example, in Sri Lanka, Pine and Eucalyptus(non-native plants) trees are introduced as a substitute to natural mountain forest, hence, other trees cannot grow in degraded soil without undergoing succession (it takes long time)and aiming to collect pulp for paper industry, but unlike indigenous varieties Pines absorb much moisture required by their huge accumulation of biomass and pine litter also reduces the infiltration

19

of rain water through soil as it is not readily decomposed like ordinary mulch due to its oiliness, this causes soil layers to dry up, and resulted in depletion of perennial river flow (which directly affects the country's hydro power generation). In addition, dry soil layers tend to move apart, this resulted in landslides in many areas during rainy season. Furthermore, they also caused forest fires during dry weather, thus it is important to study the possible impacts before implementing invasive species or any advanced techniques in terms of weather it suits the environment or not. In silviculture selecting the right variety is initially considered as a key element, rather than working on ecological parameters and harvesting methods. Selection depends on the purpose, for what reason the forest to be generated mainly for.

I. Intermediate cuttings
This includes commercial thinning of trees that have attained sufficient growth and to be used for timber, pulp, fuel wood or saw. In thinning by reducing the number of trees and give independence to the most desired tree from competition, smaller and malformed trees are cut, and space, sun light and other resource provided to the desired ones. e.g., Low thinning, crown thinning (increases light penetration), selection thinning, mechanical thinning, free thinning, loose thinning and ecological thinning (aims to the development of wild life).

II. Regeneration cuts
This occurs on mature older strands that are ready for harvest, these also occur on young strands which are identified as poor in quality. This is usually done either seed tree method or shelter wood method, in seed tree method widely spaced residual trees are kept to facilitate dispersal of their seedlings in order to regenerate the forest, in shelter wood method trees are partially cut periodically for several years which is eventually culminate the final cut and give way to new generation even aged strand. Coppicing also a regeneration method and it dose depend on the sprouting of cut trees, trees such as pines that sprout from stumps are managed this way. Variable retention is a kind of harvesting and regeneration method which keeps the understory layer and forest floor undisturbed in order to preserve the structural complexity. Clear cutting and patch clearing, here all unwanted tall trees are cut to facilitate the availability of full sun light for saplings e.g., Walnut, red oak, yellow poplar, yellow pine etc.

III. Even aged and uneven aged
Usually stands that developed after pasture or heavy cutting events are generally even in age. In uneven aged strands, generally there is an over story above, so it ultimately favours the shade tolerant crops such as sugar maple, beech and hemlock. However,

shade intolerant species also can be grown if thinning and harvesting are done frequently.

IV. Group selection

Where small tree groups are removed leaving large varieties (opposite to clear cut) this method promotes uneven aged strands for the entire forest. Only shade tolerant varieties can be cultivated such as sugar maple (on better sites) and oak (on poor sites).

V. Crop tree management

Here a manager identifies good trees and species on better sites, then frees them to grow independently by clearing the rest unwanted vegetation.

VI. But log forestry

It resembles the crop tree management, in this method veneer logs are produced in relatively short time. When crowns begin to close, week trees are removed and branches of the crops are trimmed at 17 feet.

VII. High grading diameter limit cutting

Where marketable trees over certain diameter (14" DBH for pine & 10" DBH for hard wood) are cut and more suppressed and less vigorous varieties are left.
Adapted from ("Silviculture methods", n.d.); ("Silvicultural systems", n.d.).

2.11 Most popular Afforestation and Reforestation programs

Forest plantation in a land which does not have any forest in last 50 years of history is Afforestation, if it has an occurrence of forest within last five decades then it is Reforestation.

- China annually increased its forest cover by 11,500 square miles, an area the size of Massachusetts, according to a report from the United Nations in 2011. China's Great Green Wall was designed to plant nearly 90 million acres of new forest (Luoma, 2012).

- Reforestation in Korea: Between 1961 and 1995, stocked forest land went up from 4 million ha. to 6.3 million ha. Total timber rose from 30.8 million cubic meters in 1954 to over 164.4 million cubic meters in 1984. By 2008, 11 billion trees had been planted about two-thirds of South Korea is now clothed with forest.

- Reforestation in Tanzania: The Kwimba Reforestation Project: During the nine-year period of the project's run, over 6.4 million trees were planted.

- Reforestation in Mexico: Centre for Integral Small Farmer Development in the Mixteca region reforested with 1 million trees covered more than 1000 ha.

- Reforestation in the United States: the Appalachian Regional Reforestation Initiative (ARRI): 60 million trees have been planted on about 87,000 acres of active mine sites in Appalachia under ARRI's guidance.

- Reforestation in Colombia: Gaviotas villagers have successfully reforested about 20,000 acres, as a result rainfall has increased by 10%("Sustainablog.org", 2001).

- Japan after World War II, have done intensive reforestation from 1950-1970, during that period professional silviculture spread out in every Japanese village. (Marten, 2005).

2.12 Forestry projects under the Clean Development Mechanism (CDM) of the Kyoto Protocol.

General features of this mechanism are reforestation of native forests, plantations for timber, agroforestry or multipurpose tree plantations and healing barren lands. Kyoto Protocol governs Land Use, Land Use, Change and Forestry (LULUCF) and modalities and procedures for CDM. Organizations such as International Tropical Timber Organization (ITTO) carried out the task according to the discussed strategies (Timothy , Sarah, & Sandra, 2006).

2.13 Role of International Tropical Timber Organization (ITTO)

International organizations such as ITTO, encourages conservation, sustainable development, use and trade of forest resources. It has 59 members represent about 80% of tropical forests and 90% tropical timber trade worldwide. ITTO collects analyses and circulates data on production and trade of timber and allocates funds since 1987. It has funded more than 750 reforestation and afforestation projects valued US$290 million. Donors are mostly Japan, Switzerland and the USA (Timothy , Sarah, & Sandra, 2006).

2.14   CDM projects

- Pearl River Watershed Management, China: This project proposes to alleviate local poverty and reduce threats to forests by afforesting 4,000 hectares in the Guangxi Zhuang. Project also includes half of the Pearl River basin.

- Pico Bonito Forest Restoration, Honduras: This is a pilot project on agroforestry to support small scale farmers of 20 villages within the Pico Bonito National Park buffer zone of 2,600 ha. Main roles of the project are introducing agroforestry for small scale farmers, reforestation to promote conservation, establishment of sustainable commercial grade plantation.

- San Nicolás Afforestation project: This project includes both forest and agroforest plantation in an abandoned pasture land of 8,730 ha. in San Nicolás, Colombia. Adopted from: (Timothy , Sarah, & Sandra, 2006).

2.15   International Conventions related to forest ecosystem and conservation

1. United Nations Framework Convention on Climate Change (UNFCCC) or Kyoto convention.

This was made due to the increased concern on global warming due to anthropogenic means and mainly aiming to limit the emission of greenhouse gases, protocol was adopted in Kyoto, Japan, on 11 December 1997. It also discussed various forestry practices including techniques of agroforestry such as tilling use of natural fertilizers which could enhance the release of greenhouse gases. Discussions such as LULUCF and modalities and procedures for Clean Development Mechanism (CDM) are major breakthrough in forest conservation.

2.   Convention on Biological Diversity (CDB).

Treaty aims following three aspects conservation of biological diversity, sustainable use of components of biodiversity and fair and equitable sharing of benefits arising from the use of genetic resources. It covers levels of biodiversity such as ecosystem, species and genetic diversity. It covers biotechnology by Cartagena Protocol on Biosafety. In 2010 a ten-year strategic action plan (2011-2020) was adopted by relevant parties to ensure the safe guard of natural biodiversity.

3. United Nations Convention to Combat Desertification (UNCCD).

UNCCD targets those countries experiencing serious drought and/or desertification, mainly in Africa. It provides strategic plan to combat desertification, mitigating the effects of droughts, sustainable development, improving productivity of the land, living condition and expansion of the forest.

4.   International Tropical Timber Agreement (ITTA).

Its main objective is to promote the international timber trade from tropical sources. However, it is adopted in 1992 in order to achieve sustainable management of tropical forest as "Year 2000 objective" by International Tropical Timber Organization.

5.   Other conventions related to forest.

Ramsar convention on wet land (which aims to protect all kinds of wet land ecosystem), Convention on protecting World Cultural and Natural Heritage (this aims to protect heritage of outstanding universal value, forest can be considered as natural heritage), CITES (Convention on International Trade on Endangered Species of Wild Fauna and Flora: aims to restrict the overexploitation of wild plant and animal species via international trade), Convention concerning Indigenous and Tribal People in Independent Countries (aims to protect social, cultural and economic rights of indigenous people, it also includes protecting their habitats as they are mostly related to forest).
Adopted from (Ruis, n.d.).

Following problems cause deforestation

2.16   Air pollution due to deforestation

According to Demir, Dindaroğlu, & Yılmaz(Demir, Dindaroğlu, & Yılmaz, 2014), a study demonstrated the relationship between air quality and the spread of forest lands in Aras Basin, Turkey. The study included 23,770 pieces of hourly measured SO_2 and particle matter PM_{10}, concentrations for the December, January, and February in the period from 2009 to 2010 with the support of database in geographical information system (GIS) maps showing the spread of forest area. The results revealed that the Air Quality Index (AQI) values were the lowest for the forest area, and there is no health risk whereas other regions with low forest coverage (76.50%) in December depicted significantly high AQI values. A similar forest damage due to air pollution was observed in Barents region, enormous damage occurred in Russia near borders of Norway and Finland (figure 2.3).

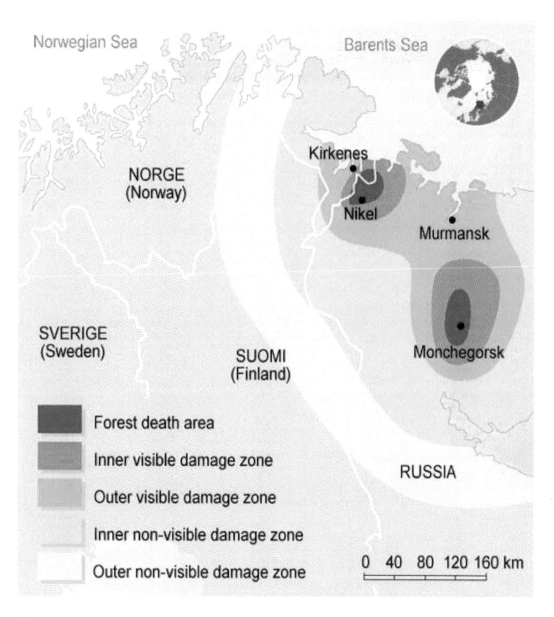

Figure 2.3 Forest damage in Barents region depicts the relationship between forest area and air quality
Source: (GRID-Arendal, 2005), License: CC BY-NC-SA 2.0

2.17 Deforestation-destruction of grasslands and mangroves due to overexploitation of natural resources

Increasing human population and needs cause an increase in the exploitation of natural resources, mainly the forest. Changing patterns of consumption and techno machinery further fuel this issue. The world's annual deforestation is estimated as 13.7 million hectares, equal to the area of Greece, if this continues at the same rate the total forest cover may get completely vanished in the next hundred years. In Central America, deforestation was carried out for cattle production, over the last four decades the forest cover has been declined by 40%, from 2004 through 2005 about 1.2 million rainforests were destroyed for soybean crop as cattle feed (Nicholson, Blake , & Lee, 1995). In Latin America forest lands are abducted for the cultivation of soy, most of the soy is used by poultry, pork, cattle, and farm fish, from 1981 to 1990 about 75 million hectares were destroyed, most of the area was converted to pasture(Kaimovitz , 1996). In South America about 4 million hectares of forest are destroyed annually this includes the most precious Amazon (figure 2.4), Argentina, Brazilian Cerrado, the Chaco, and the Atlantic Forest of South America. According to the Food and Agriculture Organization (FAO) of the United Nations, it was estimated that 30 percent of the world's land has been consumed to produce milk and meets (Berger & Green, n.d.).

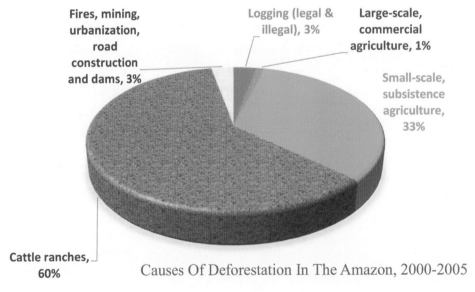

Causes Of Deforestation In The Amazon, 2000-2005

Figure 2.4 Causes of Deforestation in the Amazon 2000-2005
Source: ("The Merig", 2014)

26

Most of the mineral deposits such as Gold, copper, other precious metals, diamonds, and gemstones are found in forests. Amazon forest has been affected by the gold rush, due to its alluvial gold deposits; clearing also involved the use of heavy machinery. Before 2012, about 170,000 acres of forest were cleared by miners (Mega, 2017). However, it has been declined by the strict action taken by the Peruvian government in 2012, to protect forest biodiversity. According to a recent 2016 study showed about 1,287 acres of forest area within the Peruvian Amazon reserve were logged by miners (Mega, 2017). According to recent studies of Charles , Blake, & Lee(Charles , Blake, & Lee, 1995), it has been depicted that nearly half (49%) of the deforestation in the tropic region is due to the illegal clearing for commercial agriculture. Oil palm, soy, rubber, coffee, tea, and rice plantations have taken much of the tropical forest area worldwide ("WWF Global", 2017). In Malaysia over 3.5 million ha. of forest have been cleared for rubber and palm cultivation. Annually around 200,000 ha. of forest and woodlands are logged for tobacco farming(Geist, 1999).

Overexploitation of land resources such as construction activities, reclamation for industrial, urban, and airport development affects mangroves in the United States, Australia, and New Zealand(Saenger, Hegerl, & Davie, 1983). Mangroves were converted into paddy cultivation lands in Senegal, the Gambia, and Sierra Leone, or into coconut estates as in Sri Lanka(Salm, 1981), Mangrove lands were converted into fish ponds in the Philippines, Ecuador, Indonesia, and Costa Rica, and brine ponds and salterns in India, Malaysia, and Benin(Saenger, Hegerl, & Davie, 1983).

2.18 Global warming and climate change cause or due to deforestation, destruction of mangroves and grasslands

According to Cramer and others(Cramer, et al., 2004)that man-made deforestation affects tropical forests. Estimates of carbon emissions during the 21st century for all climate and deforestation scenarios range from 101 to 367 Gt C, resulting in CO_2 concentration increases above background values between 29 and 129p.p.m. Thus, it is possible to conclude that continued tropical deforestation will cause the building up of future greenhouse gas concentrations. According to Vale & Houston(Vale & Houston, n.d.), Environmental Defense Fund (EDF) stated that about 32 million acres of tropical rain forests were cut down each year in the period between 2000 and 2009. It is also anticipated that the forest clearing will put another 200 billion tons of carbon into the atmosphere in the future. It was also mentioned that deforestation more carbon into the atmosphere than the total vehicular emissions. According to " Causes of global warming"("Causes of global warming", n.d.), bush lands and forest trees absorb CO_2 for photosynthesis and act as carbon sinks that keep global warming to 1.5°C, as we already experienced a 1°C increase from pre-industrial times. However, clearing of forests for timber and oil palm cultivation further intensifies the warming.

It was stated in Fearnside P.(Fearnside P. , 2006)that half of the dry weight of the trees in a tropical forest is carbon, either deforestation or forest die-off releases this carbon in the form of greenhouse gases such as CO_2 and CH_4 during the process of burning and rotting tree biomass. According to Butler R.(Butler R. , Could global deforestation fight climate change?, 2007)that forests are estimated to hold 600 gigatons of carbon, and deforestation is responsible for about 20% of man-made greenhouse gas emissions (figure 2.5).

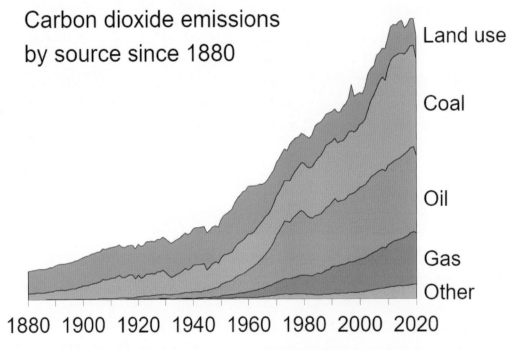

Figure 2.5 Global deforestation (Land use) and Greenhouse gas emission
Source: (Efbrazil, 2020), License: Creative Commons Attribution-Share Alike 4.0

According to Allen and others(Allen, et al., 2010), heat stress associated with climate change causes tree mortality in many regions. Also, climate change destroys forests by causing insect outbreaks and wildfires. According to Flannigan, Stocks, Turetsky, & Wotton(Flannigan, Stocks, Turetsky, & Wotton, 2009) that as suggested by recent

28

studies, climate change may cause a doubling of forest area burnt along with a 50% increase in the occurrence of fire in circumboreal regions by the end of this century. Besides, it has been mentioned in Gillett, Weaver , Zwiers, & Flannigan(Gillett, Weaver , Zwiers, & Flannigan, 2004)that human-induced climate change has had a detectable influence on the area burned by the forest fire in Canada over recent decades. Similar massage was stated by Flannigan & Van Wagner(Flannigan & Van Wagner, 1991)as the relationship between seasonal severity rating and annual provincial (in Canada) area burned by wildfire was explored, results revealed that 46% increase in seasonal severity rating, with a possible similar increase in area burned by the wildfire, in a 2 x CO_2 climate.

2.19   Deforestation and destruction of mangroves and grasslands due to the establishment of dams

According to 'Forest Asia summit'(Forest Asia summit, 2014), constructions of large-scale hydropower dams caused large areas of forest have been flooded with water. It was stated in Zarfl and others (Zarfl & et al., 2015) as cited in (Winemiller, et al., 2016)that existing dams in the Amazon, Congo, and Mekong basins are relatively small and located in upland tributaries but more than 450 additional dams are planned for these three areas alone with many already under construction.

According to Barbosa (Barbosa, 2008), the Brazilian government still plans to build several hydropower plants on the Amazon, which could increase both deforestation and greenhouse gas emission, and dams flood thousands of hectares of forest and threaten many aspects of the Amazon basin. For instance, Belo Monte Dam, the world's fourth-largest hydropower project, blocked 1000-mile Xingu River, a major tributary of Amazon, and the reservoir flooded 260 square miles of lowlands and forest (Fearnside, 2017).

2.20   Deforestation-destruction of grasslands and mangroves due to acid rain

According to Hinrichsen(Hinrichsen , 1988), from 1983 to 1984, in West Germany, acid rain killed 34% of the forests, this includes one half of the Black Forest. High aluminum concentrations damage the root system. Switzerland has recorded 14% of the forest trees lost due to acid precipitation (Ophardt, 2003). According to Auclair, Martin, & Walker(Auclair, Martin, & Walker, 1990), a paper published in 1990 stated that wet acid deposition of eastern Canada and the United States such as Alaska, British Columbia, and the Pacific Northwest United States is four times higher than that of the western region of the United States. Also, about half-million hectares of forest were damaged in Czechoslovakia and Poland. In Romania, approximately 56,000 hectares of a 6.3-million-hectare forest were affected. In Swiss, 25% of the fir and 10% of the spruce were damaged, and similar forest damages were recorded in the United Kingdom, Italy, France, the Netherlands, Austria, and Yugoslavia. In the United States, most of the Red spruce in the Appalachian mountain range was damaged as severe forest decline was recorded in the area. Furthermore, balsam fir and white birch of high elevations of New York, Vermont, and New Hampshire showed the signs of damage. Almost half of the red spruce in Camel's Hump (a mountain), Vermont, USA were dead. Pines in New Jerzy and spruce, short leaf pine, hemlock, Fraser fir, hickory, and other species in Tennessee were affected by acid precipitation.

2.21 Deforestation-destruction of grasslands and mangroves due to intensive farming

According to Vosti, Braz, Carpentier, d'Oliveira, & Witcover(Vosti, Braz, Carpentier, d'Oliveira, & Witcover, 2003) as cited in (Kovacic & Salazar, 2017), in the period between 2000 and 2011, in the Brazilian Amazon, the number of farm holdings have increased 70% caused loss of 200,000 hectares of forest area. According to FAO (FAO, n.d.), in the 1990s, the world's forest area declined at the rate of 94,000 square kilometers per year. Most of the land was cleared for agriculture and animal grazing (Figure 2.6)

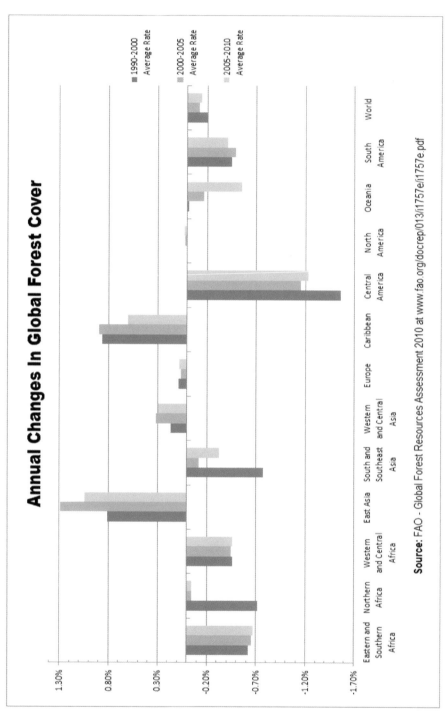

Figure 2.6 Percentage of forest area change by change process, 1990-2010

31

Also, the link between deforestation and cattle ranching is strongest in Latin America, as almost 40% of the forest cover has been declined in the past 40 years, which is accompanied by an increase in pasture and cattle population in the same period (FAO, n.d.).

According to Bradshaw (Bradshaw, 2012), Australia has lost nearly 40% of its forests. In the 18th and early 19th centuries, when European colonists expanded, deforestation occurred mainly in coastal areas. According to Norton(Norton , 1996) as cited in (Bradshaw, 2012), in New South Wales, in the period between 1892 and 1921, the rapid expansion of wheat and sheep industries caused deforestation. In the 1950s, most of the forest areas in Southwestern Western Australia were cleared for wheat cultivation. Since the 1970s, the highest rate of forest decline was observed in Southeastern Queensland and Northern New South Wales, and Victoria. Today, most of the forest decline occurs in the Northern region due to invasive weeds and wildfires.

Also, mangroves are destroyed for agriculture and shrimp farming in Latin America. According to Ong (Ong, Plants of the Merbok mangrove, Kedah, Malaysia and the urgent need for their conservation, 2003) and (Ong, The ecology of mangrove conservation and management, 1995) as cited in (Polidoro, *et al.*, 2010), mangrove species such as *Sonneratia griffithii* has lost due to rice farming, shrimp aquaculture, and coastal development. In Latin America, mangroves are destroyed for the establishment of the settlement, agriculture, and shrimp ponds (Tovilla-Hernandez , Espino de la Lanza, & Orihuela-Belmonte , 2001) as cited in (Polidoro, *et al.*, 2010).

2.22 Pollution through mining activities causes deforestation and destruction of mangroves and grasslands

According to Sonter and others (Sonter, *et al.*, 2017), a study quantified mining-induced deforestation and investigated the aspects of mining operations depicted that there is a significant increase in forest loss due to intense mining activities in the Brazilian Amazon which is up to 70km beyond mining lease boundaries, caused 11,670 km^2 of forest destruction in the period from 2005 to 2015. This extent represents 9% of all Amazon deforestation of the present time and 12 times more forest destruction that occurred within mining leases alone. The study further revealed that activities such as mining infrastructure establishment, urban expansion to support increasing workforce, and development of mineral commodity supply chain are the primary causes associated with deforestation.

Source: (Sonter, et al., 2017)

2.23 Deforestation-destruction of grasslands and mangroves due to Poverty-disease-food insecurity-war

According to Fagariba, Song, & Soule(Fagariba, Song, & Soule, 2018), economic activities such as agriculture, mining, and infrastructure improvements to meet basic human needs continuously and are being one of the major causes of deforestation. Over-resilience on forest resources by forest-dependent communities causes a high rate of deforestation in Ghana, Africa. A study includes simple random sampling and key informant interview with the aid of a semi-structured questionnaire was used to retrieve facts from the indigenous community of Sissala West District of North Ghana to find their perceptions of causes of deforestation showed poverty, high illiteracy, population growth, and lack of alternative source of livelihood were the indirect causes that trigger the livelihood economic activities such as farming, charcoal burning, wood logging and hunting lead to degradation of the ecosystem or that causes deforestation or land clearing. However, the study also stated that most of the indigenous communities are illiterate, and the unawareness of the rate of deforestation is also a significant factor here.

According to "The Beef Industry and Deforestation"("The Beef Industry and Deforestation", 2016), food insecurity is the major cause of deforestation. Even the United States, which used to produce all its needed beef has initiated the importation of Brazilian beef since 2016, and countries such as Russia imports 321,058 tonnes of beef annually. Similarly, every year Hong Kong and Venezuela imports 260,242 and 165,545 tonnes, respectively. Thus, increasing demand for beef is the major cause of deforestation in the Amazon, which attributed 65-70% of all deforestation in the area from 2000 to 2005. The Yale school of forestry and environmental studies stated that Brazil alone uses 24-25 million ha. of land for soy cultivation, where 80% of the harvest is used as animal feed. According to "What's Driving Deforestation?"("What's Driving Deforestation?", n.d.), in Latin America, beef cattle farming caused the loss of tropical forest at the rate of 2.71 million ha. per year for the expansion of grassing land.

According to Prado & Ribeiro(Prado & Ribeiro, 2011), cattle breeding motivated by increased meat consumption and its inefficiency in protein production causes increased grassification and deforestation of the Amazon Forest. The study included a literature review, data collection, and field survey in the Xapuri municipality of the State of Acre, Brazil (the site where the gasification is intense) and the Chico Mendes Extractive Reserve in Xapuri. The study verified the reasons for introducing cattle breeding in the municipality, which includes within Chico Mendes Extractive Reserve. Results revealed that historical, economic, and consumer market factors as the main causes.

2.24 Deforestation-destruction of grasslands and mangroves due to population explosion

According to Jha & Bawa (Jha & Bawa , 2006), human population and development activities affect deforestation in biodiversity hotspots. A study quantified the impact of population growth and development on the rate of deforestation also it analyzed the relationship between these casual factors in the 1980s and 1990s, and factors such as average population growth, human development index (HDI, which measures the income, health, and education), rate of deforestation, and computed correlations among these variables for countries that contain biodiversity hotspots. The deforestation rate was high when the population growth was high with Low HDI, and the rate of deforestation was low despite the high population growth when the HDI was high. The correlation among variables was significant for the 1990s but not for the 1980s. The relationship between population growth and HDI had a regional pattern that reflected the historical process of development. However, based on the changes in HDI and the rate of deforestation over time, the study identified factors such as policy choice and human development constraints as the two major drivers of deforestation. As the policy choices that do not include conservation cause deforestation even in relatively developed countries. Lack of development in other countries may increase the pressure on forests to meet the basic needs of the increasing human population. It was also mentioned that deforestation resulted from policy choices may be easier to fix than deforestation arose from human development constraints. Overall, this study indicated the relationship between population increase and destruction of natural forests, even though other factors such as HDI (including policy choices and human development constraints) played a significant role.

Rosero-Bixby & Palloni (Rosero-Bixby & Palloni, 1998)discussed the extent to which increasing population is related to massive destruction of tropical forests. Conventional regression methods and the application of spatial analyses enabled the researchers to estimate the magnitude of the relation between population and deforestation. The study also identified the factors that are responsible for establishing a linkage between them, such as a multidisciplinary geographic information system (GIS), which was developed with geo-referenced data from two population censuses and series of land cover maps. However, the key analysis was based on multivariate logistic regression, which modeled the net impact of population growth in the period from 1973 to 1983.

According to "Seeing the forest for the trees" ("Seeing the forest for the trees", n.d.), people destroy the forests for many kinds of reasons, and most of them are survival related. Even though the relationship between deforestation, harmful policies, poverty, and population growth is complicated, the fact remains that population increase causes increasing demands on existing forests. Furthermore, according to "Helpsavenature"("Helpsavenature", 2018), it was stated in the report of the United Nations Framework Convention on Climate Change (UNFCCC) that agriculture causes approximately 80% of the deforestation in the world today, where 48% subsistence agriculture and 32% commercial agriculture. Among the remaining 20%, about 14% attributed to logging and about 5% to the firewood usage, and the remaining is utilized for other purposes. However, it has been concluded that all these human activities are due to the rising human population.

2.25 Deforestation and destruction of mangroves and grasslands due to oil spills

According to Getter, Scott, & Michel(Getter, Scott, & Michel , 1981), field studies on five oil spill sites depicted their effects on mangroves. Three studies are in Florida (two in the Florida Keys and one in Tampa Bay) and two in eastern Puerto Rico were visited in 1978, 1979, and 1980. The compartmental method was used to access the oil spills impact on mangroves. Tree mortality responses such as leaf defoliation, deformation, and stunting, seedling mortality and deformation, lenticel expansion, adventitious growth of pneumatophores, and changes in the density were observed, besides, changes in the distribution of plants and animals also noticed. Based on the magnitude of the spill, each site differed. According to Chindah, Braide, Amakiri, &Onokurhefe(Chindah, Braide, Amakiri, & Onokurhefe, 2007), the acute effect of crude oil (Bonny Light) affected the mangrove plants in Niger Delta, Nigeria. Openings of breathing roots of mangroves are blocked by crude oil and cause an intense threat to the mangrove population in the Delta over the past three decades, as 70% of the oil exploration and exploitation activities in Nigeria are held in mangrove habitats.

2.26 Deforestation and destruction of mangroves and grasslands due to urbanization-urban sprawl-settlements

According to Butler (Butler, 2012), a centrally planned urban experiment in Indonesia caused huge forest destruction. Massive transmigration program moved around 730,000 families to the outer island of New Guinea, Borneo, Sumatra, and Sulawesi to reduce the population pressures on crowded central islands of Java and Bali. However, in the hinterlands, the farms established by the immigrants were not a success. Frequent forest fires occur in once-forested lands. Also, a study on the Brazilian Amazon(Richards & VanWey, 2015), where deforestation leads to urbanization, depicted that severe destruction of tropical rain forests occurred in the Amazon region to establish a farm, pasturelands, and mining sites. The study explored the impacts of Amazon land use and environmental changes such as the creation and development of urban areas.

Deforestation effects into following problems

2.27 Water pollution-water scarcity due to deforestation

According to Mapulanga & Naito(Mapulanga & Naito, 2019), the study examined the effect of deforestation on households' access to clean drinking water in Malawi. The study revealed a 1% increase in deforestation decreases the access to clean drinking water by 0.93%. Besides, the study also stated that deforestation in the last decade in Malawi is 14%, and it has had the same level of effect on clean drinking water access due to a 9% decrease in the rainfall after deforestation.

2.28 Land degradation- sedimentation- soil erosion due to deforestation and destruction of mangrove sand grasslands

As the human population increases, the need for land and resources also get increased. This made the clearing of forest land unavoidable. Deforestation is mainly due to various reasons such as extending agricultural lands, timber harvest, mineral mining,

36

encroachment, slash and burn cultivation, development activities for irrigation, power plants, industries, housing schemes, and oppression or war. After the removal of plant cover soil gets loosen and become more susceptible to erosion, exposure to sunlight causes oxidation of nutrient cause depletion of soil fertility, a natural mineral, and hydrological cycles get collapsed, loss of soil water by evaporation causes ultimate degradation of soil. According to Poole & Berman(Poole & Berman, 2001) as cited in (Norén, 2016), increased sedimentation could alter the morphology of the channels and lead to channel widening.

According to Mohammed & Butswat (Mohammed & Butswat, 2005) as cited in (Emmanuel, 2017), the annual rate of deforestation between 1980 and 1990 in northern Nigeria is about 92,000 ha. This is mainly due to the intensive removal of vegetation, and this has resulted in severe land degradation and soil erosion in the region. Also, several socio-economic problems have emerged, such as wood shortage, famine, flooding, erosion, habitat destruction, biodiversity loss, and increased poverty in rural areas (Otegbeye, 2003). A study on nutritional and organic matter differences between forest and deforested areas to measure land degradation due to deforestation depicts the following results

2.29 Deforestation and destruction of mangroves causes coral destruction and bleach

According to Hallock-Muller (Hallock-Muller, 2005), tannic acid is the substance of plant origin that involves the preservation of coral reefs mainly from UV radiation. A study revealed that the destruction of mangroves in coastal wetlands decreases the number of natural tannins in the water. Thus, corals are getting bleached by the effect of sunburn. The case study demonstrated the linkage between the destruction of mangroves and the loss of coral reefs.

2.30 Biodiversity loss due to Deforestation-destruction of grasslands and mangroves

Deforestation in Indonesia and Malaysia such as forest clearing, habitat fragmentation, and intentionally set fires caused the loss of 80% of Orangutan habitats in the last two decades (scientific american, 2018). A 2007 survey of the United Nations Environment Program (UNEP) stated that orangutan will be virtually eliminated in two decades if the current rate of deforestation continues (scientific american, 2018). The International Union of Conservation Nature (IUCN) has declared that Bornean subspecies of orangutan as endangered and Sumatran subspecies as critically endangered (scientific american, 2018). A non-profit orangutan conservancy estimated there are 54,000 Bornean orangutans and 6600 Sumatran orangutans remain in wild (scientific american, 2018).

Also, according to Gaworecki (Gaworecki , 2016), in the State of Pará that occupies 25% of the Brazilian Amazon Forest, deforestation of 92,000 to 139,000 square kilometers of pristine forest have reduced its biodiversity. This is mainly due to activities such as road construction, selective logging, and wildfires. It was also mentioned that a team of researchers from 18 different institutions have looked at 1538 plants, 460 birds, and 156 dung beetle species throughout the region, and they estimated disturbed forest had lost 46-61% of its conservation value.

According to Platt J. R. (Platt J. R., 2014), 19 authors of science paper warned that 90 of the 101 lemur species in Madagascar are threatened with extinction, 22 are critically endangered, and the number of northern sportive lemur (*Lepilemur septentrionalis*) is down to 18 individuals due to deforestation. Trees are being chopped or burned; lemurs are also hunted for meat. However, habitat loss due to illegal timber harvesting and clearing land for crops severely affected their population.

In addition, according to Polidoro and others(Polidoro, et al., 2010), the mangrove population is declining worldwide. The primary causes of the destruction are coastal development, aquaculture, timber harvest, and firewood. A study was conducted on known 70 species of mangroves, eleven of 70 species (16%) are under threat of extinction, genus *Heritiera* is the most threatening species where 2 of the 3 species (66%) in threatened categories. Over the past 60 years in parts of India and Southeast Asia have lost about 80% of all mangrove areas within its patchy range, this includes the rare *Sonneratia griffithii*. On the Atlantic and Pacific coast of Central America, about 40% of mangrove species are threatened with extinction.

2.31 Ocean acidification due to Deforestation-destruction of grasslands and mangroves

According to Brovkin and others(Brovkin, et al., 2004), a study of the historical datasets of past 150 years on land cover changes and atmospheric CO_2levels, using an earth system model of intermediate complexity It is further stated that there is a significant relationship between land cover changes (deforestation) and atmospheric CO_2 levels, as CO_2causes ocean acidification. Results revealed that changes in land cover (loss of forest cover) are responsible for 25–49% of the observed increase in the atmospheric CO_2levels and this contribution decreased from 36 to 60% during 1850–1960 to 4–35% during 1960–2000. And the land cover contribution to atmospheric CO_2 growth increase from 68% during 1900-1960 to 12% in the 1980s. However, the study showed that there is a decline in the relative role of land cover for the atmospheric CO_2increase during the last 150 years. However, during this period the pH of the oceans has dropped from 8.18 to 8.07.

2.32 Human and animal conflict due to Deforestation-destruction of grasslands and mangroves

According to Chakravarty, Ghosh, Suresh, Dey, & Shukla (Chakravarty, Ghosh, Suresh, Dey, & Shukla, 2012), deforestation increases the incidents of human-animal conflicts. For instance, elephant habitat at northern West Bengal in India is part of the Eastern Himalaya biodiversity hotspot and characterized by a high degree of fragmentation. High fragmentations increased the incidence of human-elephant conflict and the loss of human and elephant lives as well as agricultural crop loss. The mortality of 50 persons and 20 elephants recorded each year from this area(Sukumar, et al., 2003); (Mangave, 2004) as cited in (Chakravarty, Ghosh, Suresh, Dey, & Shukla, 2012). According to Chartier, Zimmermann, & Ladle(Chartier, Zimmermann, & Ladle, 2011), in Assam, India, a combined study using social surveys and remote sensing to analyze the patterns in human-elephant conflict and land-use change overtime depicted that experience of human-elephant conflicts increased dramatically in the 1980s, which is associated with dropping of forest cover from 30 to 40%. According to Gunawardhana & Herath(Gunawardhana & Herath, 2018), deforestation with habitat fragmentation and food and water scarcity human-elephant conflicts are more frequent in Sri Lanka than before. Annually 200-250 elephants and 60-80 people die, the cost of crops and property damage exceeds USD10 million in Sri Lanka.

According to Kartika & Koopmans (Kartika & Koopmans, 2013), on human-tiger conflict (HTC) that tigers visit villages to look for food as forest degradation, fragmentation, and habitat loss are incoherent with decreasing habitat of tigers and their prey, the decline in the prey population is the main reason for their entry into villages, prey on domestic cattle and cause conflicts with people and become man-eating tigers. As mentioned in 'world bank'(world bank, 2010), it has been agreed to double the number of tigers by 2022 in 13 tiger range states as they signed the tiger conservation initiative, but the report(Kartika &Koopmans, 2013)emphasized that increasing tiger population without increasing the volume of their habitat will most likely increase the number of HTC.

2.33   Deforestation as a keystone environmental problem

The rising human population and needs cause an increase in the exploitation of natural resources, mainly the forest. Changing patterns of consumption and techno machinery further fuel this issue. The world's annual deforestation is estimated at 13.7 million hectares, equal to the area of Greece. If this continues at the same rate, the total forest cover may completely vanish in the next hundred years. However, still, 30 percent of the land cover is occupied by forests. According to the DCCEE (Department of Climate Change and Energy Efficiency), the 2012 report estimated the current average net CO_2 emission as 27 Mt-e, and it is projected to be 43 Mt-e in 2020. We are inevitably committed to involving in the reconstruction of socio, economic and environmental factors to promote an inclusive developmental strategy to ensure the sustainability of forest ecosystem as it leads to the firm existence of life on our planet. Man started clearing forests several thousand years ago, mainly for agriculture and ranching purposes. In the nineteenth century transformation of Modern man in terms of industrialism, urbanism, liberal democracy, and capitalism resulted in him overexploiting nature, mainly nature's forest resource; this caused various negative impacts on the entire ecosystem, the change in weather patterns, global warming, the outbreak of epidemics, droughts, desertification, existence and distributional changes in the entire biota and its diversity. There is evidence of clearance of rain forest at least 3000 years ago in Africa, 7000 years ago in the south and Central America, and possibly 9000 years ago in India and New Guinea. Also, evidence of the slash and burn technique been practiced in Northern South America, South East Asia, and Central Africa 12,000 years ago. Land hunger, increased economic needs for resources caused the destruction. Historically, English, and Dutch migrants lured by a gold rush, collecting spices and monoculture plantations such as tea and rubber are the pioneer reasons for the destruction of forest cover in Brazilian Amazon, North

America, and South Asian regions. When considering tropical rainforests, in Bangladesh, Haiti, India, and Sri Lanka almost all rainforests were lost by 1988, China lost 50% in Xishuangbanna province. By 1960-85 Philippines and Thailand loss 55 and 45 percent of their rain forest respectively (Chris , 1992). In the year between1990 and 2000 the world is estimated to have suffered a net loss of 8.9 million hectares of forest each year. But, in the period 2000-2005 this declined to an estimated 12.9 million hectares per year. The recent deforestation rate is annually 7.3 million ha. (Parry, Canziani, Palutikof, Linden, & Hanson, 2007). Overall, the world lost about 3 percent of its forests during the period 1990 to 2005, while at present we are losing about 200 square kilometers of forest each day. Deforestation can be considered as a keystone environmental problem, because solving deforestation may mitigate various other related issues such as air pollution, human and animal conflict, biodiversity loss, and desertification or land degradation (figure2.7).

Evidence 1: Deforestation causes air pollution

According to Miteva, Loucks, & Pattanayak (Miteva , Loucks , & Pattanayak , 2015), "between the period of 2000 and 2008 Forest Stewardship Council (FSC) has reduced the aggregate of deforestation by 5% points, and the incidence of air pollution by 31% points. It had no statistically significant impact on fire incidence or core areas, but increased forest perforation by 4 km^2 on average".

Evidence 2: Deforestation causes biodiversity loss

According to Grosberg, Vermeij, & Wainwright (Grosberg, Vermeij, & Wainwright, 2012), 80% of the species in the world are found in the terrestrial environment. Thus, deforestation causes habitat loss and subsequently leads to loss of biodiversity. Also, most of the human-animal conflict occurs due to the destruction of forest habitats.

Evidence 3: Deforestation causes desertification or land degradation

Worldwide 35 million km^2 or 24% of the land area is degraded. And globally, 28% of the land is forest, and deforestation causes 47% of land degradation (Bai, Dent, Wu, & Jong, 2013).

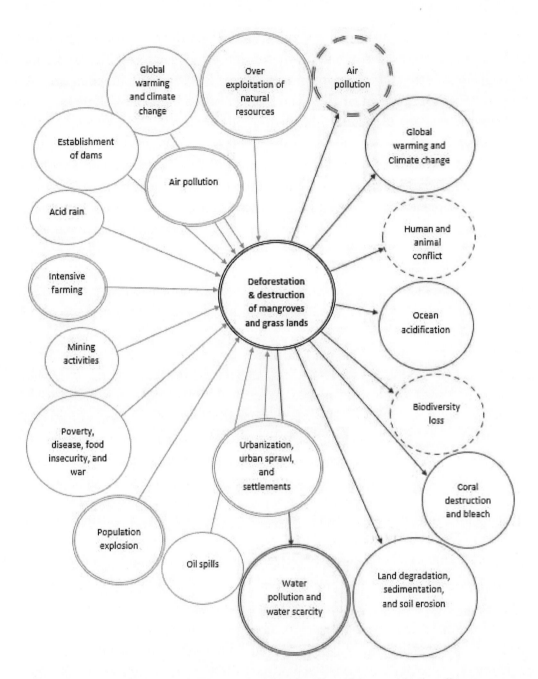

Figure 2.7 Deforestation as keystone environmental problem with the disappearance of desertification/ land degradation, air pollution, biodiversity loss and human& animal conflict on its mitigation (hypothetical diagram)

[In the figure black circle is the problem being examined, blue circles are cause man-made environmental problems, red circles are effect man-made environmental problems, double lined circles are keystone man-made environmental problems, and circles with dashed lines (either single or double lined) are the man-made environmental problems that disappear when the problem being examined (black circle) is mitigated]

Deforestation is a **keystone environmental problem**, which causes human-animal conflict, loss of biodiversity, land degradation and soil erosion, water pollution and scarcity, and exacerbates the impacts of air pollution, global climate change, ocean acidification, and coral destruction. However, the precursor for deforestation is population explosion. It has been found there is a complete dependency on causative deforestation shown by certain environmental issues such as human-animal conflict. Thus, mitigation of deforestation also prevents the occurrences of human-animal conflicts.

Regenerative vs. Sustainable vs. Conventional solutions

There are several unsustainable methods are used to surmount the human-animal conflict as an immediate and **conventional solution**, such as chasing the problem animals using fire crackers and shot gun without physically harming them, rubbing chilli, pepper and engine oil mixture on string or fences wrapped around or spraying chilli-pepper mixture to attacking elephants, chilli-dung bomb, acoustic deterrents such as beating drums and tins, whistling and other loud noises, strong lighting, e.g. flashlight, spotlight and floodlight at night (figure 2.8). Adapted from "Jannah Firdaus Mediapro Art & Story" (2022) and early detection and warming, e.g., watch towers. Further, establishment of physical barriers such as trenches and steep slopes could be used as conventional barriers because these land alteration methods accompanied with mild environmental hazard such as solid erosion, flooding and landslides. They also require high human energy on their construction.

However, prevailing gruesome practices such as hunting problematic animals either by shooting or using lethal animal traps e.g., 'Hakkapattas' in Sri Lanka are **not** solutions, but they are crimes, falls under another environmental crisis, animal slaughter and cruelty.

Greener solutions maintain the system without degrading them, such as prevent wild animal from moving into human settlements such as electric fencing, trenches and biofencing (e.g., beehive fencing), greener solutions cause minimal harm to the environment, for instance, electric fences also kill non-targeted species including humans and cattle. **Sustainable solutions** for human-animal conflicts (net-zero environmental impact, or neither benefit nor harm to sentient beings) prevent human encroachment and poaching into animal habitats while ascertaining safe dwelling of animals within their habitats and territories, such as the declaration of forest-protected areas and wild buffer zones, e.g., sanctuaries, national parks, forest reserves, and jungle corridors. This is because, according to the definition of sustainable development stated in the 1987 Brundtland commission report, "development that meets the needs of the present without compromising the ability of future generations to meet their needs." However, sustainable solutions are often very expensive due to their high energy requirements such as arduous patrolling, the requirement of equipment such as tags and GPS belts for tracking, patrolling, and fencing with continuous electricity supply, which requires labour and relatively expensive materials and technology, e.g. using wireless or infrared sensor networks or seismic data gathered from geophones, etc. (Wijesekera, Amarasinghe, Dassanaike, De Silva, & Kuruwitaarachchi, 2021).

Reforestation and afforestation to improve elephant habitat (habitat enrichment) such as salt licks and plantation for elephants are **restorative** practices, which reduce the chances of conflict by expanding the territorial habitat of the problem animal or merely expanding the area of buffer zone. And cultural or traditional and aboriginal practices such as controlling problematic elephants using trained elephants, using beacons and fire balls, hooting or shouting in groups are **reconciliatory solutions**. Establishing *customized*-agroforestry systems is a **regenerative solution**. Here, natural repellents are used against problem animals at buffer zones such as beekeeping (apiculture), and plantation of crops that elephants hate such as ginger, citrus plants, cocoa, sisal, tea, tobacco, oil seed, agave, turmeric, radish, *Coleus* sp., kale, peanuts, pepper and chilli and change the timing of certain crops e.g. sunflower as alternative crop, keep the crops clustered together or fencing using thorny plants such as prickly pear, barrel cactus, cholla cactus and saguaro cactus ("Jannah Firdaus Mediapro Art & Story", 2022). Regenerative solutions are less expensive due to low energy and high systemic vitality. It can also co-evolve (adapt) with nature.

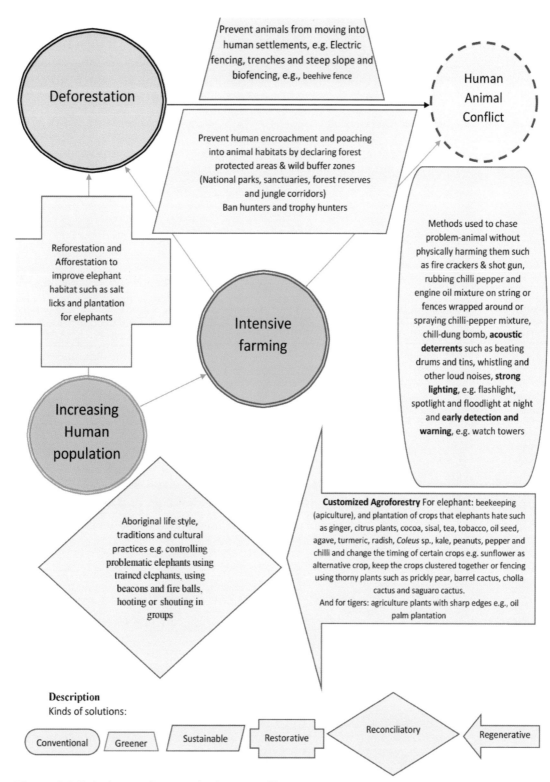

Figure 2.8 Solutions to human elephant conflict

Black circle: problem under concern, Blue circle: cause, Red circle: effect, Double-lined circle: keystone environmental problem, Single lined circle: environmental problem, Dotted lined circle: problem to be mitigated when keystone environmental problem gets solved, Black arrow: cause-effect link for which solutions are given, Blue arrow: cause-effect link

N.B.: - Each problem in the circles is connected to many other problems on the basis of cause-and-effect links, and they are not shown here.

3. Air pollution

3.1 Introduction

Air pollution is not a new for this planet even 65 million years ago during the cretaceous period the earth had experienced huge air pollution due to the clouds and smoke formed after the crash of meteorite, this caused mass extinction leads to the complete elimination of dinosaurs and various other species. Currently pollution due to natural sources such as forest fires and volcano eruption are creating several tones of greenhouse gases and other pollutants, which are unable to find human solution as they naturally occurred. However, Global emission of CO_2 reached 34.5 billion tonnes in 2012 and yearly increase was 1.4% from that of 2011(Olivier, Janssens-Maenhout, Muntean, & Jeroen , 2013). Extreme weather pattern and environment condition observed as anthropogenic air pollutants are continuously released to the atmosphere and are increasing in quantity and diversity with time. Addition to global warming, acid rain and ozone depletion are well marked for its severity. Manmade sources can be categorized by source either point or non-point sources or by its formation either primary or secondary pollutants. Most primary pollutants are emission of point sources such as factories and nonpoint source such as motor vehicle traffic of high way, whereas secondary pollutants originated by the chemical reaction of primary pollutants and generally nonpoint source of origin. Addition to naturally existing gases and particles manmade compounds such as fumes and gases of plastic, heavy metals, pesticides, fibres and chemical gases are extremely hazardous and cause severe health impacts.

After the industrial revolution air pollution become a severe problem to entire world. Various types of collectors, filters and precipitators are used by industrialists and motorists. Also, technologies for better fuels and engines of minimal emission are used, in currently emerging concept of zero emission electric and solar engines are considered as a solution for now and near future.

3.2 Sources of Air pollutants

Type and factors of air pollution vary country to country, for instance in Sri Lanka it is particles and CO, in South Africa SO_2 from Coal power plants and CO from house hold combustion and forest fires.

   I.   Sources of energy generation

This is where CO_x and SO_x and water vapour are released in the atmosphere as large amount of coal, oil, L.P/ Natural gas, gasoline and bio-fuels are used in combustion.

II. Transport

This is mobile and most leading source of CO. Combustion in engines is mainly fuelled by gas, petrol, diesel, and kerosene. Jet engines of sub sonic long-range aircrafts are major source of NO_x, Traffic on road is considered as non-point or line source, in addition, harbours and turbine engines of huge ships also emit tons of greenhouse gases and toxic particles in the air.

III. Industry

Most of the industries are directly or indirectly depend on fossil fuel, as they produce CO and CO_2, sulphur hexafluoride and particle matters. Mainly cement industry releases large amount of particle matters in the environment. There is an array of hazardous volatile compounds that are released from paints, electronics, dry cleansing and decreasing agents. Furthermore, utilization of HFC, Oxides of Nitrogen, PFC and SF_6 produce pollutants.

IV. Households

Carbon and soot emission during the cooking by the use of fossil fuels can be considered here. Volatile toxicants such as permethrine compounds from insecticides could contaminate in the air or even food and resulting in the intoxication.

V. Agricultural practices

Agriculture activities such as use of natural fertilizer release greenhouse gases. Pesticides release persistent organic pollutants (POP). Enteric fermentation in cattle ranching produces greenhouse gases mainly methane. Toxic chemicals found in pesticide and weedicide also reduce the quality of air inhaled.

VI. Land mining, earth moving activity and quarrying

Process of mining large mineral deposits in the earth accompanied with emission of dust and other chemicals. Blasting and quarrying limestone in cement manufacturing produce dust particles.

VII. Construction and repair works

Drilling, blasting, transportation, loading and unloading activities often cause dust generation. In addition, there are several non-point anthropogenic sources related to dust generation such as welding, painting, auto mobile repairing, etc.

VIII. Burning of wastes and incinerators

This is more severe threat to the environment as it contaminates the atmosphere with persistent organic pollutants (POP) such as dioxins and furans, probably their major sources are plastics and electronic wastes. In addition, as in normal combustion carbon is emitted as oxides and soot. Wastes are in a vast array such as plastic, electronic wastes, cement dust, industrial chemicals, paper, glass, steel and various derivatives of soil minerals, biological and medicinal wastes, drugs and other chemicals. Incinerators destroy the hazardous effect of any gas or particle and the remaining dust emission could be as smalls as PM10-PM2.5 or lesser, unless right particle filters are used it is also end up with adverse results.

IX.   Natural sources

Compounds released from volcanic activities such as black smoke, ash, metals, SO_x, CO_x and release of methane from thawing of permafrost regions in the northern hemisphere, wetlands and sanitary landfills are some examples of natural sources. In addition, forest fires, bush fires, dust storm, sea spray, conversion of land use and release of isoprenes and terpenes by forest (precursors of low-level ozone) are other natural means of air pollutants.

3.3 Major air pollutants and their effects

G. Primary pollutants

These are gases and particles released to the atmosphere and remain in the same form as it is from the source.

Sulphur compounds

Flue gas desulphurization plants (FGD), coal power plant (about 0.02-2% of emission)(Ray, Theory, selection and design of air pollution control equipment, 2004a)furnace oil (Sulphur content is generally 2.3 per cent by weight) (Muthukuda Arachchi, 2012), paper mills, steel industry, refineries and sewage treatment plants, petroleum refinery and vehicles engines, burning rubber, crackers and match smoke. Naturally sources such as volcanoes, marshes, bogs and swamps emit sulphur compounds. US, China and Russia are leading sulphur emitting countries. Found as SO_2, H_2S, CS_2, COS, Methyl mercaptan, Dimethyl sulphur, and Dimethyl disulphide ("Total Reduced Sulphur compounds", 2010). Health effects are generally wheezing, bronchoconstriction, chronic bronchitis, chronic obstructive, lung disease, etc. ("Carnegie Mellon University", 2003).

Nitrogen compounds

Major source is combustion such as jet engines, NH_3 come from fertilizers, livestock & poultry wastes, and vegetation, burning of biomass and ocean spray, energy production, petroleum refinery, forest fire, volcanic activity, bacterial breakdown of organic nitrates. It promotes acidification. NO_2favours photochemical smoke and reduce visibility. 77% of combustion gas of coal consist oxides of Nitrogen, in high concentrations it causes pulmonary edema, airway injury, impaired lung defences. Dissolved atmospheric NO_x as in acid rain destroys fish and plant life and N_2O is a greenhouse gas causes global warming("Carnegie Mellon University", 2003);("Total Reduced Sulphur compounds", 2010).

Carbon monoxide
Mainly from automobiles and during the combustion of fossil fuel, gas, charcoal and wood, naturally from forest fires and volcanoes cause difficulty in breathing as it competes with oxygen by forming carboxyhemoglobin, Asphyxia, damage to heart and nervous system.

Carbon dioxide
CO_2 is considered as an air pollutant as it defined by the clean air act. And it is a greenhouse gas increasing levels of CO_2 causing global warming. CO_2 emission is available from all kind of combustion both natural and manmade.

Ground level Ozone
Major sources of ground level ozone are auto mobile emission, air craft cabins and ozone generators.

Polycyclic aromatic hydrocarbon (PAH)
PAHs are released from cigarette smoke and stove smoke; it can cause lung cancer.

Radon
Released naturally from volcanic eruption, it is a radioactive material ionizes biological molecules; radon causes cell disruption and lung cancer.

Asbestos
Asbestos fibre dust released from building material, mines, mills and insulations, it causes mesothelioma, lung cancer and asbestosis.

Arsenic
Found in copper smelters and cigarette smoke, arsenic causes lung cancer.

Allergens
Allergens are particles such as house dust, pollen, animal dander, allergens cause asthma and rhinitis.

Particle matter SPM, PM_{10}, $PM_{2.5}$
Suspended particles are formed in every type of combustion and originated from various sources; $PM_{2.5}$ can even reach the blood circulation via the respiratory tract.

HCl

Released naturally from volcanic activities, cause eye irritation and damage mucus membrane and affects respiratory system.

Dioxin

Dioxin is a toxic gas produced from burning of electronic wastes and plastic materials; it could cause cancer and affects the immune system and leads to developmental reproductive disorders.

Furans

Furans are released during the burning of plastic products such as nylon, contains various harmful compounds.

Odour

Odour causes irritation, nausea and headache.

Mercury

Gold refinery is the major source of mercury and it is a known carcinogen.

Lead

Lead particle found in petrol smoke and causes health issues such as affects respiratory system, blood and kidneys also cause dyslexia and hyperactivity in children, however currently it is completely banned from fuel, due to the availability of lead-free gasoline. Burning of lead containing electronic wastes causes adverse effects to the atmosphere.

Compounds of Cadmium, Antimony, Arsenic, Zinc and Copper

These metallic elements often toxic, and irritating smoke causes adverse health effects, generally found in pesticides, fumes and gas emissions during the burning of plastic and electronic wastes.

Volatile organic compounds (VOCs)

VOCs are xylene, ethyl benzene and tri-methyl benzene compounds commonly found in Air freshener, air cleaners (with ozone), cleaning and disinfecting chemicals, cosmetics, gasoline, fuel oil, moth balls and vehicle exhaust. There is an array of compounds listed in this category such as Acetone, Benzene, Ethyl glycol, Formaldehyde, Methylene chloride, Perchloro ethylene, Toluene, Xylene and 1, 3- butadiene. Short time exposure may results irritation in eye and nose, headache, nausea, vomiting, dizziness and asthma. Continuous exposure damages central nervous system, kidney and liver, some are carcinogens causing cancer ("Minnesota Department of Health", n.d.).

Persistent Organic Pollutants (POPs)

These substances could persist in the environment, causing bioaccumulation via the food chain, they are found in chemicals which transport for long-range by air current to countries that even not produce them. Main sources are industrial products such as Poly chlorinated biphenyl (PCB), pesticides such as DDT, industrial by-products and burning of waste products such as dioxins and furans (Plastic Waste: Ecological and Human Health Impacts, 2011).

H. Secondary pollutants

These compounds are generated by the chemical reaction of primary pollutants in the atmosphere.

Ground level Ozone

It is the major component of Fog and it is produced by the photochemical reaction between NO_x and Volatile Organic Compounds. Causes breathing difficulty and aggravates the lung diseases such as Emphysema and chronic bronchitis.

Peroxyacetylnitrate (PAN)

PAN is formed due to photochemical reaction of NO_x with hydrocarbons in the sunlight, it is a component of photochemical smog, smog is a mixture of air pollutants such as gases and particles react with sun light. PAN often causes irritation to eye, and together with ozone it lowers the lung capacity and increases breathing rate (Brecher, 2003).

CFC

CFC formed by chemical reaction of fog in the atmosphere during volcanic activity, causes depletion of ozone layer. Used as propellant in sprays, deodorants and repellents, this is now completely banned.

Halons

Halons are brominated organic compounds used as fire retardant which is also an ozone depleting compound.

H_2SO_4

Sulphuric acid formed due to the reaction of oxides of sulphur with atmospheric water vapour, causes acid rain and respiratory problems.

Also refer table 3.1.

Table 3.1Effects of Air Pollutants to the atmosphere

Gas	Sources	Greenhouse effect	Ozone depletion	Acid deposition	Smog	Corrosion	Decreased visibility	Decreased self-cleansing of atmosphere
CO	Combustion of fossil fuel, biomass burning							+
CO_2	Combustion of fossil fuel, deforestation	+	+/-					
CH_4	Rice field, cattle, landfills, production of fossil fuel	+	+/-					
NO	Combustion of fossil fuel, biomass burning		+/-	+	+		+	-
NO_2	Combustion of fossil fuel, biomass burning,		+/-					
N_2O	Combustion of fossil fuel, biomass burning, deforestation, Nitrogenous fertilizer	+	+/-					
SO_2	Combustion of fossil fuel, smelting of ore	-		+		+	+	
CFC	Aerosol sprays, refrigerants, foams	+	+					
O_3		+			+			-

[+: Contribution to the effect, -: amelioration, +/-: variation in effect, empty space: not applicable](Adopted from (Ray, 2004b)

Industrial Air Pollutants

Major sources are thermal power plants, boilers, thermic fluid heaters, incinerators, cupola, blast furnace, coke oven, basic oxygen furnace, induction and air furnace and cement kilns. (Gunadasa, 2014).

3.4 Solution by limiting indiscriminate use of resources

a. Consumption of Energy

In this way, techniques such as minimizing use of raw material such as use less fuel or use of most efficient fuel which releases less quantity of pollutants are chosen. However, in developing countries coal is still being used, according to its sulphur content price of the coal differ, though there are modern boilers which use more efficient form of fuels, coal is more welcomed in the market due to the low price.

b. Afforestation and Reforestation

Forest is the natural sink to many pollutants and it has extremely high resilience It has been estimated that a hectare of forest receives 3 tons of CO_2 and releases 2 tons of O_2(Ray, 2004b).

c. Ban on hazardous compounds

Compounds such as Chlorofluorocarbon are completely banned due to the Ozone depletion.

d. End – of- pipe –add – on pollution control mechanism

Solid collectors and filters are used to collect particle pollutants and gases.

Addition of add on control devices

This is done in four different ways absorption, adsorptions, condensation and incineration.

Absorption: it is selectively isolating the pollutant, here the gaseous pollutant dissolved in a liquid scrubber are coming under this category: SO_2 scrubber, Flue gas desulphurization, selective catalytic reduction, ammonia is used to reduce NO_x into NO_2, generally lime water is used to absorb HF, HCl and SO_2, in some cases water alone is sufficient in the absorption of HCl.

Adsorption: here the molecules either enter into the adsorbent or remain outwardly attached to the surface. Common adsorbents are activated Carbon, Silica gel, alumina and zeolites. Adsorption beds are regenerative or non- regenerative. If regenerative, then the beds gain the receptivity to the pollutant again, else in case of non- regenerative beds, they have to be replaced when they are saturated.

Condensation: These process converters the gaseous pollutants into liquid form, this can be done by lowering the temperature or raising the pressure. Contact condensers: gases come into contact with cold liquid E.g.

Surface condensers: here the gas contacts cooled surface where the cold liquid or gas is circulated, its efficiency ranging from 50 to as high as 95 per cent.

Incineration: It is a process of combustion and used to control the emission of organic compounds. It involves rapid oxidation of material with combustible compounds in the presence of heat, releases CO_2 and water vapour. There are three different categories as follows.

1. Direct combustion: - air and all combustible gaseous pollutants react at the burner (efficiency 98%),

2. Thermal incinerator: - here the waste gases pass over burner flame (efficiency 99%).

3. Catalytic incinerator: - similar to thermal but after passing through the flame gases pass through the catalytic bed, here the catalyst promote oxidation so the fuel cost for high temperature generation can be minimized.

Flue gas Desulphurization: In desulphurization by injecting Ammonia, lime dissolves with SO_2 and produces sulphate and sulphites, sea water also use to absorb oxides of sulphur in wet process, in dry process $Ca(OH)_2$ slurry is used here desulphurization reaction occur after dehydration of gas. Recirculation of gas further enhance the quality of effluent air.

Flue gas Denitrification: Here the mixing of nitric or nitrous oxides with water resulted with nitric acid compounds (which is a water and soil pollutant in liquid phase).In selective catalytic reduction method ammonia is applied to the gas steam which reacts with the oxides of nitrogen at very high temperature (300°C) in the presence of catalysts such as active vanadium pentoxide and tungsten trioxide on a carrier of titanium which releases nitrogen and water. In coal burning boilers, about 80% of coal is found in fly ash while the rest remain in bottom ash. Fly ash has high tendency of deposition on wall of pipes, water tubes and furnace, this can be overcome by soot blowing, where compressed air and steam is blown.

1.   Mechanical collector

In this method dust is separated mechanically by means of gravitation or centrifugal forces.

a.   Separation by Gravity (settling chamber/ baffle chamber)

This is generally used as a pre-collector at the upstream of highly efficient collector such as fabric filter or electro static filter. In a high load of dust large particle are initially withdrawn by this method. Baffle chamber is used to prevent the entry of glowing particle towards inner fabric filter and prevent it from burning. In addition, where the dust is much abrasive and coarser, they are distracted from the flow to protect the bag of fabric filter.

b.   Separation by Centrifugation – Cyclone

This is an excellent pre-collector and protects the fabric filter from glowing and coarse particles. Mechanically driven cyclone can collect particle below 10μm more efficiently.

Cyclones are either parallel or multi-cyclones. Efficiency of cyclone can be enhanced by spraying water (wet cyclone) this agglomerates the particles and eliminates re-entrainment of dust.

2. Fabric filter

Filtration mainly depends on type of filtration size which determines the capture mechanism such as inertial impaction, direct interception, sieving, electrostatic attraction, diffusion. Generally, parameters such as Temperature, dew point & moisture, chemical composition of dust, distribution of particle size and operation pressure affect the performance.

Fabrics commonly made of cotton wool, polyester(better mechanical strength& thermo sensitive not exceed $150^{O}C$), polypropylene(PP is thermo sensitive, temperature not exceed $100^{O}C$, used in dust extraction), acrylic (or Dalton-T mechanically weak &thermo sensitive not exceed $100 ^{O}C$ cheaply available for boilers), polyamides, polyphenylene sulphide (or Rhyton, used in boilers can with stand up to $100^{O}C$), aromatic polyamide (heat & acid tolerance is high suitable for coal fired boilers), fibre glass (thermo stable and high acid tolerance used in boilers), polyterafluoroethylene (or Teflon, boiler application), Gore tex (made by W.L.Gore, formed by lamination of substrates such as polyester, fibreglass with a membrane of expanded Teflon applied on dirty side of filter) and ceramic (composite of alumina, silica, boron and Nextel 312; are extremely heat resistant up to $1150^{o}C$, used in coal fired boilers).

Efficiency also determined by type of woven such as monofilament, multifilament and spun yarn and pattern of woven fabric such as plain weave twill and Sateen.

Fabric finishing is another aspect fabrics underwent silicon treatment gives smooth surface and decreased abrasion, heating setting (heat treatment to preshrink the fabric in order to avoid loss of efficiency due to heat shrinking after application), flame retardant finish (it consists oxygen consuming substances to reduce the effect of fire, antistatic treatment (this is to handle charged particle during the flow and flammable gases and to avoid explosion), calendering (smoothen the surface by pressing the fibre for easy dust release), singeing(smoothen by passing the fabric over heated plate or flame), coated finish(improves efficiency by Teflon coating, this enhance the cake release). Durability depends on how it withstands the heat and acid chemicals. Maintenance also another aspect such as non-woven fabric is difficult to clean though they are more flexible (Ray, Theory, selection and design of air pollution control equipment, 2004a).

Bag houses are used for dry filtrates such as fly ash, grain dust; fertilizer also may combine with an SO_2 adsorption media (Gunadasa, 2014).

3. Electrostatic precipitator

Here dust particles passed through the electric field and get charged to saturation level and electrical force causes charged particle move towards an electrode and get trapped subsequently they are discarded.

It has four distinct phases 1. Ionization and corona formation 2. Charging of particles 3. Migration & precipitation of particles 4. Removal of dust deposits.

Negative corona, here electrode is negatively charged a narrow negatively charged region is generated called corona, here the electrons are absorbed by gas molecules, space outside the corona filled with negative ions and dust particles collide with negative ions and move towards collecting positive electrode. In positive corona the opposite happens in the same manner.

Negative corona is most preferred in industrial application as the industrial gases such as SO_2, CO_2, and H_2O have best ability to absorb free electrons and spark over voltage is higher in negative corona. However, negative corona generates higher level of Ozone, thus not used in air conditioners.

Receptivity of fly ash depends on sulphur content S<1 per cent gives high resistive ash, 1-2 per cent medium and greater than 2 per cent gives low resistive ash, similarly presence of SIO_2, Al_2O_3 increases the resistivity while Na_2O, Li_2O, K_2O and P_2O_5 reduce the resistance during performance of electrostatic precipitator(Ray, 2004b). Efficiency of ESP is as high as 99 per cent.

4. Scrubber

Scrubbers are most efficient pollutant removal mechanism where dust and gases are removed by liquid or/and solid droplets flow and contact intimately on the effluent pollutants similar to the removal of particle dust during the rain. Scrubber is used in foundries (iron & steel), production plants of fertilizer, chemicals and nonferrous alloys.

Advantages are micron level dust particles can be collected, liquid scrubber collects both particle and gases simultaneously, handles high temperature and corrosive gases, absolutely free from fire and explosion hazards. Only disadvantage of liquid scrubber is, it creates slurry discharge and leads to water pollution.

a. Particle scrubber
This is primarily to collect dust particle

i. **Spray tower**: here a nozzle produces droplets which fall by gravity concurrent gas flow absorbs the dust in the flow.

ii. **Centrifugal spray scrubber**: liquid is sprayed from central header gives spinning motion to the bottom entered gas stream, centrifugal force thrown the dust away with water droplets and slurry collected at the bottom.

iii. **Self-induced Spray or Impingement scrubber**: here the pollutant gas is impinged on pool of water and pass the lip of venture and flow through the water surface, contaminated water droplets agglomerates, settles at bottom of the hopper and get collected, zigzag path of the gas increases the efficiency, commonly used in grinding operation, foundries, coal plants and mining process.

iv. **Venturi scrubber**: Most efficient particulate scrubber, this is the only scrubber recommended for sticky and corrosive dust. Here gas is sent through a narrow (venture) throat where water is introduced and gas produces droplets and gas and droplets flow through a divergent section. Factors such as particle size, velocity of gas through throat, pressure drop, concentration of inlet dust, and nature of dust, rate of water flow, spray system, power and design of the scrubber determine the efficiency.

b. Gas absorption scrubber
This is applicable when the pollutant gas is soluble to the scrubber liquid; it is simply a physical transformation from gas to liquid. During the absorption a chemical reaction may occur. The process is explained by two film theory whereas bulk of liquid and gas are mixed in turbulent flow while the concentration remains the same. Concentration gradient exists only at the boundary of two different phases, mass transfer occurs as

laminar flow and there is no resistant across the interface. When the system is gas filmed, controlled gas is highly soluble in the liquid phase or about to react quickly. In liquid film, controlled the gas is either less soluble or reaction is slow with the component. Both types are commonly in use.

i. **Spray tower**: used with highly soluble gases such as HCl, NH$_3$, HF. Spray system equipped with nozzles and system maintains counter current flow of scrubbing liquid and gas, as liquid sprayed from top and gas released at bottom, and tower is provided with built-in recirculation tank at the bottom, clean gas is collected by mist eliminator at the top.

ii. **Packed bed tower**: This is suitable for meagrely soluble gases such as SO$_2$ and H$_2$S. since they are less soluble it is necessary to increase the contact of both scrubber liquid and gas phases, in order to achieve that counter current flow is established through randomly packed bed (pack is ceramic, metal or plastic-Poly propylene), gas flows from bottom and directed through the beds where the liquid from the nozzle wets the surface and meet the gas flow counter currently. Packed bed tower is also used with highly soluble gases in order to achieve high efficiency such as Acetic acid, Alkaline fume, Ammonia, Amines, Chlorine, Chromic acid, Cyanide, HCl, HF, H$_2$S, SO$_2$ and H$_2$SO$_4$.

5. Flare and Thermo Oxidizers

Flare stacks are used for burning off the flammable gas release, generally used in petroleum refineries, natural gas processing plants and chemical plants, this also used to release the pressure of the equipment. Flares are designed for short-term combustion, to avoid most hazardous methane release during fermentation in beer factories, flares are used to burn methane and releases in the form CO$_2$. Ground level flares are used in earth pits. Among thermal oxidizers regenerative thermal oxidizers are efficient up to 95%, the process is more simplified by the use of catalytic thermo oxidizers where the catalyst are used to reduce the ignition temperature and the reaction is employed in relatively low temperatures (reduction of 600 to 200°C), there are ventilation air methane thermal oxidizer, thermal recuperative oxidizer and direct fired thermal oxidizer used for the relevant purposes.

6. Conditioning Gas

This process alters the characters of gaseous effluents and removes dust particles. Addition of water (reduces the temperature of the air), Ammonia (agglomeration agent, lowers acid dew point and minimizes corrosion, eliminates the bluish plume of SO$_3$), Sulphur trioxide may reduce the receptivity of ash. Both SO$_3$ and ammonia together improve cohesiveness and porosity of the dust cake, this increases the performance of fabric filter and electrostatic precipitator.

Major component of gas conditioning is facilitated by mixing of ambient air with the effluent which dilutes the flow and reduces the temperature. However, it requires large dust collectors, due to the subsequent increase in the mass of air. In some cases where the temperature of the effluent is equal to water or acid dew point, hot air also applied.

7. Local Exhaust Ventilation systems (LEV)

LEV is generally a combination of hood, air cleaner, fan and duct. Hoods which are the essential components of the air outflow system, hoods ensure the efficient capture of dust particles which also protect the employer from the exposure to smoke and dust. E.g. Local hood, downdraft hood, side hood, booth hood, ring hood, canopy hood (more effective in furnace operations) and enclosure hood.

8. Fan

There are two different types of fans in use Axial and Centrifugal. In industrial systems centrifugal fans are widely used to move certain quantity of gas from one place to another against the system pressure. Design of blade and position may vary, as it depends on the role it is intended to, such as fan handling extremes of temperatures, abrasive dust or corrosive gas. Design of fan should aim for the task it handles, spark proof fans are used under the exposure to explosive gases, when handling toxic gases maximum air tight environment is maintained. Similarly lining of the system designed with rubber, where the effluent is acidic and glass also not reactive against most chemicals.

9. Chimney

Height of the stack is determined by considering structural, environmental parameters, the type of effluent and emission speed or flow. If the downward air current is high the chimney height has to be raised far enough to avoid the pollution risk. Generally minimum height of chimney of industries other than thermal power plant is 30m (Ray, 2004). There are two categories, self-supported and guy supported chimneys.

10. Remedies to handle explosive effluents

Explosion pressure must be released; thus, it is must to ascertain the availability of sufficient explosion vent area, earthing of the equipment ensures the discharge of any static electricity generated within the system, in fabric filter antistatic fabric ensures the safety. Dosing of inert gases prevent combustion resulting due to sparks e.g. CO_2, N_2, inert dust particles also can be used for this purpose but it is essential to conform that such practices not increase the ability of dispersal of the combustible particle (use of silica is prohibited), dosing of lime subsequently give rise to CO_2 (an inert gas).

3.5 Air pollutants during waste disposal

It is becoming a major source of air pollution. Mainly in Ghana, Africa and China also in some part of India hazardous wastes are burnt, mainly e-wastes and plastics. Toxic gases are produced during the burning of plastics and heavy metals. Release of particle matters from cement, asbestos, and other chemicals cause severe problems as they move several miles away from the sources and effects the people by various ways such as asthma and allergic responses, irritation, effecting liver and kidney. Some of such particles are carcinogens and leading to cancer. Phthalates such as DEHP in its monomer form effects the development of testis, Butylbenzyl phthalate (BBP) and dibutyl phthalate (DBP) also hazardous to reproduction, exposure to phthalates in pregnancy reduces the anogenital index in male child (distance between anus and genitals) (Swan, et al., 2005) as cited in (Brigden, Iryna , & Santillo , 2008) DINP and DIDP (diisodecyl phthalate) effects liver and kidneys. Polyvinyl chloride (PVC) is the most harmful plastic, where dioxins are released during its manufacture, dioxins cause cancer and affect the immune system and leads to developmental reproductive disease. Chlorinated compounds include Polychlorinated biphenyls (PCBs), PCB accumulates in fishes and other organisms and undergo bioaccumulation which result in high value in top- level carnivore such as humans. PCB is absorbable via skin and inhaled or ingested causing neurotoxicity, liver damage, tumours, immunosuppression, behavioural changes, reproductive disorders and abnormal sperms (Allsopp, M, Santillo, D, Johnston, & Stringer, 1999); (Allsopp, Erry, Stringer, Johnston, & Santillo, 2000) as cited in (Brigden, Iryna , & Santillo , 2008). Poly Aromatic Hydrocarbon (PAH) are formed during the incomplete combustion of coal, oil, gas, garbage and other organic substances, prolonged exposure to PAH causes lung/bladder/gastrointestinal cancer, liver damage, breathing problems, asthma-like symptoms and lung function abnormalities, and repeated contact with skin may induce skin inflammation ("toxipedia.org", 2011) as cited in (Plastic Waste: Ecological and Human Health Impacts, 2011).

Chlorobenzene causes acute and chronic effects in mammals, effects CNS (central nervous system), liver and thyroid. Increasing degree of chlorination such as tetra chlorobenzenes also affects kidneys. Hexachlorobenzene (HCB) is a group 2B carcinogen, it damages immune system, liver, thyroid, CNS, kidney and nervous system (Van Birgelen, 1998)as cited in (Brigden, Iryna , & Santillo , 2008). It is also reported the bioaccumulation of HCB. Polybrominated diphenyl ether (PBDEs) is an environmentally persistent compound, which is also reported in bioaccumulation, it causes abnormal brain development during the initial development of a foetus, it also associated with impacts on learning, memory, behaviour, thyroid, oestrogen hormone systems and effecting the immune system (Legler & Brouwer , 2003)as cited in (Brigden,

Iryna , & Santillo , 2008).When PBDEs are burnt they produce brominated dioxins/furans which are similarly hazardous. Triphenyl phosphates (TPP) are a contaminant in human blood (Jonsson, Bergstro, Blomqvist, & Drakare, 2001)as cited in (Brigden, Iryna , & Santillo , 2008), potent inhibitor of a key enzyme (monocyte carboxyl esterase) in human blood cells (Amini & Crescenzi, 2003)as cited in (Brigden, Iryna , & Santillo , 2008). Teflon and polytetrafluoroethylene (PTFE) are used as coatings of non-stick pans. Teflon cook wares should be handled carefully; when they are mistakenly placed on lit (inner side of pan) they may release harmful substances at $\geq 260°C$, Perfluorooctanoic acid (PFOA) is used during the processing PTFE and it may cause cancer.

Heavy metals such as lead may produce irreversible effects; it affects nervous system, blood, reproductive system and kidneys, it affects brain development in children (ATSDR, 2007)and (Canfield, et al., 2003)as cited in (Brigden, Iryna , & Santillo , 2008). Cadmium is a toxicant which can accumulates in tissues, exposure may affect kidneys and bones (Elinder & Jarup, 1996)and (Cadmium, 1992)as cited in (Brigden, Iryna , & Santillo , 2008), it disrupts calcium mechanism, causing hypertension and heart diseases. Cadmium oxide in fume affects the respiratory system (ATSDR, 1999), (Elinder & Jarup, Cadmium exposure and health risks: recent findings, 1996)and (WHO, 1992)as cited in (Brigden, Iryna , & Santillo , 2008), in addition it is a carcinogen causing lung cancer (DHHS, 2005)as cited in (Brigden, Iryna , & Santillo , 2008). Antimony is a toxic compound causing dermatitis, affecting skin cells, respiratory tract and affects the immune mechanism (Kim, et al., 1999)as cited in (Brigden, Iryna , & Santillo , 2008). Antimony is also stated as possible carcinogen by International Agency for Research on Cancer (IARC, 1989)as cited in (Brigden, Iryna , & Santillo , 2008). Mercury results in respiratory and skin disorders and causing chronic damage to brain. Chromium is a known carcinogen it affects the DNA and causing asthmatic bronchitis. Barium causes damage to heart, spleen and liver also leads muscle weakness, Beryllium is a carcinogen causing lung cancer, inhalation also causes chronic disease, berylliosis and skin warts (Ramachandra & Saira Varghese , 2004), and free carbon radicals are carcinogens.

Safe methods such as using incinerators, filtering the remaining particles (ceramic filters) and dumping at sanitary landfills are the best ways to avoid air pollution through waste burning.

3.6 Domestic air pollutants

Indoor air pollutants are in a broad rage such as Products of Incomplete Combustion (PIC) from stoves and house hold burning of garbage, tobacco and cigarette smoke, plastic and metal fumes, toxic sprays, pesticide and insecticides, dust and particles, Volatile Organic Compounds (VOC) and infectious agents.

Products of incomplete combustion (PIC) include greenhouse gases such as CO_2, CH_3 and Nitrogen oxides. PIC also produces eye irritating volatile organic compounds such as aldehydes, and carcinogens such as benzene, polycyclic aromatic hydrocarbons and 1,3-butidiene. There is a considerable amount of soot and particles found in (PIC) (table3.2). SO_2 fromdomestic coal combustion causes wheezing, domestic chorine and fluorine discharge also result in breathing difficulties and irritation to cell lining. Smoking causes 4 per cent of global diseases in the year 2000 (Zhang & Smith, 2003). Among 4000 chemicals produced from cigarette smoke, 69 of them cause cancer.

Table 3.2 Air pollutants and Major sources

Pollutant	Major indoor sources
Fine particles	Fuel/tobacco combustion, cleaning, cooking
Carbon monoxide	Fuel/tobacco combustion
Polycyclic aromatic hydrocarbons	Fuel/tobacco combustion, cooking
Nitrogen oxides	Fuel combustion
Sulphur oxides	Coal combustion
Arsenic and fluorine	Coal combustion
Volatile and semi-volatile organic compounds	Fuel/tobacco combustion, consumer products, furnishings, construction materials, cooking
Aldehydes	Furnishing, construction materials, cooking
Pesticides	Consumer products, dust from outside
Asbestos	Remodelling/demolition of construction materials

Pollutant	Major indoor sources
Lead	Remodelling/demolition of painted surfaces
Biological pollutants	Moist areas, ventilation systems, furnishings
Radon	Volcanic activity & Soil- under building construction

Source: (Zhang & Smith, 2003)

In many developing and least developed nations animal dung, crop residues, wood, saw and charcoal are used for stoves this resulted in PICs.

Insecticide, rodenticide and pesticide cause troubles related to kidney and skin, it also affects the inner membranes and tissues of lungs. Fungicides are extremely toxic; indeed, some compounds are cytotoxic as they affect mitochondrial and membrane respiration.

Pyrethroids such as permethrin found in insect killer (cockroach and bug spray) causes shortness of breath, coughing, wheezing, runny or stuffy nose, chest pain, or breathing difficulties when inhaled. Pyrethroids cause rash, blisters or itching when contacted to skin (Kaplan, 2014).

Air purifiers, photocopiers and laser printers generate Ozone, which causes breathing trouble due to reduction in the function of lungs; exacerbate asthma, irritation to eyes and nose, speed up aging of lung tissue and decline of resistance to colds and other infections (Zhang & Smith, 2003). HCl and HNO_3 are corrosive to body tissues are released during the thermal decomposition of polyvinyl chloride; HNO_2 resulted from the reaction of NO_2 with water films. Radon-222 is found in earth (as a product of uranium decay in earth crust) during domestic digging and drilled well water may releases Radon, it reacts with particles and induces ionization of atoms in living cells which leads to cell damage and cancer. Fibres such as Asbestos are banned in several countries for its carcinogenic effect. Cellulose fibres of saw dust also listed as human carcinogen by International Agency for Research on Cancer (IARC) also refer Table 3.3 &3.4.

Table 3.3List of hazardous compounds in household materials

Material	Compounds
Tiles of vinyl and coving	phthalate
Carpets	styrene
Linoleum	C5-C11 aldehydes and acids
Particle board	Aldehyde, ketone and formaldehyde
Electricity cable	Acetophenone, dimethyl benzyl alcohol

Adopted from (Zhang & Smith, 2003)

Table 3.4Sources of Volatile Organic Compounds (VOC)

Source	VOC
Paint	ethylene glycol, texanols, pinene, butoxy ethoxyethanol
Paint thinners	C7- C12 alkanes
Paint stripers	methylene chloride
Adhesives	benzene, alkyl benzenes
Caulks	ketones, esters, glycols
Cleaners	2- butoxyethanol, limonene, 2- butanone

Frying food	Poly Aromatic Hydrocarbon (PAH), acroline and 1, 3-butadiene
Smoke	nicotine, aldehydes, PAH and benzene
Dry cleaned clothing	trichloride ethylene
Deodorizers	p-dichlorobenzene
Moulds	sesquiterpenes
Showering	chloroform
Pesticides	chloropyrifis, dichlorvos and diazion

Adopted from (Zhang & Smith, 2003)

Mitigation methods mainly avoid the burning of compounds causing hazardous fumes such as PVC and plastics, banning asbestos, using face masks during the painting and dealing with hazardous smokes, using Electric or LPG/ LNG stoves or using well designed chimney, avoid closer blowing during incomplete combustion (or where eye protector), addition of lime to improve the quality of coal, proper handling of saw, fibres and particulate dust materials, ensure adequate ventilation during cooking, avoid low graded fuels such as cow dung which is high in sulphur, using air conditioners, ventilators and dust removers, flares are used to burn at the exit, and in thermo oxidizers, dose is relatively the same as flares.

3.7 Air pollutants in biological and hospital wastes.

In health care sector about 20% of the wastes generated may have infectious agents such as bacteria, virus or even fungi and allergens (Mohankumar & Kottaiveeran, 2011). Coughing, sneezing, raising of dust, sprays produce aerosols and droplets which are widely distributed in the air current, diseases such as Anthrax, Chickenpox, measles, influenza, smallpox, Tuberculosis and Cryptococcosis spread through air current, furthermore, fungi such as *Stachybotrys chartarum* (toxic black mold) cause severe ill effects. Best way to prevent airborne infection is to prevent the release of infectious agents from the sources such as patients, used medicinal products and equipments.

66

Wastes from health care sector generally sent to incinerators where it is completely burnt and destroyed, patients of airborne diseases are isolated such as TB patients. Some drugs also may produce odour and irritating sensation, this can be avoided by keeping them air tight.

3.8 Air pollutants from Mobile sources (Transport)

Major sources of NO_x are engine; mainly jet engines, one of the reasons behind the banning of aircrafts such as Concord was its high release of gaseous emissions. Killer smog of London in 1952 caused death of 4000; similar smog event of New York caused death of 200 in 1953 primary cause behind these events was automobile discharge (Martin, "autolife", 2010).

Pollutants of transport consists CO, HC, oxides of Nitrogen, oxides of Sulphur, Volatile Organic Compounds, lead and particulate matter, secondary pollutants such as Ozone is generated by reaction between Oxides of Nitrogen and VOC which is the main component of photochemical smog, secondary particulate matter also generated by the reaction of all of these compounds. Increased traffic in cities further increases the risk. In addition, non-exhaust particulate matter emissions produced from components such as tires, clutch and break. (Krzyzanowski , Kuna-Dibbert , & Schneider, 2005).

Upgrading fuel quality such as reformulated gasoline (RFG) during the combustion, RFG releases benzene in the concentration less than 1%, reduced levels of Volatile organic compounds, NO_x and toxic emissions, where benzene, 1,3 butadiene, aldehydes, and polynuclear aromatic hydrocarbons found in vehicle emission are known for carcinogenicity. Upgrading the standard of refineries to produce less Sulphur contented fuels.

Improving the qualities of engine, two-stroke three-wheeler and bike engines produces double the amount of particulate matter than four-stroke this is banned in certain countries such as India, China and Sri Lanka, as it is already banned in the western world, or manufactures can be given by retrofit kit to reduce the emission. Improve the performance, low fuel consumption and low emission, further improves the direct injection and homogeneous charge compression ignition engines. Removing the toxic emission and collected soot by combustion, since it required temperature as high as 500°C thus, adequate manipulations to be made in engine parameters to attain high temperatures, this may be possible by reducing the fuel additives such as cerium oxide and copper oxide. Servicing the filter is essential to avoid blockage by prolonged overloading, there are techniques to lower the nitrogen oxides such as selective catalytic reduction by adding urea.

Switch to lead free gasoline as lead effects the circulatory, nervous, kidney and reproductive systems also it causes dyslexia and hyperactivity in children. Since 2000, lead containing petrol is completely banned all over the world, reduction in olefins, benzene, Poly cyclic Aromatic Hydrocarbon (PAH) and Sulphur from patrol while reaching higher ignition quality, Similarly, limiting PAH and Sulphur contents from Diesel. In US oxygenated fuels are used to control CO emission, increase in Octane level reduces the emissions and improves performance significantly (Bose, Sundar, & Nesamani, 2000).

Government and public can find several ways to mitigate the issue such as implementing emission test and certification programmes, effective mechanisms for enforcement of vehicle compliance via periodic renewal and registration. Alternative less emission fuels such as LPG/LNG and biogas, Quality control and training programmes on upgrading engines and emission, providing better filters with advanced technology, providing repair cost waivers, switching to Hybrid, fully electric vehicles and fuel cell satisfies the demand for zero emission vehicles. Incentives such as duty free or tax reduction for zero emission vehicles (Krzyzanowski , Kuna-Dibbert , & Schneider, 2005).

3.9 Air pollution from Natural Sources.

A. Sea spray

Salt mixing with air from sea spray increases the concentration of particulate matter in the air; this contributes 80% of the particulate matter in coastal area. According to the research data of (Partanen, et al., 2014), sea aerosol provided radiative effect was -0.2 W m^{-2} (direct 0.03 W m^{-2} and indirect effect -0.07 W m^{-2}) this interferes the global radiation pattern and subsequently the weather (Partanen, et al., 2014).

B. Volcanic ash

Pinatubo mount volcanic eruption of Philippines in 1991 caused large mass of 20-million-ton sulphur dioxide cloud to the stratosphere, altitude ranging up to 20 miles, other similar eruptions are Tambora in 1815 and Krakatau in 1883. (McGee, Doukas, Kessler, & Gerlach, 1997) Smoke (fog) also reflects the sunlight back and causes temperature decline, reaction of chemical resulted in CFC which led to the destruction of Ozone. Volcanic soot and acids such as Hydrogen sulphide, Sulphur dioxide, and Hydrogen chloride causes health issues such as damaging mucus membrane, respiratory system and eye irritation. Carbon dust covered several miles and causes evacuation of people. Particles such as Radon 222 emitted from the gas releases harmful radiation which causes cell damage and eventually cancer. Rain fall with the volcanic emissions causes acid rain due to its acidic contents, in Costa Rica acid rain affects the animals and vegetation as the downwind of Poàs volcano flows over (Peterson & Tilling, 2000). Volcanic emissions also elevate the level of greenhouse gases (CO_2 and H_2O) in the atmosphere which is accompanied with H_2S, HCl, HF, H_2, CO, volatile metal Chlorides, Chlorine monoxide(McGee, Doukas, Kessler, & Gerlach, 1997).

C. Forest fires

Forest fires are more frequent in Australia, Indonesia, Brazil, Russia, Canada and Southern United States during the El Nino events. During 1997 El-Nino event Indonesian forest fire emission of CO_2 was 2 billion tons (one third of annual anthropogenic CO_2 emission) ("American Association of Advancement of Science", 2002). In 2007 forest fires in Southern California caused the release of 7.9 million metric tons of CO_2 just in a period of one week, it is also estimated that annual release of CO_2 by forest fire events alone is 290 million metric tons ("nsf.gov", n.d.). This shows there is no doubt that though we go for solutions to anthropogenic CO_2 emission such human induced changes are comparatively far smaller than natural CO_2 emission process. It is also visible that finding solutions to the natural emissions is comparatively more important, this is currently carried by pre-planned forest fire disaster mitigation programmes mainly during the events of ENSO. In addition, burning of Savannah in countries such as Zimbabwe, Zambia and Botswana, and forest fires are also the source for CO_2(Ray, Theory, selection and design of air pollution control equipment, 2004a).

D. Sandstorms (sand paper) and Desert dust

Turbulences of Sahara during extremes of hot weather condition (as high as about 50°C& lack of rain fall), Dust particles from Sahara blown across Africa and Europe ("eea.europa.eu", n.d.). According to NASAs satellite image (June 25th 2014) plume of dust particles from Africa moves towards America across Atlantic Ocean. According to Miami researchers as cited in (Patric, 2014), particle dust scatter and absorb solar radiation over tropical Atlantic which resulted in cooler temperatures. It could affect asthmatic patients or causes respiratory problems.

E. Manmade disasters and war

Vietnam War caused burning and destruction of forest trees. Destruction of forest cover by US forces during the war alone was estimated as 4.9 million hectares and changed the weather pattern (Hill, n.d.).

Gulf War oil spill explosions, during the war oil spills in Kuwait were blown up, the fire last for up to seven months and caused severe environmental problems.

Nuclear explosion of Hiroshima and Nagasaki in Japan 1945 release huge amount of Carbon and particle matters in the atmosphere addition to the radiation pollution.

Bhopal disaster in India in 1984, released more than 40 tons of methyl isocyanate gas leaked from pesticide plant, which immediately killed 3,800 and thousands later, it also resulted permanent and severe injuries to many thousands of people lived in that region.

1952 London's killer fog (consist of sulphur dioxide, nitrogen oxides and soot) killed about 4,000. Iraqi Sulphur plant Al-Mishraq fire of 2003, burnt for about a month and caused acid rain and respiratory problems. Explosion of chemical company (ICMESA) in Meda, Italy in 1976 caused dioxin release; here many children were affected by skin diseases.

Adopted from ("disasterium.com", 2013)

3.10   Ways to avoid Air pollution (Air quality management)

Air quality management refers to all activities that are directed towards creating and maintaining clean air, there are three different ways to approach the issue 1. Strategic approach 2. Technical approach 3. Educational approach. Afforestation and reforestation, implementing strict rules and regulations against deforestation, avoid slash and burn agriculture and land clearing, implementing vehicle emission test and enforcement of legislations, proper assessment on maintaining ambient air quality standards in industries and stack sampling, routine air quality checking, managing data and environmental pollution control (EPC) licensing in factories and industries, conducting proper Environmental Impact Assessment during the development activities such as industrial zones use the knowledge of air quality modelling and standard guidelines, banning of hazardous and chemically active air pollutants, implementing strict laws against solid waste burning in public places, cleaner fuels, improving engine technology, low emission fuel and engine alternatives, improving better gas and particle capture technology, increasing public awareness and introducing safe methods that would not result in harmful fumes, particle fibres and gases. Regulatory control including standard setting, granting legal authority to implement the control strategy with development of permitting programmes, collecting required funds, enforcement activities and issuing National guidelines referring to WHO Guidelines (Table 3.5).

Table 3.5 Substances and WHO Guideline

Substance	WHO Guideline (updated 2005)
PM2.5	10 $\mu g/m^3$ annual mean 25 $\mu g/m^3$ 24-hour mean
PM10	20 $\mu g/m^3$ annual mean 50 $\mu g/m^3$ 24-hour mean
O_3	100 $\mu g/m^3$ 8-hour mean
NO_2	40 $\mu g/m^3$ annual mean 200 $\mu g/m^3$ 1-hour mean
SO_2	20 $\mu g/m^3$ 24-hour mean 500 $\mu g/m^3$ 10-minute mean

Adapted from (WHO Global update 2005, 2006)

3.11 Protection from polluted air

Wearing face masks, evacuation from areas of forest fires, volcanic activity and anthropogenic pollution, improving forecasting technology of disaster events such as forest fires during el-nino, avoid burning wastes in populated areas or switch to sanitary landfills and safe incineration and dust filtering technology, using air conditioners, air filters, wind curtains, improve medications for asthma and other respiratory disorders and planting trees in the surrounding environment help to mitigate the effects of polluted air.

3.12 International Conventions on Air pollution

A. Kyoto Protocol, 1997

This is an amendment to the U.N. Framework convention on climate change, parties are committed to bring down the emission of six greenhouse gases (Carbon dioxide (CO_2), Methane (CH_4), Nitrous oxide (N_2O), Hydrofluorocarbons (HFCs), Per fluorocarbons (PFCs), and Sulphur hexafluoride (SF_6)("UNFCCC", 2014)or reducing their production as the listed gases cause global warming, parties agreed to fund research on climate change and promoting alternative energy sources in both developed and developing nations, it also includes several international partnerships such as Asia- Pacific partnership on clean development and Climate.

71

B. Effects of Industrial Accidents, 1992

Convention aimed to prevent, preparedness to industrial accidents and protecting human health and environment, indeed parties are committed to prevent industrial accidents by preventing them to certain extent by reducing their severity, frequency and providing mitigations for their effects. Parties assured the international cooperation emergency responses, research, developing, sharing the technology and information.

C. U.N. Framework Convention on Climate change, 1992.

Convention aimed to set an overall frame work for intergovernmental authorities to face the challenge of climate change. It is well recognized that the emissions of CO_2 and other greenhouse gases are the main factors affect the stability of climate system which is a globally shared resource. 192 signatories agreed to collect and share data, draw national policies and best practices, launch national strategies for addressing emissions and cooperate in preparing for adaptation to the effects of climate change.

D. Montreal Protocol, 1987

This is on substances that cause Ozone depletion in stratosphere (chlorofluorocarbons, halons, carbon tetrachloride and methyl chloroform) and committed to gradually terminate the production and consumption of such compounds and accomplished by 2000 and for methyl chloroform by 2004. 191 countries agreed to cut the production of such chemicals. And it was successfully brought down the level of such chemicals to 83,000 metric tons at the end of 2005 which was 1.8 million metric tons in 1987.

E. Geneva Convention on Long-range Transboundary Air Pollution, 1979

The Convention was the first international legal agreement dealing with problems of air pollution on a regional basis. 34 governments and members of European Union have signed that time, in the year 2008 it has increased to 51 parties. It set up an international frame work bringing together research and policy negotiation aiming to prevent the spread of pollutants emission sources to atmosphere, it is extended by 8 protocols that demonstrate specific measures to cut down the release of air pollutants.

Adopted from ("iipdigital.usembassy.gov", 2012)

Following problems causes Air pollution

3.13   Air pollution due to deforestation

Please see the chapter deforestation

3.14 Air pollution due to plastic pollution (plastic waste incineration)

According to Verma, Vinoda, Papireddy, & Gowda (Verma, Vinoda, Papireddy, & Gowda, 2016), about 12% of plastics in municipal solid waste are burnt. This releases toxins such as Dioxins, Furans, Mercury, and Polychlorinated Biphenyls into the atmosphere. Poly Vinyl Chloride (PVC) liberates hazardous halogens into the atmosphere. Toxic fumes from plastic incineration are a threat not only to human health but also to the plants and wildlife. The paper further stated that hazardous brominated compounds are carcinogens and mutagens. Dioxin (2,3,7,8 tetrachlorodibenzo-p-dioxin) also causes cancer, neurological effects, disorders related to reproductive, thyroid, and respiratory systems.

3.15 Air pollution due to the global energy crisis

According to Perera (Perera, 2018), air pollution is caused mainly due to the combustion of fossil fuels in the sectors of electricity generation, heating, transportation, and industry(USEPA, n.d.)as cited in (Perera, 2018). According to 2011 estimates, global fossil fuels represented 82% of the total primary energy supply (Council, 2013) as cited in (Perera, 2018). In the U.S., oil, natural gas, and coal account for 81% of the current fuel consumption (USEIA, 2014) as cited in (Perera, 2018). According to International Energy Agency(IEA, 2016) as cited in (Perera, 2018), the energy produced from fossil fuels in high and middle-income countries and biomass burning in low-income countries accounts for most of the global air pollution, causes 85% of airborne particulate pollution and almost all sulphur dioxide and nitrogen oxide emissions to the atmosphere. Also, black carbon, polycyclic aromatic hydrocarbons (PAH), nitrogen and sulphur dioxides, mercury, and volatile organic compounds that form ground-level ozone by reacting with nitrogen oxides in the presence of sunlight all have multiple adverse effects on human health and the most susceptible group are the children. According to WHO that only one person in 10 who lives in a city complies with WHO air quality guidelines (WHO, 2016) as cited in (Perera, 2018). It has been revealed (WHO, 2016) as cited in (Perera, 2018)that household air pollution is an important risk factor for an estimated 2.9 billion people all over the world. Furthermore, a sum of about 2 billion children live in areas that exceed the WHO annual guideline for particle matter 10 $\mu g/m^3$(WHO, 2005) as cited in (Perera, 2018). It was stated in ("Clear the Air for Children", 2016) as cited in (Perera, 2018), at present, about 300 million children live in areas where outdoor air pollution exceeds international guidelines at least six-fold. However, indoor air pollution is on a decline as the use of solid fuels has declined from 60% in

1980 to 42% in 2012(Who Indoor Air Quality Guidelines: Household Fuel Combustion, 2014) as cited in (Perera, 2018). In addition, urban ambient air pollution has increased by about 8% in the period between 2008 and 2013, and the upward trend is projected to continue ("Clear the Air for Children", 2016) as cited in (Perera, 2018).

According to International Energy Agency (IEA, 2016) as cited in (Perera, 2018), anthropogenic activities related to energy consumption annually emit about 35 billion metric tons of carbon dioxide into the atmosphere. According to National Oceanic and Atmospheric Administration(NOAA, 2017) as cited in (Perera, 2018), the annual greenhouse gas index which tracks the warming caused by the long-lived climate-altering gases depicted a 40% increase in the period between 1990 and 2016, and the rising carbon dioxide levels is responsible for the most of the change. According to "Climate Central, highest levels in 800,000 years"("Climate Central. Highest Levels in 800,000 Years", n.d.)as cited in (Perera, 2018), today, carbon dioxide levels in the atmosphere are at their peak in 800,000 years.

In the U.S., coal and natural gas are the largest contributors to carbon pollution, and this is seconded by methane released during the production of natural gas, oil, and coal {National Energy Technology Laboratory (NETL, 2015)} as cited in (Perera, 2018). In addition, methane is 34 times more effective than carbon dioxide at trapping heat over a period of 100 years(Myhre, et al., 2013) as cited in (Perera, 2018). In the U.S. natural gas is expected to surpass coal in total fuel consumption as a source of energy that emits carbon dioxide (EIA, n.d.)as cited in (Perera, 2018). International Energy Agency stated that global growth in coal consumption is predicted to decline in the period between 2015 and 2021 as developed countries continue to abandon coal and China's consumption plateaus. However, this decline will be offset by the growing demands of emerging developing nations such as India and Southeast Asia. Furthermore, the U.S. Energy Information Administration predicts that globally, coal will remain the second-largest energy source, following petrol and other liquid fuels, until 2030. And thereafter in the period between 2030 and 2040 it will occupy third place, surpassed only by natural gas and liquid fuels(EIA, 2017) as cited in (Perera, 2018).

According to International Energy Agency (IEA, 2016), global energy consumption has been remarkably stable over the past 25 years as the estimates in both 1989 and 2014 accounted for 81% of total energy consumption. However, the share of oil has declined from 37% to 31%, but the natural gas rose from 19% to 21% and coal increased from 25% to 28%, the contribution of biofuels remained steady at 10% of global energy needs.

The type and intensity of air pollution depend on the source, a gasoline car with a catalytic converter emit 1.4kt of NO_x per Mtoe (million tonnes of oil equivalent), while a diesel truck without a filter emits more than 50kt of NO_x per Mtoe. With particle matter (PM) bio-energy dominates with average emission per unit of 13 kt per Mtoe in traditional stoves. For SO_2, average SO_2 emission for coal power plants varies between less than 1kt per Mtoe to above 30 kt per Mtoe. Among all pollutants, natural gas results in much lesser emissions.

3.16   Air pollution due to e-waste

According to a journal article 'E-Waste: The next hazard wave'(E-Waste: The next hazard wave, 2007), ("eWaste Guide", n.d.), (Beary , n.d.)as cited in (Pinto, 2008)studies revealed that the Total E-waste production in India is 146,000 tonnes to 33,000,000 tonnes and it was expected to reach 47,000,000 tonnes in 2011 at that time. According to "eWaste Guide"("eWaste Guide", n.d.) as cited in (Pinto, 2008), the top states that produce the highest quantity of e-waste are Maharashtra, Andhra Pradesh, Tamil Nadu, Uttar Pradesh, West Bengal, Delhi, Karnataka, Gujarat, Madhya Pradesh, and Punjab. The leading cities that generate e-waste are Mumbai, Delhi, Bangalore, Chennai, Kolkatta, Ahmedabad, Hyderabad, Pune, Surat, and Nagpur. In India, about 80,000 people working in the recycling sector, some villages such as Seelampur has scrap markets where piles of e- wastes are separated for recycling. They separate copper from wires after burning them. Plastic and PVC codes produce noxious smoke irritable to the eyes and cause respiratory problems. Also, acid treatment is given to isolating metals; corrosive acids also released from used batteries of cell phones and computers, according to scientists of Greenpeace recycling a computer in India costs just $2 while it is $20 in the U.S. ("Keekeesocean: E Waste in India", 2012), not only cheap labor but also for the profit from recovered metals of circuit boards such as copper gives earning of $3 to $5 per day workers are spending on dismantling e- wastes rather considering their own health. However, currently, they are building an e-waste recycling plant in Bangalore, which has the capacity to handle 60,000 tons of e-waste annually. In India, about 24% of e-waste was produced from Mumbai, Delhi, Bangalore, and Chennai.

About 4 million tons of wastes are brought to Ghana from Antwerp and other parts of the western world. The government of Ghana has signed in every international treaty but the entry of e-waste is still there as the people of Ghana do not afford to purchase new electronic goods due to their poverty and slum children and young men are used as collectors and dismantlers for cheap labor. E-wastes include cameras, computers, TVs, refrigerators, drillers, and many used electronic items. They are sold for a cheap price but no warranty for its usage, while unusable items are burned and dumped there (figure 3.1). The river has now become a dark muddy stream rich in heavy metal wastes. Fishermen have almost lost their hopes and catch contains heavy metals which can cause a long-term impact on human beings {Adapted from (Dateline, 2011)}.

Figure 3.1 Combustion of e-waste in Ghana, Africa
Source:(Chasant, 2018), License: CC BY-SA 4.0

3.17   Air pollution due to wetlands or draining of wetlands

Wetland methane releases are the largest natural source of global methane budget. However, wetland methane feedbacks were not fully accessed in the intergovernmental panel on climate change fifth assessment report. However, agriculture expansion along with population increase also increases the area of wetlands such as paddy fields, which continuously release methane to the atmosphere. Boreal methane emissions are increased by 18.05 Tg to 41.69 Tg, due to the thawing of inundated areas during the cold season (December to May) and rising

76

temperature, while tropical methane emissions accelerate with a total increment of 48.36 Tg to 87.37 Tg by 2099 (Zhang, et al., 2017). Besides, annual methane emission from natural wetlands was projected to increase from 172 Tg $CH_4 \cdot y^{-1}$ at present to an average of ~225 Tg $CH_4 \cdot y^{-1}$ by 2050 and decline thereafter (according to one of the predicted scenario, RCP 2.6), however, in contrast, another scenario predicted that the methane levels are about to increase till 2070, and reaching a peak of ~246 ± 21 Tg $CH_4 \cdot y^{-1}$ and remain constant thereafter (RCP 4.5), and another scenario projected that methane emission from wetlands expected to double by 2090 (RCP8.5) (Zhang, et al., 2017).

According to United Nations University(United Nations University, 2008), it has been estimated that drained tropical swamp forests release an estimated 40 tonnes of carbon per hectare per year. Also, drained peat bogs released about 2.5 to 10 tonnes of carbon per hectare per year. Peat bogs of Siberia, North America, and Scandinavia contain a third of all carbon in the world's soil. Wetlands in Scotland contain over 90% of the carbon in British soils and forests. Furthermore, the Pantanal wetlands of Brazil spanning 160,000 square km are affected by evaporation and development pressure, which possibly result in many greenhouse gases.

3.18   Air pollution due to intensive farming

According to Bauer, Tsigaridis, & Miller (Bauer, Tsigaridis, & Miller, 2016), agricultural practices, livestock production, and nitrogen fertiliser usage affect surface air quality. According to Galloway and others(Galloway, et al., 2008) as cited in (Bauer, Tsigaridis, & Miller, 2016), increasing fertiliser usage and meat production threaten the ecosystem via Nitrate deposition. It has been calculated that globally averaged Nr deposition has increased from 49 TgN/yr during preindustrial times (1850) to 141 TgN/yr by 2010. This increase is mainly because of an increase in cereal production from 1897 Mt to 2270 Mt or a 20% increase and meat production increased from 207 Mt to 260 Mt or a 26% increase. However, these rising agricultural demands were accomplished by the Haber-Bosch process of Nr production, from 100 TgN yr^{-1} to 121 TgN yr^{-1} or 20%.

Also, the study revealed Europe, the eastern U.S., and China are the three main regions where agriculture is the prominent source of $PM_{2.5}$.

3.19   Pollution through mining activities causes air pollution

According to Ghose & Majee (Ghose & Majee, 2001), open cast coal mining activity generates a huge amount of dust and particle matter into the air. A survey using emission data from different coal mining sites including factors such as work zone air quality, ambient air quality, and seasonal variations depicted that there is high pollution potential due to the emission of suspended particulate matter (SPM) and its health hazards to humans. The study also suggested a few solutions, such as air pollution control measures, such as the implementation of a series of preventive and suppressive measures.

3.20   Air pollution due to solid wastes and sewage

According to Pathak & Kushwaha(Pathak & Kushwaha, 2013),a study held in Maihar municipality solid waste dumping site in Satna district, Madhya Pradesh, India, where the concentration of suspended particle matter (SPM), respirable suspended particle matter (RSPM), SO_2 and NO_2monitored at four directions of the dumping site during post-monsoon, winter, pre-monsoon and monsoon months in the year 2007-08 and 2008-09, and results showed that the concentrations of SPM and RSPM were above the permissible limits, whereas gaseous pollutants such as SO_2 and NO_2were within the permissible limit of (Central Pollution Control Board) CPCB, India. Maximum of $884\mu g/m^3$ of SPM and $342\ \mu g/m^3$ of RSPM was observed during winter season 2008-09 and a minimum of $250\ \mu g/m^3$ of SPM and $84\ \mu g/m^3$ of RSPM was observed during monsoon season 2007-08. All mentioned air pollutants of ambient air having a greater value at downwind direction than the upwind direction, and ultimately the study revealed a significant amount of air pollution caused by solid waste dumping site.

According to Pansuk, Junpen, & Garivait(Pansuk, Junpen, & Garivait, 2018), a study conducted on household solid waste management in areas governed by local administrative organizations (LAO) in Thailand with a questionnaire survey of random sampling on 4300 household residential areas governed by 96 LAOs depicted that a sum of 26.17 Mt of solid waste was produced every year, of which 6.39 Mt/year was not collected by the LAOs and was eliminated by households. Also, about 53.7% of waste burned on or outside the households' property or an equivalent of 3.43 Mt/year of solid waste burned in open areas. It is also evident that 0.66 Mt/year of solid waste collected by the LAOs was burned in open areas and was not eliminated properly. The total amount of solid waste from these two sources was 4.09 Mt/ year, which resulted in emissions of CO_2 equivalent, CO, SO_2, NO, and particulate matter of 1247.3 kt/year, 103 kt/year, 1.2 kt/year, 7.4 kt/year, and 19.6 kt/year, respectively.

It has been reported in Kumari, Kumar, Vineel, Khare, & Kumar(Kumari, Kumar, Vineel, Khare, & Kumar, 2017) that open burning of municipal solid waste is a source of emission of carcinogenic substances in India, the paper also listed ten major harmful pollutants such as dioxin, furans, particulate matter, CO, sulphur oxides, nitrogen oxides, benzene, toluene, ethyl benzene and 1- hexane. It was also mentioned that people who live in metropolitan areas are more affected by these emissions.

Das, Bhave, Sapkota, & Byanju(Das, Bhave, Sapkota, & Byanju, 2018)estimated the quantity of municipal solid waste that was burned in five erstwhile municipalities of Kathmandu valley, Nepal. The study includes a household survey, a transect walk survey, an experiment measuring a fraction of combustible waste, a survey on the fraction of the population burning the waste outside their houses, a survey on the fraction of municipal solid waste (MSW) burned at dumpsites. Furthermore, burning/oxidation efficiency, municipal populations, MSW generation rates, and emission factors were derived from the literature. Results showed that the total mass of MSW burned during 2016 is estimated to be 7400tons (i.e. 20 tons per day), which was 3% of the total MSW generated in the valley municipalities that year (this exceeds government estimated by factor 3). Multiplication of burned MSW mass by emission factors, the air pollutant emissions are estimated as $PM_{2.5}$ 55 tons (OC 42 tons and EC 1.4 tons), PM_{10} 60 tons, B.C. 25 tons, CO_2 11,900 tons, CH_4 30 tons, SO_2 5.0 tons, NO_x 19.2 tons, CO 630 tons, Non-methane volatile organic compounds 112 tons, and NH_3 5.7 tons per year. The study also revealed that open burning can cause health impacts such as acute and chronic respiratory disease, heart diseases, and allergic hypersensitivity, along with impacts on the local climate.

3.21 Air pollution due to agrochemicals

According to Nascimento, Rocha, & Andrade (Nascimento, Rocha, & Andrade, 2017), a study developed a green-sensitive sample preparation method for the determination of nine organophosphates, two pyrethroids, one carbamate, and one strobilurin in$PM_{2.5}$ collected in the tropical coastal area in the Southern Hemisphere. Extraction of $PM_{2.5}$ sample masses, as low as 206 μg were performed in a miniaturized device using 500 μL of a mixture containing 18% acetonitrile in dichloromethane followed by sonication for 23 minutes and injection into GC-MS. Based on the results twelve pesticides were identified and quantified, this includes eight banned pesticides. Also, a risk assessment exposure and cancer risk for possible carcinogenic pesticides such as bifenthrin, malathion, parathion, and permethrin were performed for exposure of adults, children, and infants, and based on the results Hazard Quotient and cumulative exposure for organophosphate and pyrethroid pesticides were less than 1, shows the cumulative risk is within an acceptable range. According to "Persistance organic pollutants: national implementation plan for 2005-

2020"("Persistance organic pollutants: national implementation plan for 2005-2020", 2005), in Latvia third national priority status is given to persistent organic pollutants (POPs) pesticides. However, POPs pesticides are not produced, sold, or used in Latvia but there are stockpiles, temporary storage sites found in Kņava non-marketable chemical storage facility and the Garden hazardous waste disposal site such as Toxaphene ~200 t DDT; ~5 t, Lindane ~170 t, Lindane DDT mixture of ~ 200 t. According to "anses"("anses", 2016), contamination of air by pesticides is a less documented air pollution issue all over the world. In 2000, the first measurement of pesticides in air and indoor environments was recorded by an approved French air quality monitoring association (AASQA) and French indoor air quality observatory (OQAI). And the report was published in 2010 entitled "Recommendations and outlook for national monitoring of air contamination by pesticides".

3.22 Air pollution due to nuclear explosions-radiation-nuclear wastes

According to Dowd (Dowd, n.d.), after the nuclear explosion mushroom cloud forms from the vaporized debris and disperses radioactive particles that fall on earth, contaminates air, water, soil, and food sources. Fallout can cause far-reaching environmental effects when carried by air currents. The Hiroshima explosion of 1945 destroyed everything within a 4.4 square mile radius of detonation and followed by radioactive fallout. According to Wargo (Wargo, 2009), a nuclear fallout caused by the operator error in the Chernobyl nuclear facility in 1986, affected the air and contaminated five million acres of cropland in Ukraine. The high radiation level was noticed in crops and milk from grazing cows in the contaminated region. According to Robock & Toon(Robock & Toon, 2012), the dense smoke generated from a nuclear explosion could block sunlight and plunge the area into darkness; this affects photosynthesis and causes starvation. It was also mentioned that nuclear warheads could deplete the ozone layer and could worsen the effects of global warming.

3.23 Air pollution due to hazardous wastes

According to Shen (Shen, 1981), a study conducted at municipal landfills indicated that landfill gases consist mainly of methane, carbon monoxide, hydrogen, ammonia, aromatic hydrocarbon, halogenated organics, and hydrogen sulphide (Lynton & Kenneth, 1985) on assessing toxic air pollution downwind of hazardous waste landfills to determine whether potential health threats or exceedance of air quality standards exist. Here, the emission rate of vinyl chloride from the BKK co-disposal landfill in West Covina, California was estimated. According to Tian and others (Tian, et al., 2012), a multiple year emission inventory of hazardous air pollutants (HAPs) including particulate matter, SO_2, NO_x, CO, HCl, As, Cd, Cr, Hg, Ni, Pb, Sb and polychlorinated dibenzo-p-dioxins and polychlorinated dibenzofurans (PCDD/Fs), emitted from municipal solid waste incineration in China in the period between 2003 and 2010 depicted that 28 471.1 t of NO_x, 12 062.1 t of SO_2, 6500.5 t of CO, 4654.6 t of PM, 3609.1 t of HCl, 69.5 t of Sb, 36.7 t of Hg, 9.4 t of Pb, 4.4 t of Cr, 2.8 t of Ni, 926.7 kg of Cd, 231.7 kg of As, and 23.6 g of PCDD/Fs as toxic equivalent quantity by the year 2010. The study further revealed that major hazardous air pollutant emissions are mostly in the eastern central and southeastern regions of China, where many municipal solid waste incinerators are located. In the period if 2003 to 2010 provinces, such as Zhejiang, Guangdong, and Jiangsu were ranking in the top three with the highest hazardous air pollutant emissions.

3.24   Air pollution due to urbanization-urban sprawl-settlements

It has been revealed by Singh and others (Singh, Prasad, Chauhan, & Singh, 2015), in urban areas, mainly in cities quality of air is affecting human health. As rising air pollution is due to the increased dependency on coal and petroleum as a source of energy by the rapidly increasing population. Thus, impacts of air pollutants such as carbon dioxide, sulphur dioxide, aerosols, and black carbon are increasing with urbanization as their impacts on hydrological cycles, temperature, precipitation as well as human health have become visible along with urbanization, as shown in the SCIAMACHY diagram distribution of anthropogenic aerosol particles were high over urban cities with high population densities such as Delhi, Kanpur, Kolkata, and Mumbai depicted the highest levels of aerosol in the air. And when considering the SCIAMACHY diagram of NO_2 distribution, again the same urban regions depicted the maximum level of NO_2 concentrations (Singh, Prasad, Chauhan, & Singh, 2015).

According to Song, Webb, Parmenter, Allen, & McDonald-Buller (Song, Webb, Parmenter, Allen, & McDonald-Buller, 2008), a study examined the impacts of alternative regional development patterns on emissions, dry deposition, and air quality using future visions of future land use in Austin, Texas associated with a doubling of population in 20-40 years from 2001. Here emissions and special allocation were determined based on the pattern of development or urbanization and used to predict the hourly ozone emissions between future emission levels and 2007 data ranged from -14 to 22 ppb and associated with implementing federal mobile source standards. However, differences from biogenic emissions and dry deposition from urbanization ranged between -1.4 and 0.7 ppb. These differences in the magnitude of emissions produced greater changes in air quality than the differences in regional development scenarios. In contrast, above given the 2007 range (-14 to 22), the predicted differences of future scenarios ranged from -3 to 5 ppm. Thus, the results concluded that although the effects of urbanization patterns are non-negligible, the pattern of urbanization is not as significant as reductions in emissions per capita.

Also, People in highly urbanized megacities and cities such as Los Angles, New York, Beijing, and Delhi are more often affected by polluted air such as Killer smog in London in 1952 caused the death of 4000; a similar smog event in New York caused the death of 200 in 1953 primary cause behind these events was automobile discharge (Martin, 2010).

Air pollution effects into following problems

3.25   Biodiversity loss due to air pollution

According to Sanderfoot & Holloway (Sanderfoot & Holloway, 2017), an article summarizes findings published since the 1950s regarding avian responses to air pollution depicted evidence that air pollutants such as carbon monoxide, tropospheric ozone, sulphur dioxide, smoke, particle matters including heavy metals, and various urban and industrial emissions cause respiratory distress, increased detoxification effort, elevated stress levels, and illness, immune suppression, behavioural changes, and impaired reproductive success. Also, a reduction in avian species richness, diversity, and population density in heavily air-polluted areas showed that there is a clear relationship between air pollution and biodiversity loss.

In a study, Llacuna , Gorriz , Durfort , & Nadal(Llacuna , Gorriz , Durfort , & Nadal , 1993) stated that impacts of emissions from coal-fired power plants such as SO_2, NO_x, and particulate matter on natural populations and caged specimens of birds and small mammals were studied. Results based on microscopic (x 1000) and electron microscopic (TEM & SEM) study of killed animals revealed that atmospheric pollutants from coal-fired power plants caused alterations in the tracheal epithelium. Increased mucus which covers the tracheal epithelium, shortening of cilia, and increase in the number of secretory granules and vesicles were observed in passerine birds. Similarly, variation in the uniformity of the pseudostratified epithelium with a wide stratum of mucus, shortening of cilia, and increase number of secretory granules were observed in mammals.

Uptake of heavy metals and accumulation by lichen thalli; according to Garty(Garty, 2001), the study revealed during the 1970s airborne lead affected the lichens, mercury also affected lichens in the same way. The study showed airborne heavy metal contamination caused changes of the spectral reflectance response, an increase of Malondialdehyde (MDA), a decrease of ATP, and injury to enzymatic activities in lichens.

3.26   Destruction of forest and mangroves due to air pollution

According to "Air Pollution and Forest Decline Is There a Link?" ("Air Pollution and Forest Decline Is There a Link?", 1990), since the late 1970s, scientists had reported forest decline in several parts of the world. In Europe, species such as silver fir, hardwoods, and conifers showed a population decline. It was recorded that smelters have damaged nearby forests in the United States. Low-level ozone from the Los Angeles basin caused a decline in forests of the San Bernardino Mountains, and the Sierra Nevada Mountains of California affected Ponderosa pine, Jeffery pine, black oak, and white fir. It was recorded that low-level ozone damaged white pine trees in parts of the Eastern United States, along with, forests such as high elevation spruce and fir forests of the East, natural strands of pines in the North Carolina, South Carolina, and Georgia, and some sugar maple in New England (Low-level ozone interferes with the photosynthesis and causes other damages). Thus, prolonged exposure to ozone in lower concentrations may cause similar damage to other plant species.

3.27   Poverty-disease-war-food insecurity due to air pollution

Annually, air pollution is responsible for an estimated seven million deaths, or one in eight premature deaths. Also, about 4.3 million air pollution-related deaths are due to household air pollution, and 3.7 million deaths are due to outdoor air pollution. The air pollution that caused excess deaths and diseases is $PM_{2.5}$ emitted by diesel vehicles and the combustion of biomass, coal, and kerosene. Besides, low-level ozone, which is a secondary pollutant from nitrogen oxides, also causes severe respiratory illnesses such as chronic asthma (WHO, 2016).

According to "Air pollution and food production"("Air pollution and food production", n.d.)Low-level ozone caused relative estimated global crop losses such as 6-16% loss for soy, 1-12% for wheat, and 3-5% for maize. According to a European study, the impact on ozone on 23 crops amounted to 6.7 billion Euros because crops such as wheat and soybean are highly sensitive to ozone, while potato, rice, and maize are moderately sensitive and barely is resistant to it.

3.28   Visual pollution due to air pollution

Haze resulted when light is absorbed or scattered by pollution particles such as nitrates, sulphates, organic carbon compounds, soot, and soil dust affect the vista(Stapleton, 2016), and some chemicals in the smog might cause eye irritation. Industrial boilers and vehicular emissions cause haze in cities and industrialized areas.

Peroxyacetyl nitrate (PAN) is a secondary air pollutant, PAN is formed due to the photochemical reaction of NO_x with hydrocarbons in the sunlight, PAN is a component of photochemical smog, smog is a mixture of air pollutants such as gases and particles react with sunlight. PAN often causes irritation to the eye, and together with ozone it lowers the lung capacity and increases breathing rate (Ron Brecher, 2003).

Major sources of NO_x are engines, mainly jet engines. One of the reasons behind the banning of air crafts such as Concord was its high release of gaseous emissions. Killer smog of London in 1952 caused the death of 4000; a similar smog event in New York caused the death of 200 in 1953. However, when we consider the visual pollution alone, their effect may prevent the vision along with psychological disturbances of photochemical smog (figure 3.2). In 2013 cities of Beijing, Tianjin and Hebei experienced the hazardous effects of PM 2.5. Smog affects severely in cities where coal combustion is increasingly high.

Figure 3.2 Visual pollution of photochemical smog
Source :(Kimpel, 2006), License : CC BY-SA 2.0

3.29   Ocean acidification due to air pollution

Oceans cover two-thirds of our planet. It consists of rich biodiversity that provides many key links to the food chains, it also maintains the natural balance between oxygen and carbon dioxide in the atmosphere and provides habitat for a vast amount of marine biodiversity. It consists of both biogenic and authigenic minerals. Oceans are the place where life and evolution were initiated on earth. It provides a reservoir for the biogeochemical process. Ocean acidification is the equally evil twin of climate change, and it happens alongside global warming. After the industrial revolution, the atmospheric carbon dioxide levels have been increased due to industrial and agricultural activities (highest level of atmospheric CO_2 in the past 15 million years). In that colossal sum, about a quarter of the carbon dioxide gets absorbed by the oceans every year. Absorbed carbon dioxide alters the chemical properties of the oceans (formation of carbonic acid) and causes a decrease in the pH of seawater and lowers the carbonate ion concentration and the saturation states of biologically important

85

calcium carbonate minerals. This set of chemical reactions is called ocean acidification.

It has been estimated that since the beginning of the industrial revolution (past 200 years) pH of the ocean surface has fallen by 0.1 pH units (pH 8.2 to 8.1) it depicts an approximately 30% increase in the acidity that is faster than any known change in the oceanic chemistry in the last 300 million years("ocean.si.edu", n.d.). A drop in pH by 0.1 might seem like a minor change, but like the Richter scale pH scale also logarithmic (i.e. pH 4 is ten times more acidic than pH 5 and 100 times (10 times 10) more acidic than pH 6).

Carbonate ion's saturation state can be scaled by omega (Ω). If the saturation level of aragonite (a form of carbonate required for shell formation) is less than Ω 1(Ω<1) the conditions are corrosive or under saturated. If a saturation state is above 1(Ω>1) the water is supersaturated for $CaCO_3$and favourable for shell formation, however, coral growth happens to occur from a saturation state of 3 (Ω>=3). And it has been predicted by the computer-based model that by the year 2100 in surface waters of the tropical region where corals found the Ω level will go below 3 when the oceanic acidification continues at the current rate (Ricke, Orr, Schneider, & Caldeira, 2013) as cited in ("IGBP, IOC, SCOR", 2013).

3.30   Acid rain due to air pollution

According to Wondyfraw (Wondyfraw, 2014), acid rain affects Eastern Canada and the Northeastern USA. Sulphur dioxide is released to the atmosphere from the processing of natural gas, coal-fueled large smelters in western Ontario, and steel processing plants in Indiana, Ohio. Also, forests of upstate New York and New England were destroyed by acid rain caused by the sulphur dioxide released from the power plants of the Midwest United States. In 2000, Canada released 2.4 million tons of sulphur dioxide. Besides, sources of nitrogen oxides are vehicular exhausts, furnaces, boilers, and engines. However, about 60% of all nitrogen oxide is released from vehicles. In 2000, Canada released about 2.5 million tons of nitrogen oxide into the atmosphere, which eventually caused acid rain.

In the case of China, Eastern Europe, and Russia and areas downwind from them, the impacts of the acid precipitation can spread over a wide area far from the source of air pollution. North American research revealed that in 1982, about 51,000 people died, and about 200,000 were diseased due to sulphur emission. Similarly, the Southern Norway region was severely affected by acid precipitation over the past decades, though Norway's sulphur dioxide and nitrogen oxide emissions have declined since the 1970s and 1980s. State of the Environment in Norway had reported in southern Norway 18 salmon stocks have lost, and 12 are endangered due to the acidification {Adapted from (Wondyfraw, 2014)}. According to Yibing Lu & Hiroaki Yagoh(Yibing Lu & Hiroaki Yagoh, 2007), acid rain led to a pH of less than 3.0 and caused acute damage to plants that were observed in two megacities of China. Records from city Chongqing revealed that in the period between 2000 and 2006, about 76.2% of collected samples showed a pH of less than 5.0 and 2.4% less than 4.0. And the records from city Kawasaki showed, in the period between 1988 to 2005 depicted, the pH of the samples varied from 3.8~6.6, and the pH below 5.0 was 75.1%. However, emission of SO_2 from industrial sources in Chongqing did not show a considerable increase along with socio-economic development. But the seasonal variation of SO_2 was noticeable with the higher values in winter. Considerable impacts of acid deposition on soil, plant, and ecosystem were observed in Chongqing. Also, forest destruction of 1982 remains to be determined, but it is well believed that the acid deposition from SO_2 may have been the major causes of the problem.

3.31   Global warming and climate change due to air pollution

According to Nuccitelli (Nuccitelli, 2013), in 2004, Naomi Oreskes performed a survey of 928 peer-reviewed papers on climate published in the period from 1993 to 2003, findings showed no paper rejected human causes of global warming. However, this work further expanded by a team of researchers by performing a keyword search of peer-reviewed scientific journal publications for the terms 'global warming' and 'global climate change' published in the period from 1991 to 2011, and subsequent rating of over 12,000 abstracts. Each paper was rated by at least two individuals, and altogether 24,000 ratings were obtained from volunteers from countries including Australia, USA, Canada, UK, New Zealand, Germany, Finland, and Italy. Besides, scientists also asked to rate their own papers. Finally, based on abstract ratings, over 4000 papers took position on the cause of global warming, 97.1% of that endorsed human-caused global warming and in the self-rated papers by the scientists, nearly 1400 papers were rated as taking a position, in that 97.2% of which endorsed human-caused global warming. However, out of these 1400 papers, many papers did not have a position on whether global warming is caused by humans. The consensus had grown to reach about 98% by 2011. However, this resembles the outcome of several previous surveys finding 97% consensus on the human cause of global warming.

Naturally, variation in solar irradiance, variations in orbital parameters of the earth, and volcanic activities cause climate change. A portion of incoming solar energy reflects the space. However, a portion of such outgoing energy is absorbed by atmospheric gases, this also helps to keep the temperature warmer (This is the reason the earth is warmer than the moon). In case if these natural heat-trapping properties are not available, the average surface temperature of the earth would be about 33°C lower (Shine, Derwent, Wuebbles, & Morcrette, 2001)the gases which trap the heat energy is known as greenhouse gases. In recent decades, after the industrial revolution, the amount of greenhouse gases (GHG) in the atmosphere has greatly increased because of human emission of GHG and removal of natural sinks such as deforestation and oceanic pollution. This process of increase in the greenhouse effect causes warming of the earth's surface and alters the energy transfer between the atmosphere, space, land, and the oceans. This phenomenon is referred to as global warming. Besides, solar energy or temperature is the driving force of the earth's weather pattern as it drives the wind, ocean currents, humidity pattern, movement of clouds, etc., thus, the global climate gets changed. This also intensifies the effect of natural disasters such as storms, flooding rain, landslides, droughts, land degradation, and agricultural loss, species loss, and epidemics.

Greenhouse gases give positive radiative forcing (net increase in the energy absorption by earth) due to an increase in radiatively active natural greenhouse gases such as CO_2, CH_4, water vapour, N_2O, O_3. In addition, HFCs, PFCs, and $SF_6$are anthropogenic in origin and are accounted for national greenhouse gas inventories. Several gases are influencing the global radiation budget such as CO, NO_2, $SO_2$and secondary pollutants such as tropospheric ozone (formed in reaction with volatile organic compounds with oxides of nitrogen under UV radiation). Begin with industrialization burning of fossil fuel alone causes a 30% increase in the concentration of greenhouse gases (GHG). Earth's surface temperature has risen by 0.18°C during the last century and the projected rise of current (21st) century is ranging between 1.1 and 6.4°C (Nabuurs, et al., 2007). In the period ranging from 1750 to 2001 increase in CO_2 was by 31%, 150% for methane, and 16% for nitrous oxide in the atmosphere (table 3.6). Since 1880, Earth's average temperature has been warmed by 0.8°C (1.4°F). This has reached a peak in 2014, even though it is an El-Nino neutral year. The warming of the earth has been increasing more steeply during the last three decades (NASA Global Climate change, n.d.).

According to John Cook (John, 2010) as cited in (Anup, 2015), writing the popular Skeptical Science blog (2010), 10 indicators of a human fingerprint on global warming were observed. They are shrinking thermosphere, rising tropopause, less oxygen in the air, the release of over 30 billion tons of CO_2 annually, nights warming faster than days, more fossil fuel carbon in coral, more heat return to earth, more fossil fuel carbon in the air, cooling of stratosphere and less heat escapes to space. Throughout history, earth's climate has changed several times before. For the last 650, 000 years our planet has undergone several glacial advances and retreats including catastrophic events. These changes occurred due to the small variation in solar energy received by the earth during those events and often change the global atmospheric CO_2 levels. After the last ice age (7000 years ago) modern climatic era begins with the emergence of human civilization. The last three decades have shown a rapid increase in global atmospheric CO_2 levels, which never happened before.

Table 3.6 Major sources of Greenhouse gases

Sector	Activities	Gases
Energy	Forest fuel combustion Natural gas leakage Industrial activities Biomass burning	CO_2, CH_4, N_2O, O_3
Forest	Harvesting Clearing Burning	CO_2, CH_4, N_2O
Agriculture	Paddy fields Animal husbandry (ruminants) Fertilizer usage	CO_2, CH_4, N_2O
Waste management	Sanitary landfill Incineration Biomass decay	CO_2, CH_4, N_2O, O_3, CFCs
Industrial	Metal smelting & processing Cement production Petrochemical production Miscellaneous	CO_2, CH_4, N_2O, CFCs, SF_6, CF_4, C_2F_6

Source: (Kemp D. , 2004)

Swedish chemist Svante Arrhenius the first person who predicted the rise of temperature as the CO_2 concentration in the atmosphere rises his findings were published in 1896 (Kemp D. , 2004). CO_2 contributes to 56% of global warming, as other geochemical cycles CO_2 also used to be a self-regulating one until the

89

anthropogenic vast emission and deforestation alter the balance. The major source of CO_2 is fossil fuel burning, it contributes over 75% of atmospheric CO_2in the 1990s, further chemical changes during the production of lime, cement, and ammonia augment and increasing litter and garbage decomposition are other anthropogenic means. Natural sources such as volcanic eruption and forest fires account for a large efflux of CO_2.Increased deforestation, degradation of oceanic algal photosynthesis due to marine pollution also reduces the uptake of $CO_2$from the atmosphere, according to Michael Gunson and Charles Miller of NASA on Global climate change, current CO_2levels exceeds 400 ppm (400.06 in March 2015) and expected to reach 450 ppm or more and the rate of increase is more than 2.75 ppm /year ("NASA GCC", 2015).

Methane naturally exists in the atmosphere mainly from an anaerobic decaying process in natural wetlands, methane has a GWP of 21 and its radiative forcing is 11%, its rate of increase in the atmosphere is twice the rate of CO_2. However, the life span of methane is relatively shorter than that of CO_2as it reacts with hydroxyl radicals and produces water and CO_2 (which are less potent greenhouse gases than methane). Anthropogenic sources account for half of its release to the atmosphere. Agricultural activities such as paddy fields, increased number of cattle and pig dairy farming and non-dairy cattle (ruminants release methane through their digestive process), termite concentrated areas such as tropical grasslands and forests release a considerable amount of methane to the atmosphere (Crutzen, Aselmann, & Seiler, 1986).Also, forest fire events contribute a large amount of methane efflux, particularly during ENSO. Paddy cultivation and various other cultivation produce flooded wetlands that generate methane during anaerobic decomposition. Coal mining processes, leakage through the pipelines, and drilling for oil are major anthropogenic sources (Kemp D. , 2004). Anaerobic decaying of landfill organic wastes and piling of garbage and fertilizer is another source of methane, also venting, flaring at oil and gas wells, enteric fermentation, biomass burning and burning of fossil fuels are few other anthropogenic sources. Besides, a tremendous amount of methane is trapped in higher latitude permafrost and deep ocean sediments as methane hydrates and clathrates. With the effect of warming, permafrost is about to melt and temperatures of oceans gradually increase, this causes decaying of clathrates and release of methane, such methane release is observed in the Pacific Ocean floor and Siberian permafrost(Ruddiman, 2001). Hydroxyl reduction of methane is also minimized due to the reactions with other pollutants, such as CO("Education Global Methane Inventory", 2010). Emission from natural sources alone accounts for ~180-

380 Tg per year. Current total methane emission has risen to~450-500 Tg per year, which is twice the amount of pre-industrial times.

The total amount of carbon dioxide emission caused by an individual, event, organization, or product is measured as carbon dioxide equivalent (CO_2e) or equivalent tons of carbon dioxide. Carbon footprint refers both direct (e.g., Fuel combustion in cooking and own vehicle transport (scope 1) and indirect emission of greenhouse gases (e.g., purchasing thermal power (scope 2), purchasing food or products and employee's business travel (scope 3).

E.g., when we cook food, the production of food using fuel contributes to carbon footprint by the emission of CO_2. When we buy food from the shop, food manufactured in one place and transported to another, causes an additional CO_2 emission during transportation, and packaging using electric machinery contributes to carbon footprint (in case of thermal power generation), travel to purchase food causes CO_2 emission from the transport to be considered (when we use private transport its contribution is more than using public transport), and the bag that is given with food also comprises its own greenhouse gas emission during its production and transportation, thus, cooking food contributes less to the carbon footprint than purchasing. Also, when food waste is disposed of, waste is transported by a municipal truck this causes CO_2emission, during waste storage other greenhouse gas methane is generated due to anaerobic digestion, and disposal methods incineration causes direct CO_2emission to the atmosphere and open dumping also may lead methane generation, thus, every human activity is associated with greenhouse gas generation and contributes to the carbon footprint (Table 3.7). {Adapted from ("Timeforchange.org", n.d.)}.

Table 3.7 CO_2 emission by fuel and the resulted carbon footprint

Fuel type	Unit	CO_2 emitted per unit
Petrol	1 gallon (UK)	10.4 kg
Petrol	1 liter	2.3 kg
Gasoline	1 gallon (USA)	8.7 kg
Gasoline	1 liter	2.3 kg

Diesel	1 gallon (UK)	12.2 kg
Diesel	1 gallon (USA)	9.95 kg
Diesel	1 liter	2.7 kg
Oil (heating)	1 gallon (UK)	13.6 kg
Oil (heating)	1 gallon (USA)	11.26 kg
Oil (heating)	1 liter	3 kg

Source: ("Timeforchange.org", n.d.)

Nitrous oxide is the third-highest greenhouse gas. N_2O has a varying growth rate of 0.1–0.7% per year (Saikawa, et al., 2014). GWP of N_2O is 298, and it accounts for 6% of total radiative forcing by greenhouse gases (Shine, Derwent, Wuebbles, & Morcrette, 2001)as cited in (Kemp D. , 2004). N_2O released from fertilizers mainly during the intermittent stages of nitrification and denitrification, breakdown of nitrogen from livestock manure, and urine account for 5% of global efflux. Transportation is another major source, and supersonic engines and rockets release N_2O. Nitrous oxide is released as a byproduct during the industrial production of nitric acid, mainly in the production of inorganic fertilizer and adipic acid used in the production of fibers such as nylon(EPA overview of greenhouse gases, 2015).

Halogenated carbons such as CFCs were used as refrigerants, insulating foams, aerosol sprays. Its GWP is 12,000 its radiative forcing is 24%(Shine, Derwent, Wuebbles, & Morcrette, 2001) as cited in (Kemp D. , 2004). However, the use and production of CFC are completely banned by the Montreal protocol, thus, current levels of global CFC in the atmosphere are declining.

3.32   Ozone depletion due to air pollution

Commercial use of CFC was started in the 1930s (CFC-12), its reaction with ozone under the UV radiation was initially published by M.J.Molina and F.S.Rowland in 1974. Studies further revealed that about 7% of the ozone layer would be depleted in 60 years by CFC. U.S. banned CFC aerosols in 1978. A Japanese Scientist Dr. Shigeru Chubachi measured the low ozone levels above Syowa, Antarctica and reported at the Ozone commission meeting in Halkidiki, Greece in 1984 in the same year recurring springtime Antarctic ozone hole was discovered by British Antarctic survey scientists Joesph Farman, Brian Gardiner, and Jonathan Shanklin and was published in Nature in May 1985. The study revealed, there is a 10% decline of ozone than norm level during the spring season in Antarctica when the stratospheric temperature goes below -80°C ("The Ozone hole", n.d.). In the period between 1980 and 1990 at northern mid-latitude (Europe) and over the southern regions such as Australia, New Zealand, Argentina, and South Africa the ozone concentration has declined by 4% and 6-7% respectively, and a significant rise in ground level UVR at the DNA damaging wave band was observed(McMichael A. , 2003). Then the Vienna Convention for the Protection of the Ozone Layer, held in 1985, was a multilateral agreement though it acted as a framework, it did not legally bind the use of CFC. After the Montreal protocol in 1987 phasing out of ozone-depleting gases began, and the protocol was tightened further after the 1990s, this put the levels of ozone-depleting substances (ODS) down. In the period from 1986 to 2006, annual worldwide consumption of CFCs declined from 1.1 million tons to 35,000 tons, and the Antarctic ozone layer is expected to attain its normal state by 2050(UNEP, 2008) as cited in (Globalization 101, 2015).{Adapted from (WHO&UNEP, 1995)}.

3.33   Water pollution due to air pollution

According to Wong C. , Li, Zhang, Qi, & Peng (Wong C. , Li, Zhang, Qi, & Peng, 2003), samples of atmospheric deposits were collected in urban, suburban, and rural locations in the Perl River Delta of China (including Hong Kong) during summer and winter seasons in 2001 to 2002. According to the results, atmospheric deposition of Cr, Cu, Pb, and Zn in the Perl River Delta are 6.43±3.19, 18.6±7.88, 12.7±6.72 and 104±36.4 $mg/m^2/yr$, respectively. This is significantly high as the Great Lakes region in North America and the North Sea in Europe. The study also found the concentration of Cu, Cr, and Zn was greater during the summer season than winter (due to the washout effect of rain). Also, the Pb isotopic composition of the air deposits ($^{206}Pb/^{207}Pb$ 1.161–1.177) depicts that the atmospheric input of Pb is mainly from anthropogenic sources such as vehicular emission.

3.34   Air pollution as a keystone environmental problem

Air pollution is not new for this planet because 65 million years ago, during the Cretaceous period, the earth had experienced huge air pollution due to the clouds and smoke formed after the crash of a meteorite. This event caused mass extinction led to the complete elimination of dinosaurs and various other species. Currently, pollution due to natural sources such as forest fires and volcano eruption is creating several tonnes of greenhouse gases and other pollutants, which are unable to find a human solution as they occur naturally. However, Global emission of CO_2 reached 34.5 billion tonnes in 2012, and the yearly increase was 1.4% from that of 2011 (Olivier, Janssens-Maenhout, Muntean, & Jeroen , 2013). Extreme weather patterns and environmental conditions observed as anthropogenic air pollutants are continuously released to the atmosphere and are increasing in quantity and intensity with time. In addition to global warming, acid rain and ozone depletion are well recognized for its severity. Man-made sources can be categorized by source as either point or non-point sources or by its formation as primary or secondary pollutants. Most primary pollutants are the emission of point sources such as factories and non-point sources such as motor vehicle traffic on high ways, whereas secondary pollutants originate by the chemical reaction of primary pollutants and generally non-point source of origin. In addition to naturally existing gases and particles, manmade compounds such as fumes and gases of plastic, heavy metals, pesticides, fibers, and chemical gases are extremely hazardous and cause severe health impacts. Air pollution is a global issue, it is a growing challenge since the time of industrialization and according to the World Bank report in 2013, China lost nearly 10% of its GDP, India 7.69%, Sri Lanka and Cambodia roughly 8%, among developed countries the UK lost $7.6bn, the U.S. $ 45bn and Germany 18bn annually through lost workdays and welfare cost from premature death. According to WHO Global Ambient Air Quality Database, both in urban and rural areas an estimated 3.7 million premature deaths were caused all over the world in 2012. Yet 3 billion people still depend on coal and biomass fuel (indoor), which emit annually several billion tonnes of CO_2, and other greenhouse gases to the atmosphere. Industries, power plants, and transport are some major anthropogenic sources. In the post-industrial era, air pollution can be considered as a keystone man-made environmental problem because termination of CFC air pollution and Sulphur dioxide air pollution would result in a complete solution to the ozone depletion and acid rain, respectively (figure3.3).

Evidence 1: Air pollution causes acid rain

During the 1970s and 80s acid rain was a huge environmental issue, and its impacts such as dead lakes, corroded statues, and increasing rate of asthma were the headlines of that time. According to Nixon & Curran (Nixon & Curran, 1998), in 1985, 21 countries including Canada signed the Helsinki Protocol; Accordingly, Canada was targeting to reduce SO_2 emissions by 30% from the 1980 levels. In 1993, the Canadian acid rain control program was introduced, and this was targeted to reduce the SO$_2$ emission by 50% from the 1980 level of 4.6 million tonnes. In 1990, the Clean Air Act amendments were introduced in the United States. And in 2000, title IV of the amendment promised to cut the SO$_2$ emissions by 9.1 million tonnes. Furthermore, in 1991, Canada and the United States signed a bilateral agreement on air quality. This addressed acid rain and its causative trans-boundary air pollution issues. Nixon & Curran (Nixon & Curran, 1998)stated that the area of North America receiving loadings of wet sulphate over 20 kg/ha/yr. depicted a significant reduction between 1980-82 and 1985-87. However, nitrate loading did not show any significant change during the same period.

According to Owens(Owens, 2019), Gene Likens, an ecologist at the University of Connecticut who first discovered the impacts of acid rain in 1963 at Hubbard Brook Experimental Forest in New Hampshire said that acidity in Hubbard Brook is now 80% less than it was in the 1960s. "It has been a big success story," said Gene Likens.

Levels of SO$_2$ in the USA in the 1970s were 31,218 thousand tons, and the level of SO$_2$ in the USA in 2017 was 2,815 thousand tons(Tiseo, 2020). Thus, the reduction of SO$_2$ in the atmosphere in the period between 1970 and 1917 is 28,403 thousand tons, and the percentage of reduction is 91%. Thus, when it is assumed that the difference between 1960 and 1970 SO$_2$ levels are small and negligible, it is possible to say a 91% reduction in SO$_2$ air pollution caused an 80% reduction in the acidity (acid rain) in Hubbard Brook. This is a general conclusion; the raw data of each value for the reduction in the acidity was not available for statistical calculations.

Evidence 2: Air pollution causes ozone depletion

After the Montreal protocol (1987) on substances that deplete the ozone layer, the Chlorofluorocarbon (CFC) ban was implemented, and the CFC refrigerators were replaced by ozone friendly product. As a result, the ozone layer is recovering. And the ozone hole is expected to heal completely by 2040-2070. Thus, solving CFC air pollution extenuate the resulted ozone depletion issue.

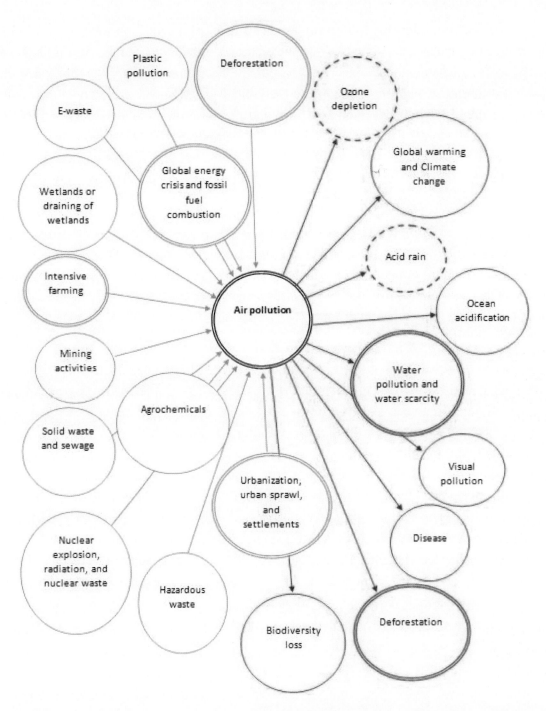

Figure 3.3 Air pollution as keystone environmental problem with the disappearance of ozone depletion and acid rain on its mitigation (hypothetical diagram)

[In the figure black circle is the problem being examined, blue circles are cause man-made environmental problems, red circles are effect man-made environmental

96

problems, double lined circles are keystone man-made environmental problems, and circles with dashed lines (either single or double lined) are the man-made environmental problems that disappear when the problem being examined (black circle) is mitigated]

Air pollution is a keystone environmental problem, which causes acid rain (SO_x & NO_x air pollution), ozone depletion (CFC air pollution), global warming and climate change (greenhouse gas air pollution), respiratory diseases (particle air pollution), and visual pollution (smog air pollution). However, the precursor for air pollution is population explosion in urbanized areas, and pesticide air pollution is usually noticeable in agricultural village regions. To completely overcome acid rain, it is mandatory of getting rid of air pollution caused by oxides of sulphur and nitrogen.

Regenerative vs. Sustainable vs. Conventional solutions

For SO_x flue Gas desulphurization (FGS), Lime Injection Multi stage Burning (LIMB), Fluidized Bed Combustion (FBC or circulation dry scrubbers) and for NO_x Selective Catalytic Reduction (SCR) and catalytic converters provide **greener** solution because it gives minimal harm to the environment (figure 3.4). Furthermore, establishing alternative renewable energy sources of zero emission to replace coal combustion also leads to greener solution because solar for instance generate hazardous heavy metal waste after the use. Similarly, windmill affects birds and causes visual pollution, hydropower dams cause land degradation or soil erosion, and aggravate flooding, biodiversity loss, and etc. wave and tidal power generation affect fish population by obstructing their migratory routes and cause visual pollution. Thus, greener solutions have minimal harm to the nature.

Coal ban is a **sustainable** solution because it causes neither benefit nor harm to the ecology and sentient beings and according to the definition of sustainable development stated in 1987 Brundtland commission report, "development that meets the needs of the present without compromising the ability of future generations to meet their needs" Thus, aforesaid solutions could be categorized as sustainable solutions. However, greener and sustainable solutions are often very expensive due to their high energy requirement such as requirement of equipments and relatively expensive technology. And unlike smart regenerative solutions they cannot adapt or co-evolve with the nature, they cannot affirm the wellbeing, and depicts relatively low systemic vitality and low resilience.

In addition, some **conventional** solutions are unsustainable solutions because they create or exacerbate another environmental problem. This phenomenon can also be referred as succession of environmental problems, for instance, after EPA has reduced the emission of particles larger than 2 mm by 78% (U.S.EPA, 1996) as cited in (Environmental challenges, 1997), the air became clearer but it caused another problem of acid deposition in the region of north-eastern United States. This is because the larger particles in the emission were alkaline and it neutralizes the acidity caused by smaller sulphur oxide particles. And in the absence of alkaline large particles, smaller acid sulphur oxide accumulated in the air and leads to *acid deposition*. Mitigation to SO_x also reduced the concentration of acid aerosol. This has created another unexpected problem that the sulphuric acid aerosol also served as nuclei for the formation of clouds. More nuclei or smaller droplets were present. These droplets scatter incoming solar radiation before reaching the earth's surface resulting in dimming or global cooling effect. Absence of aerosol in the air intensified the impact of *global warming* (NRC, Aerosol Radiative Forcing and Climate Change, 1996) as cited in (Environmental challenges, 1997). Aboriginal or traditional life style with low carbon footprint is a **reconciliatory** solution.

Afforestation and reforestation are **restorative** means of solving the problem because human domination such as watering and monitoring are there, and agroforestry and holistic farm management are **regenerative** solutions because both ascertains the co-evolution with the nature with no human superiority.

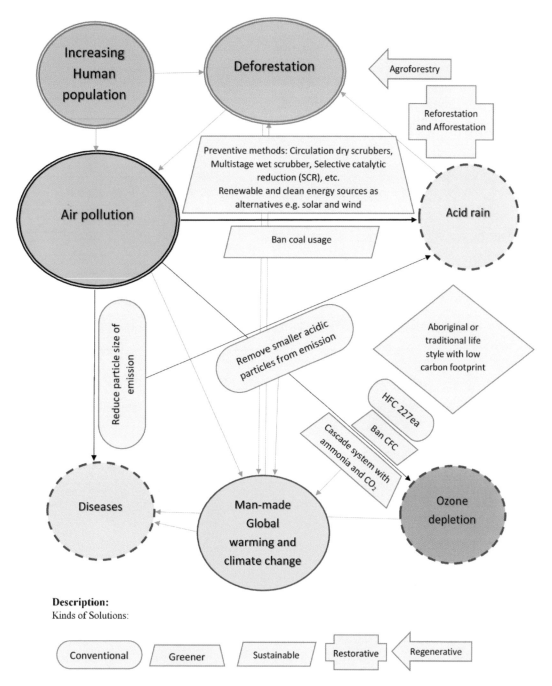

Figure 3.4 Potential solutions for air pollution, acid rain and ozone depletion

Black circle: problem under concern, Blue circle: cause, Red circle: effect, Double lined circle: keystone environmental problem, Single lined circle: environmental problem, Dotted lined circle: problem to be mitigated when keystone environmental problem get solved, Black arrow: cause-effect link for which solutions are given, Blue arrow: cause-effect link

N.B.: - Each problem in the circles is connected to many other problems on the basis of cause-and-effect links, and they are not shown here.

4. Over exploitation of natural resources

4.1 Introduction

It is clear that much of the environmental issues are due to overconsumption of resources, wasteful life style and negligent technologies and this is further elevated with the population growth and the living standards rise. Climate changes, fresh water resources, wet lands, fish stocks and forests get shrunk. There are new areas opened up for agriculture: parts of the Amazonian jungles are deforested for agriculture, high way construction and various developmental purposes. Overloading of crops as monoculture causes nutrient depletion, over consumption of ground water causes water shortages in many areas this also causes sea water intrusion in coastal regions.

According to ("foe.co.uk", 2009), today humans extract and use about 50% more natural resources than 30 years ago, around 60 billion tons of raw materials extracted each year and this is further expected to increase to 100 billion tonnes by 2030, this massive extraction causes environmental problems as well as human right violations due to poor working conditions. World economy today uses around 30% fewer resources to produce one Euro or Dollar of GDP than 30 years ago and overall consumption is still rising. People in rich countries consume up to 10 times more natural resources than the people of poor developing, most resource intensive areas are housing, food and transport, utilization rhythm varies vastly between developing countries and developed nations, an average British family comprises two children but their resource consumption is as high as the resource utilized by 10 children of developing country, furthermore, resulted pollution and other environmental issues are more complicated than that of in developing countries. E.g., effects of particle matter in the air – the Great smog of London 1952.

Malthusian population trap theory has significant consequences, premature and abortive attempts to escape from such trap in long-term do more harm than benefits, and this is because the growth achieved is non-sustainable. For instance, if per capita income of a country is raised due to drawing its natural resources at high rate, the consumed resources depletes and it also resulted several environmental problems such as waste generation and pollution thus the country cannot hold that increased per capita income level, irreversible natural resources can support smaller population than previously did, thus it is difficult for the community to escape from the low-level equilibrium trap. Industrial world consumes 75% of world's commercial energy, 90% of its traded hard wood, 81% of paper, 80% of iron and steel 70% of its milk and meat and 60% of fertilizers (Polunin, 1994).

Natural resources comprise either biotic or abiotic materials. Biotic resources are cereals and timber and abiotic resources are minerals, fossil fuels, energy, water, land and fertile soil. Today's human resource consumption is 4 to 8 times higher than in that of agricultural man, and 15 to 30 times more resource consumption than people in hunter gatherer societies. Worldwide each average individual consumes over 8 tons of natural resources annually or 22 kg per day.

Renewable resources such as agricultural products, fish live stocks and timber (furniture and paper), non-renewable resources such as fossil fuels, metal ores used in the production of cars and computers, industrial and construction minerals used to build houses and roads. Overburden from mining activities accounts for 40 billion tonnes each year, overall, 100 billion tons of materials move annually. In addition, intense mining activities also leads to landslides and land degradation, each year several hundreds of people get killed in landslides associated with mining activity, in U.S. alone landslides cause approximately 3.5 billion $(year 2001 $) in damage and kill about 50 people each year. In addition, intensified material use, energy and land use often associated with environmental problems such as destruction of soil fertility, water shortages and toxic pollution, it entails several social issues such as human rights violations, poor working conditions, low wages and limited health and safety concerns.

E.g., oil extraction of Nigeria, Copper mining and processing in Peru and Palm oil production in Indonesia and Malaysia.

International trade in raw materials and products has increased in recent decades. This accelerates worldwide resource extraction, it also leads to unequal sharing of resources as more natural resources are scraped from poor developing countries to richer countries, this also associated with environmental threats especially in case of resource extraction e.g., Shell company's crude oil extraction in Niger delta, Nigeria which causes huge health and environmental problems in the area.

4.2 Ecological footprint

Ecological footprint is a measure of human impact on earth's ecosystem, measured as area of wildness or amount of natural capital consumed each year. Ecological footprint measures supply and demand on nature, supply refers biocapacity such as biologically productive lands (e.g., forest, pasture, cropland and fisheries) and demand refers productive area required by the renewable resources for human consumption and to the absorption of waste. Adapted from ("footprintnetwork.org", 2016).

4.3 Solutions to over consumption

"If we fail to bring population growth and overconsumption under control then we will inhabit a planet where life becomes increasingly untenable" -Ehrlich and Ehrlich (2008).

Negative effect of the population increase and overconsumption can be expressed by the equation I=PAT (P: population; A: average affluence or overconsumption per individual; T: technology that serve and drive the consumption). Automobiles using fossil fuel creates much greater T than fully electric or hybrid cars. The product of P, A and T gives the Impact or a rough estimate of ecosystem degradation by man. As explained in (Ehrlich & Ehrlich, 2008)2 billion rich people disrupts the climate more than 2 billion poor people, three hundred million Americans consume more petroleum than 1.3 billion Chinese and driving a sport utility vehicle (SUV) is more harmful to environment than the public bus or a bike. New consumers such as China and India will also have a considerable impact on overall resource consumptions.

According to (Ehrlich & Ehrlich, 2008) a billion or more people experiencing problems of under consumption, as their basic needs are yet to be fulfilled, they are unable to contribute for sustainability. It is very unfair that talking about preserving wild resources or conserving a forest or mitigations to air pollution to a person with empty stomach, person who has urgent basic needs may put his maximum efforts on utilizing the natural resources despite of conservation laws and environmental protection measures. Even though strict environmental laws are in practice it is hard to implement them unless the poachers change their own idea of poaching or making illegal money. However in history Easter Island, classic Mayan civilization and Nineveh all collapsed by environmental degradation but modern man still has some over confidence on his technological advancements and most advanced scientific knowledge such as use of biotechnology and nanotechnology may help him to beat the challenge, however, effects of such technologies or finding shelter in other planet or moon are still at crawling stage, the great examples for such human failure is natural disasters, still man cannot predict the earth quack, tsunami or a severe cyclone, man cannot overcome terrorism, even man cannot control his kind of being cruel to the society and the environment, how can he win the nature and the challenges of protecting ecosystem services, on the whole the inner beauty of every human being is the future's big need.

4.4 Overexploitation of resources, degradation of habitats, diseases and pollution

Over fishing causes severe problem in fish population and genetic diversity, according to WWF, 53% of world's fish population are completely depleted, 32% are overexploited, depleted or recovering from depletion ("wwf.panda.org", 2015) global fishing rate is more than 2-3 times larger than what oceans can sustainably support. Increased catching of juvenile fish, pirate fishers who does not obey fishing laws, degradation of breeding grounds or spawning or nurseries by destructive fishing techniques, non-selective fishing methods such as bottom trawling destroys coral reef, reed beds, and shallow sea grass beds, cyanide fishing killed coral reef fishery in Mainland China, Hong Kong, Philippines and Singapore, explosives such as dynamite fishing affects South East Asian coral reef fishery, Ghost fishing is where ghost net is released in the sea and it moves while catching dolphins, turtles and fishes unselectively such as about 1000km of Ghost nets often released in pacific ocean. ("Destructive fishing", 2015), trawlers with modern fish finders which also eliminate juvenile forms, consequently deplete the future stocks and entire population (table 4.1).

Table 4.1 Types of over fishing

a.	**Growth over fishing:** This occurs when fish is harvested before it is grown to the appropriate size that would give maximum yield per unit. Growth over fishing reduces the fish catch and subsequently the profit.
b.	**Recruitment over fishing:** This is where the population of mature adults or the spawning biomass is depleted from the population due to over fishing, reproductive capacity can be replenished by moratoriums, quotas and minimum size limits on the fish catch.

c.	**Ecosystem over fishing:** This is where the balance of the ecosystem is altered by over fishing where the large individuals are lacking in the population and abundance of small forage type stocks; this moves the entire ecosystem towards population of smaller varieties.
d.	**Biological over fishing:** This is where the mortality of the fish population reached where the biomass of the stock has negative marginal growth. Replenishment or breeding of the population slows down due to over fishing; this reduces the number of individuals in fish population.
e.	**Economic or bio economic over fishing:** This is where the total cost of the catch exceeds the maximum economic yield. If more fishes are caught it will reduce the market price, hence reduces the profit.

Adapted from ("overfishing", n.d.)

Catching of threatened or vulnerable species such as blue whales, endangered turtles and deep-sea fishes lead to species extinction, mainly deep-sea fishes such as Orange roughy, Patagonian tooth fish and sable fish live in dark, freezing cold temperatures, less food and slow growth rate (takes 30-40 years to get matured) deep trawlers also consume such varieties and cause species decline ("overfishing", n.d.). Over fishing also worsen the impact of competitive species such as jelly fish to increase further, this affects the availability of food for fish stocks. El-Nino along with over fishing in Peruvian coast caused depletion of Anchovy during period of 5 years after 1971. Collapse of Cod fishery in off Newfoundland and 1992 collapse of Cod fishery in Grand banks, Canada and complete extinction of blue whales in Great lakes in 1980s are typical example of effects of over fishing. Improper management and weak implementation of fishing laws, lack of transparency in fishing agreements, fail to follow scientific advice and guidance and flag of convenience vessels where many countries fail to inspect their vessels and declaring marine protected areas. However, marine protected areas are too few as 1.2% of World's Ocean is declared as no take zones ("poor fisheries management", 2015). Implementation of international regulations such as harvest control rule, harvest control rule is a model with set of rules and protocols proposed in 2010 to maintain sustainable fishery.

Some stocks are affected by diseases. Species of shrimps, mollusks, crabs, lobster and fishes face disease outbreak by virus, bacteria, protists and metazoans, this severely increases the mortality. Manmade pollution such as ocean dumping, sewage and warm water effluents increase the vulnerability of species; as it increases the susceptibility to diseases. Furthermore, pollution also alter the breeding grounds and fish's behaviours and, in some cases, chemicals affect the fertility or produce toxic effects, sewage and waste effluents also reduce the available dissolved oxygen (mainly thermal pollution) and light penetration, increased turbidity made difficulties to find their mates and also it affects the primary production required by the food chain. Particles in stormwater or industrial effluents injure the gills and soft skin of the fish and made them more susceptible to diseases, warm water effluents also kill the fish directly by thermal shock and destroys the eggs and juvenile forms. Ocean acidification increases nitrogen fixing bacteria and subsequently the phytoplanktons, this may affect the entire food chain and acidification also affects the eggs, shellfish, corals and other calcareous biota ("www.niwa.co.nz", 2009). Oil spills from tankers, ships and storm runoff caused fish kills, reduce the taste of the fish, reduction in fish growth, coral reefs get destroyed, lobsters, crabs, sea stars, sea urchins are affected, mangroves will perish as they are very sensitive to oil, affects sea birds ("waterencyclopedia.com", n.d.) and pollute the beach and also affect the fishing gear. Floating plastic pollutants clog the digestive system of fish and marine birds. Pollutants of anionic surfactants cause swelling of gills and increased mucus secretion this reduces the gas diffusion and affects breathing, further more surfactants reduce the surface tension, if surface tension goes below 50 dyn/ cm it is lethal in fish (Pearson & Frangipane, 1973). Persistent chemicals such as DDT and heavy metals increase in concentration with trophic levels of the food chain and affect the behaviour, reproduction and survival in highest level organisms. Chlorinated pesticides and PCB affect the growth in Oysters and increases the susceptibility to diseases (usually by fungal pathogens). Disasters such as tsunami destroy coral reefs, causes massive fish death and habitat destruction, this affects coastal fisheries.

Manmade dams are barriers to migratory fishes, disposal of unwanted fishing gears and baits, boating in sensitive areas, coastal development programmes, harbours and dockings affect the marine ecosystem. Natural effects such as climate change causes bleaching of coral all around the world due to global warming, this made severe loss of habitats for reef fishes. Invasive species also cause destruction of indigenous fish population by being their predators or competitors or parasitic and disease-causing agents, such as lion fish in Atlantic Ocean is an invasive species caused severe destruction of native plants and compete with native fishes ("oceanservice.noaa.gov", 2014).

Adapted from ("greateratlantic.fisheries.noaa.gov", 2014); ("wwf.panda.org", 2015); ("overfishing", n.d.)

Following problems causes over exploitation of natural resources

4.5 Overexploitation of natural resources causes or due to poverty-disease-disability-inequality-war-food insecurity

According to Moore, Gould, & Keary (Moore, Gould, & Keary, 2003) as cited in ("Environmental History Resource Guide for South Africa", n.d.), it has been mentioned both cause and result of resource stripping is poverty, as the following statement expresses the poverty resulted in overexploitation of natural resources "in developing countries people rely heavily on available resources as poverty leads to resource stripping as means of survival", and the other statement expresses the cause of poverty is overexploitation of natural resources "many of these developing countries have histories of colonialism led to the impoverished state". Thus, poverty and overexploitation of natural resources are cyclic processes as one causes the other or one to result in the other.

Poverty also leads to foreign debt burden and subject to exploitation by developed countries. Developing nations of South and Southeast Asian countries use the money of developed nations for their infrastructural development, and they pay the loan with their natural resources including timber countries such as Japan utilizes their forest resources and granting loans for various development schemes (Colchester & Lohmann, 1993) as cited in ("Rainforestinfo", n.d.). Research carried out to find the links between natural resource exploitation, environmental degradation, and poverty by using Ghana's gold mining as a case study depicted that there is a negative relationship exists between the abundance of natural resources and economic growth and development, and the study demonstrated how the overexploitation leads to poverty (Aubell & Mensah, 2007).

It was stated in Godfray and others (Godfray, et al., 2010) that increasing competition for land, water, and energy resources and overexploitation of fisheries will affect our ability to produce food for the growing population.

4.6 Overexploitation of natural resources due to intensive farming

Globally 80% of deforestation occurs for agricultural needs ("onegreenplanet.org", n.d.). In Latin America, two-third of forest area was destroyed for commercial agriculture. According to the government web page for Natural Resources of Canada, about 43% of deforestation in 2010 was for pasture and crop ("onegreenplanet.org", n.d.). A total area of 1,389 of 157,896 hectares of forest resource has been destroyed for soybean cultivation in Brazilian Amazon since July 2006 to date (Butler, 2012). According to the documentation of Earth sight, approximately 500 sq. km of forest area had been cleared for rubber and oil palm plantation in Central Africa in the past five years (till 2018). It has been found that companies hold a license to clear another 8,400 sq. km for industrial agriculture, and it has been warned thousands of acres in the Congo basin (the world's second-largest rain forest) could fall to industrial agriculture(Cannon , 2018).

About 3.5 million hectares (8.7 million acres) of forest land in Indonesia, Malaysia, and Papua New Guinea were destroyed for the cultivation of oil palm in the period of 1990-2010. This deforestation causes a vast area of habitat destruction and depletion of forest resources(Butler R. , 2013).

Historically, English, and Dutch migrants lured by a gold rush, collecting spices and monoculture plantations such as tea and rubber are the pioneer reasons for the destruction of forest cover in Brazilian Amazon, North America, and South Asian

108

regions. When considering tropical rainforests, in Bangladesh, Haiti, India, and Sri Lanka almost all rainforests lost by 1988, China 50% loss in Xishuangbanna province, by 1960-1985 Philippines and Thailand loss 55 and 45 percent of rain forest respectively(Chris , 1992). In the year between1990 and 2000 the world is estimated to have suffered a net loss of 8.9 million hectares of forest each year, but in the period 2000-2005 this was declined to an estimated 12.9 million hectares per year, recent deforestation rate is annually 7.3 million ha. Overall, the world lost about 3 percent of its forests in the period 1990 to 2005, at present we are losing about 200 square kilometers of forest each day(Parry, Canziani, Palutikof, Linden, & Hanson, 2007).

In the Peruvian Amazon 12,000 acres of rain forests have been destroyed for the oil palm industry since 2011("rainforest resque.org", n.d.).

4.7 Overexploitation of natural resources due to the global energy crisis

According to McCarthy (McCarthy, 2017), Since the beginning of 2015 more than 99 billion barrels of oil, nearly 25 billion tons of coal, and more than 10.6 trillion cubic meters of natural gas have been exploited due to the energy crisis (fossil fuel burning causes air pollution that kills estimated 6.5 million people each year). Furthermore, it was stated(McCarthy, 2017)that in 2012, about 804,000ha. of the forest was destroyed by palm oil companies to produce bio-energy (Indonesian rainforests are more carbon-rich than Amazon forests).

According to "Greenpeace" ("Greenpeace", 2016), from 1930 to 2000, about 2.4 million ha. of natural landscape mostly forests were exploited for coal mining. In China, about 3.2 million ha. of land has been degraded due to coal mining and only 10-12% of such lands were restored. According to "Greenpeace"("Greenpeace", n.d.) Russian oil giant Gazprom has already begun producing a small quantity of oil from the Arctic in the ocean of northern Russia. In addition, Shell and Exxon are aggressively involved in the oil rush in the Arctic Ocean. Oil excavation also caused severe spills such as 1989, Exxon Valdez spilled 11 million gallons into the Alaskan waters, and in 2010, BP Deep Water Horizon spilled about 200 million barrels in the Gulf of Mexico.

In addition, according to Al-Amin(Al-Amin, 2014), according to the 2000-2005 Global Forest Assessment of the Food and Agricultural Organization (FAO) of the United Nations, Nigeria has the world's highest annual deforestation rate of primary forests at 55.7%.

According to the 2000-2005 Global Forest Resources Assessment of the Food and Agricultural Organization of the United Nations (FAO) (FAO, "Global Forest Resource Assessment 2005", 2005), Nigeria has the world's highest annual deforestation rate of primary forests at 55.7%. The country is one of the two largest losers of annual natural forests in Africa. Energy shortages are the increasing challenge in Nigeria, such as grid electricity and other conventional sources that are in short supply or not reliable. However, 52% of the population in Nigeria does not afford to pay for fuel or electricity, and 70.8% are in absolute poverty. Al-Amin (Al-Amin, "Domestic Energy Crisis and Deforestation Challenges in Nigeria", 2014) stated that Africa accounts for over one-quarter of global fuel wood production. According to FAO (FAO, 'State of the world's forests', 2009) as cited in (Al-Amin, "Domestic Energy Crisis and Deforestation Challenges in Nigeria", 2014), in 2006, about 13% of Africa's fuel wood is produced in Nigeria. This includes refined charcoal. According to Odihi(Odihi, 1993) as cited in (Al-Amin, "Domestic Energy Crisis and Deforestation Challenges in Nigeria", 2014), since the late 1980s, in the Sudan Sahel region (in the North) exploitation of trees for fuel wood has been increasing significantly. According to Singh (Singh, 1993) as cited in (Al-Amin, "Domestic Energy Crisis and Deforestation Challenges in Nigeria", 2014), in the period between 1980 and 1990, the Northern region has lost the forest cover from 4.37×10^7 to 4.0×10^7 ha.

4.8 Overexploitation of natural resources due to population explosion

The increasing population causes deforestation, which leads to the loss of valuable genes, water regulators, flood controllers, watersheds, protectors of inland and coastal fisheries, and climate stabilizers. This also leads to the destruction of mineral cycles and several food chains, which are essential to keep the environment unchanged.

As mentioned by Paul Ehrlich in Population Explosion, I=PAT, where

I - The impact in the environment equals population

A- Affluence (the amount of energy and food supply the population consumes)

T- Technology (a country has)

Thus, with the increasing population, there are impacts on the environment.

More people need more space, more food from agriculture, fisheries, poultry and meat, more jobs, more vehicles, more energy, more water supply, more infrastructures such as apartments, shopping malls, factories, industries, more roads, railroads and highways, hospitals, schools, and playgrounds.

According to Robert Criss, professor of earth and planetary sciences in Arts & Sciences as stated in(Fitzpatrick, 2008), in the United States, population growth leads to resource problems such as water and energy crisis. In Arizona, the water level has dropped many hundreds of feet due to low aquifer levels, saltwater intrusion also recorded in certain areas of the United States. At present (2018.August) U.S. population is 328 million, and it is continuously in an increasing trend, and about half of the U.S population depends on groundwater for drinking. Thus, the question of future water source for the U.S remains unanswered. However, Repetto & Holmes (Repetto & Holmes, 1983) stated, pressure on renewable resources in developing countries originates from population growth is often overshadowed by the raising world market demands.

4.9 Overexploitation of natural resources due to urbanization-urban sprawl-settlements

According to Chen J. (Chen J. , 2007), China is already facing land scarcity. Rapid urbanization along with skyrocketing economic growth further worsens the shortage of agricultural land over the last two decades. It has been demonstrated that urbanization caused land-use changes such as a small share of agricultural lands are converted into urban settlements or industrial areas. Urbanization also affects soil quality. Thus, China's cultivated land is shrinking at a very high rate.

Over exploitation of natural resources effects into following problems

4.10 Water pollution-water scarcity due to overexploitation of natural resources

In the river of Cauvery of Southern India, uncontrolled sand mining alters the course of the river and causes pollution. Rivers such as Coleroon, Amaravathi, Palar, and Vellar in Tamil Nadu and Kapila and Suvarnavathi in Karnataka face a similar issue. In addition, agricultural and industrial encroachments affect the water bodies in both states, for instance, the bank of Bhavani in Tamil Nadu have been used for the cultivation of paddy, banana, and turmeric, for which the water is diverted and affecting the supply to others in Erode district. In addition, the Arkavathy river valley of Bangalore is encroached by industrial buildings. This affects the water level in the Thippagondanahalli Reservoir. However, the main cause of water scarcity in the Cauvery River is that the river has been occupied with crops that require a huge amount of water such as paddy (1,200mm) and sugarcane (1,800 mm) respectively. It has been suggested that farmers can cultivate dry land crops such as ragi, which consumes only 500 mm of water but provide similar support prices. Farmers in Tamil Nadu grow paddy three times every year (in June, August, and September) and according to the recent observation as the decreasing rainfall and lowering groundwater levels, it has been recommended that switching to water-intensive crops, at least for one or two seasons, can help to overcome the water scarcity in the region. Source:(Sattiraju, 2017).

It has been revealed (Oppenlander, 2014), globally, 92% of freshwater is consumed for agriculture of which 30% goes to factory farming or pasture or crops to feed them. In the southwest United States, such as California requires over 4,000 gallons of water to produce just one pound of beef and over 1,000 gallons to produce just one gallon of milk. The California state raises over 6 million cattle and 2 million dairy cows, the water requirement of each animal is 20 gallons and 40 gallons, respectively. Furthermore, an additional 2 million annual gallons are used in the entire production process, including the production of grains to feed them. In addition, 900,000 acres of land in California is dedicated to the cultivation of alfalfa whereas 90% which are cattle feed, each acre of alfalfa consumes 1 to 2 million gallons per year (50-80-acre inches per acre per year) and the sum of water consumed for hay production in California for just one year is 1.8 trillion gallons. In addition, about one-fifth of all water from the Colorado River is diverted through the Imperial Canal and 70% is used in one way or another for livestock. However, average rainfall in the Valley is less than 3 inches; thus, the water is sparse in other areas of California where alfalfa is cultivated.

4.11 Pollution through mining activities due to overexploitation of natural resources

It was stated (Goswami, Das, & Guru, 2010), in the Odisha state of India, extensive chromite mining in Sukinda, coal mining in Talcher-Angul, Belpahar-Brajarajnagar and Gopalpur areas, iron and manganese mining in Mayurbhanj and Keonjhar districts, limestone mining in Baragarh district, graphite mining in Boangir and bauxite mining in Damanjori affected the state since many years as they degrade the environment such as releasing fly ash and red mud.

According to "Vietnam News" ("Vietnam News", 2016), in the coastal central Binh Thuan Province of Vietnam, 67 titanium exploiting sites were recognized, but, only three have obtained the license from the environmental department and exploited titanium causes air and water pollution. In addition, the Viet Nam Association for Conservation of Nature and Environment revealed that in the region of Central Highlands, red mud and wastewater are produced during the exploitation of bauxite, more precisely, generation of 1 tonne of alumina from bauxite causes 1.5 tonnes of red mud generation and air pollution. According to the estimates, the Nhan Co bauxite mining site expels over 11 million cubic meters of wastewater and red mud each year. Whereas, this is 0.8 million cubic meters in Tan Rai bauxite mine.

4.12 Coral destruction due to overexploitation of natural resources

Non-selective fishing methods such as bottom trawling destroys coral reef, most of the ocean floor to a depth of 2000m could be destroyed. In heavily fished areas such as around seamounts off southern Australia, almost 90% of the surface where coral used to grow is now bare rock. In addition, cyanide fishing killed coral reefs in Mainland China, Hong Kong, Philippines, and Singapore, explosives such as dynamite fishing affects South East Asian coral reef fishery over the past 20 years("WWF Global", 2017).

It has been investigated in Mcmanus, Rodolfo , & Cleto(Mcmanus, Rodolfo , & Cleto , 1997), effects of blast fishing, sodium cyanide fishing, and anchor damage on live coral were investigated on a heavily exploited fringing reef in Bolinao, Philippines in the period between 1987 and 1990. Results projected through simple balance sheet

113

model depicted blast fishing caused the loss of hermatypic coral cover at the rate of 1.4%/yr., cyanide caused 0.4%/yr. and damaged by anchors caused 0.03%/yr. In addition, the potential coral recovery rate is reduced by one third from 3.8%/yr., whereas in the disturbance's absence it is 2.4%/yr. (possibly subjected to compound errors). The study also showed reefs with patchy coral cover are more susceptible to damage from blast fishing as they are targeted by fishers. Reefs with smaller corals have greater resilience because each unit of radial colony growth contributes a greater percent increase in areal cover. Blast fishing also reduced the resilience to natural perturbations led to small, sparse corals and reduced patches.

4.13 Land degradation- sedimentation- soil erosion due to overexploitation of natural resources

According to Saad, Shariff, & Gairola(Saad, Shariff, & Gairola, 2011), it was stated that overexploitation of natural resources is the major cause of desertification in Libya. Anthropogenic causes of land degradation are deforestation, shifting cultivation, overexploitation of vegetation, resurfacing of soil, overgrazing, indiscriminate use of agrochemicals, lack of soil conservation activities, and excess consumption of groundwater (Osman, 2014). It has been revealed in Kaur & Sharma(Kaur & Sharma, 2016)that inappropriate use of land, overexploitation of surface and groundwater resources are the major causes of loss of soil fertility, development of acidity, salinization, alkalization, deterioration of soil structure, soil erosion, and loss of organic matter.

Overexploitation of resources of the Usambara Mountains in Northern Tanzania resulted in deforestation, soil erosion, flooding, sedimentation, and disturbance of the hydrological balance. The major factor is increasing pressure on the marginal hill forest, which has been used for the consumption of firewood and animal fodder(Ezaza, 1988).

4.14 Groundwater contamination-depletion-salinization due to overexploitation of natural resources

The movement of seawater into freshwater aquifers is known as seawater intrusion. Seawater intrusion may happen naturally or by increased human consumption of groundwater. When the freshwater in the aquifer decreases by human consumption, the seawater tends to move towards the vacant areas and rising seawater levels also

114

cause intrusion. This has happened in many parts of the world such as Jaffna-Sri Lanka, coastal areas in the U.S., and coastal plains of Hersek, Taşköprü, and Altinova in Yalova region-Turkey, coastal aquifers in India, coastal aquifers in South Korea and the Gulf of Mexico. In Jaffna, saltwater exclusion bunds were established in selected locations adjacent to the lagoon and sea. However, improper maintenance caused intrusion of saltwater in certain locations such as Thondamanaru, Ariyali, and Araali. In these areas, hundreds of acres of land and hundreds of wells are in the abandoned stage (Sivakumar, 2013).

4.15 Deforestation-destruction of grasslands and mangroves due to overexploitation of natural resources

Please see the chapter deforestation

4.16 Animal slaughter and cruelty due to overexploitation of natural resources

According to Pendergrast (Pendergrast, 2015), the paper discussed the media hegemony of cruel live animal transport for slaughter from Australia. The live shipping of cattle from Australia was shown in the footage. The animals were densely overcrowded and suffocated during the voyage. Some of them died on board before reaching the slaughterhouse. In August 2017, Awassi Express on its way from Fremantle, Australia to the Middle East carried 64,000 sheep. According to Animals Australia, about 2400 sheep died from heat stress before reaching its destination. Previously, in October 2003, the Cormo Express disaster, 6000 of the shipment of 58,000 died as Saudi Arabia had refused to accept the live cargo and 30 other countries refused to offload them. It has been revealed by the media that in the latest 2017 event 72 days of shipment under the weight of the survivors, urine, and excrement. The death occurred mainly due to the extremes of temperatures and stifling humidity. Furthermore, it has also been revealed that more than 10% of them die from stress. Overexploitation of live animal resources leading to abuse or cruel death has been taken place in various forms all over the world.

In addition, the Chinese consume shark fins from the market in order to prepare the soup, sharks are caught alive and after cutting the fins, sharks are thrown back to sea as waste, sharks cannot swim or maintain their position in the water without fins, affected sharks stayed at the bottom seafloor with agony and die slowly with the pain and without food or eaten by predators while they are alive. Shark fins have a broad market area such as China, Hong Kong, Taiwan, Singapore, Malaysia, Viet Nam South America, and Europe. Major importers are Italy, Brazil, Uruguay, Spain, and South Korea (Towers, 2015).

4.17 Biodiversity loss due to overexploitation of natural resources

Destruction of forest threatens both fauna and flora, indeed it leads to severe extinction of entire biota, there are several species completely become extinct due to anthropogenic means such as Tasmanian wolf, Moa, Wooly mammoth, Cape lion, Atlas bear, and several wild plants in prehistoric times. Today, there are many species red-listed as critically endangered (CR) and plenty of species become vulnerable. It was stated (FAO, 2002), roughly about two-thirds of the world's fish stock is fully fished or overexploited. Overfishing causes several fish species under threat as the juvenile fishes are being caught. Bottom trawling destroys the coral reefs and dependent biodiversity. Global consumption of fishing is increasing along with the population increase, according to FAO (FAO, The State of World Fishereies and Aquaculture opportunities and challenges, 2014) report, world fish production is 93.7 million tons in 2011, the second-highest (it was 93.8 million tons in 2006) catch of tuna alone hits 7 million tons in 2012, the annual global catch of the sharks, rays and chimaeras species 760, 000 tonnes since 2005, 2012 global total shrimp catch hits about 3.4 million tons and cephalopods exceeds 4 million tons. About 58.3 million people all over the world engaged in fishing or other forms of aquaculture (FAO, The State of World Fishereies and Aquaculture opportunities and challenges, 2014). According to 2013 estimates, China is leading in global fish production which is 16,274,926 metric tons in the year 2013 followed by Indonesia (6,101,725 MT) and Peru (5,854,233 MT). The world's annual catch is expected to rise further as the population grows; this may lead to the extinction of certain aquatic species and increases the threat to aquatic life due to over consumption (FAO, The State of World Fishereies and Aquaculture opportunities and challenges, 2014).

According to Keledjian and others (Keledjian, et al., 2014), 40% of the global fish catch is bycatch (catching non-targeted organisms), it is around 63 billion pounds annually. Also, bycatch injures and kills thousands of whales, dolphins, seals, sea turtles, and sharks. According to federal fisheries managers, tens of thousands of sea turtles are killed annually by commercial fisheries and this is mainly by shrimp trawlers in the Gulf of Mexico, over 3400 dusky sharks get caught as bycatch in two bottom long line fisheries in the Southeast United States. Another study states over

116

40% of the global catch is discarded overboard, millions of pounds of halibuts or cots are wasted when fishermen reach their quota. Over 300 pilot whales and 700 sea turtles entangled and killed each year in Atlantic and Mexican long lines, overfishing of tuna or bycatch removal of sea turtles cause jellyfish population to boom due to lack of predators, in addition, overfishing of small pelagic fish such as sardine and herring which are a competitor of jellyfish for zooplanktons also cause acceleration in jellyfish number as consequence stinging jellyfish attack on swimmers increases.

Today oil palm plantations cover over 27 million hectares of the earth's surface. It was stated that the forest and human settlement have been destroyed and replaced by "green deserts", and an area of the size of New Zealand lacks biodiversity. Endangered wildlife such as the orangutan, Borneo elephant, and Sumatran tiger are pushed towards extinction. About 70,000 orangutans are still living in the forest of Southeast Asia, but the biofuels policy of the European Union pushes them to extinction {Adapted from ("Rainforest-rescue", 2017)}.

For instance, tortoise *Geochelone radiate* endemic to southern Madagascar heavily harvested for food and pet trade (Brien, Emahalala, Beard, & Rakotondrainy, 2003). According to the estimates annually about 45,000 adults radiated tortoises are harvested. The overall population of the tortoise is declined by one-fifth over the last 25 years. If human overexploitation of this species continues, they soon become extinct in wild.

4.18 Wetlands or draining of wetlands due to overexploitation of natural resources

In Africa, Yala swamp wetland, Kenya does not have protected status. Since the 1960s the wetland has been subjected to land reclamation mostly for agricultural purposes such as growing rice, groundnuts, cassava, yams, and sugarcane. Similarly, wetlands such as Nakivubo urban wetland in Uganda and the Hadejia-Jama'are wetland in Nigeria and Lake Chilwa, Malawi are facing degradation due to land reclamation. However, Zambezi basin wetlands, South Africa faced an overuse issue by the local population as well as land reclamation for infrastructure developments by outside influences (Schuyt, 2005). An economic valuation of Zambezi basin wetlands using the Contingent valuation method (CVM) the value was estimated as $4,229,309(Seyam, Hoekstra, Ngabirano, & Savenije , 2001). According to the given Table 4.2, the values given for wildlife services and goods, resulted in a negative value for the Zambezi basin wetlands, the reason is the costs of managing the wildlife in the wetlands exceed the income derived from tourism; it is guessable that the value of measures taken to control overexploitation of wildlife resources was high. Overconsumption of groundwater for irrigation purposes drains most of the wetlands in Spain and Greece. Spanish wetlands such as Doñana reserve the water table is falling by one meter every two years (United Nations University, 2008).

Table 4.2 Economic values of the Zambezi basin wetland

Wetland benefit	Economic value (U.S.$ per year)
Flood plain recession agriculture	50 million
Fish production	78.6 million
Wildlife services and goods	-1 million
Livestock grazing	70.6 million
Ecotourism	814,000
Biodiversity	68,000
Natural products and medicine	2.6 million

Source: (Seyam, Hoekstra, Ngabirano, & Savenije , 2001)

4.19 Overexploitation of natural resources as a keystone environmental problem

According to "Overconsumption? Our Use of the World's Natural Resources" ("Overconsumption? Our Use of the World's Natural Resources", 2009), today humans extract and use about 50% more natural resources than 30 years ago, around 60 billion tons of raw materials extracted each year, and this is further expected to increase to 100 billion tonnes by 2030.This massive extraction causes environmental problems as well as human right violations due to poor working conditions. The world economy today uses around 30% fewer resources to produce one Euro or Dollar of GDP than 30 years ago, and overall consumption is still rising. People in rich countries consume up to 10 times more natural resources than the people of poor developing countries. Most resource-intensive areas are housing, food, and transport, while the utilisation rhythm varies vastly between developing countries and developed nations. An average British family that may comprise two children would consume resources as high as the resource utilised by 10 children of a developing country. Furthermore, resulted pollution and other environmental issues are more complicated than that of in developing countries. E.g., effects of particle matter in the air–the Great Smog of London 1952.

Overfishing causes a severe problem in fish population and their genetic diversity. According to WWF, around 53% of the world's fish population is completely depleted, 32% are overexploited, depleted or recovering from depletion ("Unsustainable fishing", 2015) Global fishing rate is more than 2-3 times larger than what oceans can sustainably support.

The many destructive practices and operations that contribute to this situation are: -

- increased catching of juvenile fish,
- pirate fishers who do not obey fishing laws,
- degradation of breeding grounds or spawning or nurseries by destructive fishing techniques,
- non-selective fishing methods such as bottom trawling destroys coral reef, reed beds, and shallow seagrass beds,
- cyanide fishing killing coral reef fishery in Mainland China, Hong Kong, Philippines, and Singapore,
- use of explosives such as dynamite fishing affects South East Asian coral reef fishery,
- Ghost fishing, where ghost nets are released into the sea and it moves while catching dolphins, turtles and fishes unselectively. Sometimes about 1000km of Ghost nets are released in the Pacific Ocean. According to "Destructive fishing practices" (" Destructive fishing practices", 2015), trawlers with modern fish finders which also eliminate juvenile forms, consequently deplete the future stocks and entire population.

Such similar overexploitation of natural resources are keystone links because it causes biodiversity loss (to a great extent), deforestation, land degradation, coral destruction, wetland loss or draining of wetlands, animal slaughter and cruelty, groundwater contamination, water pollution-water scarcity and pollution through mining activities. Furthermore, the problem varies based on the type of resource being exploited. When the resource depletion comes to an end, then problems such as biodiversity loss (almost) may get eliminated. Similarly, deforestation, land degradation, coral destruction, wetlands or draining of wetlands, animal slaughtering and cruelty, groundwater contamination, water pollution and scarcity, pollution through mining activities, all may disappear (figure 4.1).

Evidence 1: Overexploitation of natural resources causes biodiversity loss

According to Waldman(Waldman, 2018), "Human overexploitation of wildlife resources has caused 60% of biodiversity loss, a new report revealed in the last 40 years 60% of wildlife population has declined due to human pressure".

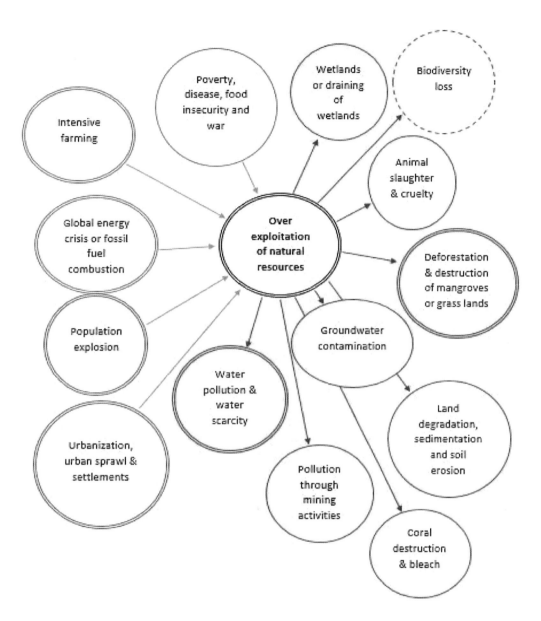

Figure 4.1 Overexploitation of natural resources as keystone environmental problem with the disappearance of biodiversity loss on its mitigation (hypothetical diagram)
[In the figure black circle is the problem being examined, blue circles are cause manmade environmental problems, red circles are effect man-made environmental problems, double lined circles are keystone man-made environmental problems, and circles with dashed lines (either single or double lined) are the man-made environmental problems that disappear when the problem being examined (black circle) is mitigated]

121

Over exploitation of marine fish resources is a keystone environmental problem because virtually complete dependency of the problem biodiversity loss on overexploitation of natural resources is depicted by the scenario. Thus, mitigating over exploitation will protect the biodiversity and ensure its existence.

Restorative vs. Sustainable vs. Conventional solutions

Solutions for overexploitation of natural resources are explained from the following epic. Overexploitation of coastal fish resources is a threat to the fisheries and biodiversity in the Palk Strait region between India and Sri Lanka. It has been blamed those Indian bottom trawlers haul vehemently in the region. However, in Sri Lankan water trawlers are banned. Trespassing Indian fishing trawlers into the Sri Lankan waters is an unsolved issue between the fishermen of two nations. Technically, arresting and imprisonment, seizing fishing vessels, and penalties are **conventional** solutions being administered by both nations, and they are unsustainable way of handling the tragedy. Yet banning bottom trawling is a **sustainable** solution because according to the definition of sustainable development stated in 1987 Brundtland commission report, "development that meets the needs of the present without compromising the ability of future generations to meet their needs" could be considered as sustainable development. In addition, keeping a cap value for fishing, fishing ban during spawning seasons, creating awareness and sensitizing fishermen are **greener** solutions (figure 4.2).

However, greener and sustainable solutions are often very expensive due to their high energy requirement such as coastal patrolling by coast guards and need for expensive satellite technologies. And unlike smarter restorative solutions they cannot adapt or co-evolve with the nature, they cannot affirm the wellbeing, and depicts relatively low systemic vitality and low resilience.

Due to the aforementioned negative reasons sustainable development path is not so successful for developing countries. However, Sri Lanka has implemented complete ban on bottom trawling (sustainable solution) via an amendment to Section 28A of the Fisheries and Aquatic Resources Act No 02 of 1996 on 6th of July 2017. According to the legislation (a Supplement to Part II of the 2017 Gazette of the Democratic Socialist Republic of Sri Lanka) the fishermen who engaged in bottom trawling or individuals who causes the practice (trawler owners) should be charged a penalty not less than Rs.50,000 or imprisonment not exceeding two years ("extwprlegs1.fao.org", 2017). In addition, it is high time to go for most vital and low energy (less costly)

restorative solutions such as establishing 'no catch zone' and marine protected areas (marine reserves) as buffer zone by both nations, coral and mangrove restoration in the archipelago or implantation of artificial coral reefs at the region along the International Maritime Boundary Line (IMBL). Restorative solutions are wise, vital and less expensive way to handle the crisis.

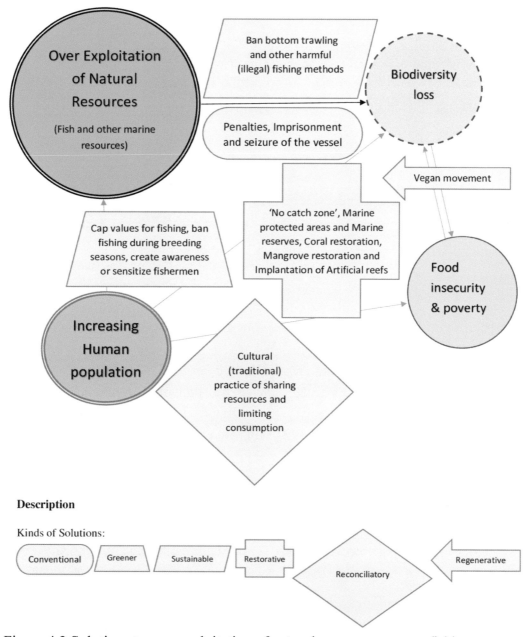

Figure 4.2 Solutions to overexploitation of natural resources or over fishing

123

Black circle: problem under concern, Blue circle: cause, Red circle: effect, Double lined circle: keystone environmental problem, Single lined circle: environmental problem, Dotted lined circle: problem to be mitigated when keystone environmental problem get solved, Black arrow: cause-effect link for which solutions are given, Blue arrow: cause-effect link. N.B.: - Each problem in the circles is connected to many other problems on the basis of cause-and-effect links, and they are not shown here.

5. Global energy crisis

5.1 Introduction

Increasing industries around the world causes increasing consumption of non-renewable energy such as fossil fuels- coal, oil and gas. Over 80% of current energy needs depend on fossil fuels. In addition, electricity generation, transports and various industries still depend on fossil fuels as sole source of energy. Energy demand is expected to rise almost half over the next two decades but energy resources are started to run out. Potential for an energy crisis when sources of non-renewable energy get deplete is very true, however, in the past two decades proven gas resources have increased by 70% and proven oil reserves by 40%, and it has been estimated that we have enough for thirty years supply. In addition, new oil and gas fields are being discovered all the time, advanced recovery technologies open up several unconventional sources such as tar sands, shale gas and ultra-deep water. Furthermore, with the emergence of nuclear energy and increasing usage technologies of renewable energy sources would pacify the future emerging energy needs; however, at present usage of renewable energy is too small amount compare to non-renewable sources (fig.5.1). Adapted from (Ehrlich & Ehrlich, 2008)

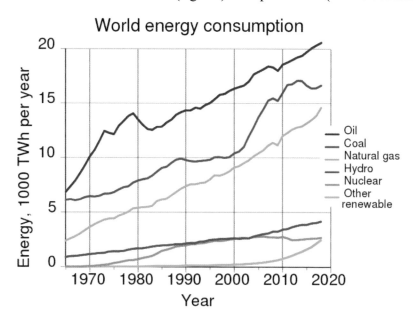

Figure 5.1 World Energy Consumption by fuel
Source: https://commons.wikimedia.org/wiki/File:World_energy_consumption.svg

License: CC by 3.0

5.2 Trend of energy consumption and causes for crisis

When considering the developing world, emerging energy needs are filled by fossil fuels while rich countries switching to other renewable sources (fig. 5.2 & 5.3).

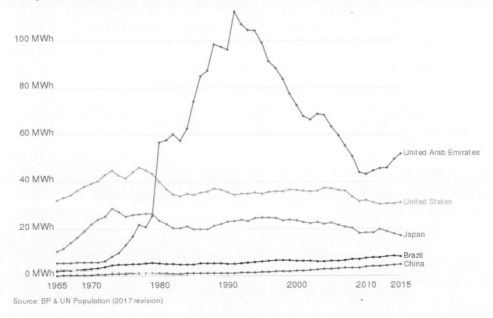

Figure 5.2 Oil consumption by part of the world
Source:
https://commons.wikimedia.org/wiki/File:Oil_consumption_per_capita,_OWID.svg
License: CC by 3.0

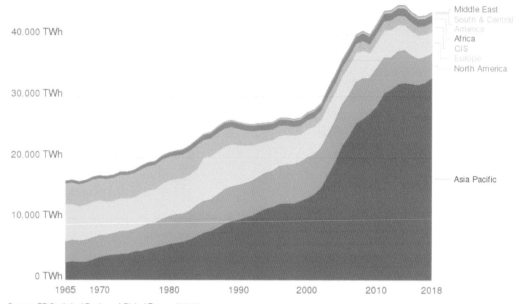

Coal consumption by region
Annual coal consumption, measured in equivalents of terawatt-hours (TWh) per year.

Middle East
South & Central America
Africa
CIS
Europe
North America
Asia Pacific

40,000 TWh
30,000 TWh
20,000 TWh
10,000 TWh
0 TWh

1965 1970   1980   1990   2000   2010   2018

Source: BP Statistical Review of Global Energy (2019)
Note: CIS (Commonwealth of Independent States) is an organization of ten post-Soviet republics in Eurasia following break-up of the Soviet Union.

Figure 5.3 Global Coal Consumption by part of the world
Source:
https://commons.wikimedia.org/wiki/File:Coal_consumption_by_region,_OWID.svg
License: CC by 3.0
Major cause for the energy crisis is increasing population and their needs for quality life style, which also lead to over consumption of oil, gas and coal. However, it associates several other factors as given below.

- Poor infrastructure: Aging of infrastructure of power generators is another cause old and non-upgraded fuel engine consume more fuel than modern or upgraded generators or engines.
- Unexplored renewable energy options: renewable energy still remains unused in many countries, unlike fossil fuels renewable energy does not result in greenhouse gases, thus worldwide movement towards clean energy is now a major concern.

- Delay in commissioning of power plants: In many developing countries there is a delay in commissioning new power plants that can fill the gap between demand and supply of energy.
- Wastage of energy: energy is wasted in many ways such as fail to switching off the electric equipment when there is no need, use of vehicles to travel short distances, not using energy efficient lights and fail to use the maximum from day light (using lights in sunny days) and energy leakages.
- Poor distribution system: This causes frequent tripping and break downs
- Accidents and natural calamities: accidents such as oil spills and get burnt due to tanker accidents, explosions in refineries or storage, bursting of pipeline. Natural calamities such as volcanoes, floods and earth quakes cause destruction and severe loss of fuel e.g. Fukushima Daiichi nuclear disaster following an earthquake on 11th March 2011 caused several thousands to evaluate from the area and resulted economic loss ranges between $ 250-500 billion.
- Wars and terror attacks: Wars between countries could hamper the global energy supply if it happens in Middle East countries e.g. Gulf war in 1990 caused severe rise in oil prices due to oil shortages. 2022 Russia's invasion into Ukraine caused global surge in oil price.
- Miscellaneous factors: tax hikes, strikes, military coup, political events, extreme climatic events may cause increase demand for energy or affects the fuel or energy supply.

(Rinkesh, 2016)

- Pandemic – oil prices have even gone negative, uncertainty is very high, and thus production cutting happens.

5.3 Solutions for energy crisis

- Move towards renewable energy sources such as solar, wind, ocean tide, hydro power and geo thermal energy.
- Encourage the use of energy efficient products such as CFL and LED bulbs, LED television or monitor and energy efficient air conditioners.
- Use of Lighting controls help to conserve large amount of energy such as preset lighting controls, slide lighting, touch dimmers and integrated lighting controls or using energy recovery units.
- Provide incentives such as less or no tax for hybrid and electric cars or easy payment schemes and encourage the public for using alternative renewable

energy sources or clean energy sources, encourage electricity saving by giving discounts on bills for low electricity usage.

- Energy simulation by using energy simulation software reduce business energy source and reduce carbon footprint.
- Perform energy audit: it helps to identify the areas of waste energy and improves the efficiency
- Common stand on climate change: both developed and developing countries adopt a common stand to reduce greenhouse gas and on saving energy.

Adapted from (Rinkesh, 2016)

Following problems causes global energy crisis

5.4 Global energy crisis due to poverty

According to Hosier & Kipondya (Hosier & Kipondya, 1993), the paper presented the findings of the urban household energy survey of Tanzania conducted by the Tanzanian urban energy project. Household energy use varies by income group according to local fuel availability. Also, the considerable difference between the marginal costs of supplied and its market price by consumers led to major misallocations of resources. A comparative analysis with the (past) records of 1987 depicted that in 1990, a significant shift by households from fuel wood, charcoal, and LPG toward kerosene and electricity occurred. The study also revealed the major reason for the shift towards modern fuel is fuel prices.

According to Dagoumas & Kitsios (Dagoumas & Kitsios, 2014), the study revealed the impacts of the economic crisis on energy poverty in Greece. It was stated that the power cuts made due to the economic crisis and the social policy of the government for sensitive social groups. The study also provided evidence that economic crisis or poverty has a considerable effect on electricity consumption and the capability of people to pay their bills. The primary reason for power cuts here is the unwillingness of consumers on paying electricity bills continuously.

5.5 Global energy crisis due to Urbanization

5.6 Global energy crisis due to Population Explosion

(Both 5.5 and 5.6 are merged into the following paragraph)

Increasing industries around the world causes increased consumption of non-renewable energy such as fossil fuels-coal, oil, and gas. Over 80% of current energy needs depend on fossil fuels. In addition, electricity generation, transports, and various industries still depend on fossil fuels as the sole source of energy. Energy demand is expected to rise almost half over the next two decades, but energy resources are started to run out. The potential for an energy crisis when sources of non-renewable energy get deplete is very true, however, in the past two decades proven gas resources have increased by 70% and proven oil reserves by 40%, and it has been estimated that we have enough for thirty years supply. In addition, new oil and gas fields are being discovered all the time, advanced recovery technologies open up several unconventional sources such as tar sands, shale gas, and ultra-deep-water. Furthermore, the emergence of nuclear energy and increasing usage technologies of renewable energy sources would pacify future emerging energy needs; however, at present usage of renewable energy is too small amount compare to non-renewable sources {Adapted from (Ehrlich & Ehrlich, 2008)}.

When considering the developing world, emerging energy needs are filled with fossil fuels while rich countries switching to other renewable sources. The growth of the global population, economy, and urbanization cause increased energy demand. According to the United Nations, world's population is expected to hit 9.8 billion by 2050, and two-thirds of the world's people will live in urban areas by 2050 ("World Energy Needs and Nuclear Power", 2018). Meeting this rapidly growing demand, while reducing the greenhouse gases, is a hard challenge. Global energy demand rose by 2.1% in 2017, while global energy-related CO_2 emissions increased by 1.4% in 2017 (International Energy Agency, 2018). Furthermore, over 70% of growth in global energy demand was met by oil, natural gas, and coal, while renewables accounted for the rest. However, carbon emission has hit the historical high of 32.5 Gigatons in 2017, which is driven by most major economies except the U.S., UK, Mexico, and Japan and the steepest decline in emissions recorded from the USA due to deployment of renewables yet fossil fuel account for 81% of total energy demand in 2017 (International Energy Agency, 2018).

5.7 Global energy crisis due to (Marine) oil spills

On 9th January 1909, Lake View Gusher oil spill caused the leak of 9 million barrels of oil into the sea this largest oil spill lasted for 18 months.

During the Gulf war 240 to 336 million gallons of crude oil deliberately flowed into the Persian Gulf, Kuwait, on the 19th of January 1991, this is one of the biggest oil spills in history, it was dumped by the Iraqi forces to prevent American intrusion(Laura, 2012). Deep-water Horizon oil spill of the Gulf of Mexico also known as BP oil spill 10th April 2010 caused the loss of 172 to 180 million gallons of crude oil into the environment("Conserve Energy Future", n.d.).The Ixtoc oil spill caused a loss of 3.3 million barrels of oil crude oil at sea on 3rd June 1979. The Atlantic Express oil spill on 19th July 1979 caused 2.1 to 2.4 million barrels of oil into the ocean. Fergana Valley oil spill of 2nd March 1992 caused due to the blowout at well number 05 in Uzbekistan caused the loss of over 2 million barrels of oil. The oil spill of the Iran Iraq war caused the loss of over 1500 barrels of crude oil per day for 9 months caused the loss of 1,094,761 barrels of oil on the coast. ABT summer, a Liberian registered transport tanker exploded and caused the loss of 1.8 to 1.9 million barrels of oil spill on the 28th of May 1991.

The Castillo De Bellver commenced on 6th August 1983 caused the loss of 1.85 million barrels this occurred in an environmentally sensitive area and affected the abundance of seabirds and marine life. Amoco Cadiz oil tanker collided with a sand bar and sunken on 16th March 1978, released 1.6-1.7 million barrels of oil into the sea. Adapted fromDenison (Denison, 2014).In addition, it was stated in"Research paper"("Research paper", n.d.)that oil spills renewed the sense of urgency of finding alternative sources of energy.

5.8 Global energy crisis due to poverty

According to Hosier & Kipondya (Hosier & Kipondya, 1993), the paper presented the findings of the urban household energy survey of Tanzania conducted by the Tanzanian urban energy project. Household energy use varies by income group according to local fuel availability. Also, the considerable difference between the marginal costs of supplied and its market price by consumers led to major misallocations of resources. A comparative analysis with the (past) records of 1987 depicted that in 1990, a significant shift by households from fuel wood, charcoal, and LPG toward kerosene and electricity occurred. The study also revealed the major reason for the shift towards modern fuel is fuel prices.

According to Dagoumas & Kitsios (Dagoumas & Kitsios, 2014), the study revealed the impacts of the economic crisis on energy poverty in Greece. It was stated that the power cuts made due to the economic crisis and the social policy of the government for sensitive social groups. The study also provided evidence that economic crisis or poverty has a considerable effect on electricity consumption and the capability of people to pay their bills. The primary reason for power cuts here is the unwillingness of consumers on paying electricity bills continuously.

Global energy crisis effects into following problems

5.9 Global warming and climate change due to the global energy crisis

According to Gunnemyr (Gunnemyr, 2019), man-made global warming is just like pouring a glass of water into the flood caused by torrential rain. Similarly, the global energy crisis leads to air pollution with greenhouse gases. Man-made greenhouse gases also contribute to global warming but in a minuscule amount which is negligible. However, according to Lewis D. (Lewis D. , 1973), "C influences D, and D influences E, then C causes E, and this is true even if C does not influence E, in the most trivial case where C influences E directly, C does of course cause E." and in reality, 95% of the natural global warming is from water vapor (H_2O) is a greenhouse gas that occupies 95% in the atmosphere (figure 6.4), whereas natural carbon dioxide emission took only 3.6% in the atmosphere. In that 3.6%, man-made carbon dioxide is just 3.5%. Thus, man-made greenhouse gas emission is negligible as a glass of water poured in the flood caused by torrential rain.

Despite these denials of significant man-made climate change, research on quantifying the census in anthropogenic global warming in the scientific literature (Cook, et al., 2013)showed that 97.1% of the scientific literature endorsed anthropogenic global warming (AGW), while 0.7% rejected and 0.3% was uncertain on the AGW. This survey documented 11 944 peer-reviewed climate abstracts published in the period between 1991 and 2011.

5.10   Nuclear explosions, radiation, and nuclear wastes due to the global energy crisis

According to Horvath & Rachlew (Horvath & Rachlew, 2016), increasing demand for electricity as fossil fuel engines are being substituted by electric battery motors, and the need for electricity can also be provided by nuclear power generation. This may result in nuclear wastes and nuclear disasters. E.g. Fukushima Daiichi nuclear disaster 2011 (fig. 5.4).

Figure 5.4 Fukushima Daiichi nuclear disaster 2011
Source: ("commons.wikimedia.org", 2011)

5.11   Air pollution due to the global energy crisis

Please see the chapter air pollution

5.12   Intensive farming due to the global energy crisis

Demand for palm oil to produce biofuel increases every year. According to Nasution, Afriani, & Erwinsyah(Nasution, Afriani, & Erwinsyah, 2014), Indonesia faced problems in the importation of fossil fuel which was challenging the national energy security in 2013. However, energy production from biodiesel, biogas, and biomass from palm products was used to generate electricity 2 GWh, 4 GWh, and 2.16 GWh respectively. Indonesia as the world's largest palm oil producer was projected to explore palm oil as a potential energy alternative.

Since the 1990s area occupied by oil palm cultivation has expanded globally by around 43%. This had caused massive destruction of the rainforest at an alarming rate, mainly using slash and burn techniques. This is mainly due to increasing energy demands from India, China, and entire Europe (RSPO , 2011) as cited in (UNEP,

2011). Oil palms are high yielding and profitable source of biofuel. Varieties produced by breeding programs can produce up to 20 tonnes of fresh fruit bunches/ ha./ Year under ideal conditions and this is equivalent to 5 tonnes oil/ ha./ Year (excluding the palm kernel oil) (FAO, 2002) as cited in (UNEP, 2011). In recent years production of biodiesel from palm oil is on a hike, mainly in Africa and Latin America(FAO, Global Forest Resources Assessment 2010, 2010); (Mitchell , 2011) as cited in (UNEP, 2011). However, oil palms are restricted to tropics and cultivated in Indonesia, Malaysia, and Thailand in Southeast Asia, Nigeria in Africa, Colombia and Ecuador in South America, and Papua New Guinea in Oceania(FAO, FAOSTAT online statistical service., 2009) as cited in (UNEP, 2011).

Traditionally, oil palm production was maintained as part of mixed farming practices in West Africa. And now it has been expanded as industrial-scale mono-crop(Colchester , 2010) as cited in (UNEP, 2011). Modern oil palm cultivation is characterized by monocultures of uniform age structure, low canopy, sparse undergrowth, a low stability microclimate, and intensive application of chemical fertilizers and pesticides(Fitzherbert , et al., 2008) as cited in (UNEP, 2011).

The global demand for palm oil is expected to double by 2020. Surveys and assessments are being conducted to find suitable locations for the palm oil plantation, new plantations continue to be established, and existing ones are being expanded(WWF, 2011) as cited in (UNEP, 2011). Also, environmental threats due to intensive farming of the oil palm have been broadly examined, particularly in Indonesia and Malaysia, where 85% of global production is taking place.

5.13   Pollution through mining activities due to the global energy crisis

The energy crisis led to oil exploration in environmentally sensitive areas such as protected wetlands and forest reserves. For instance, Oil mining in Niger Delta affects the components of the environment (ASA, 1998) as cited in (Ohimain, 2003). Nigeria is the sixth-largest petroleum producer and the eighth largest exporter, with a crude oil production rate of 2.4 million barrels per day. Its crude oil and gas reserve stand over 20 million bbl and 3.4 trillion cubic meters respectively(Imevbore, 2001)as cited in (Ohimain, 2003). Niger Delta is a wetland ecosystem that supports a large amount of biodiversity, including the mangroves. In November 2001 dredging activities in the Western part of Niger Delta, which included the construction of 3km long access canal to oil wells affected red mangrove (*Rhizophora racemosa*) and about four months later in March 2002 about 120 ha of primary mangrove forest showed severe mortality, and thereafter, about one year later fish kills were observed within the

134

dredged canal. In addition, habitat modification, erosion, flooding, and subsidence were observed in the region. Furthermore, enormous numbers of man-made canals, the presence of four export terminals, 159 oil fields, 1481 production wells, and several hundreds of pipelines and flow lines have severely changed the natural environment of the site. Furthermore, impacts on topography, hydrology, soil conditions, acidification caused by oxidation of sedimentary pyrite, and its severe and long-term impact on mangrove vegetation were crucial in this scenario, adapted from(Ohimain, 2003).

In addition, the energy crisis also led to the exploration of oil deposits in comparatively incredibly remote locations such as marine deep-water oil wells in Arctic and Antarctic regions. Antarctica's predicted levels of oil have been estimated at 203 billion barrels (Fogarty , 2011). Furthermore, according to Waldman (Waldman, 2017), Adam Paul Zukunft stated that even cleaning of Deepwater Horizon oil spill in 2010 in the Gulf of Mexico where the conditions were much favorable, depicted extreme difficulty of handling similar oil spill recovery in the Arctic and Antarctic. Also, there is a controversy on opening oil drilling in Alaska's arctic national wildlife refuge. Furthermore, in April 2017, President Trump signed an executive order that lifted the ban on oil and gas exploration in the Beaufort and Chukchi seas. However, Russia and China have already constructed their deep-water ports and have begun the dredging operation. But the U.S. is not prepared for the oil spills or it does not have adequate ice breakers either. According to Sen. Lisa Murkowski (R-Alaska), it has been estimated that 30 billion barrels of oil as wells as more than 200 trillion feet of natural gas reserves to be opened in the region, {adapted from (Waldman, 2017)}.

5.14   Overexploitation of natural resources due to the global energy crisis

Please see the chapter over exploitation of natural resources

5.15   Establishment of dams due to the global energy crisis

According to Sonoda (Sonoda, 2007), in Sri Lanka, at the beginning of the 1990s due to economic expansion and development, electricity demand was increased by more than 8% on average, and the balance between supply and the electricity demand had tightened after the second half of the decade. It was estimated that Sri Lanka could be hit by a critical supply-demand situation for electricity in any dry year. To overcome the crisis a multipurpose reservoir, type hydroelectric power plant with an output of 144 MW was launched with the funds from the United Nations Development Programme (UNDP) the plant is constructed with the establishment of a dam across Kukule Ganga River.

According to Mujeeb (Mujeeb, 2017), the Kalabagh dam hydroelectricity project is a rising hope to mitigate Pakistan's energy crisis, which is one of the major problems in Pakistan. At present, the hydropower generation of the country is solely dependent on Tarbela and Mongla dams, and thermal power accounts for 68.12% of the country's energy production. Since 1970 power cuts frequently occur in Pakistan, and in May 2013, power cuts were severe enough to put 70% of Pakistan without electricity at any given amount of time, and the proposed project is expected to produce about 3600 MW of electricity. Thus, the Kalabagh dam project is an urgent need for Pakistan to mitigate its long-lasting energy crisis.

According to Atkins (Atkins, n.d.), about 24% of the world's electricity is generated from hydropower. In 1998, the hydroelectric power of Norway and Congo provided 99% of each country's power and 91% of Brazil's electricity is generated from hydropower. Also, the U.S. has increased its hydroelectric power generation from about 16 billion KW hours in 1920 to about 306 billion KW hours in 1999, which made hydropower as 8% of total U.S. power generation. It was stated that only 2,400 of the 80,000 dams in the U.S. are used for hydroelectricity generation. Furthermore, Canada is the world's largest hydroelectricity generating country; the Former Soviet Union, Brazil, China, and Norway are the world's leading hydropower producing countries.

5.16   Global energy crisis as a keystone environmental problem

Increasing industries around the world demand energy. This is primarily generated by consumption of non-renewable energy resources such as fossil fuels, coal, oil, and gas. Over 80% of current energy needs depend on fossil fuels. Further, electricity generation, transports, and various industries still depend on fossil fuels as the sole source of energy. Energy demand is expected to rise by almost half of the present demand over the next two decades but energy resources have started to run out. The potential for an energy crisis when sources of non-renewable energy gets deplete is very true, however, in the past two decades available gas resources have increased by 70%, and oil reserves by 40%, and it has been estimated that we have enough for thirty years supply(Finding Solutions Together. Proposal - The Energy Crisis and Climate Change, 2016). Besides, new oil and gas fields are being discovered all the time. Advanced recovery technologies open up several unconventional sources such as tar sands, shale gas, and ultra-deep-water are been considered. Furthermore, nuclear energy and increasing usage of technologies of renewable energy sources would pacify future emerging energy needs. However, at present the usage of renewable energy is too small compared to non-renewable sources.

Global energy crisis and burning of fossil fuels cause overexploitation of coal and other fossil fuel resources. Furthermore, pollution through mining activities including fracking; deforestation through intensive farming of oil palm, also cause air pollution (carbon sinks and particle filtration activity are lost through deforestation), the establishment of dams for hydropower generation, etc. Solving the global energy crisis may eliminate several of the above-mentioned problems such as pollution through mining activities (for crude oil & gas), air pollution, and up to certain extent deforestation and intensive oil palm cultivation. It will also solve indirect links such as groundwater contamination by pollution through mining activities - fracking, and biodiversity loss because of deforestation. (Figure 5.5).

Evidence 1: Global energy crisis causes air pollution

According to the International Energy Agency (IEA) WEO-2016 Special Report Energy and Air Pollution(International Energy Agency (IEA) WEO-2016 Special Report Energy and Air Pollution, 2016) as cited in (Perera, 2018), energy-related fossil fuel combustion in high and middle-income countries and biomass burning in low-income countries account for most of the global air pollution, generating 85% of airborne respirable particulate pollution and almost all sulphur dioxide and nitrogen oxide emissions to the atmosphere.

Evidence 2: Global energy crisis causes global warming and climate change

According to the "OECD report"("OECD report", 2011), fossil fuel combustion accounted for 84% of global greenhouse gas emission in 2009.

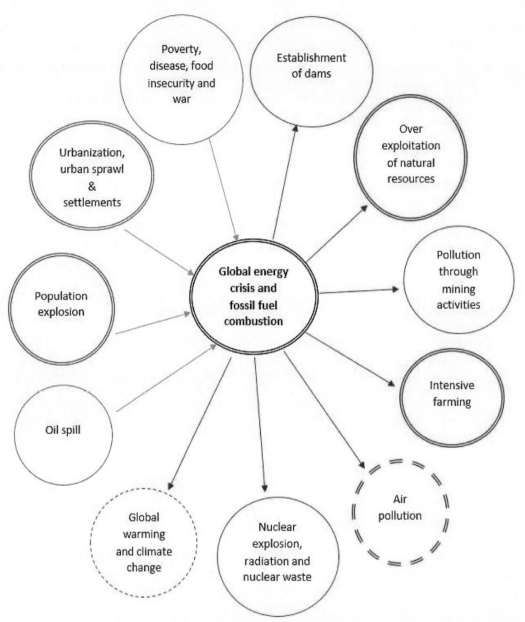

Figure 5.5 Global energy crisis as keystone environmental problem with the disappearance of air pollution on its mitigation (hypothetical diagram)

[In the figure black circle is the problem being examined, blue circles are cause man-made environmental problems, red circles are effect man-made environmental problems, double lined circles are keystone man-made environmental problems, and circles with dashed lines (either single or double lined) are the man-made environmental problems that disappear when the problem being examined (black circle) is mitigated]

Global energy crisis and fossil fuel burning is a *keystone environmental problem*, which causes air pollution which includes acid rain (SO_x & NO_x air pollution), ozone depletion (CFC air pollution), global warming and climate change (greenhouse gas air pollution), respiratory diseases (particle air pollution), and visual pollution (smog air pollution). However, the precursor for air pollution is population explosion in urban areas, and pesticide air pollution occurs usually in the agricultural village regions.

Sustainable vs. Greener vs. Conventional solutions
A. Conventional energy

Fossil fuels such as coal, kerosene, diesel, petrol, and liquid petroleum gas (LPG), liquid natural gas (LNG) and waste-to-energy are considered as malefic to environmental health because they impart additional carbon in the form of greenhouse gases that was sequestered by ancient plants many million years ago. Thus, they are not green energy, often placed under **conventional** solutions of the energy crisis **with** the appropriate mitigations such as scrubbers and air purifiers. If these mitigations are not given, then fossil fuels **cannot** even be considered under conventional solutions because without mitigatory measures they directly break the law (not a solution).

In addition to fossil fuels hydropower schemes are also **not** placed under greener energy (except mini and micro hydro projects) because the construction of dams and reservoirs cause **major** environmental threats such as alteration of the water current, and excavation of soil causes severe land degradation leading to erosion and flooding events. And dam and reservoir construction may cause deforestation or resettlements of human and wildlife. This leads to habitat destruction; in some cases, it may also result in species extinction. Sedimentation effect of the dams and reservoirs cause water pollution. Altered water currents may affect the natural migration of fish species and their spawning or breeding grounds. Due to the high energy requirements hydropower projects are costly, and they are placed under the category of **conventional** energy.

Nuclear energy is **not** inexhaustible, and it is not reconstituted in mines. Thus, it is a non-renewable resource ("citizen.org", 2023). Even though uranium is recyclable, it is stock energy, and if the stock is exhausted, no more resources are available for energy generation. In addition, nuclear power is considered as fissile energy that results from the fission of atoms within nuclear reactors. According to nuclear experts ("Orano", n.d.), annually, nuclear power prevents the release of 2 billion tonnes of carbon dioxide. But it cannot be placed under greener fuels because mining, milling and enrichment of uranium is energy intensive and contributes to an increase in the carbon footprint. Estimated energy recovery time for a nuclear plant is 10-18 years, this waiting time for energy retention is relatively longer period depends on the richness of the uranium ores, according to US Nuclear Regulatory Commission 12 cancer deaths can be expected for each 20-year term during the reactor's operation and this excludes the radiation released from nuclear waste and its disposal, thermal pollution from the coolers immensely affects the marine ecosystem and causes anoxic environment that leads to death of marine biota, from a typical reactor about 20-30 tons of high level nuclear waste is generated annually that remains hazardously radioactive for a quarter of a million years, nuclear power has immense security threat, disasters could lead to mass massacre e.g. Chernobyl, Three Mile Island and Fukushima, and also, nuclear plants are expensive, the initial cost, maintenance and security related expenditure is relatively high. Due to the aforementioned negative environmental facts nuclear fission power is placed under **conventional** energy.

In the waste-to-energy-process, several techniques such as the gasification process where synthetic gas (Syngas) is produced and used as fuel. Dried sludge after dewatering, char, and waste oil which are released during the incineration/ pyrolysis/ gasification process can be used as boiler fuels in industries or power plants. However, use of plastic waste for incineration may cause toxic fumes that are even carcinogenic. Thus, waste should undergo screening prior to incineration. However, resulting smoke, fly, and bottom ash often consist of hazardous heavy metals, other toxic products, and greenhouses gases. Thus, it is placed under **conventional** energy with appropriate mitigatory measures.

Animals are used as a source of energy since ancient times for transportation, grinding, pumping water from wells, as carriers, to plough paddy fields, etc. Yet when compared to machines animals are less efficient and need human husbandry. However, using the animal energy is now being considered as animal cruelty. And animal cruelty is a serious environmental problem that questions the continuity of life in this planet because cruelty of any form is hazardous in nature and affects the peaceful existence of all life forms in reality. Thus, use of animal energy cannot be considered as green or sustainable. And today, use of animals for aforementioned purposes as a source of energy is banned in many countries with the support of animal activists. Even placement of animal energy under the conventional energy category is breaking the law. However, if animals used for energy should be cared well with human love and compassion, then it is eligible to be considered as **conventional** energy.

B. Greener energy

Greener solutions are almost sustainable, but they cause **minimal damage to the environment at any part of their lifecycle**. For instance, photovoltaic panels are zero emission and no carbon emission on its usage. Yet, when its carbon footprint is considered, its manufacturing and transporting process take a significant amount of carbon emission. Photovoltaic panels need larger land space for mounting. Thus, it may cause deforestation or habitat degradation (e.g. destruction of tortoise habitat in Southern Nevada deserts in the United States). Photovoltaic panels need batteries for electricity storage. Thus, they also produce considerable amount of electronic waste. Ironically, the electronic waste (E-waste) from photovoltaic panels has **hazardous heavy metals** such as silver, lead, arsenic and cadmium. Thus, E-waste from the photovoltaic system is hazardous, and needs to undergo a safe disposal mechanism. Due to aforementioned reasons photovoltaic panels cannot be considered as sustainable solutions (net zero) to the energy crisis, and they are placed under greener solutions. Similarly, wind turbines are also placed under greener solutions because they cause nearly zero impact to the environment. Yet when we consider the entire life cycle, it has a considerable amount of carbon footprint on its manufacture and transportation. At the end of their life cycle they produce plastic waste that is hardly biodegradable because the turbine blades are made up of non-recyclable plastics. In addition, they also occupy considerable space in the ground and sea, and may affect the areal and water navigation. Wind turbines kill large birds and impose a threat to the biodiversity. And similar to photovoltaic panels, wind turbines also cause visual pollution. Also, wind turbines cause noise pollution.

In case of biomass, biofuel (ethanol), bioenergy, and biogas (including landfill gas and wastewater treatment digester gas), anaerobically produced methane or renewable natural gas (RNG) the carbon sequestered by (present day) plants is released back to the atmosphere during the fuel combustion, the added carbon to the atmosphere is cyclical, and thus it is carbon neutral, and yet there are certain negative impacts such as particle pollution (PM_{10} and $PM_{2.5}$) and generation of carbon soot and carbon monoxide that are harmful to human health. Methane emitted during their combustion can stay in the atmosphere only for 12 years on average {a 25 times stronger greenhouse gas than CO_2 ("US EPA", 2022)}, and later it becomes CO_2 (which is also cyclical and carbon neutral) Also, forest clearing for palm tree cultivation palm oil (a biofuel) causes severe threat to biodiversity in Indonesia. Orangutan (an ape) is facing destruction of their own habitats due to increasing palm oil plantations. However, virtually, merely considering their carbon neutrality, they are placed under **greener** fuels.

C. Sustainable energy

The sustainable solution for the air pollution and energy crisis is the implementation of a permanent ban on fossil fuels, because here the impact on the environment is net zero. Thus, the resource is being utilized without compromising the use and environment (air, climate, mineral resources and biodiversity) of future generation (as mentioned in the 1987 United Nations Brundtland commission's definition of sustainable development). According to (Hollaway, 2023), the energy that can be replenished in the human time scale and cause no long-term impact to the environment. Here, the long-term environmental impacts are serious environmental threats such as climate change or global warming, hazardous heavy metals, hazardous radioactive waste, or radiation emission, deforestation or loss of habitat, land degradation or soil erosion or sedimentation, diseases (cancer and respiratory illnesses) and biodiversity loss. And the energy generator may cause these environmental threats at any part of their life cycle (during manufacture or at the time of operation or at the time of disposal).

Aforementioned definition pushed following renewable energy sources into a green energy source (minimal environmental impact) and conventional energy sources (serious or long-term environmental problem).

✘ Photovoltaic panel (solar panel) – **Unsustainable and greener** energy because at the end of its life cycle it produces hazardous heavy metal containing waste, in addition, solar farms caused habitat loss for certain wildlife and in some cases caused deforestation (visual pollution is a minor threat). And even though it causes serious environmental threats, they are not placed under conventional because those serious environmental threats do not always occur, for instance roof top solar

142

panels and desert land solar farms never cause deforestation or habitat loss, and heavy metal waste can be properly disposed without harming the environment, thus, it is considered greener energy.

×Windmill – **Unsustainable and greener energy**- because turbine blades cause non-recyclable plastic waste at the end of their life cycle, kill birds, etc. (noise and visual pollution by changing the panorama including their flickering lights are minor threats). And even though it causes serious environmental threats, they are not placed under conventional because those serious environmental threats do not always occur, for instance bird kill happens rarely with these turbine blades and non-recyclable plastic waste can be reused for other making purposes or considered for other sanitary disposal methods, thus it is considered greener energy.

× Hydropower (large)- **Unsustainable and conventional energy** because hydropower schemes when establishing dams and reservoirs often cause deforestation, habitat loss, relocation of people and animals, land degradation, soil erosion, floodings, and landslides. Unlike solar and wind, hydropower schemes cause mass destruction to the environment and they are irreversible and cause long term environmental threats, and merely by considering its zero-carbon emission it is not possible to keep them in the green energy category, thus, hydropower (large) is placed under conventional sources. However, mini and micro hydropower are placed under the sustainable energy category.

× Nuclear fission- **Unsustainable conventional energy** because they generate hazardous radioactive waste on their operation, and their radiation pollution causes cancers among the citizens live close by the plant. And merely by considering its zero-carbon emission features it is not possible to keep it under the green energy category. Thus, nuclear fission is a conventional energy source. However, unlike nuclear fission, nuclear fusion is placed under the sustainable energy category.

× Bioenergy, biofuel, biomass, biogas (Renewable Natural Gas) and hydrothermal decarbonization (HTC) – **Unsustainable and greener energy** sources because even though they are carbon neutral (the carbon emission here is from the CO_2 sequestered by present green plants via photosynthesis from the atmosphere), they produce particle matter emission $PM_{2.5}$ and PM_{10} and this is a threat to human health. And along with fossil fuels biofuels (all kinds of bioenergy and biogas) cause nearly 7 million premature deaths annually. In addition, it also causes deforestation and habitat loss (e.g., oil palm - Indonesia) and causes biodiversity loss (orangutan-

Indonesia). Thus, by considering aforementioned long-term or serious environmental threats it should be placed under the conventional energy category, yet by considering its possibility of environmentally friendly production (e.g. oil palm agroforestry (Hoffner, 2021)) and its carbon neutrality it is placed under the green energy category.

✗ Animal power- **Unsustainable and conventional** energy because animal cruelty is considered as a serious environmental threat (Sivaramanan & Kotagama, 2022). And many animal welfare groups and activists are against it. Yet if the animals used for energy needs are not treated well with care and compassion, it is not even eligible to be placed under the conventional energy category because it directly breaks the law.

Yet in reality, **the maximum level of source categorization given for the presently available energy sources is sustainable energy.** Since sustainable solutions are high-energy solutions, they are mostly accompanied by a high initial cost.

✓Green hydrogen and green ammonia also cannot be considered as net zero in terms of environmental impact. This is because the initial electricity for the electrolysis comes from other renewable sources such as solar or wind energy. And they require frequent maintenance, which causes a significant amount of carbon emissions such as transportation of equipments, maintenance staff, etc. However, by ignoring the source of energy initiation and the carbon footprint it generates during its manufacture, transport, and usage, green hydrogen and green ammonia are placed under sustainable energy solutions because they produce no harmful emissions or hazardous waste throughout their entire life cycle. In addition, tidal and wave energy are environmentally also placed under sustainable solutions. Even though they are emission-free, but they might impair marine shipping routes, or alter the habitats of marine biota and cause a positive carbon footprint during manufacture, transport, implementation and maintenance of the generators. Yet these impacts are negligible and do not involve any serious environmental threat. Thus, by considering the zero carbon emission features, green hydrogen and ammonia are placed under the sustainable energy category.

✓Solar thermal, ✓geothermal energy and ✓mini-hydro, and ✓micro-hydro are also emission-free natural sources. Yet by ignoring the carbon footprint required for its manufacture, transport, implementation and maintenance of the generators, and considering their zero-carbon emission feature these renewable sources are placed under the sustainable (net zero, neither harm nor benefit to the natural environment) energy category. Furthermore, it has been envisaged that energy generation from ✓nuclear fusion is going to be the dominating sustainable energy source of the future. Helium is the only emission from fusion power generation, which is an inert gas. Thus, it is carbon-free, and raw elements deuterium and tritium are heavy isotopes of hydrogen. Deuterium can be extracted from seawater, and tritium can be produced from lithium, which is also abundant in nature. Yet fusion energy also required batteries for its storage. Thus, may contribute a little amount of waste. In addition, initial input energy for fusion is very high. Thus, the initial energy requirement should be facilitated from the grid energy. Also, the initial production, implementation and maintenance of fusion plants contribute towards increasing the carbon footprint significantly. By ignoring all these minimal drawbacks to the environment and by considering its zero-carbon emission feature, fusion technology is placed under sustainable energy. In addition, ✓manpower also placed under sustainable solution, human energy used in Gymnasium can be used to generate electricity. The use of manpower to ensure a healthy lifestyle reduces the risk of cancer and obesity. Thus, it is a sustainable energy source (environmentally net zero, neither benefit nor harm to the nature and other living beings).

There are **no** restorative or reconciliatory solutions available in the energy sector (fig.6.6). However, it is believed that photosynthesis of green plants, green algae, and cyanobacteria is the only naturally existing **regenerative** solution for the energy crisis, and this argument is supported by the 2nd law of thermodynamics that as energy is transferred or transformed, more and more of it is wasted.

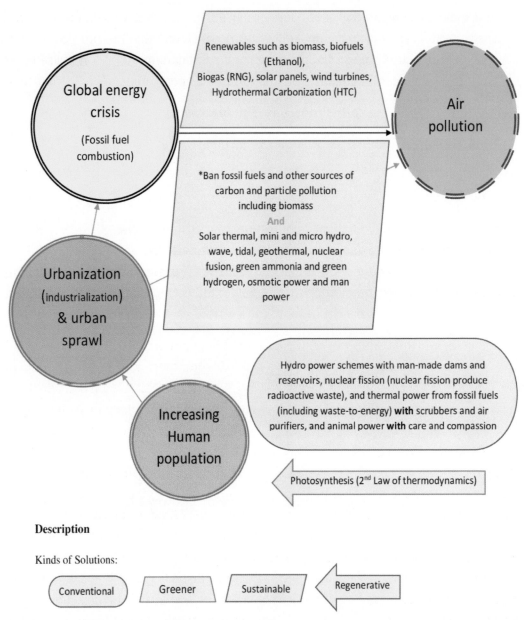

Figure 5.6 Solutions for global energy crisis

Black circle: problem under concern, Blue circle: cause, Red circle: effect, Double-lined circle: keystone environmental problem, Single lined circle: environmental problem, Dotted lined circle: problem to be mitigated when keystone environmental problem gets solved, Black arrow: cause-effect link for which solutions are given, Blue arrow: cause-effect link

N.B.: - Each problem in the circles is connected to many other problems based on cause-and-effect links, and they are not shown here.

146

6. Intensive farming

6.1 Introduction

Since the time of Rachel Carson, when the book Silent Spring was published on 27th of September 1962, the whole world was shocked to know the impacts of agrochemicals on our ecosystem and human health. The book was an eye opener at that time. The book revealed the stories those pesticides in the environment killing non-targeted pests such as butterflies and bees, which are essential for pollination, it emphasised on declining flora and fauna populations due to the toxic effects of bio-magnification and bioaccumulation of chemical pesticides. It harbingers the today's despeciation and unidentified chronic kidney diseases and cancers.

When an agriculture system of crop plants or animals with higher levels of input and output per unit of land area it is considered as intensive farming. In other words, increased utilization of farmland to collect high yields to gain profits and to support human food needs; it uses large number of labour and capital relative to land area.

The high yield has been obtained by the increased use of chemical fertilizers, abundant irrigation, heavy use of machinery and land treatment, planting high yielding variety or hybrid varieties or genetically modified crops, expansion of arable land, etc.

Due to the high yield from small territory intensive farming and less labour, it is believed to be the aid for growing population. However, intensive farming is to blame for 80% of deforestation on earth. Furthermore, intensive chemical fertilizer, pesticide, weedicide, and fungicide application caused loss of bees and various links in the biota. When the bee population decline, pollination is affected and subsequently destroys the vegetation cover and the habitats. Leachate of harmful chemicals also affects the aquatic life, in addition, inorganic fertilizer residues causes eutrophication in the water bodies. Intensive chemical fertilizer farming causes soil salinization and result in desertification. According to Vandana Shiva (Deiters, n.d.), *"when the green revolution was introduced to India in the 1960s through U.S. conditionalities and Word bank conditionalities the driving force was the corporations, but the implementor was the government. Today the driving force is still the corporations but the state structures that were created in 60s & 70s are being dismantled, such as government subsidies and minimum support price (price above the production cost) were completely withdrawn today. Thus, today it has become non-sustainable agriculture in Panjab. In addition, today's global rule also requires of farmers to stop government support, including the termination of government regulation of imports. In combination of these international prices started to destabilise domestic prices".* Vandana Shiva further mentioned that *"two main factors have worsened the situation in Panjab, first corporations have directly got in to the seed supply and chemical supply (no involvement of government authoritative bodies), high-cost seeds and huge implementation of chemicals, roughly 700% increase in pesticide expenditure by farmers in the last few decades. Thus, the cost is shooting up by ten-fold and the prices for yields are dropping. This situation squeezes the small farmers, and they are getting into death by committing suicides".*

Low and uncertain harvest from this method has put them into a state of anxiety and had led to suicides. In India, averages of over 10 farmers apparently have committed suicide daily during the period between 2017 and 2018because of their debts. The immediate withdrawal of applications from the fields may yield low harvests, as the soils been "almost barren and dead" would not be able to provide the nutrients for the plants for higher yields. Thus, creating a low yield dilemma and a financial crisis.

Due to its high impact on carbon foot print, intensive farming is also a major known cause for the climate change. It has been found vegetables and grains produced from intensive agriculture are the root causes of congenital abnormalities and cancers.

Mono cropping such as soy bean, corn, paddy and wheat reduce soil fertility, enhance pest outbreaks and diseases. Methane generation from paddy fields and cattle farms cause significant impact on global climate change.

6.2 Health hazards of agro-chemicals

Interestingly 99.9 percent of the pesticide residues remain in the soil, water and air environment or consumed by the non-targeted organisms, with time they undergo physiochemical changes, undergo evaporation, volatilization, photodecomposition, breakdown by microbial activity, plant uptake and travel through the food chain (bioaccumulation and bio magnification). Persistent compounds such as organochlorine pesticides may concentrate in tissues of organisms and also its concentration through the food chain increases, they affect more on organisms in higher trophic level. Pesticide Action Network (PAN) an international organization has listed highly hazardous pesticides (HHP) according to the categorization of WHO.

The pesticides based on their toxicity can be classified as:

a). **neurotoxic substances** such as Organochlorine compounds or Organo phosphates, carbamates and Pyrethroids, which affect nervous system by affecting perception, motivation, habituation, learning and memory may cause depression of acetylcholinesterase (AChE) activity in serum. Organochlorines such as DDT, Cyclodienes and Chlordecone may result in acute convulsive seizures with brain ischemia, anoxia and neural cell loss (Tardiff, 1992).

b). **immune toxic substances**, autoimmune disease was reported in workers with chronic pesticide exposure, antibodies developed against liver and kidney. Exposure of Organochlorine or Organophosphate insecticide caused pulmonary hypersensitivity in animals because of pesticide exposure(Yonemoto, Gellin , & Epstein, 1983); (Ecobichon, et al., 1990) as cited in(Tardiff, 1992).

c). **dermal toxic substances**, where spraying or dusting of pesticides leads to penetration through skin which is more than that of reaching respiratory tract, which result in allergic reactions(Morisset, Ahluwalia, Nagy, & Urban, 2001)as cited in (Tardiff, 1992).

d). **reproductive toxic substances** that cause abortion in females and infertility in males. Effects of Dibromochloropropane (DBCP) on male fertility, such as chromosomal damage, reduction in sperm count, sperm motility, it also affects the reproductive mechanism on females (Tardiff, 1992).

e). **chronic toxic substances** affect the human health by continuous exposure, accumulation of pesticide chemical in tissues also cause lethal health hazards in long terms.

f). **developmental toxic substances**, causes malformations and injuries to embryo and foetus, decreased birth weight, mortality of the foetus or neonate and functional changes in neonates (Tardiff, 1992).

g). **genotoxicsubstances**, result in forward and reverse mutations, frame shift mutation, deletions, transpositions exchange of sister chromatids, unscheduled DNA synthesis, neoplastic transformation and chromosome breakage (Tardiff, 1992).

h). **carcinogens** such as Dichlorodiphenyltrichloroethane (DDT) and chlordane are known human carcinogens.

i). **heavy metal toxic substances**, heavy metals such as lead, cadmium, chromium, copper, arsenic and thallium (rodenticide) are naturally existing persistent compounds. Heavy metals when added through pesticides or fertilizers could cause several health effects such as skin lesions, kidney and bone troubles, respiratory problems, neurotoxicity, heart diseases, muscle weakness, reproductive problems, reduced white blood cells (suppression of immune system) and cancers (As, Cd and Cr are carcinogens) when concentrated in tissues of the organisms.

All these toxic substances undergo bioaccumulation (persistent pesticide increase in concentration in the tissues of first organism) and biological magnification (increasing concentration of pesticide residue along the food chain e.g., DDT & heavy metals) in the bodies of consumers to enhance the impact up the food web.In addition, high levels of fluoride from agrochemicals along with heavy metals such as cadmium, lead, arsenic, and uranium in soil and water are believed as contributory factors of CKDu and cancers. It is believed that CKD found in Rajarata (North Central Province of Sri Lanka) is due to Calcium Arsenate from pesticides. This also causes Arsenicosis (chronic illness caused by drinking water contaminated with high levels of Arsenic) (Chandrajith , Seneviratna , & Wickramaarachchi , 2010). In addition, several health problems such as neurobehavioural, neuropathic effects, problems related to memory and intellectual function, reproductive effects, steatosis (fatty liver), cardiovascular disease, Ischemic Heart Disease (IHD), carotid atherosclerosis, Respiratory illnesses, hormonal affects, and diabetes mellitus.Adapted from ("ejatlas.org", 2016).

6.3 Environmental implications of chemical applications

Anthropogenic changes in the soil chemistry through application of agrochemicals leads to soil salinization, soil acidification and erosion, ultimately cause loss of macro and micro fauna. Fungicides kill the mycorrhizae of the higher plants, which are essential for soil moisture, soil structure and for the establishment of micro habitats for different kinds of soil fauna, from earth worms to insects. Also, tillage and other mechanical ploughing practices kill earthworms and mycorrhizae (Chan, 2001). Pesticide chemicals directly kill soil's insect population unselectively, along with molluscs, and earthworms, such as neonicotinoids and some herbicides (e.g., glyphosate) can remain in soil surface for years and kill non-targeted soil organism (Bünemann, Schwenke, & Zwieten, 2006). Loss of saprophytic soil fauna leads to incomplete natural cycling of nutrients, and unavailability of nutrient due to the incomplete cycles, increases the needs for artificial fertilizers. Alteration in the soil pH from synthetic fertilizers reduces soil microbes, including nitrogen fixing bacteria. Furthermore, a study of (Vieira, Morales-Hojas, Santos , & Vieira, 2007)depicts the

Sulfentrazone pesticide affects the nitrogen fixing micro flora in soybeans and reduces the plant growth. Another study by (Fox, Snyder, Vincent, & Raichle, 2007) showed, use of organochlorine pesticides affects the recruitment of *Rhizobium* sp., decline in the activity of nitrogenase enzyme, this reduces the harvest. Phenoxylkanoic acid herbicide (2,4-D) affects *Rhizobium* sp. (Guenzi, , Ahlrichs, Chesters, Bloodworth, & Nash, 1974).

A study of (Ma, 2005), showed the effect of five organotins and pyrethroid pesticides on cyanobacteria such as *Anabaena flos-aquae, Microcystisflos-aquae, and Microcystis aeruginosa* and green algae (*Selenastrumcapricornutum,Scenedesmus quadricauda, Scenedesmus obliqnus, Chlorella vulgaris,* and *Chlorella pyrenoidosa*) resulted in adverse results in the treated varieties. This further leads to the formation of nitrogen deficient soils and further increases the dependency on the inorganic nitrogen through chemical fertilizer. Unlike in the silvopasture system, lack of shady higher plants and their mulching litter leads to prolonged exposure of soil to direct sunlight causes soil nutrient loss via oxidation. In nature, phosphate cycling occurs via droppings of birds sitting on trees lack of trees also questioned this mineral availability. Thus, loss of both above ground and below ground soil biodiversity leads to nutrient loss and eventually creating infertile soil. In contrast, no-input agriculture and agroforestry systems root mycorrhizae, and natural nitrogen fixation by soil microbes *Nitrosomonas* sp. and *Nitrobacter* sp. is not disturbed.

In addition, floating pesticide and weedicide chemicals in the atmosphere, according to Nascimento, Rocha, & Andrade (Nascimento, Rocha, & Andrade, 2017), a study developed a green-sensitive sample preparation method for the determination of nine organophosphates, two pyrethroids, one carbamate, and one strobilurin in $PM_{2.5}$ collected in the tropical coastal area in the Southern Hemisphere. Extraction of $PM_{2.5}$ sample masses, as low as 206 µg were performed in a miniaturized device using 500 µL of a mixture containing 18% acetonitrile in dichloromethane followed by sonication for 23 minutes and injection into GC-MS. Based on the results twelve pesticides were identified and quantified, this includes eight banned pesticides. Also, a risk assessment exposure and cancer risk for possible carcinogenic pesticides such as bifenthrin, malathion, parathion, and permethrin were performed for exposure of adults, children, and infants, and based on the results Hazard Quotient and cumulative exposure for organophosphate and pyrethroid pesticides were less than 1, shows the cumulative risk is within an acceptable range. According to "Persistence organic pollutants: national implementation plan for 2005-2020" ("Persistance organic

151

151

pollutants: national implementation plan for 2005-2020", 2005), in Latvia third national priority status is given to persistent organic pollutants (POPs) pesticides. However, POPs pesticides are not produced, sold, or used in Latvia but there are stockpiles, temporary storage sites found in Kņava non-marketable chemical storage facility and the Garden hazardous waste disposal site such as Toxaphene ~200 t DDT; ~5 t, Lindane ~170 t, Lindane DDT mixture of ~ 200 t. According to "anses" ("anses", 2016), contamination of air by pesticides is a less documented air pollution issue all over the world.

The concentration of nitrates, phosphates, and dissolved oxygen in surface water of the Tunga-Kawo irrigation scheme affected the water quality according to Jimoh, Ayodeji, & Mohammed (Jimoh, Ayodeji, & Mohammed, 2003). In a study on three sampling points of surface water, at the downstream site, the nitrate level increased from zero to 74.1 mg l^{-1} just after the fertilizer application, this is more than the WHO maximum safe limit of 50 mg l^{-1}, and the phosphate level increased from 1.2mg l^{-1} to 19.2 mg l^{-1} during the same period in the year 2000. In addition, hydrazine level in the same section was increased from 62 μg l^{-1} to 102 μg l^{-1} and the dissolved oxygen levels were lower in the downstream location than the upstream, and the level was lower than the minimum amount required to support fauna and flora. Although, the quantity of the fertilizer applied by the farmers is below the required optimum to get the maximum yield.

A review (Konstantinou, Hela, & Albanis, 2006) on long-term research projects, monitoring programs, and published papers concerning the surface water pollution of Greece, which revealed that pesticide classes that are mostly detected in surface water are herbicides used in corn, cotton, and rice cultivation. Organophosphorus insecticides and banned organochlorine insecticides due to their persistence in the aquatic environment. The most frequently detected compounds were herbicides such as atrazine, simazine, alachlor, metolachlor, and trifluralin, insecticides such as diazinon and parathion methyl and endosulfan lindane, and organochlorine pesticides such as aldrin. Rivers were found to be more polluted than lakes. Detected pesticide concentrations were subjected to seasonal variation as higher levels were found during late spring and summer, followed by a decrease in winter. Greek rivers also depicted similar trends compare to other rivers in Europe.

In addition, groundwater contamination of agrochemicals affected the drinking water quality in Jaffna peninsula. The higher nitrate content in the groundwater causes methemoglobinemia (blue baby syndrome), and may causes oesophageal and

152

stomach cancers. Heavy metal contamination in water bodies from agrochemicals is one of the speculated causes for chronic kidney disease in North Central province of Sri Lanka.

According to University of Sydney's research associate and the study's lead author Dr Fiona Tang (Tang , Lenzen, & McBrat, 2021), about 64% of world's arable land is at risk of pesticide pollution. A UN backed study published in 'TheGuardian.com' (Watts, 2017) stated that third of earth's soil is acutely degraded due to (intensive or chemical based) agriculture. The study also revealed that globally fertile soil is being lost at the rate of 24bn tonnes a year. Furthermore, increasing demand for food and productive land leads to risk of conflicts in Sudan and Chad.

Crop plants sequester carbon through photosynthesis. However, intensive monoculture farms contribute comparatively less in carbon sequestration than the regenerative agroforestry systems. In addition, amount of carbon stored by the soil depends on the addition of organic matter naturally available from the litter. Inorganic fertilizers often cannot provide the required soil carbon, which is depleting through soil respiration and decomposition. A survey revealed that in the United States forests and crop lands currently sequester 12% of the carbon dioxide emission from energy, transport, and industrial sectors (Huber, 2008).

6.4 Intensive farming increases animal cruelty

There are sufficient evidences for the conflicts between ancient man and animals cause complete extinction of few species such as Dodo, Moa, Woolly mammoth, Siberian tiger and Tasmanian wolf, such extinctions are taken place by chasing and killing in groups, use of traps, use of fire, sharp weapons and stone or wooden rods when man spent his life as hunter gatherer. Even today increasing human population and needs cause over consumption of animals for food and for other human needs, destruction of natural habitats of many animals and plants, poaching, trading animal products, abusing, animal cruelty lead to suffering of animals and human- animal conflicting situations in many parts of the world. White rhinos are almost extinct; the only available male white rhino is being guarded by armed men day and night in Kenya and allowed to access with females to maintain species continuity. Rhinos are still being hunt by poachers for its priceless horn and the same is happening for elephants for their tusks and tiger for their skin and Chinese medicine, trading of wild animal is illegal in many countries, list of threaten and vulnerable species of animals lengthens, animal abuse and cruelty are not a rare incident or an accident, it is now industrialized, technology and machines also take part in this devastation gruesome

153

act, use of killing machines, electric prod, burning or corrosive chemicals against innocent animals are taken place in almost every meat, fisheries, poultry, fur, wool and other animal related product manufacturing, entertainment, sport and servicing industry.

Following problems causes Intensive farming

6.5 Intensive farming due to population explosion

According to Singh & Narayanan (Singh & Narayanan, 2015), technology-driven intensive agriculture helps to mitigate the rising food demand due to the increasing population. Intensive agriculture increases the yield, facilitates land use in more productive ways and decreases the fallow period to a great extent, and increases the available land that mirrors the land augmenting aspect of technology. This study examined the impacts of these two aspects of technology on cropland expansion for Andhra Pradesh, India, using district-level data in the period between 1970 and 2009. Also, the study evaluated the impact of population growth, urban population, and literate population on cropland expansion. To measure the relative impact of affluence, population, and technology on resource usage, a regression model based on the IPAT framework was used. Results rejected the land-sparing hypothesis in the state after the implementation of modern technology. However, population pressure on cropland seems to have declined due to the technology-driven intensive agriculture.

According to Conelly & Chaiken (Conelly & Chaiken, 2000), a study on the impact of increased population densities and agricultural intensification on-farm diversity and food insecurity depicted those farmers in Hamisi, in western Kenya, which is one of the most densely populated areas in all of rural Africa, engaged in a wide variety of sophisticated technology that maintain exceptionally high levels of agricultural diversity. The intensification includes a complex variety of inter-cropping, poly variety, and emphasis on multi-purpose crops, and the close integration of crops and livestock. However, despite the crop diversity, the population pressure in Hamisi increased the threat, such as food insecurity and limited availability of nutritionally dense food.

According to Josephson, Ricker-Gilbert, & Florax (Josephson, Ricker-Gilbert, & Florax, 2014), a study based on household-level panel data on smallholder farmers in Ethiopia aimed to estimate the relationship between rural population density (RPD) and the agricultural intensification and productivity revealed that higher RPD is

154

associated with smaller farm size, and has a positive effect on input demand such as increased fertilizer usage per hectare. In conclusion, increasing inputs does not result in high yields, thus, farm income falls as the rural population density increases. Thus, farmers stuck in place, as they are unable to sustainably intensify agriculture as the rising RPD declined the farm sizes.

6.6 Intensive farming due to the global energy crisis

Please see chapter global energy crisis

Intensive farming effects into following problems

6.7 Intensive farming causes solid wastes and sewage

According to Obi, Ugwuishiwu, & Nwakaire (Obi, Ugwuishiwu, & Nwakaire, 2016), agricultural wastes are residues from growing and processing raw agricultural products such as fruits, vegetables, meat, poultry, dairy products, and crops. For instance, animal waste consists of manure and animal carcasses, food processing waste are that in some cases such as in the production of maize only 20% is canned and the remaining 80% is waste, crop waste consists of corn stalks, sugarcane bagasse drops and culls from fruits, vegetables and prunings and insecticides, and herbicides. According to Agamuthu (Agamuthu, 2009) as cited in (Obi, Ugwuishiwu, & Nwakaire, 2016), it has been estimated that globally about 998 million tonnes of agricultural waste are generated each year. According to Dien & Vong(Dien & Vong , 2006) as cited in (Obi, Ugwuishiwu, & Nwakaire, 2016), estimates of the Plant Protection Department (PPD) stated about 1.8% of the chemicals remain in their packaging or containers. These containers are thrown or cast in the field or ponds and that are potentially harmful to the environment. Also, in a properly managed farm, about 30% of the feed used will become solid waste(Obi, Ugwuishiwu, & Nwakaire, 2016). According to Cooke(Cooke, 2016), North Carolina's factory farms produce 15000 Olympic pools worth of waste each year. According to "www.humansociety.org" ("www.humansociety.org", n.d.), annually in the United States 10 billion land animals are raised and killed for meat, eggs, and milk. Confined farm animals produce almost 500 million tonnes of manure each year. This is three times more raw waste than generated by Americans. Besides, improper handling of farm waste led to severe environmental disasters such as in 1995 an eight-acre hog waste lagoon released 25 million gallons of manure into the nearby river. This spill killed 10 million fish and resulted in the closing of 364, 000 acres of coastal wetlands used for shell fishing.

According to quantitative research with a 19-point questionnaire applied to 59 farmers, managers, and leaseholders with agricultural cattle raising activities and analyzed with SPSS held in Brazil as mentioned in Souza Mazza and others(Souza Mazza, et al., 2014), results revealed that major problems are related to handling waste residues, disposal sites, the dearth of information, etc. It was also mentioned that more than 60% of the farms do not undertake solid waste collection.

6.8 Human and animal conflict due to intensive farming

According to Huang, Li, Shi, & Jiang(Huang, Li, Shi, & Jiang, 2018), patterns and drivers of human-wildlife conflict were examined using a questionnaire survey around Daxueshan Nature Reserve, Yunnan, China. The study found Asiatic black bear (*Ursus thibetanus*) was the most conflict-prone animal around the reserve, followed by the rhesus macaque (*Macaca mulatta*) and Southeast Asian sambar (*Cervus equinus*). Poisson models depicted that human-bear conflicts were negatively related to distance to the reserve and proportion of forest, but positively correlated to the proportion of cropland, and negatively correlated with distance to the reserve, where communities affected by livestock depredation were negatively correlated with the proportion of cropland. The study suggested that eliminating food crops near the reserve boundary and livestock grazing at conflict hotspots could potentially reduce the human-bear conflict. According to Jonas, Abram, & Ancrenaz(Jonas, Abram, & Ancrenaz, 2017), intensive palm oil cultivation in Borneo increases the risk of human-orangutan conflict. Also, the Bornean orangutan population is declining steeply due to massive deforestation for intensive oil palm plantation and by the combination of harassment, poaching, and killing.

6.9 Land degradation- sedimentation- soil erosion due to intensive farming

Intensive farming practices such as tilling or ploughing, water-logging, application of agrochemicals all coming under this category. Physical deterioration occurs during the process, such as coalescence (slow deposition of fine particles between individual aggregates), slaking (collapsing of soil structure when dry soil aggregates are wetted by rain or irrigation), dispersion (products of slaking break apart due to high forces of repulsion between particles), consolidation (decrease in soil volume by the disappearance of soil space) and aggregate pulverization (when highly dry soil become fine particles due to tilling). This overall physical deterioration can further be categorized as surface sealing, surface crusting, hard setting, compaction, water-logging, lowering of the water column, subsidence of organic soil, and desertification. {Adapted from Osman (Osman , 2014)}.

In India, the green revolution has intensified the land use while increases agriculture production from 50 Mt to over 250 Mt over the last five decades, and it increased the land area under irrigation and increases the use of chemical fertilizers and pesticides. Furthermore, various agricultural practices such as land clearing through clear-cutting, deforestation, overgrazing, excessive irrigation, and over-drafting of groundwater affected soil fertility (Bhattacharyya, *et al*., 2015). National Bureau of Soil Survey and Land Use Planning (NBSS&LUP, 2004) as cited in (Bhattacharyya, et al., 2015) stated that in India, ~146.8 Mha is degraded out of 264.5 Mha of agriculture, pasture, forest, and biomass production lands. Degraded land includes 94 Mha from water erosion, 16 Mha from acidification, 14 Mha from flooding, 9 Mha from wind erosion, 6 Mha from salinity, and 7 Mha from a combination of factors (Bhattacharyya, et al., 2015).

Water erosion has been identified as the major cause of land degradation in India, which results in the loss of topsoil and terrain deformation. Based on the first approximate analysis, the rate of average soil erosion was ~16.4 ton ha^{-1} $year^{-1}$result in annual total soil loss of 5.3 billion tons throughout the country (Dhruvanarayan & Ram, 1983)and nearly 29% of total eroded soil is permanently lost to the sea, 61% transformed to other places and about 10% deposited as silt in reservoirs (Bhattacharyya, et al., 2015). Besides, improper planning and management and expansion of canal irrigation projects such as the Indira Gandhi Nagar project caused widespread water-logging and salinization problems in areas such as Indo-Gangetic Plains. Similarly, the Mahaweli irrigation expansion project in Sri Lanka depicted salinity problems in the Mahaweli H area. According to Environmental Assessment of Accelerated Mahaweli Development Programme (TAMS/USAID, 1980) as cited in (Thiruchelvam & Pathmarajah, n.d.), In Sri Lanka almost half a million ha. of lands in coastal areas and under irrigation in the dry zone are being degraded due to salinity and water-logging.

6.10   Deforestation-destruction of grasslands and mangroves due to intensive farming

Please see the chapter deforestation

6.11   Intensive farming causes draining of wetlands

It has been estimated that the dead zones are created in the Gulf of Mexico due to the nitrogen fertilizer runoff from farms. Dead zones are created when the nutrient flow overwhelms the capacity of some wetlands to filter pollutants. As a result, algal blooms replace the wetland community (Clark & Malamud, n.d.).

It was stated by World Wildlife Fund for nature ("WWF", n.d.) that hundreds of thousands of hectares of lands have been drained for agriculture. According to Maltby (Maltby , 1986); (Maltby & Immirzi , 1993); (Hooijer , Silvius , Wösten , & Page , 2006) as cited in (Verhoeven & Setter, 2010), about 45% of the tropical peatland area in South East Asia (270, 000 km^2, represents 12% of the total land area in the region) has been drained for oil palm plantation during the last 50 years. According to Elizabeth (Elizabeth, 2015), in the period between 2008 and 2012, about 250, 000 acres of land in Minnesota were converted into agricultural croplands. Most of it was grassland, but 25,000 acres were wetlands. It was stated in United Nations University (United Nations University, 2008)that mostly threatened wetlands are found in the Mediterranean where the people drained most of the wetland for agriculture purposes for two millennia.

6.12   Intensive farming causes the establishment of dams

According to Ashraf, Kahlown, & Ashfaq (Ashraf, Kahlown, & Ashfaq, 2007), the state of Punjab in Pakistan has constructed 32 small dams in water scares areas of the Pothwar region to store and conserve water for agriculture. Dams increased the agricultural productivity of wheat and vegetables and increased farmers' income. A case study on Mashi earth dam Katsina state depicted harnessing the dam for improving agricultural productivity. Data for the study was retrieved from field visits, observations, and interviews with farmers. Small scale and large-scale dams were constructed in northern Nigeria following the impacts of 1972-1975 draught in the Sahel. Food shortages have overcome by establishing small scale dams which provide year-round water for irrigation. In the year 2000, the Kano state government has created three major dams such as Tiga, Challawa Gorge, and Kadawa and 20 small-scale dams (Oyeniyi, 2000) as cited in (Ladan, 2016). Even though the Mashi dam provides water for the Mashi local government area and the neighboring regions, the study revealed that the dam was not harnessed efficiently (Ladan, 2016).

In Western Australia, yabbies (shrimps) are cultivated in farm dams. To examine the variation between farm yabby productions between individual farm dams, a survey was held. The survey covers the area of 750,000 km^2 ranging from Northampton in the north, Esperance in the South, and east to Mukinbudin. About 30 dams were examined for harvests, feeding, and management practices. Results depicted for the

1995-96 harvest season correlations between farm dam production and environmental parameters were obtained (Lawrence, 1998).

6.13   Intensive farming causes poverty-disease-war-food insecurity

According to Woodward (Woodward , 2016), it has been found that the agricultural policies aimed at alleviating poverty in Africa are making things worse, as the poor farmers in Africa cannot afford to buy necessary inputs of seeds, fertilizers, and pesticides, and they live in fear of government agencies seizing and relocating their lands. The article further revealed that 90% of people in Africa are smallholder farmers completely dependent on traditional agriculture. Changes towards modern intensive agriculture disrupt subsistence practices, exacerbate poverty, impair local systems of trade, knowledge, and threaten land ownership. Also, intensive farming practices lead to soil salinization and depletion of water resources, which ultimately ends up in desertification.

According to "The Human Society of the United States" ("The Human Society of the United States", n.d.), almost one billion people are malnourished, but half the world's grain production is used as animal feed to produce meat, milk, and egg. Most of the nutrients from grain are converted into inedible parts of the animal, such as bones, faeces, and metabolic energy. Thus, meat consumption puts more people in hunger while satisfying a few. Most of the soybeans cultivated in the world are used as animal feed. Also, animal farming increases global warming as the methane generation from cattle contributes to the greenhouse effect, and this further worsens food insecurity. It was stated in Baroni, Cenci , Tettamanti , & Berati(Baroni, Cenci , Tettamanti , & Berati , 2007) as cited in ("The Human Society of the United States", n.d.)that a 2007 article in the European Journal of Clinical Nutrition suggested that plant-based diets could play a vital role in preserving environmental resources and reducing hunger and malnutrition in poor people.

6.14   Biodiversity loss due to intensive farming

It was stated in Dalton (Dalton, 2018) that scientists have stated that the world is now facing sixth extinction. In the UK number of grey partridges, corn buntings and tree sparrows have dropped by at least 90% in 40 years. In addition, according to Bird Life International, as given in Dalton (Dalton, 2018), 95% of turtle doves have vanished in 20 years. The hedgehog population is halved in the countryside since 2000. Nearly two-thirds of skylarks and lapwing have disappeared. Intensive farming techniques such as sawing large areas of monoculture (identical) crops and end of

159

crop rotation have reduced the diversity of habitats for different species. In addition, according to the book Dead Zone, as given in Dalton (Dalton, 2018), it has been mentioned that the application of chemical fertilizer and insecticides have adversely affected many species. Intensive farming causes the loss of the bee population, a variety of birds, amphibians, reptiles, and small mammals everywhere (Dalton, 2018). In addition, ornithologist Philip Lymbery worried that many policymakers and scientists put the blame on climate change for this extinction process instead of finding the actual causes in hazardous intensive farming techniques (Dalton, 2018).

6.15   Eutrophication due to intensive farming

According to Hubbard , Newton , & Hill (Hubbard , Newton , & Hill , 2004), it was stated that several studies have measured a high number of cattle or livestock farms that have been shown to discharge as much as 5 to 10 times more nutrients than the crop or forestry lands. According to Folke, Kautsky, & Troell (Folke, Kautsky, & Troell, 1994)salmon fish farming caused eutrophication in the Nordic region. Also, Honkanen & Helminen (Honkanen & Helminen, 2000) stated that the Archipelago Sea, Southwest Finland has been affected by coastal eutrophication over recent decades. A study analyzed data collected among three fish farms in the period between 1983 and 1997 in Rymättylä, southwest Finland revealed that plank-tonic chlorophyll-a and the growth of periphyton were significantly high in the area adjacent to the fish farms. According to Oh, Edgar, Kirkpatrick, Stuart-Smith, & Barrett (Oh, Edgar, Kirkpatrick, Stuart-Smith, & Barrett, 2015), the broad-scale nutrient enrichment effect of salmonid farms on Tasmanian reef communities was assessed by comparing macro algal cover at four fixed distances from active fish farms across 44 sites. Macro algal assemblages were measured in the distances of 100m to 5km. Epiphyte density varied with the distance from fish farms, both sheltered and exposed locations.

Green algae such as *Chaetomorpha* spp. dominated the swell-exposed sites whereas filamentous green algal forms were high near the sheltered fish farms and canopy-forming perennial algae found everywhere unaffected by fish farm distance.

6.16   Global warming and climate change due to intensive farming

According to Fiala (Fiala , 2009), at present, meat production generates 1.4 and 22% of the 36 billion tons of "CO_2 equivalent" annual global greenhouse gas production. Based on carbon footprint, an experiment held by Daniel J. Morgan of the University of Washington and his co-workers observed that growing half-pound of the asparagus vegetable in Peru emits greenhouse gases equivalent to 1.2 ounces of CO_2 as a result of the application of agrochemicals. Also, refrigeration, transportation of vegetables to an American dinner table took another 2 ounces, and ultimately 3.2 ounces of CO_2 is generated. When considering factory farming, it has been found by the ecological economist Susan Subak of the University of East Anglia in England that cows emit 2.5 and 4.7 ounces of methane for each pound of beef depends on the production method, which is equivalent to 3.6 and 6.8 pounds of CO_2 released into the atmosphere because methane has 23 times the global warming potential of CO_2. In 2003, Lucas Reijnders of the University of Amsterdam and Sam Soret of Loma Linda University showed that producing a pound of beef protein to the dinner table requires over 10 pounds of plant protein, including all the emissions of greenhouse gases in the production of grains. Besides, Subak estimated that producing a pound of beef in a feedlot, or concentrated animal feeding operation (CAFO) system, produced the equivalent of 14.8 pounds of CO_2 pound for pound, over 36 times the CO_2-equivalent greenhouse gas emitted in the production of asparagus. Similarly, pork produces CO_2-equivalent of 3.8 pounds, and chicken generates CO_2-equivalent of 1.1 pounds.

It was stated in the United Nations' report Livestock's Long Shadow that the livestock sector contributes 18% of the global greenhouse gas emissions, and this is more than the transport sector, which is usually thought to be the largest cause of greenhouse gases(FAO, 2006a) as cited in (Cristina Ilea, 2009). Also, 70% of all agricultural land and 30% of the Earth's land area is directly or indirectly involved in livestock production(FAO, 2006b) as cited in (Cristina Ilea, 2009), and by 2050 it is expected to double (Cristina Ilea, 2009). Thus, a significant increase in greenhouse gas emissions from farming is expected, and this may lead to a significant rise in the global temperature that causes a devastating impact on the climatic factors all over the world.

6.17   Animal slaughter and cruelty due to intensive farming

Millions of animals such as cattle and birds are killed for meat each year. Several poultries and slaughterhouses are mechanized and use techniques not to keep them alive longer and avoid agony. However, there are many traditional hunters still using cruel methods to consume their meat. Increasing population increases the need for slaughter. Dogs and cats are killed for meat in Taiwan, some parts of the USA, the Arctic, Korea, Mexico, China, French Polynesia, Switzerland, and Vietnam, in these countries several cruel incidents were recorded when animals concentrated in cages before slaughter or in few in incidents, dogs are starved to death. About 19% of the worlds' beef is produced in the USA, which is seconded by Brazil (16%) and thirdly the European Union (13%), in case of Pork production China is topping with 53,400 metric tons, seconded by the European Union (23,675Mt) and thirdly the United States (11,610Mt) in 2017("pork checkoff", n.d.). In case of poultry, the USA (18.29 million Metric Tonnes) is the largest producer of poultry products, which is followed by Brazil, China, India, and Russia. It has been estimated annually about 50 billion chickens are raised for food (Source: ("whichcountry", n.d.)), in case of sheep meat China is topping as contributing about 15% of global sheep meat production, followed by India (6.4%), Australia (6.3%), Sudan (4.4%) and Iran (4.1%)("faostat data", 2014). It has been found that the demand for chicken and turkey is skyrocketing compare to other animal meat sources, as the overall global meat consumption is in an increasing trend with the increasing population.

Factory farming: To maximize their profit farms, keep the animals squeezed into tiny spaces, many animals die from infection, hens are kept in small cages, chickens and pigs are kept in jam-packed sheds, cows are kept in crowded filthy feedlots. Antibiotics are used to grow them faster and keep them alive, most such animals are genetically manipulated to grow larger to produce milk or eggs, and thus they suffer from starvation, dehydration, and inability to reach their food. They are crowded in trucks during transportation to the slaughterhouse, and they suffer from starvation and extremes of weather. Survived individuals have their throats slit while they are conscious, and they are punched into boiling water for defeathering or hair removal while their bodies skinned or hacked apart. Source:("peta.org", n.d.)

Cows: Cows are burnt with hot irons (branded), their horns are gouged out, cut, or burnt off, and testicles of male cattle removed from their scrotums (castrated) without painkillers. Cows are fattened for slaughter, and this causes chronic digestive pain, breathing impairment, bloat (stomach full of gas), fatal liver abscesses, increased stomach acid, ulcers, and acute acidosis. Since feedlot air is saturated with urine and dung, high saturation of ammonia, methane, and noxious chemicals may cause chronic respiratory problems. To keep them alive, higher doses of antibiotics are given, several cows die out with their fatal injuries made by keepers as uncooperative animals beaten or prod poked in their faces or rectums, dairy cows repeatedly impregnated and permanently separated from their newborn calf, mother cows frantically cry for their calves for several days, and they are fitted to milking machines more than twice a day, calves are shot on the head by a captive bolt gun to death.

Cattle are transported without food or water to slaughterhouses, they are hung up by one leg, and their throats are cut, skinned, and gutted. Source: ("peta.org", n.d.)

Turkey: Turkeys are genetically bred for faster growth and crippled under their own weight. Birds are crowded, and to avoid pecking each other to death, portions of the toes and upper beaks are cut off with hot blades, males denuded without any pain relievers, sick birds are beaten to death by a pole, their leg bones may get broken during the transfer, they are transported to the slaughterhouse with no food or water, at slaughterhouse they hung upside down, their heads are dragged through an electrified stunning tank, their thoughts are slit, if the knife fails to cut, they are scaled in boiling water for feather removal alive. Source: ("peta.org", n.d.)

Pigs: Mother pigs spend most of their lifetime in gestation crates that are too smaller for them to turn around. They are impregnated again and again until their body gives out and then sent to slaughter. Piglets are torn from their mother after few weeks, their tail is chopped off, and ends of their teeth are snipped off by pliers, males are castrated under extreme agony without providing any painkillers. Pigs spent in crowded pens on the tiny slap of dirty concrete. Many die during the transportation to the slaughterhouse, by getting exposed to extreme cold or warm weather in the congested truck, sick pigs are kicked, struck with electric prods to make them move, they scream, and some may die by a heart attack and they are hanged upside down and cut at the neck. In some cases, they are conscious and squeal when they reach the hog scalding tank for softening their skin and fur removal. Source: ("peta.org", n.d.)

Ducks and geese: Ducks and geese raised for slaughter spent their entire life in filthy dark sheds, even after the electric stunning birds are conscious as their throats are cut or when they are scalded into hot water for defeathering, as ducklings grown in stress condition they do peck and injure each other or pull out feathers, to prevent this their sensitive upper beak is cut off without any painkillers, this also increases the chances for infection and die from malnutrition, their legs are crippled or deformed, they are transported in congested trucks in unfavorable weather conditions, at slaughterhouse they are kept upside down and neck slit. To produce foiegras (fatty goose liver) pipes are driven in the throat of a male duck twice each day about 2.2 pounds of grain and fat are pumped into the stomach for geese thrice a day up to 4 pounds daily known as gavage, this forced feeding causes the liver to get swollen ten times than normal, cages are so tiny, birds are unable to stand or bath or preen their secretion thus get coated with excess oily secretion on feathers,   they are affected by foot infections, esophagus, fungal infections, diarrhea, impaired liver function, heat stress, lesions,

163

and fractures of the sternum and many die by aspiration pneumonia, since foiegras is only made from males all female ducklings are tossed into the grinder and used as cat food or fertilizer. Source: ("peta.org", n.d.)

Chickens: Chicken are raised for meat called broilers, they are isolated from the parents since the day they hatch, and intense crowding and confinement increase the chances of diseases such as heart attacks, organ failure, crippling legs, and deformities. They are kept in very unsanitary conditions along with their urine and faeces, and many suffer from chronic respiratory conditions, weak immune system, bronchitis, and ammonia burn. At a young age, part of their sensitive beaks are cut by hot blades without giving any painkillers, antibiotics are given to live in such unsanitary conditions, during the transportation farm keepers often break their legs by rough handling, when egg production wane after two years, hens are sent for slaughter, birds are hung upside down at crates, their throats are cut by machine, then they are scalded in hot water for feather removal, they are not even stunted before all these processes. Source: ("peta.org", n.d.)

6.18   Intensive farming causes agrochemicals

According to Wickramasinghe, Harris, Jones , & Jennings (Wickramasinghe, Harris, Jones , & Jennings, 2004), bats (*Chiroptera* sp.) feed on insects. In the United Kingdom, bats feed over agricultural habitats. Due to intense agriculture practices, which comprise the heavy utilization of chemical pesticides, the insect population went down, and ultimately the foraging bat population gets declined. A study demonstrated the impact of intensive agriculture in the ecosystem, evaluated the impact of intensive agriculture on bat foraging, as available bat prey was quantified by comparing nocturnal aerial insects captured within 24 matched pairs of organic and conventional farms. The comparison was made by quantifying the abundance of 18 insect families commonly fed by bats in the UK between farm types and evaluated for correlations of abundance with bat activity. Factors such as insect abundance, species richness, and moth species diversity were significantly high in pastoral, woodland, and water habitats of organic farms than on conventional farms. And the activity of bat that eats Lepidoptera was significantly correlated with the abundance of this order. In conclusion, intensive agriculture (with the use of agrochemicals) reduces the nocturnal insect population, and this reduction in prey population subsequently reduces the bat population.

164

According to Bengtsson, Ahnstrom, & Weibull(Bengtsson, Ahnstrom, & Weibull, 2005), organic agriculture is more environmentally sound than intensive agriculture, which depends on chemical herbicides, pesticides, and inorganic fertilizers in the production of crops and animals. A study analysed the impacts of organic farming on species richness and abundance using meta-analysis of published literature before December 2002. It has been evidenced that species richness is 30% higher in organic farming than in conventional farming. However, yet 16% of the literature actually depicted the negative effects of organic farming on species richness. Thus, the data is divided into different organism groups based on the spatial scale of the study. The study showed 50% more abundance in organisms in organic farms than in conventional agriculture.

Agrochemicals include pesticides, insecticides, herbicides, fungicides, rodenticide, chemical fertilizers, synthetic hormones, and concentrated manure. Pesticides and some fertilizer manures comprise heavy metals. Heavy metals in phosphate fertilizers are arsenic, cadmium, manganese, uranium, vanadium, and zinc. Furthermore, poultry and pig manure comprise zinc, arsenic, and copper and pesticides consist of arsenic, copper, manganese, lead, zinc(Towhid, 2014). Also, agrochemicals consist of a wide range of organic pollutants such as chlorinated hydrocarbons, organophosphates, and carbamates.

The pesticide is a chemical used to control pests in agriculture, e.g. herbicides (weeds), insecticides, molluscicide, nematicide, fungicides, bactericides, and rodenticides (vertebrate poisons). World pesticide consumption in 2007 was 5.2 billion pounds (USEPA, 2007). The number of pesticides reaching the targeted organism is just 0.1 percent, and the remaining contaminates soil, flora, and water. Also, certain amounts are transferred via the food chain and causing bioaccumulation in the first organism. Pesticides interfere with many biochemical reactions in nature. It contaminates soil nutrients and affects the micro flora. Toxicity leads to health hazards such as cancer, reproductive impairment, and irreversible neurotoxicity other than humans. It also affects fishes, birds, and much other soil fauna. Pesticides cause a change in biodiversity, such as stimulates the reproduction of natural enemies and suppress the production and survival of beneficial organisms. As shown by Rachel Carson's Silent Spring, the impacts of persistent pesticide chemicals in birds, fishes, mammals, and other non-targeted organisms are severe in the long run.

Types of pesticides used in intensive agricultural practices

Insecticides

Insecticides are applied either indoor and in the field. Insecticides can be categorized as organophosphorus compounds, organochlorines, carbamates, and pyrethroids {Adapted from (Towhid, 2014)}.

I. Organophosphate compounds

These compounds are neurotoxins. They are fumigants (produce fume), contact poisons, and synthetic pesticides. Most of them are used in warfare during WWII, such as tetraethyl pyrophosphate (TEPP) and Sarin. Other organophosphates are less toxic to mammals and were designed to kill insects such as Malathion, Dibrom, chlorpyrifos, temephos, diazinon, and terbufos {Adapted from(Towhid, 2014)}.

II. Organochlorines

Organochlorine pesticide such as DDT (dichlorodiphenylchloroethane) is completely banned. Similarly, hexachlorocyclohexane (lindane), DDE, DDD cyclodienes(aldrin, heptachlor), Mired, and chlordecone are persistent compounds and can pass through the food chain and undergo biomagnification as it affects the higher tropic level fauna in increased concentration. {Adapted from (Towhid, 2014)}.

III. Carbamates

Carbamates are esters, also known as urethanes, and they are low persistent compounds. Persistency only for a few hours to several months after its application; however, it is fatal to birds as it affects the breeding potential. They act on acetylcholinesterase enzyme and reversibly inactivate the enzyme, e.g., aldicarb, carbaryl, propoxur, oxamyl, and terbucarb {Adapted from (Towhid, 2014)}.

IV. Pyrethroids

It is a natural compound extracted from dried pyrethrum or chrysanthemum flowers. It consists of 6 active ingredients such as pyrethrum I & II, cinerins I&II, and Jamolines I & II. Pyrethroids are desirable for its lower persistency (rapid degradation in heat and sunlight, thus unsuitable for agriculture), lower toxicity, and quick knockdown action. Synthetic pyrethroids are more toxic than natural ones.

Pyrethroids are generally used for domestic bug and cockroach killer sprays. There are 4 groups of synthetic pyrethroids in use, such as permethrin, allethrin, bioresmethrin, and fennvalerate. And they are highly toxic to aquatic organisms and bees. Adapted from (Towhid, 2014)}.

V. Herbicides

This includes several hundreds of both organic and inorganic chemicals. Synthetic growth-regulating hormones such as 2,4-D, 2,4,5-trichlorophenoxyacetic acid, 2-methyl-4,6-dichlorophenoxyacetic acid (MCPA). Organochlorine herbicides include aniline derivatives such as propanil and alachlor. Organophosphorus herbicides are desirable for its non-carcinogenic nature and efficient weed killing. E.g. Glyphosate. Carbamic acid derivatives, urea derivatives, and Triazine herbicides such as atrazine (banned in some countries for high persistency) are few other examples. {Adapted from(Towhid, 2014)}.

VI. Fungicides

Fungicides are compounds either organic or inorganic. They also contain natural and synthetic compounds e.g., heavy metal compounds: Bordeaux contains copper, organometallic compounds: organotins, derivatives of phthalic acid e.g., phthalimide (Captan). Benzimidazoles are synthetic fungicides. {Adapted from (Towhid, 2014)}

VII. Calcium carbide

Calcium carbide is used to ripen fruits as it produces acetylene gas when it reacts with water, which mimics ethylene and accelerates the ripening process. It is commonly applied to mango, papaw, banana, pears, etc. It has been widely used, as it is cheap and readily available in the market. Calcium carbide contains carcinogenic properties, commercially available calcium carbide contains a small amount of Arsenic and phosphorous hydride compounds which are also malefic to humans, initial symptoms are vomiting, diarrhea with or without blood, burning sensation of chest, abdomen, thirst, weakness, difficulty in swallowing, irritation on burning in the eyes and skin, permanent eye damage, skin ulcers, sore throat, cough and shortness of breathing and causing the build-up of fluids in the lungs. It affects the nervous system, including prolonged hypoxia, causes headaches, dizziness, mood disturbances, sleeplessness, mental confusion, memory loss, and cerebral oedema. {Adapted from(Towhid, 2014)}

Persistence of pesticides

Persistent is the tendency of a pesticide to conserve its molecular integrity and chemical, physical, and functional characteristics in a medium in which it is transported and distributed after its release into the environment. Compounds that resist its biodegradation are recalcitrant molecules (Towhid, 2014). Organochlorine pesticide such as DDT is completely banned; similarly, hexachlorocyclohexane (lindane), DDE, DDD cyclodienes (aldrin, heptachlor), Mirex, and chlordecone are persistent pesticides. Similarly, herbicides such as triazines, uracils, phenylurea, sulfonylurea, dinitroanilines, imidazolinones, and plant growth regulators (clopyralid, picloram, triclopyr, and chlorimuron) are persistent chemicals. Plants, floods, and tillage affect the persistence of pesticides. In the presence of plant cover, persistence increases than the fallow soil. The behaviour of pesticides also depends on ionizability, water-solubility, polarizability, volatility, formulations, rate of application, placement, nature of soil particulate matter such as clay minerals, organic matter, metallic hydrous oxides, Biological activity of adsorbed organic chemicals, and biological activity of adsorbed pesticides. {Adapted from(Towhid, 2014)}

6.19   Groundwater contamination-depletion-salinization due to intensive farming

It has been revealed by Moiwo, Yang, Li, Han, & Yang(Moiwo, Yang, Li, Han, & Yang, 2010), in Northern China overconsumption of water resources in the Baiyangdian Lake Catchment caused considerable depletion of storage and hydrology of Baiyangdian Lake. The study was conducted in the period between 1956 and 2008 for over five decades using three different methods such as WetSpass (water and energy Transfer between soil, plants, and atmosphere under Quasi-Steady State), WATBUD (water budget) and MODFLOW (USGS three-dimensional finite difference groundwater flow model). As per the results, the primary water source of lake storage depicted a steady decline. This is mainly due to multiple dam construction and reservoir impoundments in various locations, including headwater valleys and rivers in the catchment. Furthermore, the major cause of the depletion of groundwater is agriculture consumption due to intensive farming practices.

According to Michalopoulos, Tzamtzis, & Liodakis(Michalopoulos, Tzamtzis, & Liodakis, 2016), intensive hog farming operation on a geologic fault in East Mediterranean caused groundwater contamination. The plot of land where the treated fog farm discharge met the soil surface was examined in a study. Evaluation of chemical oxygen demand (COD), biochemical oxygen demand (BOD$_5$), total viable count (TVC), and total coliform (TC) of contaminated groundwater showed a significant increase in all these factors. Besides, precipitation further increases the loading of organic content and microbes into the aquifer.

6.20   Water pollution-water scarcity due to intensive farming

According to Ryder (Ryder, 2017) the global agriculture sector is responsible for 70% of water abstractions worldwide. According to Schneider (Schneider, 2014), state documents depicted that since 2002 at least 80 serious instances of factory farms polluting Illinois waterways were recorded. It has been revealed by the Illinois EPA that more than 672 miles of Illinois streams and more than 25,000 acres of lakes have been polluted by animal feeding operations. In 2001, in wood Dairy in Peoria country caught by the Illinois EPA for dumping approximately 2 million gallons of liquid cow manure into a ravine flows into West Fork Kickapoo Creek caused large fish kill and contaminated the creek with foam released by the manure. In 2004, manure from a swine farm in McDonough country disposed into a waterway led to troublesome Creek. The creek was filled with foul-smelling brown sludge about 10 inches deep. The Creek was too polluted to support any aquatic life. In 2009, a swine farm operator in Morgan country dumped 27,000 pounds of solid manure into a ravine flows into a nearby pond cause a severe threat to aquatic biota. In the period between 2009 and 2011, about 40 swine farms were accused of polluting Taylor Creek on multiple occasions. In 2001, about 24 miles of Taylor Creek were polluted to extents, which no longer support aquatic life. {Adapted from (Schneider, 2014)}.

According to Hooda, Edwards, Anderson, & Miller (Hooda, Edwards, Anderson, & Miller, 2000), in the UK, increased loss of nutrients from farm effluents (livestock wastes), pesticides such as sheep-dipping chemicals, bacterial and protozoan contamination were major causes of degradation of water quality. This is the same in Europe and China. A paper revealed that more than 10,000 pig carcasses were found in Huangpu River in Shanghai, China, in March 2013, which made the water inconsumable for residents (Dai, 2014).

In a survey (Thuyet , Luong-Van, & Austin, 2012)on water pollution from the effluents of intensive shrimp farming in Coastal Areas of the World Heritage-Listed Ha Long Bay, Vietnam, water samples were collected from three spatially different locations such as the inside section of creeks directly receiving farm effluent, from main creeks adjacent to points of effluent discharge outside the farm and few kilometers away from the farm, of the bay at three different times, and analyzed for nutrient pollution. Results revealed that significant increase in the concentrations of TAN (Total amount of Nitrogen), NO₂, NO₃-N, TP (Total Phosphorus), PO₄-P, BOD (Biological Oxygen Demand), COD (Chemical Oxygen Demand) and Chl-a (Chlorophyll a), among all three locations after shrimp crops (main seasonal crop) in North Vietnam. The results from the inside section of creeks directly receiving farm effluent depicted an increasingly high level of TAN, NO₃-N, TP, BOD, COD, Chl-a, and TSS (Total Suspended Solids), which is higher than the recommended levels to support aquatic biota.

6.21   Hazardous waste due to intensive farming

According to Loehr (Loehr, 1978), a large amount of food processing, crop, forestry, and animal solid waste are generated in the USA each year. Major components of these wastes are biodegradable. However, thy poses nitrogen, human and animal pathogens, medicinals, feed additives, salts, and certain metals those are hazardous to living things, including human being. It was also mentioned that such hazards usually come from soil or trash animal feed. It was stated in Knobbe (Knobbe, 2018) that millions of pounds of hazardous air pollutants are generated from U.S. factory farms each year. The wastes include particulate matter, ammonia, and hydrogen sulphate that contribute to respiratory disease and other health problems.

It was stated in Alberts (Alberts, 2018) that the North Carolina region has around 2000 factory farms that are overcrowded with thousands of pigs, chickens, or turkeys. North Carolina produced about 10 billion gallons of fecal waste each year. During the hurricane Mathews in 2016 millions of pigs, chickens and turkeys died in factory farms in North Carolina and resulted in contamination of state waterways by hazardous animal waste.

An Iranian case study (Golbaz, Farzadkia, Vanani, & Emamjomeh, 2017), investigated waste management in the cattle slaughterhouse with the objectives, such as identifying the existing waste management practices concerning sources, quantity, and characteristics of wastes. Study aimed to identify the situation of production, collection, storage, transportation, processing and recycling, and final disposal of wastes and problems of existing waste management practices in three slaughterhouses (see Table 6.1).

Table 6.1 Characteristics of study cattle slaughterhouse

Slaughterhouses No	Slaughterhouse capacity		Produced waste (ton/year)	Per capita waste (kg/day)	
	Heavy livestock (per cattle)	Light livestock (per sheep)		Heavy livestock (per Cattle)	Light livestock (per Sheep)
Ahvaz	392	1960	7836		
Dezful	85	390	1755	54.6	11.1
Shushtar	36	180	661.5		

Source: (Golbaz, Farzadkia, Vanani, & Emamjomeh, 2017)

Here that total production of industrial waste in the study units was 10,252y/year, among which, 76.5% were produced by Ahvaz slaughterhouse, 17% by Dezful, and 6.5% by Shushtar's slaughterhouse. The daily per capita waste generation was reported as 54.6kg/cattle and 11.1kg/sheep. However, it has been revealed that about 97%, 99%, and 98% of the produced industrial wastes in Ahvaz, Dezful, and Shushtar respectively. Thus, slaughterhouses were hazardous and could be infectious.

6.22   Overexploitation of natural resources due to intensive farming

Please see chapter Overexploitation of natural resources

6.23   Invasive species due to intensive farming

According to Raposo, Pinto-Gomes and Nunes (Raposo, Pinto-Gomes, & Nunes, 2020) in the Alentejo (South of Portugal), spreading of *Robinia pseudoacacia* species has increased with intensive farming practices of vineyards, olive groves, and almond trees. The availability of water and nutrients enabled the species to disperse further and now become a threat to the environment and native biota.

6.24   Intensive farming as a keystone environmental problem

Intensive agriculture is one of the largest contributors to man-made climate change, accounts for around 12% of total emissions, and a quarter of greenhouse gas emission (Smith, Martino, Cai, Gwary, & Janzen, 2007). Animal agriculture accounts for 37% of methane emission and 65% of nitrous oxide(FAO/LEAD, 2006). Also, runoff from farms causes eutrophication. Poor living conditions in industrial farms cause animal diseases and animals are said to be subject to cruel handling. Agrochemicals such as pesticides, fungicides, herbicides, and chemical fertilisers lead to toxic effects on waterways and the atmosphere and affect non-targeted biota such as insects, birds, and other animals. Agrochemicals also affect soil microflora and fauna, cause soil

171

salinization and desertification. A high concentration of nitrate in groundwater from chemical fertiliser causes methemoglobinemia (blue baby syndrome). Nitrate and phosphate effluents from excessive chemical fertilisers lead to eutrophication resulted in algal blooms that clogs the fish gills, and increases the biological oxygen demand. Intensive palm oil agriculture causes deforestation in Indonesia and affects orangutan habitats. Intensive farming including slash and burn techniques cause severe biodiversity loss and a threat to indigenous people. According to the Department of agriculture in the United States, the number of factory farms increased by 230% from 1982 to 2002. Besides, in the period between 1990 and 2015, pesticide usage worldwide has increased by 73%. Antibiotics and growth hormones used in animal farming also affect humans (Bridgeman, 2020).

Intensive farming results into problems, such as overexploitation of natural resources, desertification, deforestation, biodiversity loss, animal slaughtering and cruelty, agrochemicals, solid waste and sewage, eutrophication, groundwater contamination, the establishment of dams, water pollution-water scarcity, wetlands or draining of wetland, and hazardous waste from toxic pesticide chemicals. If intensive farming comes to an end, then problems such as resource depletion, desertification, deforestation, animal slaughtering and cruelty, agrochemicals, eutrophication, groundwater contamination, wetlands, and biodiversity loss (to a certain extent) get eliminated (fig.6.1).

Evidence 1: Intensive farming causes agrochemical pollution

Intensive farming with the use of chemical fertilizers and pesticides may result in several environmental issues such as eutrophication, land degradation-sedimentation- soil erosion, loss of biodiversity, overexploitation of natural resources, heavy metal contamination, water pollution, groundwater contamination, hazardous waste, deforestation, air pollution, global warming, solid waste and sewage, dam construction, coral destruction, animal slaughter, and cruelty and food insecurity diseases and poverty. However, based on the concept diagram (fig. 6.1) if intensive farming techniques are abandoned and replaced by organic farming or permaculture techniques then agrochemical problems get cease completely. Thus, intensive farming is a keystone environmental issue.

According to Feuerbacher, Luckmann, Boysen, Zikeli, & Grethe (Feuerbacher, Luckmann, Boysen, Zikeli, & Grethe, 2018), the study revealed that Bhutan's large-scale conversion to 100% organic agriculture by abandoning the agrochemical methods resulted in 24% lower yields than conventional yields. The study also found a considerable reduction in Bhutan's GDP, substantial welfare losses, particularly for non-agricultural households, and adverse impacts on food security. The reduction in agricultural yield was largely compensated by imported foods from India. And this situation also weakened the country's cereal self-sufficiency. Even though soil phosphorus and potassium remained unchanged, soil nitrogen levels gone down by (-22.4%). Because nitrogen release from animal manure was too slow. However, the study also suggested overcoming these pitfalls Bhutan should improve fertilization management, crop protection, and integration of livestock to obtain better yield as truly holistic, organic farming. Thus, Bhutan's present agriculture policy and its implementation revealed that the absence of intensive farming brought the use of agrochemicals to a halt. Thus, it is clear that intensive farming is a keystone man-made environmental problem (based on the definition). However, increasing food demand as the result of an increasing population may question Bhutan's 100% organic policy in the future and it may further increase food insecurity and poverty in the country. Thus, the population explosion acts as the precursor link of major man-made environmental problems.

Evidence 2: Intensive farming causes water pollution and scarcity

According to FAO (FAO, 2011) as cited in (Water for Sustainable Food and Agriculture: A report produced for the G20 Presidency of Germany, 2017) "agriculture accounts for 70% of total freshwater withdrawals on average worldwide, thus, agriculture is the largest water user in the world." and "these amounts can reach as much as 95% in some developing countries" (FAO, n.d.)as cited in (Water for Sustainable Food and Agriculture: A report produced for the G20 Presidency of Germany, 2017). Besides, "agriculture is the major source of water pollution such as nutrient loading, pesticide, and other contamination" (Water for Sustainable Food and Agriculture: A report produced for the G20 Presidency of Germany, 2017).

Evidence 3: Intensive farming causes deforestation

According to the report 'Agriculture is the direct driver for worldwide deforestation' (Agriculture is the direct driver for worldwide deforestation, 2012), "agriculture is estimated to be the direct drive for deforestation. 80% of deforestation worldwide is due to agriculture or intensive farming".

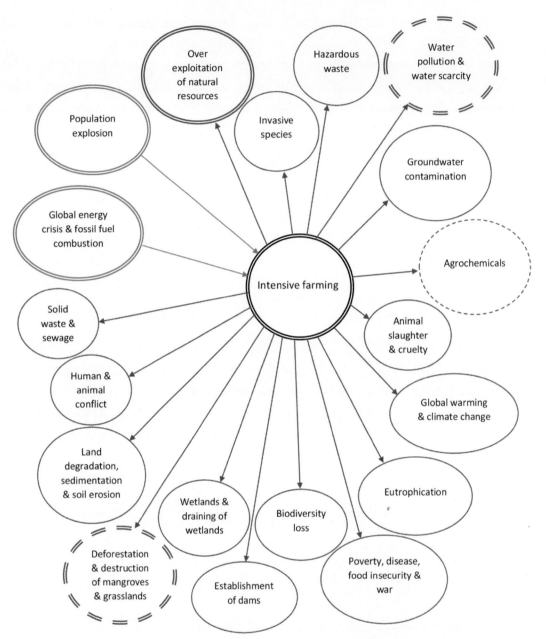

Figure 6.1 Intensive farming as keystone environmental problem with the disappearance of agrochemicals, water pollution-water scarcity, and deforestation on its mitigation (hypothetical diagram)

[In the figure black circle is the problem being examined, blue circles are cause man-made environmental problems, red circles are effect man-made environmental problems, double lined circles are keystone man-made environmental problems, and circles with dashed lines (either single or double lined) are the man-made

174

environmental problems that disappear when the problem being examined (black circle) is mitigated]

Regenerative solution vs. sustainable solutions vs. greener solutions

It has been shown in the above scenarios that intensive farming is a keystone environmental problem, and seeking high energy sustainable solutions often come up with a huge cost. Thus, seeking regenerative solutions are the viable means.

When mitigating agrochemical contamination, **conventional** techniques such as pump and treat (chemical, physical and biological water treatment) - advanced oxidation, activated sludge, ion exchange, membrane bioreactors and membranes-reverse osmosis & electro dialysis are unsustainable because they are costly (high energy) and not providing permanent solutions to the problem. Techniques such as reduce chemical fertilizer and prevent mixing of agriculture runoff into waterways, intercropping with cover crops which enhance nitrogen ion assimilation, crop rotation and reduce tillage at sensitive soils, ban crops requiring high amount of chemical fertilizers (e.g. tobacco) can be considered as **greener** solutions because they do a minimal harm to the environment. Agrochemical ban is a **sustainable** solution because the impact is net zero, and according to the definition of sustainable development stated in the 1987 Brundtland commission report, "development that meets the needs of the present without compromising the ability of future generations to meet their needs" could be considered sustainable development. However, its socio-economic consequences are usually malefic. Floating wetlands, bioremediation (in-situ denitrification), carbon farming and intercropping with biological nitrogen fixing crops such as *Azolla* sp. are the **restorative** solution for the agrochemicals because positive things happen in a system still dominated by man. In addition, cultural or traditional methods such as using Neem oil as pesticide, applying seaweeds as organic fertilizer and biological control such as introducing ducks and crabs into the field for pest-control are **reconciliatory** practices, which consider human as a part of the nature and not a dominant factor. Agroforestry and holistic farm management are the **regenerative** solutions because they require low energy and provisioned high systemic vitality and high resilience. And agroforestry systems are adaptable to the changes in the environment (Figure 6.2).

175

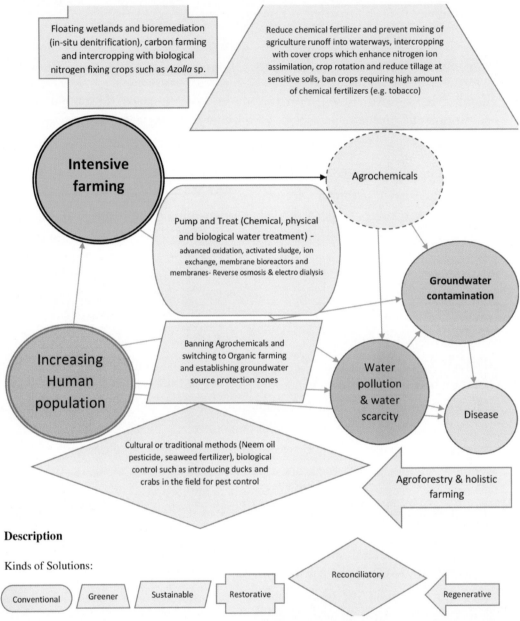

Figure 6.2 Sustainable and regenerative solutions to agrochemicals, which is caused by intensive farming

Black circle: problem under concern, Blue circle: cause, Red circle: effect, Double lined circle: keystone environmental problem, Single lined circle: environmental problem, Dotted lined circle: problem to be mitigated when keystone environmental problem get solved, Black arrow: cause-effect link for which solutions are given, Blue arrow: cause-effect link

N.B.: - Each problem in the circles is connected to many other problems on the basis of cause-and-effect links, and they are not shown here.

It has been shown in the above scenario that intensive farming is a keystone environmental problem, and seeking high-energy sustainable solutions often comes at a huge cost. As a result, the only viable option is to seek restorative, reconciliatory, and regenerative solutions.

According to Bill Reed, "When compared with a sustainable system, regenerative systems have higher efficiency, lower cost, reduced generation of waste, faster time to market, result in a variety of products and benefits, and are the only way towards the realization of the exponential value of the social, ecological, financial, and human qualities of the project, community, and ecosystem." And according to Wahl (2016), a regenerative human culture is healthy, resilient, and adaptable; it also includes the wellbeing of the system, cares for the planet, and cares for life in the awareness that this is the most effective way to create a thriving future for all of humanity.

Regenerative development design should be considered the highest priority when handling *keystone environmental problems*. The interconnected nature of the man-made environmental issues should be studied using the concept maps. The co-evolving (auto-correcting) feature of the regenerative development should be tested prior to implementation (with respect to other environmental parameters). All smart alternatives have to be examined when choosing the right solution.

Since all man-made environmental problems are linked as causes and effects. Establishing sustainable solutions (link cutters) is often affected by human adaptability factors, such as economic, political, and social. This can be overcome by regenerative solutions (creating bridges to the linked manmade environmental issues). The following diagram depicts different kinds of available solutions for the issue.

7. Water pollution, scarcity and salination

7.1 Introduction

Water pollution problems escalated following World War II as it is caused by dramatic increase of urban population and industrialization. Disease such as cholera epidemics of 1854 in London increases the public attention that time, this concern on water pollution reached a peak at 1970 in United States and Canada, this is same in Europe, United Kingdom, Japan and other industrialized countries. Water pollution is now a global problem effecting both industrialized and developing nations. Sources of water pollution can be either point sources such as sewer outfall and industrial discharge or non-point sources such as urban, agricultural runoff and droppings from polluted air. Any chemical or physical change in water that has an adverse effect on organism can be considered as pollution such as synthetic organic compounds, human and animal wastes, chemicals, particles, sediments, oils, toxic metals, acids, pathogens and heat. Waste water collection and several levels of treatments are being conducted. Remnants of drains were identified from the historic Minoan civilization (3000 B.C.) in Crete, Greece. Pipes for stormwater and drains of few houses were used during Romans, however during middle of the nineteenth century human waste discharges into sewers were begun, and early sewers were admitted to dual function as it carries both the human waste and stormwater. In addition, these systems often created problems such as solid deposition, basement flooding, blockage, odours and become unhygienic, this has created to the need for treatment plants, in 19th and early 20th century combined sewage treatment plants are used, combined treatment plants required large spaces than sanitary sewers. During middle of the 20th century separate treatment systems are used to handle stormwater and sewage systems, this overwhelmed the overflowing or blockage issues of combined system and facilitated to increase the Biological Oxygen Demand (BOD), Chemical Oxygen Demand (COD) levels to most acceptable standards. Currently advanced treatment method up to the tertiary level of treatment gives the drinkable quality water and ensures the reuse and saving of water resource. Adapted from (Metcalf & Eddy, 1995)

7.2 Reasons and Needs of water treatment process

Reasons for waste water treatment such as decomposing waste material could produce malodours gases, sewage consume dissolved oxygen in the water bodies for its decomposition and raises the Biological Oxygen Demand (BOD) which lead to the fish kills, waste water rich in nutrients can accelerate the algal blooms and causing eutrophication, as wastewater contains pathogens, toxic chemicals and heavy metals. Purpose of development of water treatment plants was initially to satisfy the environmental and health standards. As cities become larger and development of industrial processing zones creates huge amount of waste water every day, when this increased amount of waste water exceeds the natural self-purification capacity of streams, ponds and rivers. This resulted with several environmental pollution issues including water born disease outbreaks, thus accelerated the need for waste water treatment system. In early 20th century treatment was held for 3 main objectives such as removal of floating and suspended material, treatment of biodegradable organic compounds (BOD removal) and to destroy the pathogenic microorganisms. However, those early methods lacking understanding of environmental effects caused by discharged waste water and long-term impacts of some specific constituents of wastewater. Adapted from (Metcalf & Eddy, 1995)

7.3 Types of Water Pollution

7.3.1 Nutrients pollution

Organic nutrients are the major source for bacterial and fungal pathogens, this leads to oxygen depletion and production of Hydrogen sulphide, Ammonia and methane cause foul smell. Biological oxygen demand rises, subsequently fish death increases and productivity get declines as the elevated level of turbidity hinder the available light for photosynthesis of aquatic flora. Major sources of organic nutrients are municipal sewage, stormwater, feedlots, agricultural wastes, leaf litter and industries such as meat packaging plant, paper mills, other food processing, beverage and dyeing industries. Natural oxygen recovery will be abated if the pollution loading is continuous and it is more difficult during dry weather condition.

Inorganic plant nutrients often stimulate the plant and algal growth and lead to eutrophication. Nitrogen, Phosphorus, Iron, Sulphur, Sodium and potassium released to waterways via agricultural fertilizer runoff, laundry detergents and effluents of chemical industries.

7.3.2 Eutrophication and Natural succession

Accumulation of nutrients such as nitrogen and phosphorus from sewage treatment plants and agriculture and detergent effluents stimulates algal blooms, and the activity of aerobic microbes, this increases the BOD levels, causes death of aquatic fauna and loss of primary production due to low light levels by algal blooms and sediments.

179

Subsequently, anaerobic decomposition occurs and it produces foul smell due to noxious gas production such as hydrogen supplied, ammonia and methane. Gradual rise in sediments may lead to the formation of land at the end of succession.

7.3.3 Aquatic weeds

Water weeds causes many problems such as increased level of BOD causing fish kills or stunted fish growth, Alter the flavour of the fish, thus fish loses its market, odour at the water due to the generation of hydrogen sulphide, Ammonia and Methane due to anaerobic decomposition of plant and animal debris, water becomes unsuitable for consumption where it initiated with change in taste of drinking water (Helfrich L. , Neves, Libey, & Newcomb, n.d.)as cited in (Pieterse & Murphy , 1990).

7.3.4 Infectious Agents

Major sources for infectious agents are untreated or poorly treated sewage, human and animal wastes, meat packaging plants, tanning plants, parasitic vectors and vector breeding grounds (mosquitoes). Faecal pollution is determined by the presence of coliform bacteria, which is common in human intestine along with pathogenic forms. Diseases such as cholera, typhoid, tuberculosis, hepatitis and dysentery are water born.

7.3.5 Toxic Organic water pollutants

Many of these are non-biodegradable, some magnified via food chain, and some are carcinogens causing cancer, kills fish and other organisms or make the water distasteful. Polychlorinated biphenyls (PCB) used in electrical capacitors and transformers they are hardly biodegradable and magnified via food chain. Phenols are released from rotting vegetation and sewage treatment plants, phenols are related with fish kills as their toxicity increased by warm water, increased salinity and lower oxygen levels, Chlorinated phenols may alter the taste of water and fish.

Proteins and carbohydrates are found in nine tenth of the domestic sewage. They are mostly biodegradable such as excreta, urine, food wastes, laundry runoff, oils and dyes.

7.3.6 Toxic Inorganic water pollutants

These consist of chemicals, metals, acids and salts from various sources such as industrial discharge, urban run-off, mining, soil erosion, sewage effluents and air pollution fallout.

Heavy metal pollutants

Sources of heavy metals are agricultural runoff, urban runoff, soil erosion, volcanic activities and aerosols. Agricultural effluents receive heavy metals from pesticides they are As, Cu, Pb, and Hg. Effluents such as textile dyes consist of Cr, Cu, Pb and Ni. Cooling waters of nuclear generators often contain copper and zinc. Metal mining and querying activities releases various types of heavy metals. Wastewater from tanneries may contain chromium, glass industries release selenium, metal finishing and electroplating events release Ni, Zn, Cr, Cd and Cu. In addition, Cd, Hg, Pb and Ni are also released from damaged batteries and used LED bulbs contain Ni, Pb and Cu, Natural volcanic activities release As, Hg, Al, Rb, Mg, Cu, Pb and Zn. Commonly Cd, Cr, Cu, Pb and Zn found in industrial waste waters Adopted from (Ogphenerobor, Gladys, & Tomilola, 2014).

Mercury

It is a toxic heavy metal. Outbreak of mercury in 1950s causes Mina Mata disease in Japan, as it develops numbness of the limbs, lips, tongue and loss of muscle control, also affect the mental condition. Methyl mercury effects the brain and causing retardation, cerebral palsy and birth defects. Mercury is a waste of tube lights and CFL bulbs, PVC manufacturing, chemical industry, incinerators, power plants, laboratories and hospitals.

Nitrates and Nitrites

Nitrates and nitrites are common inorganic pollutants found in effluents of septic tanks, agro-fertilizer runoff, barnyards and sewage treatment plants are converted into toxic nitrites in human intestine. When nitrite forms methemoglobinemia by binding with heme groups in blood and reduces the oxygen carrying capacity and in the fresh water environment nitrate accumulation causes eutrophication.

Phosphates

Phosphates are released mostly from domestic waste water effluents as soap, shampoo and various other detergents contain phosphate ions, causes eutrophication of water bodies.

7.3.7 Salts

Salts such as sodium and calcium chlorides used as to melt the snow on roadside, brine from oil-drilling works and agricultural inorganic fertilizers increased the salt in waterways and ground water, in addition, sea water mixing also can lead to increased saline condition in ground water. Salt affects the salt tolerant plants and microorganisms.

7.3.8 Oils

Oil mixing or spills on water bodies alter the taste and quality of water. It also affects mammals, amphibians, birds (stick to feathers) and fish (reduces oxygen mixing to water). Crude oil mixing events occurred both in marine and freshwater environments mainly from ships, ballast water, leaching to ground water from power plants, oil storage tanks and stormwater runoff.

7.3.9 Colours / Dyes

Dyes are more common in textile industrial wastes; dyes often reduce the light penetration and organic dyes feed the harmful microorganisms. Dyes also hinder the prey; thus, fish and other fauna faces hardship to locate the prey. It was noticed that some dyes retain in the water even after the secondary treatment process.

7.3.10 Acids

Acids are released from underground coal mines and industries such as sulfuric acid in cleaning steel. Furthermore, acid rain also increases the acidity in waters causing the degradation of calcareous shells of mollusks, coral reefs and affecting the microorganism.

7.3.11 Chlorine

It is highly reactive chemical, used to kill bacteria in drinking water, destroys harmful organisms in treated wastewater of sewage treatment plants. Released chlorinated water from effluents may eradicate fishes. Many chlorinated compounds act as carcinogens and teratogens cause cancer in liver and intestinal tract.

7.3.12 Sulphates

Sulphates are found in sewage effluents, and they are found in large amount in oxidized food wastes.

7.3.13 Sediment

Sediment particles arise from various sources such as silviculture, agriculture, ranching, mining, construction of road and buildings. It also carried by sewage and stormwater runoff. Sediments destroy spawning, feeding places of fish and other fresh water life forms. In addition, it decreases the light intensity of the water and causes decline in primary productivity of the system and harbour pathogens and other active pollutants such as pesticide chemicals, nitrogen and phosphate ions from agricultural fertilizers.

7.3.14 Thermal pollution

Water used for cooling of nuclear power plants, thermal power generators, steel and paper mills and refineries are discharged into waterways, several billions of litres are emitted from such plants every day. It directly kills fish and several other organisms by thermal shock and it also retard the hatching of eggs and the development of juvenile forms. In addition, heat lowers the dissolved oxygen content and increases the metabolism of aquatic organisms, thus, increase the need for dissolved oxygen. Some species may get eliminated if there is a temperature rise by 10°C. Thermal pollution also increases the susceptibility of aquatic organism to the pathogens, parasite and certain toxins. In addition, elevated temperatures accelerate the lethality of salts, acids and toxins. Adapted from (Metcalf & Eddy, 1995)

7.4 Sources of pollution

7.4.1 Municipal wastewater

Sanitary sewage (human excreta), domestic sewage such as kitchen, bath, laundry, floor drain wastes, industrial and commercial establishments are generally known as municipal wastes. This is generally collected via sewers, manholes and pumping stations. Grey water consists 50- 80% residential runoff. Domestic waste water is high in pathogens and it is usually alkaline as it consists soap, shampoo and various detergents.

7.4.2 Industrial wastewater

Industrial wastewaters include employees' sanitary wastes, process waste from manufacturing, wash waters and comparatively uncontaminated water from heating and cooling actions. It may consist of metals, metalloids, volatiles, semi-volatiles. Wastes from meat packaging, textiles, dyeing, paint industry, plating, tanning, beverage, food production, steel making, electronic and automobile are different from each other. They have to undergo monitoring for toxic products, pH, BOD, microbial content and COD after treatment process.

7.4.3 Agriculture runoff

Wastewater from irrigation canals may consist harmful pesticide residues, these are toxic to low-level organisms such as worms and small mammals, pesticides also consist of heavy metal residues, some chemicals has long lifespan in the soil and water, and their toxicity remains in the environment for long time. In addition,

183

Nutrients from fertilizers such as Nitrate, nitrite, phosphate, and potassium increase the nutrient content in nearby waterways or proliferate into ground water and cause toxic effects. In ground water, increased nitrate level causes nitrate toxicity and methemoglobinemia, and in surface water bodies it causes algal blooms and subsequent eutrophication, which are most significant environmental hazards.

7.4.4 Stormwater

Rainfall, snowmelt and street washing runoff are less polluted than municipal wastewater. Thus, it gets little or no treatment and discharged directly into receiving water bodies. Stormwater discharge is lesser than the sewer discharge as per annual discharge quantity, but during the storm event the runoff is several times higher than the all other wastewater sources. Stormwater runoff is common in cities as paved roads, roofs, parks and fields collects the flood water, and it carries dusts, grease, oils, leaf litter, particle wastes and fallout form polluted air. Adapted from (Metcalf & Eddy, 1995)

Following problems causes water pollution, scarcity and salinization

7.5 Water pollution-water scarcity due to overexploitation of natural resources

Please see the chapter overexploitation of natural resources

7.6 Land degradation- sedimentation- soil erosion due to water pollution-water scarcity

According to Pottinger (Pottinger, 2009), most of the rural Africans directly depend on surface water sources. At present, 20 African countries experiencing water scarcity and another 12 will be added in the next 25 years. It has been revealed that the dams are expected to affect water quality and quantity for millions of downstream users.

Dams trap nutrients and lead to eutrophication causes massive algal blooms that are generally toxic and the water becomes unsafe for drinking. E.g., Reservoirs in the former USSR, South Africa, and California. Besides, four hydro dams in California have nearly closed, e.g. the fisheries of the Klamath River made the river unsafe for drinking and swimming (Pottinger, 2009).

184

Water stored for a long period behind a dam may become lethal to most life forms in the reservoir and the river for a long distance below the dam. This problem is more common among the rivers receive treated effluents from the upstream urban area. Furthermore, dams also cause the deepening of river beds for tens or even hundreds of kilometers below the reservoir. However, riverbed deepening can lower the groundwater aquifers along a river. It has threatened vegetation and local wells in the floodplain, and it also created a need for irrigation in places where it was previously not in need(Pottinger, 2009).

In tropical reservoirs, colonization of aquatic weeds and toxic algal blooms may adversely affect the water quality. Furthermore, when considering water scarcity issues, water loss by evaporation and transpiration in weed-covered reservoirs can be six times higher than that in open waters (Pottinger, 2009). It has been revealed that annually about 170 cubic km of water evaporated from the world's reservoirs, and this is more than 7% of the total freshwater consumed by all human activities. For instance, that annual average of 11.2 cubic km of water evaporated from the Nasser reservoir behind the high Aswan Dam, and this is 10% of the dam's total water capacity, and it is roughly equal to the total withdrawal of water for residential and commercial use throughout Africa. It was predicted that the Epupa Dam reservoir could have evaporated more water than that is consumed by the nation's capital city in a year. Water scarcity caused by a series of dams upstream, reduced high floods in Kenya's Tana River, this has affected the Tana River floodplain forests by reducing its ability to regenerate, and thus, the forest is dying. {Adapted from (Pottinger, 2009)}

7.7 Water pollution-water scarcity due to overexploitation of natural resources

Please see chapter over exploitation of natural resources

7.8 Pollution through mining activities causes water pollution-water scarcity

According to Khan, Israili, Ahmad, & Mohan(Khan, Israili, Ahmad, & Mohan, 2005), a study revealed that untreated mine water discharge, fly-ash pond water, and industrial effluents of opencast lignite mines, pit-head thermal power plants, and Neyveli mining and industrial complex cause heavy metal contamination at natural reservoirs such as Peria, Kolakudi, Walaza, and Perumal Ponds, and the Paravannar River in Tamil Nadu, India. Importantly, the concentrations of Cu, Zn, Mn, Fe, Ni,

185

Cd, Cr, Co, Pb, and Hg in surface water in the study area are from 2 to 1200 times higher than the average concentrations of river water all over the world. These waters are used for bathing, washing, and animal watering for a long time. Also, untreated mine and industrial wastewater and natural reservoir water have been used by villagers for more than four decades, which led to the deterioration of soil, surface water, and groundwater. Analytical experiments from mine water, fly-ash pond, and industrial effluents and the natural reservoirs depicted that Co, Cr, and Hg concentration above the recommended irrigation water quality standards in 17%, 75%, and 100% of the samples, respectively. It has been suggested that in high concentrations these metals can accumulate in soils and enter the food chain, leading to serious health risks.

7.9 Water pollution-water scarcity due to Establishment of dams

According to Sharma (Sharma, 2016), the initial consequence of dam construction is the creation of a reservoir that submerges large tracks of land, where an enormous amount of vegetation and biomass undergo decomposition. A riverine ecosystem change into the lacustrine system ultimately affects the water quality as the dynamics of the oxygen transfer mechanism in the river water gets altered. Water quality of the impounded river both upstream and downstream get affected mainly towards the reservoir bed due to factors such as duration of storage, nutritional load, depth of the reservoir, turbidity, and temperature. The study conducted by Sharma (Sharma, 2016)aimed to assess the variation of water quality from dams depicted depletion of oxygen content in both vertical and longitudinal water quality profiles of the river. Increased concentrations of heavy metals were observed in the bed level samples as compared to samples of flowing water.

According to Pearce(Pearce, 2017),to investigate the hydrological impact of dams Ted Veldkamp and her colleagues at Vrije University in Amsterdam, the Netherlands created a detailed modeling study that divided the world into 50km squares and accessed water scarcity between 1971 and 2010 and identified the hydrological winners and losers from dam interventions. Results showed that most people upstream benefits from the capture of river flows, but those downstream left high and dry. She also stated that almost a quarter of the global population experiences a significant decrease in water availability through human interventions on rivers.

7.10   Water pollution-water scarcity due to intensive farming

Please see the chapter intensive farming

7.11 Water pollution-water scarcity due to urbanization-urban sprawl-settlements

According to Pires and others (Pires, *et al.*, 2015), a study on the impact of urbanization on the surface water quality of Preto River throughout the town of Formosa, Goiás, Brazil. Water samples were collected at five different points along the river. Spatially distributed along one side to other of the town, from May to October 2012. Data were subjected to descriptive statistics, variance, and cluster analysis. The water from the second sampling point from the city depicted the worst water quality indicators based on the presence of fecal coliforms and higher nitrate levels. The collected location was not within the town (urban area) or too far from the town (rural area), it is on the outskirts of the town, the area under urbanization and problems such as sanitation, absence of sewage collection and treatment are found. Thus, due to the mixing of high domestic sewage concentration of ions such as F^-, SO_4^{2-}, NO^{3-}, and Na^+ were high. Urban expansion had been taken place at the riverbanks and watercourses. Besides, monitoring data also produced public health issues due to bathing (in parts of Feia Lagoon) and environmental concerns such as eutrophication and the presence of aquatic weeds also recorded in the region.

According to a case study(Luo, et al., 2018), the study was aiming to access the impacts of urbanization on water quality on the composition and distribution of micro invertebrates revealed that rapid urbanization in China affects the quality of surface water and affects the aquatic life. In this study environmental variables over multi-spatial scales and micro invertebrate community data were collected in April (dry season) and September (wet season) in2014 and 2015 at 19 sampling sites in the Liangjiang New Area. Among them, 9 sites had a high urbanization level, 6 had moderate urbanization levels and 4 had low urbanization levels. In the results, a significant variation in the micro invertebrate assemblage was observed. Sensitive species were mainly found in Low urbanization level area, whereas tolerant species such as families of Tubificidae (17.3%), Chironomidae (12.1%), and Physidae (4.61%) exhibited its highest relative abundance in the low urbanization area. Also, the values of the family biotic index and biological monitoring working party indicated the **deterioration of water quality along the urbanization gradient**. However, seasonal and interannual changes in micro invertebrate communities were not observed. It was also observed that increasing nutrient content of the water favours the tolerant species, whereas high water flow and substance coarseness community taxa and diversity richness.

187

7.12   Water pollution-water scarcity due to agrochemicals

The concentration of nitrates, phosphates, and dissolved oxygen in surface water of the Tunga-Kawo irrigation scheme affected the water quality according to Jimoh, Ayodeji, & Mohammed (Jimoh, Ayodeji, & Mohammed, 2003). In a study on three sampling points of surface water, at the downstream site, the nitrate level increased from zero to 74.1 mg l^{-1} just after the fertilizer application, this is more than the WHO maximum safe limit of 50 mg l^{-1}, and the phosphate level increased from 1.2mg l^{-1} to 19.2 mg l^{-1} during the same period in the year 2000. In addition, hydrazine level in the same section was increased from 62 µg l^{-1} to 102 µg l^{-1} and the dissolved oxygen levels were lower in the downstream location than the upstream, and the level was lower than the minimum amount required to support fauna and flora. Although, the quantity of the fertilizer applied by the farmers is below the required optimum to get the maximum yield. However, excess agrochemicals in the surface waters are attributed to the techniques and timing of application.

A review (Konstantinou, Hela, & Albanis, 2006) on long-term research projects, monitoring programs, and published papers concerning the surface water pollution of Greece, which revealed that pesticide classes that are mostly detected in surface water are herbicides used in corn, cotton, and rice cultivation. Organophosphorus insecticides and banned organochlorine insecticides due to their persistence in the aquatic environment. The most frequently detected compounds were herbicides such as atrazine, simazine, alachlor, metolachlor, and trifluralin, insecticides such as diazinon and parathion methyl and endosulfan lindane, and organochlorine pesticides such as aldrin. Rivers were found to be more polluted than lakes. Detected pesticide concentrations were subjected to seasonal variation as higher levels were found during late spring and summer, followed by a decrease in winter. Greek rivers also depicted similar trends compare to other rivers in Europe.

7.13   Water pollution-water scarcity due to deforestation

Please see chapter deforestation

7.14   Water pollution-water scarcity due to invasive or exotic species

According to Binns, Illgner, & Nel(Binns, Illgner, & Nel, 2001), South Africa is experiencing a serious water crisis. High water demands were found in both rural and growing towns and cities. Even though new dams and water transfer schemes are being constructed, but they are not sufficient to meet the water demand. It has been observed that alien trees and plants are established everywhere in the country, and they replace the native indigenous varieties. The study further revealed that invasive plants consume more water than native plant species. Thus, invasive plants are also a cause for current water scarcity.

According to Chamier, Schachtschneider, le Maitre, Ashton, & van Wilgen(Chamier, Schachtschneider, le Maitre, Ashton, & van Wilgen, 2012), in South Africa, more than 200 varieties of invasive plants spread in the riparian ecosystem causes loss in native plant varieties. Historically, the impact of invasive plants on water quantity has been recorded. However, this study revealed their impacts on water quality as well. Exotic plants increase the evaporation rates and reduce stream flow and dilution capacity. Nitrogen fixers such as *Acacia* spp. can increase the nutrient levels in groundwater. Besides, invasive plants also may cause wildfires and subsequent soil erosion and sedimentation, and thereby deteriorate the water quality.

7.15   Water pollution-water scarcity due to Solid waste and sewage related problems

According to Maysonet (Maysonet, 2011), in the Greater Caribbean region, the constant increase in solid waste caused water pollution in River Port-au-Prince along with various other factors. It was stated that only 25% of the population in the region have access to sewage services, with 52% have latrines. This is more critical in Haiti, St. Kitts, Montserrat, and Grenada. In addition to solid waste, improper disposal of sewage water also has become a threat to public health. Furthermore, the number of people has access to portable water also on a hike (in millions), and this is an added health risk in the region.

According to Alemayehu (Alemayehu, 2001), the Akaki river and four water reservoirssuch as Legedadi, Gefersa, Dire, and Aba-Samuel represent the surface water bodies of Addis Ababa city of Ethiopia. Akaki River has two branches that are Big Akaki and Little Akaki. Improper waste disposal such as septic tanks, open dumps, surface impoundments, and land application is the major threat to the surface water quality here. The streams receive a major part of the waste produced by residents. In the southern part of the city, the river water is used for horticulture, drinking water for cattle, washing, and other domestic purposes. Based on regional sampling through the entire waters, which includes streams, rivers, and reservoirs on chemical, physical and organoleptic properties of water, the nitrate and chromium concentrations were higher than the background levels. Results of *E-coli* test, for instance, that inlet of Aba Samuel reservoir Big Akaki River has 1010 total coliform

189

per ml. of water, while Little Akaki River contains too many bacteria to count (TMC) which is above the counting range. Besides, the Lideta spring, which is used as holy water, contains 290 total coliforms per ml, and this is well above the WHO standard limit of 10 total coliforms per ml.

According to Marques, Silva, Rodrigues, & Coelho (Marques, Silva, Rodrigues, & Coelho, 2012), in the cities of Southern Minas Gerais state of Brazil, the impact of urban solid waste facilities on surface water quality was examined such as Campo Belo sanitary landfill on Varões River, the controlled landfill of Santo Antônio do Amparo on Fabiano River, and the closed dump of Elói Mendes on Mutuca River. The sampling was done on five occasions, which includes rainy and dry seasons. Each site had three collection locations, such as upstream to the solid waste facility, downstream nearby point of influx from the sewage treatment plant or drainage point in the landfill, and downstream of the solid waste facility. However, it was **not possible** to detect the significant impact of solid waste on the rivers as various other pollution factors play a major role in polluting the surface water environment. Thus, this is **not proving evidence** of the link between solid waste and water pollution. However, our previous two examples from River Port-au-Prince of the Great Caribbean region and Addis Ababa, Ethiopia, more clearly depicted the positive relationship among both environmental issues.

7.16   Water pollution-water scarcity due to plastic pollution

According to Corcoran, Belontz , Ryan, & Helm (Corcoran, Belontz , Ryan, & Helm, 2018), a study on microplastic pollution of Thames River in Ontario, Canada, where 35 samples and duplicates were collected from river bottom sediment using a Petite Ponar Grab from November to December in 2016 depicted that every sample taken along the 400 km river including both urban and rural agricultural areas that went through organic debris splitting, wet sieving, sodium polytungstate density separation, and microspy and the 63 μm to 2 mm grain size grade filtering contain microplastics and the counts ranged from 16 to > 10,000 particles /kg dry sediment with an overall fragment-fibre-microbead ratio of 27:67:6. Most abundant fragments were mainly blue and red, fibers were mainly blue and black, and beads were mainly black and gray. However, a weak correlation was noted between river flow and microplastics abundance with moderate flow region averaging greater counts than low and high. Also, results revealed that mud, clay, and organic matter in the samples were all contaminated with microplastics and the samples from the urban region showed greater particle count than samples from rural areas.

According to Palatinus, Centa, Viršek, & Peterlin (Palatinus, Centa, Viršek, & Peterlin, 2018), a microplastic sampling in the Ljubljanica River and Lake Bled of Slovenia using methods such as using water pump (suitable in lakes), surface-epi-neuston net, water column-water pump and sediment-Van Veen grab through the entire water column was done. The results from 38 samples (all) depicted that microplastics are already present in Slovenian waters and lead to ecological problems.

According to Eo, Song, Han, Hong, & Shim (Eo, Song, Han, Hong, & Shim, 2018), the Nakdong River in South Korea is an important pathway for transporting plastics to the oceans. A study using surface water sampling upstream, midstream, and downstream in February (dry season), May (intermediate), and August (wet season) including the bottom waters downstream depicted that microplastics abundance was 1.8-3.7 times higher in surface water than the bottom waters in all season. Besides, microplastics less than 300 micrometers accounted for 66%, 81%, and 71% of the total abundance in February, May, and August, respectively. Dominant polymers were polyesters in February accounted for 32%, polypropylene accounted for 66% in May, and 38% in August. Furthermore, microplastics in the Nakdong River were estimated as 1.2×10^{13} n/yr. (surface water of top 20 cm 9.9×10^{11} n/yr. and subsurface water 1.1×10^{13} n/yr.).

According to Jambeck and others (Jambeck, et al., 2015), 275 million metric tons of plastic trash was generated in 192 coastal countries in 2010, with 4.8 to 12.7 million metric tons entering the ocean. According to Derraikn (Derraik, 2002), plastic debris causes marine plastic pollution. According to Ritchie & Roser(Ritchie & Roser, 2018), 80% of the ocean plastics come from land-based sources, and 20% from marine. According to "oceanconservance.org" ("oceanconservance.org", n.d.), Ocean Conservancy has documented more than 220 million pounds of trash from the world's beaches for more than 30 years in volunteered beach cleanup programs, with participants from 153 countries. A study (Sivaramanan & Kotagama, 2018) on beach trash from the coastal belt of Colombo district, Sri Lanka, depicted the beach trash as the major source of marine plastic pollution. And another Island wide beach survey held in Sri Lanka revealed that among the debris counted, plastics contributed the largest portion (93%) (Jang, et al., 2018).It was stated in UNEP (UNEP, 2009) report that coastal based sources are, illegal domestic and industrial garbage dumping, tourist resorts, hotels, restaurants, boutiques found along the coastal belt, fishing harbors, fish anchorages, and fish landing sites, urban centers bordering the coast, waste from construction sites and beach visitors, etc. According to the recent work

191

done by Hettige, Weerasekara, & Azmy(Hettige, Weerasekara, & Azmy, 2012), a trash survey was conducted on monthly basis from November 2012 to February 2013 at Kaluwamodara, Kalutara, Panadura, Mount Lavinia, Dehiwala, Wellawatte, and Negombo coastal beaches in Sri Lanka. A location at the beach (30 x 20 square meter area) was selected by a random sampling method. Plastics were identified as the highest type of waste in each location such as Kaluwamodara (41.60%), Kalutara (35.97%), Wellawatte (40.65%), Mount Lavinia (35.64%), and Negombo (40.65%) areas respectively. Polythene took second place as 54.59% of all wastes collected in Panadura and 49.16% in Dehiwala.

According to Eriksen and others (Eriksen, et al., 2014), plastic pollution is everywhere. A study estimated the total number of plastic particles and their weight floating in the world's oceans from 24 expeditions from 2007 to 2013 across all five sub-tropical gyres, coastal Australia, Bay of Bengal, and the Mediterranean Sea, an estimate of the total number of plastic particles and their weight floating in the world's oceans from 24 expeditions from 2007 to 2013 across all five sub-tropical gyres, coastal Australia, Bay of Bengal and the Mediterranean Sea using surface net tows (N = 680) and visual survey transects of large plastic debris (N = 891). Also, calibrated data of the oceanographic model of floating debris dispersal and correcting for wind-driven vertical mixing depicted an estimate of a minimum of 5.25 trillion particles weighing 268,940 tons. According to Lebreton and others(Lebreton, et al., 2017), a study evaluated the river input of plastic debris into oceans from waste management, population density, and hydrological information estimated that annually, plastic waste ranging between 1.15 and 1.41 million tonnes enter the oceans through rivers (figure 7.1). Over 74% of emissions occur during May and October, furthermore, the world's top 20 polluting rivers are mostly located in Asia, which represents 67% of the global total.

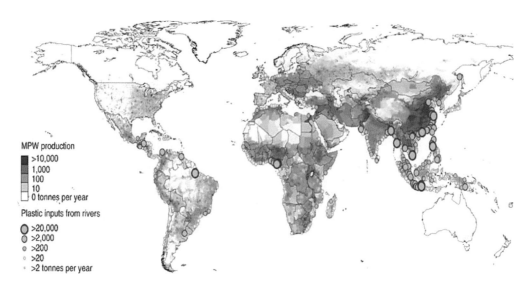

MPW production
■ >10,000
  1,000
  100
  10
□ 0 tonnes per year

Plastic inputs from rivers
◉ >20,000
◉ >2,000
◦ >200
· >20
· >2 tonnes per year

Figure 7.1 Mass of river plastics flowing into oceans in tonnes per year
Source: (Lebreton, et al., 2017), License: CC BY-SA 4.0

River contributions are derived from individual watershed characteristics such as population density (in inhab km^{-2}), mismanaged plastic waste (MPW) production per country (in kg inhab^{-1} d^{-1}), and monthly averaged runoff (in mm d^{-1}). The model is calibrated against river plastic concentration measurements from Europe, Asia, North and South America. Source: (Eriksen, et al., 2014).

7.17 Water pollution-water scarcity due to e-wastes

Streams in Guiyu, China are black and pungent due to pollution from electrical wastes. Guiyu receives electronic wastes from the developed world where it is dismantled for precious metals and reusable or recyclable parts. According to Kevin Brigden from Greenpeace laboratories that river of Guiyu is acidic because of the expelled acid baths used in the disintegration of circuit boards. Higher levels of lead have been observed in the children's blood ("Greenpeace", n.d.).

According to Huang, Nkrumah , Anim , & Mensah(Huang , Nkrumah , Anim , & Mensah , 2014), in Ghana, Africa the amount of e-waste dumped has been increasing each year by about 20,000 tonnes. Surface water bodies such as Odaw River and the Korle Lagoon are polluted by contaminants from e-waste that are mostly carried through floodwaters during the heavy rain. This includes heavy metals such as lead, cadmium, copper, and organic pollutants such as PCDD/Fs, and PBDEs have been detected in the sediments of local waters and this affects the aquatic biodiversity in the region.

7.18   Water pollution-water scarcity due to heavy metal contamination

According to Salwa and others (Salwa , et al., 2016), in Sudan, water and fish resources were sampled from three different states such as Khartoum, Nahrelnile, and Sinnar. Samples were assayed for heavy metals such as lead, cadmium, mercury, arsenic, and copper. Based on the results, fish samples showed a significantly higher level of lead than acceptable levels, while zinc, cadmium, and copper showed lower than the acceptable limits. In water samples, all water samples depicted significantly higher levels of lead compared to standard acceptable levels. Zinc and copper concentrations were significantly lower than the acceptable limits, while the cadmium level was higher at the Gabalawalia dam area of Khartoum state. Also, mercury and arsenic showed a high and low level than acceptable limits, respectively.

Buriganga River flows beside Dhaka in Bangladesh. The population of the city is around 12 million. City dwellers largely depend on Buriganga's water for drinking, fishing, and carrying merchandise. However, the river is now polluted and the odour from black water sensed even from half a kilometer distance (Mohiuddin, Ogawa, Zakir, Otomo, & Shikazono, 2011). In a study, where water and sediment samples from 20 locations of the river collected in summer and winter in 2009 depicted that levels of chromium, lead, cadmium, zinc, copper, nickel, cobalt, and arsenic in water samples mostly exceeded the severe effect level values, at which the sediment is considered as heavily polluted. The study also estimated that on average 72% chromium, 92% lead, 88% zinc, 73% copper, 63% nickel, and 68% of total cobalt was associated with the first three labile sequential extractions phase, which portion is readily bioavailable and might be associated with the frequent negative biological effect. The enrichment factors showed that the lead, cadmium, zinc, chromium, and copper in most of the sediment samples were enriched severe to very severely. Furthermore, the pollution load index value hits 21.2 in summer and 24.6 in winter. Thus, the study concluded the progressive deterioration of the site and estuarine quality due to severe heavy metal pollution (Mohiuddin, Ogawa, Zakir, Otomo, & Shikazono, 2011).

7.19   Water pollution-water scarcity due to hazardous wastes

According to Fick and others (Fick, et al., 2010), a study investigated hazardous chemical waste from the pharmaceutical production area, whereas water samples from an effluent treatment plant near Hyderabad, India that receives processed water from nearly 90 bulk drug manufacturers and analysis of surface water from recipient stream and from two lakes that are not contaminated from treatment plant were tested for the presence of 12 pharmaceuticals with liquid chromatography-mass spectrometry. Results revealed that a very high concentration of ciprofloxacin (14mg/L), and cetirizine (2.1 mg/L) along with a high concentration of seven additional pharmaceuticals were detected in the effluent of the treatment. In addition, samples from two lakes depicted very high concentration of ciprofloxacin (up to 6.5 mg/L), cetirizine (up to 1.2 mg/L), norfloxacin (up to 0.52 mg/L), and enoxacin (up to 0.16 mg/L). These clearly evidenced insufficiently treated industrial hazardous wastes resulted in pollution of the lake and affect the water quality as the effluents contain wastes of broad-spectrum antibiotics highly exceeding the allowable limit for drinking water of 100 ng/L, and that could harm the human as well as entire biota that depends on the lake.

According to Mathur, Bhatnagar, Nagar, & Bijarnia (Mathur, Bhatnagar, Nagar, & Bijarnia, 2005), Sanganer town, in Jaipur district, Rajasthan, India, about 400 industries involved in the textile dyeing and printing process. The effluents are discharged into nearby ponds, drains, and reach the Kaduna River basin without treatment. The effluents contain highly toxic dyes, bleaching agents, salts, acids, alkalis, and heavy metals such as cadmium, copper, zinc, chromium, and iron. This has adverse effects on the environment and the health of the textile workers as well as residents of Sanganer town. A study using Ames *Salmonella* or microsome mutagenicity assay depicted that the effluents and the surface water of Amani Shah Drainage have high mutagenic activity and the drainage water and dry bed of the drainage (during the summer) are not acceptable for agricultural or other recreational purposes.

7.20 Water pollution-water scarcity due to nuclear explosions-radiation-nuclear wastes

Fukushima Daiichi Nuclear Power plant's breakdown of the reactor's cooling system resulted in overheating of fuel in three reactors that were in operation during the earthquake (Wakeford , 2011) as cited in (Mark, Wakeford, Bouville, & Simon, 2016). Subsequent radionuclide release affected the atmosphere and the sea as most of which was deposited on the Pacific Ocean (Yoshida & Kanda , 2012) & (Black & Buesseler , 2014) as cited in (Mark, Wakeford, Bouville, & Simon, 2016). Concentrations of ^{137}Cs in sea waters were very high near the site at the time of the accident and for a few weeks afterward and decreased to relatively low levels within a year (Buesseler & al., 2012) as cited in (Mark, Wakeford, Bouville, & Simon, 2016).

According to Loew (Loew, 2016), it has been reported that a single sockeye salmon, sampled from Okanagan Lake during summer 2015 depicted the presence of cesium-134 in it. However, according to Cullen, who leads the team which accesses the radiation pollution in the ocean waters, the level was more than 1000 times lower than the action level determined by Health Canada and does not have any significant risk to consumers. In the United States, a team lead by Ken Buesseler detected the cesium-134 in the samples collected from Oregon in January and February 2016, according to the analysis 0.3 becquerels per cubic meter of cesium-134 was measured. However, cesium-134 has a half-life of two years (it is down to a fraction of what it was five years ago), but cesium-137 has a 30-year half-life and the recent data from Buesseler concluded that cesium-137 levels have increased considerably in the central northern Pacific, although they are at levels that imply no concern. Scientists reported that the plume spread throughout this vast area from Alaska to California and moving at roughly twice the speed of a garden snail. However, Cullen stated that the levels are closer to shore, and about to increase over the coming year.

7.21 Water pollution-water scarcity due to population explosion

According to Taft (Taft, 2015), exponential population growth in a world with uneven freshwater distribution may cause water scarcity. Overconsumption of groundwater leads to salinization in coastal areas. It was stated that "according to World Bank estimates, 25-30% fresh water is wasted, costing the global economy $14 billion annually" (Taft, 2015). According to Mcnally and others(Mcnally, et al., 2019), globally four billion people are suffering from acute and chronic water scarcity. These values may increase with increasing population and demand for food and energy production.

7.22 Groundwater contamination-depletion-salinization causes water pollution-water scarcity

According to Sharma S.(Sharma S. , 2008), salinization due to seawater intrusion has become a major reason for water scarcity on the eastern coast of India. Also, this region is often hit by cyclones every year. It has been estimated with the population growth, by the year 2025 the water abstraction from aquifers will increase by 50% in the region. In the Krishna-Godavari basin area of Andhra Pradesh, the landward movement of saline-freshwater interface occurred for several kilometers as saltwater intrusion caused by overexploitation of groundwater. The groundwater quality assessment data depicted, total dissolved solids (TDS) 1912 / 1948 mg/l, TH 365/393 mg/l - Ca^{++} + Mg^{++}, Na^+ 721/ 739 mg/l, Cl^- 781/ 797 mg/l, SO_4^{++} 122/ 112 mg/l and F^- 1.6/1.9 mg/l, these concentrations are higher than the recommended WHO domestic and industrial water quality standards. Excessively high fluoride levels (more than 1.5 mg/l) in groundwater, which is toxic, caused several health issues, as discoloration of teeth and crippling skeletal effects are prominent in the region. Millions in the region are affected by chronic fluorosis disease.

7.23 Global warming and Climate change cause Water pollution-water scarcity

Climate change can result in water scarcity in several ways such as increased temperatures and prolonged drought periods cause strain on water demand, reduce soil moisture, deplete existing water resources, reduce soil moisture, variation in quantity, and seasonal distribution of precipitation. Furthermore, degradation of water resources caused by flooding events of climate change, as the heavy rain and floodwater carries pathogens and various contaminants into the water sources and make them inconsumable. According to a literature survey(EricaDeNicola, Aburizaiza, Siddique, Khwaja, & David , 2015), the Middle East and certain North African region are now in a water crisis, including Saudi Arabia and the other countries of Gulf Cooperation Council (GCC) as classified by United Nation's water scare nations. Except for Oman, all other Middle East countries are placed well below the severe water scarcity threshold of 500 cubic meters per capita per year.

According to Sowers, Vengosh, & Weinthal(Sowers, Vengosh, & Weinthal, 2011) as cited in (EricaDeNicola, Aburizaiza, Siddique, Khwaja, &David , 2015), Regions in the Middle East and North Africa are vulnerable to the effects of climate change on water resources. It was also mentioned that the combination of a greater than the average population growth rate of 2.5% along with an 8.8% annual increase in water demand and the changes brought by climate change will have a significant impact on the future available quality of water resources in Saudi Arabia (Al-Suhaimy , 2013) as cited in (EricaDeNicola, Aburizaiza, Siddique, Khwaja, &David , 2015).

According to Mekonnen & Hoekstra (Mekonnen & Hoekstra , 2016) as cited in (Gao, Schlosser, Fant, & Strzepek, 2018), two-thirds of the global population about 4 billion people live underwater scarcity at least one month of the year and half a billion people in the world face severe water scarcity all over the year. According to Chellaney (Chellaney , 2012) as cited in (Gao, Schlosser, Fant, & Strzepek, 2018), more than half of the global population resides in Asia, however, the availability of fresh water

197

is less than the global annual average of 6380 m^3 per inhabitant, and per capita, water availability in Asia has been declining over the decades by 1.6% per year. Besides, climate change further exacerbates the issue by altering the hydrological cycle (Oki & Kanae , 2006) as cited in (Gao, Schlosser, Fant, & Strzepek, 2018). It has been predicted ("Water Futures and Solutions: Asia 2050", 2016) as cited in (Gao, Schlosser, Fant, & Strzepek, 2018) that up to 3.4 billion out of predicted 5.2 billion people in Asia could be living in water-stressed areas by 2050. A study on the population under water stress based on multiple climate projections from general circulation models (GCMs) of six projected future scenarios in China, India, and Southern and Eastern Asia (SEA) is depicted (Table 7.1), as per values in China, regardless of socioeconomic growth or climate change or their combination, the additional population under threat is approximately 80 million, this is equivalent to 40% of its projected population increase, in India, the population under stress attributed to socioeconomic growth nearly doubles the current estimate, and the resulting total population under stress reaching up to 1 billion. However, under the mitigation policy, climate change reduces the affected population by nearly 145 million, and the overall mitigation policy results in 70 million fewer people in India under water-stressed conditions. Across the entire Southern and Eastern Asia (SEA), all scenarios project an increase in the number of people under water stress.

It has been predicted that by 2050 an additional 200 million people are under threat of at least high water-stressed conditions. However, a modest mitigation pathway could reduce this additional population under threat by 60 million (30% of the expected number).

Table7.1 Changes in total population and population exposed to water stress (in millions) for China, India, and SEA under three impact scenarios and two policy scenarios

	Total population			Population exposed to water stress (WSI > 0.6)						
	2000	2041–2050	2041–2050 (change)	2000	2041–2050 (changes relative to 2000)					
					C_UE	G_UE	CG_UE	C_L2S	G_L2S	CG_L2S
China	1278	1480	202	524	80	83	81	83	83	83
India	1018	1555	537	567	−96	449	−11	−143	443	−73
SEA	2930	4144	1214	1241	143	657	195	104	651	135

The total population of 2041–2050 is the average from 400-ensemble projections. Bold numbers indicate decreases in population. Source: (Gao, Schlosser, Fant, & Strzepek, 2018)

7.24 Water pollution-water scarcity causes or due to Eutrophication and hypoxia

According to Qin and others(Qin, et al., 2010),in Lake Taihu, which is the third-largest freshwater lake in China, massive toxic *Microcystis* spp. bloom caused a severe water crisis in late May 2007. Taihu was the sole water supply of Wuxi city in southern Jiangsu province of China. The water crisis put over 2 million people without drinking water for at least a week. Continuous nutrient loading and multi-annual warming trend extended the period of blooming. Besides, the prevailing wind also caused the toxic blooms to accumulate near the shoreline where the intake of the water plant is located. It has been mentioned that both human and climatic factors together contributed to this blooming event. Nutrient loading from domestic and agricultural wastewater discharges caused eutrophication in Sagar Lake, Sagar city, Madhya Pradesh, India for several decades. In a survey(Pathak & Pathak, 2012), physiochemical characters of water samples from six sampling points during three seasons were analyzed for contaminants. The results showed that the samples were highly polluted and well above the WHO standards. Due to the degradation of water quality by eutrophication, changes in vegetation pattern increased decay was recorded. Hypoxic conditions also observed which led to undesirable changes in the diversity of aquatic fauna.

According to Rabalais, Turner, Díaz, & Justić(Rabalais, Turner, Díaz, & Justić, 2009), in coastal Atlantics, harmful algal blooms are caused by cumulative effects of environmental issues such as climate change, increased population and intensive industrialization and agriculture activities resulted in reduced water quality and loss of habitats. Also, hypoxia (oxygen depletion) resulted from eutrophication formed dead zones in the estuaries and coastal waters of the United States, a survey on oxygen levels in July 2004 and 2005 showed the following results.

7.25 Water pollution-water scarcity due to acid rain

According to Cronan & Schofield (Cronan & Schofield, 1979) as cited in (Singh & Agrawal, 2008), Aluminum concentration was found to be abnormally high in Scandinavia and North America. According to Dickson (Dickson, 1978)as cited in (Singh & Agrawal, 2008), a high concentration of heavy metals such as Al, Cd, Hg,

Fe, and Zn was found in acidified lakes. The identified sources of these heavy metals are soil and rocks from in the catchment areas.

7.26 Water pollution due to air pollution

Please see chapter air pollution

7.27 Water Pollution-water scarcity due to draining of wetlands

According to ("awe.gov.au", 2016), wetlands are the kidneys of the world. Wetlands improve the water quality in Australia. Thus, draining of wetlands also remove the natural water purifying capacity of the ecosystem, and leads to scarcity for potable water. In many parts of the world wetlands are used for establishment of human settlements, highway development and various other purposes. According to United Nations Framework Convention on Climate Change (UNFCCC), globally wetlands disappear three times faster than forest ("unfccc.int", 2018).

Water pollution- water scarcity- salinization effects into following problems

7.28 Vector-borne diseases due to water pollution

Polluted waters are breeding grounds for *Culex* sp. mosquito vectors that transmit diseases such as West Nile virus, Japanese encephalitis, and Filariasis. According to Chandra(Chandra, 2008), water pollution with organic matters increases the habitats and breeding grounds of *Culex* sp. Mosquitoes.

7.29 Water pollution-water scarcity causes Poverty-disease-food insecurity-war

According to Harada (Harada, 2008), in May 1956, Minamata disease, methyl mercury poisoning was observed in those who feed on ingested fish and shellfish from waters contaminated by wastewater of a chemical plant. The disease was initially observed in the inhabitants of the Minamata city of Japan's Kyushu Island. The marine products displayed high levels of mercury contamination from 5.61 to 35.7 ppm, mercury content from the hair of patients was a maximum of 705 ppm. Symptoms of the disease were sensory disturbances, ataxia, dysarthria, constriction of the visual field, auditory disturbances, and tremor. Besides, extensive lesions of the brain were also detected. The fetus of the affected mother also showed congenital Minamata disease. For the past 36 years of identified 2252 patients, 1043 have died.

According to Kessler (Kessler, 2013), in addition to food insecurity in the Shiranui Sea and the horrific symptoms of the disease, the disease also caused disabilities in affected people. There were patents reported to have memory loss, dizziness, vision and hearing problems, and neurological problems such as unable to lift the head or unable to walk.

According to Kasuya and others (Kasuya, et al., 1992), in the early 1950s, Jinzu River Basin in Toyama, Japan was heavily polluted by cadmium from a zinc mine. Paddy field soil was also contaminated by cadmium from the river water. Ingestion of cadmium caused Itai-itai disease, caused severe bone pain, pseud fracture, renal tubular dysfunction, and osteomalacia, and decreased bone mass accompanied by osteoporosis.

7.30   Biodiversity loss due to water pollution-water scarcity

According to the Ministry of Water Resources of India as stated in "Hindustan times"("hindustantimes", 2018)at least ten species that are listed as endangered in the IUCN Red List are now facing extinction in Ganga River, India such as Ganges river dolphin, Gharial (fish-eating crocodile), black-bellied turn, Indian skimmer, northern river terrapin, three stripped roofed turtle, red-crowned roofed turtle and golden, mahseer fish. Furthermore, the Sarus crane, the mugger crocodile, and snow trout are listed as vulnerable. It is further mentioned the dolphin population of Ganga was about 10,000 in the late nineteenth century, reduced to 3,526 in 2014. According to UNICEF as stated in "Helpsavenature" ("Helpsavenature", 2018), more than 3000 children die every day due to the consumption of contaminated drinking water. It was also stated that according to the U.S. EPA that every year about 1.2 trillion gallons of untreated sewage, industrial wastes, and a large amount of surface water due to heavy rain are dumped into the lakes, and annually, over one million seabirds, 100,000 sea mammals and an excessively large amount of fish population wiped-out due to pollution. Pollution affects top-level carnivores such as polar bears and otters indirectly through the food chain by bioaccumulation. Biomagnification of heavy metals may affect the top-level carnivores and causes disease and tumors, e.g., lake trout and herring gulls. Chemicals such as dioxins and PCBs cause birth defects and tumors in fish and amphibian populations ("Helpsavenature", 2018). According to the United States' Fish and Wildlife Service, as stated in "Helpsavenature" ("Helpsavenature", 2018), annually 6-14 million fish death occur due to pesticide pollution. A survey by food and water watch stated as mentioned in "Helpsavenature"

("Helpsavenature", 2018), by 2025 two-third of the world's population will face scarcity of water, and five times as much land is likely to undergo drought.

7.31   Water pollution-water scarcity as a keystone environmental problem

According to "www.worldwildlife.org"("www.worldwildlife.org", n.d.), about 1.1 billion people all over the world lack access to freshwater, and 2.7 billion people find water scarcity for at least one month of the year. Inadequate sanitation is a problem for 2.4 billion people in the world, where diseases such as cholera, typhoid, and diarrhoea affect. Furthermore, 2 million people, mostly children, die each year from diarrhoeal disease alone. It has been predicted by 2025 two-third of the world population will face water shortages ("www.worldwildlife.org", n.d.). Also, agriculture accounts for 70% of the global freshwater access, but 60% of this water used in irrigation are wasted through leaky irrigation.

In the wastewater, decomposing waste material could produce malodorous gases, sewage consumes dissolved oxygen in the water bodies for its decomposition and raises the Biological Oxygen Demand (BOD) which lead to the fish kills, wastewater rich in nutrients can accelerate the algal blooms and causing eutrophication, as wastewater contains pathogens, toxic chemicals, and heavy metals. The purpose of the development of water treatment plants was initially to satisfy the environmental and health standards. As cities become larger and as the development of industrial processing zones created a huge amount of wastewater every day it increased the amount of wastewater exceeding the natural self-purification capacity of streams, ponds, and rivers. (Figure 7.2).

Evidence 1: Water pollution causes disease and food insecurity

According to the Cornell University study (Epstein, Ford, Puccia ,& Possas , 1994); (Robbins, 2000) as cited in (Pimentel, et al., 2007), "water-related diseases responsible for 80% of all infectious diseases worldwide, and 90% of all diseases in developing world." Thus, if water pollution is solved completely, we can get rid of 80% of infectious diseases. This is a statistically significant solution. Thus, water pollution can be considered as a keystone issue.

Evidence 2: Water pollution causes eutrophication

According to the editors of Britannica (Britannica, 2019), cultural eutrophication (man-made and not natural) occurs due to human water pollution by sewages, detergents, fertilizers and other anthropogenic nutrient sources into the ecosystem. Thus, water pollution can be considered as a keystone environmental problem.

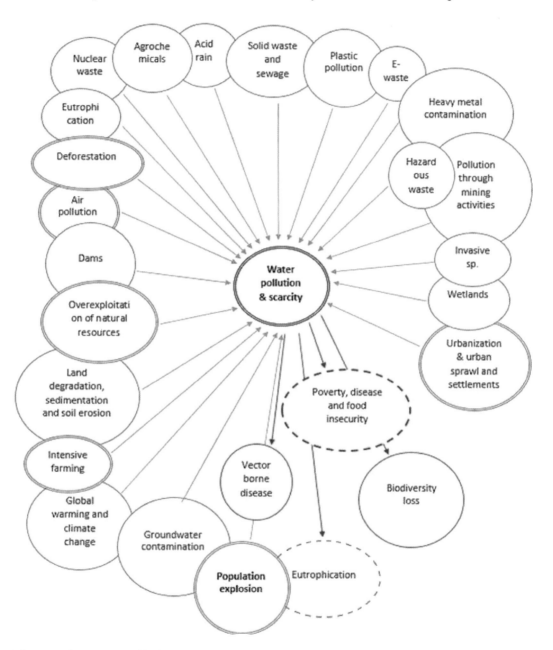

Figure 7.2 Water pollution-water scarcity as keystone environmental problem with the disappearance of disease and food insecurity on its mitigation (hypothetical diagram) [In the figure black circle is the problem being examined, blue circles are cause man-made environmental problems, red circles are effect man-made environmental

problems, double lined circles are keystone man-made environmental problems, and circles with dashed lines (either single or double lined) are the man-made environmental problems that disappear when the problem being examined (black circle) is mitigated]

Regenerative solution vs. Sustainable solution vs. Conventional solutions
Regenerative solutions are smarter than sustainable solution and include other pillars of development, such as economic factors and social factors. Co-evolving and high resilient nature of regenerative development are some advantages over sustainable solutions (figure 7.3).

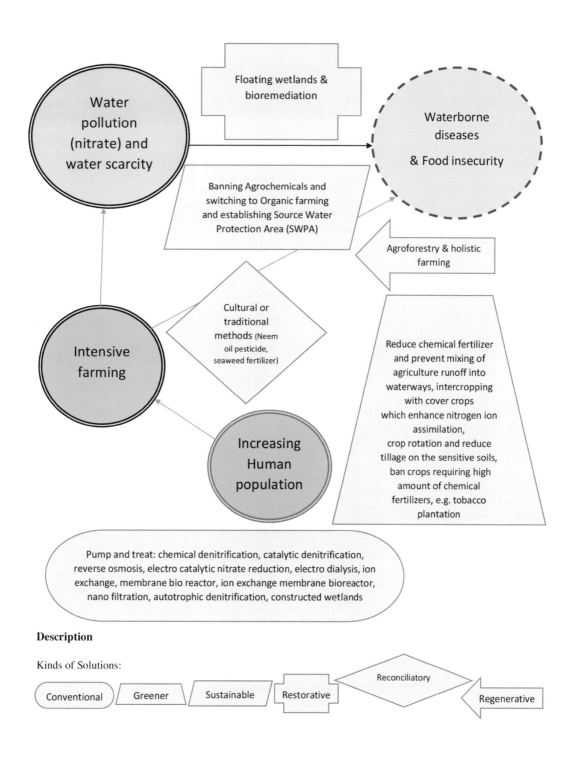

Description

Kinds of Solutions:

Figure 7.3 Solutions for water pollution

Black circle: problem under concern, Blue circle: cause, Red circle: effect, Double lined circle: keystone environmental problem, Single lined circle: environmental problem, Dotted lined circle: problem to be mitigated when keystone environmental problem get solved, Black arrow: cause-effect link for which solutions are given, Blue arrow: cause-effect link

N.B.: - Each problem in the circles is connected to many other problems on the basis of cause-and-effect links, and they are not shown here.

Banning chemical fertilizer and switching to organic farming and declaring source water protection zones are **sustainable** solutions because the impact is net zero (neither benefit nor harm to ecology and sentient beings) and according to the definition of sustainable development stated in 1987 Brundtland commission report, "development that meets the needs of the present without compromising the ability of future generations to meet their needs" could be considered as sustainable development. However, sustainable solutions are often very expensive due to their high energy requirement, unlike smart regenerative solutions they cannot adapt or co-evolve with the nature, they cannot affirm the wellbeing, and depicts relatively low systemic vitality.

Due to the above given negative reasons sustainable development path is not suitable for developing countries, where their economic factors are not strong enough to support it. In Sri Lanka, as a consequence of the implementation of sustainable solution in May 2021(banning agrochemicals) the entire country had experienced a severe economic crisis a year later by May 2022, which led to surge in prices of all basic needs including fuels, foods, raw vegetables, cereals, etc. Subsequently, country is also facing political instability and social unrest, or protests against the leadership. On the 18th of April 2022 the president himself accepted that he had committed a mistake by banning agrochemicals that are necessary for crops and to maintain market economy. 13% of the Sri Lanka's income is from Tea exports, and a similar but smaller portion from other agri-product exports. Depletion in tea production also affected the foreign exchange. However, prices of vegetable and cereals are also sky rocking, which never occurred ever before in the country's history.

Pump and treat methods such as chemical denitrification, catalytic denitrification, reverse osmosis, electro catalytic nitrate reduction, electro dialysis, ion exchange, membrane bio reactor, ion exchange membrane bioreactor, nano filtration, autotrophic denitrification, constructed wetlands are high energy **conventional** practices. In addition, **greener** solutions cause minimal harm to the environment, they are: reducing chemical fertilizer application and preventing mixing of agriculture runoff into waterways, cover crops with enhanced nitrogen assimilation, crop rotation and reduced tillage in sensitive soil and banning the cultivation of crops that require high fertilizer application such as tobacco. Floating wetlands and bioremediation are **restorative** solutions because they can adapt according to the level of pollution and the system requires human maintenance. Traditional practices such as use of Neem-based pesticides, seaweed application as organic fertilizer can be considered as **reconciliatory** methods of handling the issue. Reconciliatory methods consider human as part of the nature (not dominated by human). Agroforestry (permaculture) and Allan Savory's holistic farm management are **regenerative** methods because they ascertain co-evolving with nature as cyclical beings. And they require low energy, and ascertain high systemic vitality and high resilience.

8. Urbanization (industrialization)-Urban sprawl-settlements

8.1 Introduction

Since ancient times, evolution of cities occurs. It is believed, *Sprawl is the spreading out of city and its suburbs over more and more rural land at the periphery of an urban area. More specifically, conversion of rural land into built-up or developed land overtime.* Most of the activities of the nation happen in cities, such as flow of people, information, finance, and goods. The extensive land use, lack of choice in ways to travel, fragmented open space, lack of choice in housing type and prices lack of public space and community centres, separation of uses into distinct areas, repetitive one-story development, etc.

Human population has doubled over the last four decades, population increase and its developmental needs are the main causes of urbanization and urban sprawl. According to UN estimates over the second half of the 20th century total population of the world increased at an average annual rate of 1.75%, while world urban population increased at an average annual rate of 2.68%. When we consider the population density in the year 2000, population density in US was 28% per square kilometers, in China, it was at 130 people per square kilometers, and in India it was 307 People per square kilometers. In 1998, the world's population density was almost 40 people per kilometers (Rain, Long, & Ratcliffe, 2007) as cited in (Bekele, 2005). Population density increases not only form the increased birth rate, and also from international migration.

Increasing densities increases land scarcity and the need for protection, need for energy conservation and the need for households. Density also determines the functionality of the city. Urban sprawl also associated with high environmental cost. Urban sprawl causes air pollution, water pollution and water scarcity, noise, erosion, loss of biodiversity, draining of wetlands, resource depletion, energy crisis, deforestation, visual pollution, poverty and diseases etc. It also has an impact on human psychology such as increased crime, traffic accidents, increased transportation time and psychic costs.

Urbanization and urban sprawl also have economic impacts such as high maintenance fee, expensive schooling and hospitals, high utility bills such as gas, water, electricity, and telephone. And expensive public services and facilities, such as police, waste collection, library, and health care.

208

8.2 Mega cities

According to United Nations, megacities are urban agglomeration with a population that exceeds eight million. However, in some other literature it is 10 million (Bekele, 2005). In 1950s New York was the only megacity with the population over 10 million. However, number of megacities reached 23 in the year 2000. Beijing, Bangkok, Tokyo, Calcutta, Jakarta are few examples of Asian megacities. These cities improve economically as well as increase in population. Megacities have highest level of economy, health care, education, and other services. Megacities also control the small cities and towns. However, megacities are the source of several environmental issues, air pollution, water pollution, noise pollution, visual pollution, etc. Lot of crimes and narcotic problems often occur in the suburbs of the megacity. Adapted from (Bekele, 2005).

Following problems causes urbanization- urban sprawl- settlements

8.3 Urbanization-urban sprawl-settlements due to population explosion

According to a case study on population growth and its impact on urban expansion in Bahawalpur, Pakistan(Khan, Arshad, & Mohsin, 2014), it has been evidenced that in Pakistan urban areas are expanding than rural counterparts due to both natural increase and rural-urban migration. The urban area has increased from 590 acres to 11,500 acres between the years 1951 and 2012 whereas, the population has increased from 41,646 to 5,60,588. The expansion of urban areas reached its peak from 1960 to 1970 (maximum of 27% urban change). At present, the population is increasing, and developments such as road construction and widening, residential built-up, commercial rise, and industrial expansion are taking place. Also, a saturation of the city has reached the stage of urban sprawl, over 25 squatters also contributing to urban sprawl. Thus, local municipal authorities are now facing several challenges mainly related to services such as solid waste management, wastewater management, water supply, and urban transportation management.

8.4 Land degradation- sedimentation- soil erosion causes or due to urbanization-urban sprawl-settlements

According to Babiker (Babiker, 1982), in the arid region of Sudan desertification leads to rural-urban migration of the population. The results of overcrowding of population in town, negative over–urbanization diseconomies imposed more pressure

209

on the natural resources, such as in the immediate hinterland of urban centers leads to deforestation, soil erosion, and depletion of water resources. This situation further accelerates the desertification process (figure 8.1), for instance, Khartoum the largest urban centre in Sudan underwent rapid urbanization and ended up in intensified desert conditions.

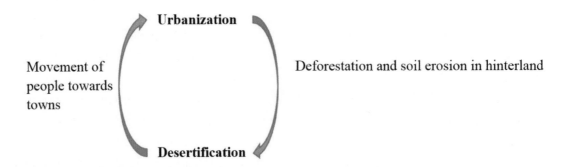

Figure 8.1 Urbanization and Deforestation in Sudan occur cyclically, as one causes another

According to Esetlili, Kurucu, Turk, & Ozen(Esetlili, Kurucu, Turk, & Ozen, 2016), over the last 26 years in coastal areas of Izmir, population increase causes rapid urbanization mainly due to migration, commercial development such as industry, residential growth, and tourism. This is followed by severe damage to natural resources such as agricultural soils, forests, and foraging lands, resulted in rural unemployment, as well as the creation of economic and ecological problems. More importantly, the native population of farmers is replaced by a population of individuals who are employed in tourism, and individuals who no longer preserve aesthetic values. Besides, the new population demands the improvement of urban requirements such as housing and infrastructure, with no specific regard to nature. A study on land-use changes in coastal areas of the Izmir region, which are under rapid growth in the period between 1984 and 2011 using aerial and satellite images taken over this period, depicted a considerable expansion of the urban areas. Up to 552,481 and 439% increase has been observed in the coastal districts of Cesme, Karaburun, Foca, respectively due to tourism, the establishment of new industrial regions, increase in marine transportation, secondary residences, etc. Expansion of Aliaga district from 780 to 3580 ha. and this showed a total increase of 459%. Furthermore, losses in agricultural lands of this area depicted 1497 ha. of land area in the I and II land use capability class LUCC and 10,597 ha. in the III and IV LUCC (table8.1).

Table 8.1 Land use or Land cover changes in areas

LUCC	Area (ha.)
I	7914
II	7060
III	4732
IV	5865
V	7080
VI	6197
VII	203
Total	39,052

Source: (Esetlili, Kurucu, Turk, & Ozen, 2016)

According to Xue-li, Ya-lin, & Bu-li(Xue-li, Ya-lin, & Bu-li, 2007), in a study relationship between urbanization and desertification has been examined using RS, GIS, and GPS techniques and statistical data from 1987 to 2003 in Kubuqi desert. As per the results, urbanization levels of Dalate Banner depicted a gradual increase from 9.1% to 19.1% from 1987 to 2003. Also, the highest increasing trend of urbanization was observed after 1998. The urbanization level of the yearly average increase ratio was 0.7% and higher than 0.53% of that before. However, the changing trend of the degree of desertification was decreased from 0.269 to 0.214 in this period. The changing trend was induced by area fluctuation of semi-mobile and semi-fixed dunes because 2.6% area of semi-mobile dunes and 12.3% area of semi-fixed dunes were unchangeable during the period from 1987 to 1995. Furthermore, the most changeable area of the semi-mobile and the semi-fixed dunes is transferred to other sand-dune types and cropland. Besides, analysis of the relationship between urbanization and desertification depicted that there was a significant linear relation in

211

the 0.05 level when the urbanization levels were less than 14%. But there was no significant relationship when the urbanization levels were over 14%. Thus, the study concluded that urbanization and its impact on desertification have a period character in the semi-arid region of northern China.

Urbanization- urban sprawl- settlements effects into following problems

8.5 Solid waste related problems due to urbanization-urban sprawl-settlements

According to the survey of Federation of Indian Chambers of Commerce and Industry (FICCI Report, 2009), on the current status of waste management in Indian cities, which includes small cities such as Shimla, which generates 65 TPD (Tonnes Per Day) to Delhi, which generates 6,800 TPD depicted that cities where the rate of urbanization is high, rate of waste generation also high such as Chandigarh and cities where the rate of urbanization is low, rate of waste generation low such as Shimla, this clearly shows the **direct link between urbanization and waste generation** (Vij, 2012). Furthermore, based on the quantity of waste generated cities can be classified such as cities that generate a large quantum of waste more than 1000 TPD of municipal solid waste e.g. Ahmedabad, Delhi, Greater Mumbai, Jaipur, Kanpur, Lucknow, Pune, and Surat. The cities those generate municipal solid waste between 500 and 1000 TPD e.g. Ludhiana and Vadodara; and cities that generate less than 500 TDP of municipal solid waste e.g. Agartala, Asansol, Chandigarh, Faridabad, Guwahati, Jamshedpur, Kochi, Kozhikode, Mangalore, Mysore, and Shimla (table 8.2). {Adapted from (Vij, 2012)}

Table 8.2 Waste generation trends in India

Year	Per capita waste generation (g/day)	Total urban municipal waste generation (MT/ yr.)
1971	375	14.9
1981	430	25.1
1991	460	43.5
1997	490	48.5
2025	700	Double the amount of 1997

Source: India Energy Portal (FICCI Report, 2009)

However, study (FICCI Report, 2009), showed there is an inadequate allocation of dumpsites, which is regardless of the quantity of waste handled in the cities. For instance, cities that generate more than 1000 TPD have single dump sites, whereas cities generate less than 450 TPD have two dumpsites, e.g. Asansol, Faridabad, and Jamshedpur. Also, it was depicted in the results that Greater Mumbai and Ludhiana supplies the entire quantum of waste to their dumpsites, whereas cities such as Vadodara, Jaipur, Pune, Surat, Kanpur, Ahmedabad, and Delhi supply 80-90% of waste to their dumpsites. City Indore supplies 54% of waste to its dumpsite. However, some cities such as Lucknow supplies 1050 TPD waste for disposal, but it lacks dedicated dumpsite, and the waste spread on the outskirts of the city center. Furthermore, the study also revealed that there is an inadequate number of sanitary landfills in Indian cities. Out of 22 surveyed cities, only 6 have sanitary landfills, e.g. Ahmedabad, Chandigarh, Jamshedpur, Mangalore, Surat, and Vadodara. Even large cities such as Greater Mumbai, Delhi, and Kanpur lack sanitary landfills (FICCI Report, 2009).

It was also revealed that improper planning and inadequate exploration of other vital options such as composting and waste to energy plants amplifies the effects of urbanization in this regard. However, during this survey, several municipal councils have accepted that they lack technology, manpower, and funds to handle the increasing quantity of waste. In semi-urban areas and rural towns, this is even worse as they have more public open dumping sites (road site garbage) that create more health problems as well.

According to Muneera & Kaleel (Muneera & Kaleel, 2016), in Kalmunai, Eastern Sri Lanka, urbanization caused several problems, primarily solid waste disposal (figure 8.2). Most of the solid wastes generated here are ended up in landfills or dumps. In Kalmunai municipal area, about 27 tons of waste produced every day, and of that, only 50% are collected, and the remaining wastes lie here and there in the neighborhood and pollute the environment. In the past, there were a lot of freely available degraded lands where the waste can accommodate, but rapid urbanization caused land scarcity in the region. Thus, waste handling has become an arduous task for the Kalmunai Municipal Council, and it also has been evidenced during recent years spreading of chronic diseases in a hike due to the unsanitary environment.

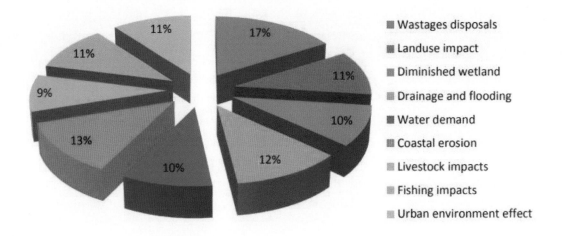

Figure 8.2 Impacts of urbanization in Kalmunai Municipal Council, Sri Lanka
Source: (Muneera & Kaleel, 2016)

8.6 Air pollution due to urbanization-urban sprawl-settlements

Please see chapter air pollution

8.7 Deforestation and destruction of mangroves and grasslands due to urbanization-urban sprawl-settlements

Please see chapter deforestation

8.8 Water pollution-water scarcity due to urbanization-urban sprawl-settlements

Please see chapter water pollution-water scarcity-salinization

8.9 Visual pollution due to urbanization-urban sprawl-settlements

It has been realized that environmental graphics (visual pollution) in Nigeria embarrassed city planning as erection of billboards, posters, city traffic, waste disposal, and other constructions cause an eyesore. It also affects the reputation of the city (Bankole, 2013). According to Durotoye (Durotoye, 1998) as cited in (Bankole, 2013), mainly in developing countries, visual pollution is closely associated with urbanization (figure 8.3 and figure 8.4).

214

Figure 8.3 Visual pollution in an Indian urban area
Source: (Hogue, n.d.)
License: CC0

Figure 8.4 Visual pollution Times Square, New York
Source: (Jean-Christophe, 2012)
License: CC BY 3.0

8.10 Noise and vibration pollution due to urbanization-urban sprawl-settlements

According to Singal (Singal, 2005) as cited in ("Noise Solutions", 2015), it has been evidenced that in the days of Julius Cesar, the annoying clatter of horse-drawn chariots on the Cobblestone streets of Rome was considered a source of noise pollution that caused discomfort to the residents. Thus, the relationship between urbanization-urban sprawl-settlements and noise and vibration pollution are well understood since ancient times.

In a study on noise levels associated with urban land use(King, Mieszkowski, Jason, & Rainham, 2012), the effects of the urban environment and land use on levels of environmental noise was examined on two selected different urban study locations based on a combination of small area census geography, land use information, air photography, and ground-truthing. The first location consists of residential lands with several two to three-storied houses, and the second location was characterized by mixed urban lands such as apartments and commercial institutions. Both locations were sub-divided into six grids, and each grid was sampled four times over a 24h day, resulted in a total of 24 samples from each of the two locations. Results depicted that both locations exceeded recommended noise limits when compared with World Health Organization guidelines and yielded average noise events values in the moderate to serious annoyance range with the potential to obscure normal conversation or lead to sleep disturbance.

A survey (Oloruntoba, et al., 2012), using a structured questionnaire aiming to assess the sources, noise levels, and possible impacts in selected residential neighborhood groups in

215

Ibadan, Nigeria depicted that noise levels, sources, and the period the noise level reaches its peak vary with population density and were shown on GIS maps. The mean noise values of the three residential neighborhood groups were low density (LD): 53.10±2.80dB, medium-density (MD): 68.45± 2.10dB, and high density (HD): 68.36±1.92dB, where the medium density neighborhood group had the highest mean value. However, there is a significant difference in noise levels in three neighborhood groups (F value=11.88 and p=0.000). Differences in noise levels between HD/LD and LD/MD areas were significant (p=0.000), while between HD/MD areas was insignificant (p=0.975). In the survey, the highest noise level 85.80dB was recorded at Bere junction, and the lowest noise level was recorded at Bowers tower at Oke Are (48.65dB). However, according to WHO 16-hour DNL criteria of 55dB for residential areas, only 16 (23.2%) neighborhood groups had noise values within the WHO recommended limit. A recent WHO study found that Guangzhou in china has the worst noise pollution, seconded by Delhi, while Zurich in Switzerland had the least noise pollution ("KNOPS", 2017).

8.11   Light pollution due to urbanization-urban sprawl-settlements

A study using a calibrated satellite radiometer showed in the period between 2012 and 2016 earth's artificially lit outdoor area grew by 2.2% every year, with total radiance growth of 1.8% year-1. However, only a few countries depicted differences in nocturnal growth rates with lighting remains stable or decreasing (Kyba, et al., 2017).

A study using a false-color image of polarization on a night sky with moon showed that a clear pattern of lunar polarization was observable in rural or outside the Berlin city and in the Berlin cityit was not visible. Similar to sunlight, the moonlight also produces a celestial compass that stretches across the sky, and some nocturnal animals have the ability to use these patterns for their navigation. But, anthropogenic light pollution in urban cities unpolarized this natural moonlight, thus, urbanization increases light pollution (Kyba, Ruhtz, Fischer, & Hölker, 2011).

8.12   Disease due to urbanization-urban sprawl-settlements

According to Acuto (Acuto, 2020), the COVID-19 pandemic affected many of the urban cities all over the world, which was originated in Wuhan city of China in December 2019.According to Hamidi, Ewing, & Sabouri (Hamidi, Ewing, & Sabouri, 2020), a study investigated the impacts of development density on the spread and mortality rates of COVID-19 in metropolitan areas in the United States using the Multilevel Linear Modeling (MLM) technique revealed that large metropolitan size (higher population) leads to significantly higher COVID-19 infection rates and higher mortality rates.

According to Iram, Rasool, Shahzad, & Saeed (Iram, Rasool, Shahzad, & Saeed, 2012), a survey (semi-structured interview) on the relationship between urban sprawl and public health conducted in Ravi Town, Lahore, Pakistan depicted, among 120 respondents, about 82.5% stated that lack of physical activity caused overweight 90% of them stated that overweight increases the risk of various disease and high extent of people was sad and in a high possibility of being affected by mental illnesses (Table 8.3 and Table 8.4). Besides, studies also noted a high prevalence of diarrhea, malaria, and obesity in the urban society in Ravi Town, Lahore.

Table 8.3 Urban sprawl effects on physical health

Statements	Not at All		To Some Extent		To Great Extent	
	f	%	f	%	f	%
Lack of physical activity is the risk factor for being overweight	06	05	15	12.5	99	82.5
Overweight is a well established risk factor for a number of diseases	00	00	12	10	108	90

Source: (Iram, Rasool, Shahzad, & Saeed, 2012)

Table 8.4 Mental Health Problems Faced by Urban Sprawl

Statements	Not at All		To Some Extent		To Great Extent	
	f	%	f	%	f	%
Worthlessness due to segregation from the main city	00	00.0	51	42.5	69	57.5
Sadness due to low social connections	00	00.0	45	37.5	75	62.5
Hopelessness due to low connectivity from the people	06	05.0	42	35.0	72	60.0

Source: (Iram, Rasool, Shahzad, & Saeed, 2012)

8.13   E-waste due to urbanization-urban sprawl-settlements

According to Lu and others (Lu, et al., 2015), in China from 2000 to 2012 amount of e-waste collected and dismantled, and the growth rate of five major electronic equipment types depicted a steep increase along with urbanization.

8.14   Hazardous waste due to urbanization-urban sprawl-settlements

Study (Elliott & Frickel, 2013)investigated the accumulation of hazardous waste over time and space during urbanization. Data collected from a dataset containing geospatial and organisational information on more than 2800 hazardous manufacturing sites operating in the period between 1956 and 2006 in Portland, Oregon. The study also compared the data with historical data from the U.S. population census and Oregon Department of Environmental Quality (DEQ) and examined the records on the hazardous waste accumulation in those urban regions.

The study recorded historical heavy metal contamination and dumping into the Columbia River floodplain (1957-1969) and on-site after 1969. However, subsequently, about 900 tons of contaminated soil and sludge were remediated, treated, and disposed into the offsite landfill. Today, about 69% of such hazardous sites were converted into non-hazardous commercial enterprises. However, in Portland over recent decades numbers of small producers have increased, and the transformation happened both inside and outside of the historic industrial zones resulted in an expansion in the cumulative land area they transformed. Thus, the study has shown that "the churning of hazardous manufactures across a growing number of urban parcels over time".

8.15   Global energy crisis due to Urbanization

Please see the chapter global energy crisis

8.16   Overexploitation of natural resources due to urbanization-urban sprawl-settlements

Please see the chapter over exploitation of natural resources

8.17   Plastic pollution due to population explosion

8.18   Plastic pollution due to urbanization-urban sprawl-settlements

(8.17 and 8.18 are merged into following epic)

Population plays one of the major roles in plastic pollution. Across many low and middle-income countries, countries such as South Asia and Sub-Saharan Africa, 80-90% of plastic waste is inadequately disposed of and polluting rivers and oceans(Ritchie & Roser, 2018).Also, the population in South Asia and Sub-Saharan Africa also relatively high as South Asia depicted a population of 1,899 million in 2018,24.78% share of the world population, and Sub Saharan Africa showed a population of 1,050 million in 2018, 14.00% share of the world population, respectively. Thus, it seemed that there is a possible linkage between population increase and the amount of mismanaged plastic garbage. A study documented an increasing trend in plastic consumption in India, however, it did not show any significant correlation between the population increase and plastic consumption (as plastic consumption showed a steeper increase, whereas population growth depicted a steady increase in the periods of 1975-1985 and 1990-2000). Also, many countries ban plastic bags and Styrofoam (single-use plastics), and many developing countries have now established several plastic recycling facilities. Besides, countries such as Indonesia provide incentives as they swap plastic bottles for bus rides (in 2018).

However, according to "Earth eclipse"("Earth eclipse", n.d.), increasing urbanization and population growth is a significant drive for plastic pollution because of the increasing population demand for cheaper and readily available materials increases. In the first decade of this century, more plastics were produced than any other time in history, and this is due to rapid urbanization. Furthermore, it was stated that in many urban regions, plastic comprises a greater part of landfills and constitutes about 80% of all municipal waste. Thus, it is possible to conclude that the linkage of plastic pollution with population increase and urbanization is true.

8.19 Global warming and climate change due to urbanization-urban sprawl-settlements

According to UN-Habitat, 60% of the global greenhouse emission is from urban cities (Climate Action Summit, 2019), or 60% of man-made global warming is due to urban cities. Urban dwellers continuously depend on fossil fuels, and this makes urban populations are highly responsible and vulnerable to global climate change. The report further added that by 2050 another 2.5 billion people will reside in urban areas and nearly 90% of them in cities in Asia and Africa.

8.20 Biodiversity loss due to urbanization-urban sprawl-settlements

According to Forys & Allen (Forys & Allen, 2005), a study on the relationship between sprawl and biodiversity, using data collected from ant species in 46 different habitat patches found in highly suburbanized Florida Keys, the USA depicted that sprawl affects the species composition by increasing the rate of invasion by non-native species and decreasing number of native species. Urban sprawl was quantified by the proximity of roads and the amount of development surrounding a habitat patch. Also, 24 native and 18 non-native ant species were observed using the bait transects. It was evidenced that native ant species of Florida Keys did not appear to be influenced by the sprawl, however, increasing development activities caused an increase in non-native ant species and many of them have been decreasing the native ant fauna. Furthermore, if development plateaus, the native ant species could persist and could decrease the non-native ant population through competition and predation.

According to Blair (Blair , 2001) as cited in (Mckinney, 2002), urban development replaces the native species that are lost with widespread distribution of "weedy" non-native species, and this process is constituted by a process called biotic homogenization. It was noted in Mckinney (Mckinney, 2002)that increasing fragmentation of natural habitat by anthropogenic disturbances in the direction toward urban centers will reduce the richness of biodiversity.

This is a very generalized and simplified depiction of changes in surface area, species richness, and composition, as compiled from several sources discussed in the text. Two basic conservation strategies concerning urban sprawl are shown at the top(Mckinney,

2002). According to Blair (Blair , 2001) as cited in (Mckinney, 2002), a study on bird diversity along the urban-rural gradient used certain categories such as "urban avoider", "urban adapters" and "urban exploiters". It was also mentioned that even in highly modified environments species are non-randomly assembled in ways that approximate the community assembly process in nature, and each of these assemblages has a distinct set of ecological characters that reflect the impacts of urban sprawl on native species and one of the main traits that involved in the separation of three categories is the extent which species depend on human subsidized resources to exist in an area (Johnston , 2001) as cited in (Mckinney, 2002).

8.21 Coral destruction and bleach due to urbanization-urban sprawl-settlements

According to Baum, Januar, Ferse, & Kunzmann(Baum, Januar, Ferse, & Kunzmann, 2015), growing urbanization, industrialization, and coastal development exert multiple stressors on coral reefs. Reefs in Thousand Islands off the coast of Jakarta, one of the largest megacities worldwide, have degraded dramatically over recent decades. The study says urbanization plays a major role in changing the bay environment in Jakarta, and this is seconded by agriculture and aquaculture. Over 80% of the variation in benthic community composition is due to sedimentation rate, NO_2, PO_4, and Chlorophyll a.

8.22 Urbanization-urban sprawl-settlements causes draining of wetland

According to Davis & Froend (Davis & Froend, 1999), about 70% of the wetlands have been lost in the coastal region of Southwestern Australia since British settlement (in 1829), mostly due to infilling or drainage of wetlands to create lands for agriculture and urban development. It was stated that infilling or drainage of wetlands to create land for agriculture or urban development. Australia's urban sprawl is at least partly responsible, it is expected many of the residents of Perth and the small cities and towns in southwestern Australia will live in single dwellings on areas of land ranging from 0.2 to many ha., resulted from direct loss of wetlands through draining and infilling.

According to Mao and others (Mao, et al., 2018), in the period between 1990 and 2010 (20 years) China has lost 2,883 km^2 of wetlands to urbanization. The rate of urbanization or wetland loss was 2.8 times higher in the period from 2000 to 2010 (213 km^2 $year^{-1}$) than between 1990 and 2000 (75 km^2 yr^{-1}). Most of the lands were lost due to urban built-up areas than industrial or transportation lands. Reservoirs, ponds, and marshes were severely degraded. However, it has been expected in the next few decades urban expansion mainly in middle and small-sized cities and urban traffic networks will about to encroach most of the wetlands.

According to United Nations ("UN.org", 2018), today 55% of the world population lives in urban areas, and by 2050 68% of the world population is projected to live in urban areas. The human population has utilized lands for various developmental needs, intense urbanization converts rural and untouched wild habitat areas into more intense use areas such as towns and cities. However, every human occupational role such as agriculture, fisheries, hunting, gathering, poultry, dairy, food, and beverage industry, textiles, fibre, leather, steel, energy, product manufacturing, transportation, and waste management faces the environmental challenges which cannot be combated in the absence of biodiversity and ecosystem services. Anthropogenic urban sprawl results, nuclear proliferation, war, global warming, coral mining, poaching, ozone depletion, acid rain, overexploitation (e.g. overfishing), ocean acidification, heavy metal pollution, noise pollution, generation of toxic gases and chemicals, garbage generation, and improper dumping, sewage, oil spills, heavy metal pollution, spreading of carcinogenic pollutants, habitat destruction including deforestation, destruction of mangroves, invasive species, intense sand mining, and desertification all threaten surrounding environment and continuity of life on earth. Also, pandemic diseases such as COVID 19 affected urban cities, e.g., Wuhan, New York, Ahmedabad, and Gujarat.

Besides, urbanization-urban sprawl-settlements causes solid waste and sewage, air pollution, water pollution and scarcity, visual pollution, deforestation, light pollution, noise and vibration pollution, global energy crisis, draining of wetland and biodiversity loss. If it is possible to find a clear solution for urbanization and urban sprawl, then most of the environmental problems such as solid waste and sewage, air pollution, water pollution and scarcity, visual pollution (by man-made structures), light pollution, noise and vibration pollution, global energy crisis, draining of wetlands, deforestation (almost) and biodiversity loss (to a certain extent) could be eliminated. Indirect links such as climate change and global warming may be reduced (fig. 8.5).

Evidence 1: Urbanisation-urban sprawl-settlements causes Global energy crisis

According to UN-Habitat, urban cities consume 78% of the world's energy (Climate Action Summit, 2019). If this relationship is statistically significant in an imaginary situation where there is no urbanization or urban cities, then 78% of the causes of the energy crisis would have been solved.

Evidence 2: Urbanisation-urban sprawl-settlements causes air pollution

According to UN-Habitat, 60% of the global greenhouse emission is from urban cities (Climate Action Summit, 2019).

Evidence 3: Urbanisation-urban sprawl-settlements causes man-made global warming and climate change

60% of man-made global warming is due to urban cities, as 60% of greenhouse gas emission is from cities(Climate Action Summit, 2019).However, in reality, removing keystone links is not possible due to the presence of human adaptability factors such as economic, social, political, health, genetics, evolution, and behavioural factors (Mandal, 2010).

Evidence 4: Urbanisation-urban sprawl-settlements causes light pollution

According to "energy.gov"("energy.gov", 2013), at 4.00 PM on August 14, 2003, Midwest and Northeast United States and Canada experienced a cascading power cut which prolonged for four days. About 50 million people were affected by the event. However, they were able to see the clear night sky in the absence of light pollution. Even now the clean sky is observable in abandoned cities in California where urban city living is no more. According to "darksky.org"("darksky.org", 2016), 80% of the world's population lives under a sky glow. In the USA and Europe, 99% of the people cannot see the natural night sky. USA and Europe have converted regions of the world from cities to megacities with a huge urban network. Thus, if urbanization disappears, the light pollution also will disappear.

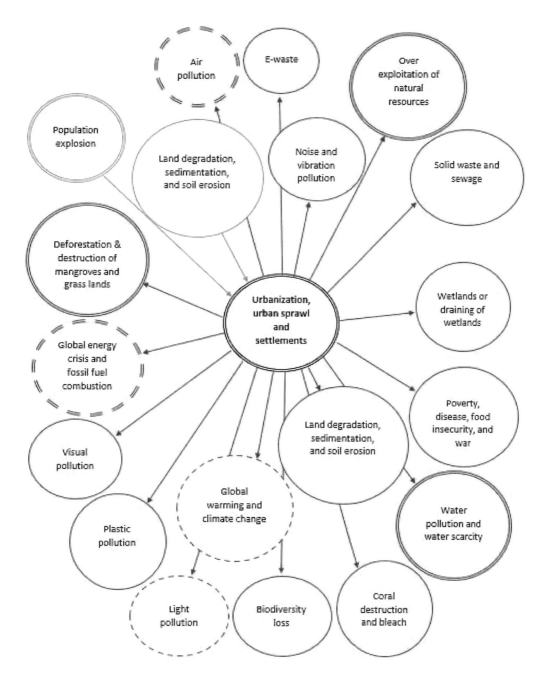

Figure 8.5 Urbanization-urban sprawl-settlements as keystone environmental problems with the disappearance of air pollution, global energy crisis, and light pollution on its mitigation (hypothetical diagram).

[In the figure black circle is the problem being examined, blue circles are cause man-made environmental problems, red circles are effect man-made environmental problems, double lined circles are keystone man-made environmental problems, and circles with dashed lines (either single or double lined) are the man-made environmental problems that disappear when the problem being examined (black circle) is mitigated]

Reconciliatory vs. Sustainable vs. Conventional solutions

There is **no regenerative** solution found for plastic pollution caused by urbanization (Figure 8.6). Yet using traditional and aboriginal product alternatives for plastics is the **reconciliatory** solution e.g., using natural fibre craft bags knitted from the bark of the cane plant instead of plastic bags, urban forestry by planting mangroves and mangrove associates along the coast with plastic free zone is a **restorative** solution.

Banning single-use plastic and switching to biodegradable alternatives is a **sustainable** solution because, according to the definition of sustainable development stated in the 1987 Brundtland commission report, "development that meets the needs of the present without compromising the ability of future generations to meet their needs" could be considered sustainable development, and it produces net zero impact on the environment (neither increment nor degradation to sentient beings). As of 2023, over 100 countries have imposed a partial or full ban on single-use plastic with varying degrees of enforcement (Elton, 2023). However, sustainable solutions are often very expensive due to their high energy requirements, as the manufacturing or importation cost of plastic alternatives such as cellulose-based bags may be relatively high, and there will be an immediate need for technology and advanced machinery. Thus, it is very difficult for developing and least developed countries to switch from plastics immediately. And unlike smart regenerative solutions, they cannot adapt to or co-evolve with nature; they cannot affirm well-being; and they depict relatively low systemic vitality. **Greener** solutions depict minimal harm to the environment and sentient beings, e.g., reduce, reuse, recycle, redesign, upcycle, have extended producer responsibility (EPR), a deposit refund scheme (DRS), incentives, and penalties. **Conventional** solutions are merely a step ahead of pollution, such as waste-to-energy, source-level categorization and segregation, beach clean-ups, enabling waste bins in required locations, including public transportation, sensitizing the public via billboards, educating through awareness programmes, and screening floating plastics at river deltas and canals. Here, clean-up programmes provide a temporary relief, source-level categorization and segregation aid in waste management, but they never stop the pollution, and waste-to-energy projects disguised as smart generate harmful gases and ash remains; thus, it is mandated for the system to use scrubbers and air purifiers and safe disposal of fly ash and bottom ash.

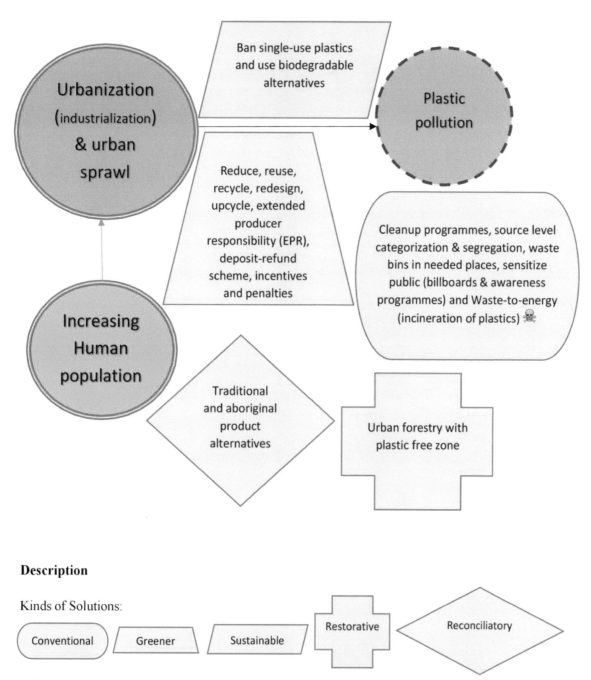

Description

Kinds of Solutions:

Conventional Greener Sustainable Restorative Reconciliatory

Figure 8.6 Solutions to urbanization-urban sprawl-settlements

Black circle: problem under concern, Blue circle: cause, Red circle: effect, Double lined circle: keystone environmental problem, Single lined circle: environmental problem, Dotted lined circle: problem to be mitigated when keystone environmental problem get solved, Black arrow: cause-effect link for which solutions are given, Blue arrow: cause-effect link N.B.: - Each problem in the circles is connected to many other problems on the basis of cause and effect links, and they are not shown here.

9. Population explosion

9.1 Introduction to Population crisis

Increasing human population is a threat to the nature, environment, wildlife and entire biodiversity, as the population increases human needs increase, consumption of natural resources increases, it leads to deforestation, loss of natural habitats and species extinction, animal abuse and cruelty, decline in non-renewable resources such as minerals and fuel (energy crisis), air, water and land pollution or degradation, global warming or climate change, deficiency in drinking water and food (insufficiency of cultivable land), famine, war and social unrest, terrorism and disasters (fig. 9.1).

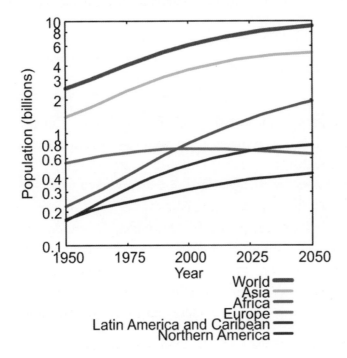

Figure 9.1 World population 1950-2050

Source: (donarreiskoffer & casito, 2005), License: CC BY-SA 3.0

Global population has now reached to approximately 7.3 billion; it is expected to reach 8 billion by 2024; this will increase the pressure on every human being, it is difficult to estimate how many can sustain on the earth as individual preference to obtain a wealthy and happy life differs. In addition, everyone wants to enjoy more space to live and lots of resources such as food, cloths, vehicles, stationeries, tools, instruments, machines and utensils to fulfil their needs, this cannot be provided unless the number of individuals has declined. However, in the past with low number of individuals resources were well-managed and preserved, renewable resources have sufficient time to re-establish after the human consumption, thus. there was a peaceful interaction found among human beings and nature, this is now collapsed and resulted in competition for resources, depletion of renewable resources and lacking of non-renewable resources, man is pushed into a machine life in order to seek even his own needs, increasing greed towards wealthy life causes destruction of several natural resources which are essential to ascertain the continuity of life in this planet. Hunger, malnutrition and poverty still prevail in several underdeveloped and developing countries. It is important to consider that the growth rate of food production is declining faster than growth rate of population.

Increasing population causes deforestation which leads to loss of valuable genes, water regulators, flood controllers, watersheds, protectors of inland and coastal fisheries and climate stabilizers. This also leads to destruction of mineral cycles and several food chains which are essential to keep the environment unchanged. As mentioned by Paul Ehrlich in Population Explosion I=PAT, which means I: - impact in the environment equals population multiplied by the A: - affluence (the amount of energy and food supply the population consumes) multiplied by the amount of destructive T: - technology a country has, thus with increasing population there are impacts on the environment. More people need more space, more food from agriculture, fisheries, poultry and meat, more jobs, more vehicles, more energy, more water supply, more infrastructures such as apartments, shopping malls, factories, industries, more roads, rail roads and highways, hospitals, schools, play grounds, etc., this result in more pollution, more land degradation, more waste generation, more deforestation, more greenhouse gas emission and global warming, ozone depletion, more spreading of epidemics, more animal abuse and killing for meat, more acid rain and more chances for disasters such as radiation emission from nuclear power reactors, more chances for hazardous chemical discharge, oil spills, more excavation of soil and minerals cause more deadly landslides, increased terrorism and war.

In human history First revolution(cultural revolution) was occurred in 100,000 ago during the time of Ice Age when man lived as hunter gatherer, human had more culturally expanded communities than earlier human forms. Food supply increases, resulting dramatic increase in population. By the end of Ice Age human population was about 5 million (Ehrlich & Ehrlich, 1990). Second revolution was around 8000 B.C., which is agricultural revolution, here man was able to cultivate their crop at desired location, agriculturists develop villages and town, population starts rising. However, there were certain setbacks such as Black Death (1346-1353) a bubonic plaque killed around 75-200 million people in europe.In 1650s, the world's population reached 500 million, then in 1760, the industrial revolution (third revolution) begins, this deeply changes the human life style, as the fossil fuel replaced the wood, wind and water, improvements found in fields such as medicine, economy and sanitation, by the year 1800 the hypothetical human population reached one billion, in the beginning of 19th century machines replaced human employees, this led to further improvement in the social status and standard of living in Europe and North America, by the year 1900 the global population was reached to 1.6 billion, and hit 2 billion by 1927(100% increase), and from 1943 green revolution (fourth revolution) it further sky rocketed and during the 20th century it was boomed steeply to 6 billion

(400% increase in just 100 years). This exponential growth led to high consumption of natural resources and manmade resources, this brought environmental problems such as deforestation, soil degradation and erosion, air water and land pollution, green house gas emission, waste accumulation, increased demand for fresh water etc. In addition, there are 0.01 and 0.1% of all species become extinct each year (if 0.01% is true: 200-2000 and if 0.1% is true: 10,000-100,000 species become extinct annually)("wwf.panda.org", 2016). Further more, urban sprawl causes habitat destruction, invasive species , increased pollutants and negative effects on human health such as obesity, stress and hypertension.

9.2 Causes of Over Population

General causes of over population are increased birth rate, increased longevity, reduced infant mortality, decreased death rate, lack of education, cultural and religious oppose on birth control, in case of a particular country, immigration also causes over population.

(Adapted from ("ukessays.com", 2016)

9.3 Theories on population

A. Malthusian

Thomas Robert Malthus in principles of population (1978), he pointed out that because of the strong attraction of two sexes population could increase by multiples, population doubles every 25 years, though population increase geometrically/ exponentially (1,2,4,8,16,32,64,128,256) the subsistence form the land increase in arithmetic progression (1,2,3,4,5,6,7,8,9) thus, even food supply increases, that is insufficient to meet the needs of expanding population. Furthermore, famine and other natural calamities cause wide spread suffering and increase the death rate which is nature's check against population. At Malthus's time in early nineteenth century hypothetical global population was one billion and he predicted it would increase to 256 billion within 200 years as the population growth is exponential but to feed them, subsistence were only capable to increase up to nine billion as the resources grow arithmetically, this brings the future generation into struggle for limited resources, therefore the population increase should be kept down by the operation of various checks such as preventive and positive checks. Preventive checks are moral restraint or sexual abstinence or strict celibacy, abortion, infanticide, marry later in life (he was clearly aware that problems could come by postponing marriages such as illegitimate births but he thought those problems are less serious compare to the one that could arise by increasing population). However, Malthus strongly opposed to birth control (as he is from Christian background), he did not suggest that parents should try to restrict the number of children born to them. He also pointed out positive checks, that any causes that contribute to shortening of human life span such as poor living and working conditions that could give rise to diseases, epidemics, war and famine. He urged strong government action to ascertain late marriages.

B. Karl Marx

According to him population increase must be controlled by capitalist economy. As capitalist gives the labour the wage which is a small share of labour's productivity, lion share is pocketed by capitalist and capitalists also introduce machinery which also creates unemployment and reserved labours, thus the wages may go down further, poor parents cannot afford to have many children. Positive checks such as poverty, hunger and social ills affect the population growth. He further suggested the landlordism, unfavourable and high man-land ratio and uncertainties regarding land tenure system are responsible for low food production in the country. Only where the food production is inadequate, the population growth becomes a problem.

C. Neo-Malthusian- pessimistic view (Paul Ehrlich)

In 1968 world population reaches above 3 billion. Paul Ehrlich authored a book 'Population Bomb' stated that rate of population growth was outstripping agricultural growth and the capacity for renewal of Earth's resources; he also predicted certain demographic disasters in response to eventual food shortages and diseases. He added the battle to feed all of humanity is over, in the 1970s and 1980s hundreds of millions of people will starve to death in spite of any crash programs, he suggested that industrialized nations such as North America and Europe would need to undertake mild food rationing as starvation spreads on developing countries such as Asia, Latin America, and Africa. He predicted lack of food security in developing world would lead to thermonuclear war. Paul Ehrlich's population theory consists three major elements; they are a rapid rate of change, a limit of some sort, and delays in perceiving the limit.

Adapted from ("cgge.aag.org", 2011)

D. Boserup

Esther Boserup suggested that human innovation and technical advances would make the food production to keep up with the population growth. In her book "The Conditions of Agricultural Growth: The Economics of Agrarian Change under Population Pressure" she also pointed out agricultural intensification as a solution. Adapted from ("cgge.aag.org", 2011)

E. Julian Simon

He supports Boserup's view that humanity would innovate its way out of disaster in his book, as "We now have in our hands—really, in our libraries—the technology to feed, clothe, and supply energy to an ever-growing population for the next seven billion years." From: Simon along the State of Humanity: Steadily Improving in 1995(Malthus & Boserup, 2012).

F. The club of Rome

The club of Rome is composed of scientists, economists, businessmen, international high civil servants and statesmen of 10 countries. The Limits to growth was published in 1972, according to them if present growth trends in world population continues and if associated industrialization, pollution, food production and resource depletion continue unchanged, the limits to growth on this planet will be reached sometimes in next 100 years, most probably the results will be sudden and uncontrollable decline in both population and industrial capacity. However, it does not consider the human's ability to adapt and innovate such as use of alternative energy source (solar, electric cars), hybrid seeds, genetically modified varieties, etc.

9.4 Demographic Transition model

This model is based on historical trends in population characteristics such as birth rate and death rate. Both birth and death rates suggest country's total population growth rate cycles through stages as the country develops economically, each stage is characterized by a unique relationship between birth rate (number of yearly births per thousand people) and death rate (number of yearly deaths per thousand people). As each (birth rate and death rate) changes in relation to each other, their impacts greatly affect total global population. Based on the pattern of birth and death rate every country can be placed in the model at relevant stage, with the socioeconomic development country's position can be changed within the model(Grover, 2014).

Stage 1. It is applicable to most of the world prior to industrial revolution; both birth rate and death rate are high, thus population remains fairly constant but have major swings during the events such as wars or pandemics.

Stage 2. After the introduction of modern medicine, death rate gets lower at this stage (mainly among children), while birth rate remains high resulting in rapid population growth e.g. least developed countries such as Ethiopia

Stage 3. Birth rate decreases gradually, usually at increased economy, increased women's status and access to contraception, population growth continues at a low rate e.g. developing countries such as India, Sri Lanka and Brazil

Stage 4. Both birth and death rates are low, population get stabilized, countries do have strong economies, high level of education, better health care, high proportion of working women, fertility rate hovers around two children per woman, developed countries such as US and UK.

Stage 5. Fertility rate has fallen significantly below replacement level (2 children), elderly population is greater than the youth, and usually such countries often invite skilled immigrants to maintain their work force.

Limitations: there may be exceptions, other demographic variables (e.g. migration) are not considered. Source: (Grover, 2014)

9.5 Zero Population Growth

Kingsley Davis an American sociologist and demographer first coined the term zero population growth. Zero population growth occurs when birth rate and death rate become equivalent then the population remain constant. Generally, two child family policy would help to replace each parent by a single child. At present countries such as Cook Islands, Bulgaria, Montenegro, Estonia, Ukraine, Latvia, Russia, Portugal, Poland, Germany, Italy, China, Iceland, Japan, Ireland, Belgium, France, Luxembourg, Denmark, and Serbia are nearing this situation Adapted from ("buzzle.com", 2016).

9.6 Population control

Population control refers to the methods that are used to control or limit the type, location and number of people inhabits the earth. Methods are economic, administrative and educational which prevents the parents from having more children than needed (Watson, n.d.). Fertility is defined by factors such as socio-economic advancement, women's status, child mortality and family planning. When we consider socio economic advancement generally countries with high per capita growth national income has lower fertility rate, due to high women employment, education and family planning, however this is not always true, for instance, in case of Sri Lanka's fertility rate, which is 2.35 (2012) per capita GNI is US $ 3000 while in Qatar, its fertility rate around 2.1 and GNI is US$ 65,000. Low per capita income, low-level technology, inadequate savings and investments cause poverty. However, there are twice as many illiterate women as men in developing countries with poor employment, and owns less property than men and their rights, this place women more disadvantageous than men, thus, their personal preference and views on family planning is not accepted by the male dominant societies. In third world countries most of the women does not aware of contraception, still in some Middle East countries women education is prohibited. When considering the girls entering age sixteen or higher education, about 74% of them do not receive any formal financial education. An average girl receives 1.98 hours a week, compared to the 2.36 hours an average boy does receive. According to the 2013 UNESCO fact sheet there are 31 million girls of primary school age out of school, of these there are 17 million are expected never enter school, there are 4 million fewer boys than girls out of school, in Nigeria approximately five and a half million, Pakistan over three million and in Ethiopia over one million girls out of school, among adolescent girls there are 34 million out of school, almost quarter of young women aged 15-24 about 116 million in developing countries never completed primary school and lacking skills for work. Two third of the illiterate people are female (774 million), if all mothers completed primary education maternal deaths would be reduced by two third, which may save 98,000 lives and this will also reduce child death by 15%, 1.7 million children would be protected from malnutrition and 14% fewer child marriages. In case if all women had secondary education then the child death total get reduced to half, saving 3 million lives, 12 million children would be protected from malnutrition and there would be two-thirds fewer child marriages (table 9.1). In sub-Saharan Africa and South and West Asia 10% fewer girls become pregnant less than 17 years if all had primary education and almost 60% fewer girls would become pregnant less than 17 years if they had secondary education. Moreover, women with no education have an average of 6.7 births, which are 5.8 for those with primary education and 3.9 to those with secondary education ("en.unesco.org", 2013). Literature is one of the main positive factor influences reducing family size, education increases the chance of employment, in case of women improved social status and high income, greater the knowledge about modern contraceptive methods and family planning, it also delays the marriage or first pregnancy.

Table 9.1 women education in poorest countries

Percentage of poorest females aged 7-16 who have never been to school			Average years of education for the poorest 17-22-year-old females		
Rank	Country	%	Rank	Country	Years
1	Somalia	95	1	Somalia	0.3
2	Niger	78	2	Niger	0.4
3	Liberia	77	3	Mali	0.5
4	Mali	75	4	Guinea	0.5
5	Burkina Faso	71	5	Guinea-Bissau	0.8
6	Guinea	68	6	Yemen	0.8
7	Pakistan	62	7	Central African Republic	0.8
8	Yemen	58	8	Burkina Faso	0.9
9	Benin	55	9	Pakistan	1.0
10	Cote d'Ivoire	52	10	Benin	1.1

Source: ("en.unesco.org", 2013)

A. Contraceptive prevalence

Globally contraceptive prevalence is estimated as 64 % in 2015. Based on the country's developmental standard it greatly varies. Contraceptive prevalence among women of reproductive age who are married or in a union is 4 % in South Sudan and 88 % in Norway ("unpopulation.org", 2013). Based on 2011 data among 49 least developed countries 36% of married or in-union women are using contraceptive methods this level is twice as high as in other developing countries (about 66%), among developing countries contraceptive prevalence is about 50% or more (except sub-Saharan Africa: 25%) and in Melanesia,

Micronesia and Polynesia it is 37%.Over half of the 48 countries in sub-Saharan Africa it is below 30% (western and in the horn of Africa), however in Middle East and close related countries such as Afghanistan, Pakistan, Saudi Arabia, Tajikistan, Timor-Leste, the United Arab Emirates and Yemen it is below 30%, countries such as Anguilla, Dominica, Guatemala, Guyana, Haiti, Saint Kitts and Nevis, Saint Lucia, Suriname, and Trinidad and Tobago has contraceptive prevalence range between 30-50% but not below 30%. North America has the highest 75% contraceptive prevalence in the world followed by Latin America and Caribbean (73%) and Europe (70% except Bosnia, Herzegovina and Montenegro as contraceptive prevalence is less than 50%). However, in certain countries governments and/ or religious institutions are powerfully against the all form of abortions, it has been revealed by("wgo.int", 2016) that each year nearly 21.6 million women experience unsafe abortion, among this 18.5 million recorded in developing countries, about 47,000 women die due to complications of unsafe abortion annually this is close to 13% of all maternal deaths. High level of illegal and unsafe abortion is continuously prevailing in places where effective contraception is hardly available or not chosen, as no contraceptive is fool proof, however, this may be lack of awareness in poor countries strict societal or religious or government rules against safe legal abortion, this is also a reason behind high maternal death on this nature. Furthermore in some countries there is a moral opposition for the use of contraceptive methods, in Pakistan about 65% are against the use of contraception, this is 54% in Nigeria, 52% in Ghana and 40% in Malaysia. Adapted from ("unpopulation.org", 2013); ("wgo.int", 2016) and("un.org", 2015).

B. Planning parenthood

In United States every year about 1.94 million unintended pregnancies are prevented, this includes 400,000 teen pregnancies. According to a study in 2012 among 213 million pregnancies that occurred worldwide, about 85 million (40%) were unintended, thus such pregnancies often ended up in abortion, unplanned child birth and miscarriage ("guttmacher.org", 2014); ("healthypeople.gov", 2016) and ("guttmacher.org", 2015).

In order to the plan the parenthood it is essential to educate the women, men and youth with sexual and reproductive health education. Family planning comprised of birth spacing, family size and improving the health of infants, health of children, women and the whole family. This includes services such as contraceptive and associated reproductive health service including counselling, breast and pelvic examinations, breast and cervical cancer screening, sexually transmitted infection, AIDS prevention education, counselling, testing and referral, pregnancy diagnosis and counselling (Adapted from ("healthypeople.gov", 2016).Birth control methods help the women preventing unwanted pregnancy and regulating menstrual cycles. They are either reversible or irreversible methods, however among all the methods only male and female condoms provide protection against sexually transmitted infections (STI) (table 9.2).

Table 9.2 Birth control Methods

Reversible birth control methods				
Hormonal methods				
Method	**Function**	**Prescription/ application**	**Age or other recommendations**	**Efficiency**
Birth control pill	Estrogen & progestin- inhibit ovulation & prevent sperm reaching egg	Used under prescription	<35 & not having history of blot clot or breast cancer	92-99%
Mini pill	progestin- inhibit ovulation & prevent sperm reaching egg	used under prescription	For those who can't take estrogen	92.99%
Birth control shot	Progestin injection- inhibit ovulation &prevent sperm reaching egg	Shot is given every 3 months by the doctor	More convenient method	99.7%
The ring	progestin and estrogen are released by the ring in the vagina	Ring is placed in the vagina for 3 weeks and removed during period		92-99%
The patch	progestin and estrogen are released into the blood stream	Used under prescription	Less effective in woman more than 198 pounds	92-99%
The implant	Thin rod inserted under skin of a women's upper arm it releases	Implanted by the doctor		99%

	progestin into blood for 3 years			
Intrauterine Devices (IUD)				
IUD	Inserted into vagina, device contains hormones	Inserted by health care professional and last up to 10 years	No planning needed. Side effects: tough periods, effects are similar to pill if it contains hormones	99.8%
Barrier methods				
Male condom	Prevent sperms from getting in to vagina			85-98%
Female condom	Prevent sperms form getting in to vagina			79-95%
Diaphragm (with spermicide)	It covers the cervix and block the sperm, however should be used with spermicides	Proper fitting and use of right size are needed		84-94%
Cervical cap	Fits over the cervix and prevent sperms from entering, however should be used with spermicides	Proper fitting and use of right size is needed		
Spermicides	Foam, gel, cream, film, suppository or tablet kill the sperms	Placed an hour before intercourse and left in place at least 6-8 hours after intercourse		71-82% (spermicide alone)
sponge	Made of plastic foam			More effective for women

	and contains spermicide, it covers cervix and blocks sperm entry			never given birth, thus varying level of effectiveness
Fertility awareness and abstinence				
Abstinence	Abstinence or avoid sexual relationship			100%
Natural family planning or continuous awareness	Not having intercourse at certain time based on menstrual cycle also called calendar method or mucus method (keep tracking on mucus level as it changes in colour and consistency when woman is fertile) or temperature method (check body's basal temperature to find ovulation)			75-99% effective if calculated correctly
Permanent methods	**When parents want no more child**			**99%**
Female sterilization	Fallopian tubes tied and cut or cauterized/ banded/ trans-cervical sterilization (a tiny device is sent to both fallopian tubes which irritates the wall and causes the	Tubal ligation requires a surgery		

	growth of a scar tissue and blocks the tube) thus the sperm or eggs cannot enter		
Male sterilization/ vasectomy	Prevents sperm from going to penis by blocking the Vas differentia	Surgery is simpler than women's tubal ligation, sperm count must be checked to zero after wards	
Emergency contraception and other ways			
Emergency Contracepti on / plan B/ morning after/ day after pill	Type 1: Progestin Type 2: ulipristal acetate Type 3: both Progestin and Estrogen Type 4: mifepristone Copper-T Intra Uterine Device (IUD)	Used under prescriptio n IUD Can be used for five days after having sex fitted by physician	Type 1: 88% Type 3: 75%

Abortion pill	mifepristone and misoprostol			Effective up to 9 weeks after woman's last period
Abortion	in-clinic abortion: destroy the fetus clinically			
Avoid pregnancy during intercourse	Avoiding sex during menstruation because sperm can still travel through the fluid and fertilize an egg. Pulling out before ejaculation is not the right way to avoid pregnancy Avoiding close contact of exposed genitals, you may think rubbing genitals together is safe but even precum contains sperms that could travel through vagina and fertilize an egg. Avoid fingering into vagina after touching your partner's penis because sperms can be transferred that way Do not touch the condom after touching your partner's penis because sperms can transfer from fingers to condom and then vagina Avoid leaving the penis inside the vagina after ejaculation, condoms may come off when penis retracts in size and reach the vagina			

Adapted from ("marshall.edu", n.d.); ("ec.princeton.edu", 2015) and ("www.newhealthadvisor.com", 2014).

9.7 Unmet need for family planning

About 142 million married or in-union women of reproductive age are estimated to have an unmet need for family planning in 2015 worldwide this is projected to change to 143 million by 2030, however in 2011 this was 143, if women using traditional contraceptive methods are included (in 2011 data) this may rises to about 215 million. In developing countries four out of five women with an unmet need for modern contraceptive methods. The unmet need for family planning is 4% in Mauritius to 48% in Samoa. However, in Africa 26 of the 39 countries with recent data have high unmet need levels, ranging from 21% to 38 % of all women of reproductive age who are married or in a union. In Asia, Europe, Latin America and the Caribbean, by chance, majority of countries with recent data have unmet need levels below 20 %.In addition, unmet need for family planning is lowest in countries where contraceptive prevalence is already high (above 60 %) (Adapted from ("unpopulation.org", 2013); ("wgo.int", 2016); ("un.org", 2015).

9.8 China's one child policy

China began promoting birth control and family planning since 1949, by 1970s China's population was rapidly approaching one billion, thus in 1978 Chinese government conduct a volunteer program that encouraged families to have no more than two children and one child is preferable, however later, strict implementation of rules was required to control the skyrocketing population, then in 1980 one child policy has been announced by the Chinese communist party. Strict implementation of the one child policy brought down the fertility rate. However, it had so many drawbacks in the society, many parents preferred male child and female children were sent to orphanages or abortion of female foetus or even infanticide of baby girls was the major threat to the society, country's sex ratio skewed towards males. In the late 2015 and early 2016 China has given up the one child policy and all families are allowed to have two children (Pletcher, 2016).

9.9 India's sterilization program

Sterilization programmes conducted all over India to reduce the increasing population, brought the population growth rate to 1.6 which was 2.3 in 1970s. Both men and women in Indian states were under gone to sterilization and few incentives are given by the government for the individuals undergone sterilization, recruiting agents are also paid for recruitments. However, this also increases the maternal mortality in India as the intensified sterilization process brings unhygienic and unsafe environment. Adapted from (Metha, 2015).

9.10 Social measures of population control

Fixed minimum age for marriage: in developing county, India for instance it is 21 for men and 18 for women by law.

Late marriage: Now the age of marriage is 30, this reduces the period of reproduction among females ultimately bring down the birth rate.

Self-control: self-control is the best method to encourage late marriage or reduce the number of children born.

Recreational facility: exposure to recreational facilities such as cinema, sports and dance could alter the sexual drive and a means of spending time.

Increase awareness: benefits of family planning can be propagated to uneducated families using social media such as television, radio and field presentations.

Incentives: Incentives can be given to those who follow family planning and those who adopt birth control measures.

Women education, employment and status upgrading: this brings active participation of women in work force this enriches the country's economy while reducing the fertility rate.

Adoption: adoption is beneficial to both childless parents and orphan children.

Change in social outlook: marriage should no longer consider as a social binding, issueless women should not be looked inferior.

Social security: increased social security schemes prevent dependents even in old age, sickness and unemployment.

9.11 Economic Measures

More employment opportunities: this will help the man to improve the status both economically and socially and he is occupied as more issues to be handled, thus it reduces the urge for more children.

Development of agriculture and industries: this will provide more employment opportunities. Human will adopt to live in small family norms.

Urbanization and standard of living: people live in urban areas have low birth rate than people in rural area. Fertility rate declines when family income rises.

Effective implementation of population control methods brings the world population growth rate down in the period between 1950 and 2050.

Causes of human population explosion cannot be defined since it may relate to economy, favourable environment, and other social factors.

Population explosioneffects into following problems

9.12 Water pollution-water scarcity due to population explosion

Please see the chapter water pollution-water scarcity-salinization

9.13 Overexploitation of natural resources due to population explosion

Please see chapter overexploitation of natural resources

9.14 Deforestation-destruction of grasslands and mangroves due to population explosion

Please see chapter deforestation-destruction of grasslands and mangroves

9.15 Poverty-disease-war-food insecurity due to population explosion

According to Kibirige (Kibirige, 1997), the population in Africa has doubled since 1960. The continent is facing an alarming socio-economic situation. Africa has a lower life expectancy, and it is affected by a variety of diseases. Based on the study, this paper has found that population growth is the original cause of poverty and underdevelopment. Also, the paper has discussed population growth and poor health as the most significant problems that lead to poverty. Birdsall (Birdsall , 1980) has stated that the "link between absolute poverty and population growth affects 780 million people in the developing countries". Poverty is associated with high fertility, high infant mortality, lack of woman's education, less family income unable to spend for children, inequitable shares in national income and inaccessibility of family planning, etc.

9.16   Solid waste and sewage problem due to population explosion

According to AbdManaf, Samah, & MohdZukki (AbdManaf, Samah, & MohdZukki, 2009), population growth is one of the factors that made the management of municipal solid waste one of Malaysia's most critical environmental problem, where per capita waste generation rate is about 0.5-0.8 kg/person/day in which domestic waste is the primary source. According to Zhang, Tan, & Gersberg (Zhang, Tan, & Gersberg, 2010), in China, population growth along with urbanization and industrialization caused the rapid increase of municipal solid waste generation. The total municipal solid waste increased from 31.3 million tonnes in 1980 to 212 million tonnes in 2006, and the rate of waste generation was increased from 0.5kg/capita/day in 1980 to 0.98kg/capita/year in 2006.

Dhaka in Bangladesh is a faster-growing megacity in the world, its population doubling from 6 million in 1990 to 12 million in 2005. It was estimated that by 2025 Dhaka's population will reach over 20 million people. Along with population solid waste generation also in a hike, solid waste generation in urban centers of Bangladesh was estimated at a little above 20,000 metric tons per day (MTPD) in 2012 and is projected to reach 47,000 MTPD by 2025. Growing at a compound annual growth rate (CAGR) of 6.5%.

9.17   Animal slaughter and cruelty due to population explosion

According to Carrington(Carrington, 2018), the human population of the world, which is 7.6 billion, represents just 0.01% of all living things. And human has caused the loss of 83% of wild mammals and half of the plants, while livestock raised by humans is abundant. Further, it was stated that three-quarters of all earth is significantly affected by human activities.

A study reveals that farmed poultry makes up 70% of all birds on the planet, with just 30% being wild. And 60% of all mammals on earth are livestock, 36% are humans, and only 4% are wild animals. This livestock and poultry are treated as objects in factory farms, spend their entire life in a slaughterhouse, and killed for meat.

241

9.18   Plastic pollution due to population explosion

Please see the chapter Urbanization-urban sprawl-settlements

9.19   E-waste due to population explosion

According to Faiaz & Soltan (Faiaz & Soltan , 2013), the amount of e-waste generation is increasing along with the growing population. For instance, the number of mobile phone consumption increases with the number of individuals. Based on the collected data on the quantity of e-waste produced and the population in various countries in the period from 2006 to 2010 depicted that there is a sub-liner relationship between population and quantity of e-waste.

In conclusion, there is a sub-linear relationship between e-waste and population. Each year's increase is indicated in table 9.3.

Table 9.3 E-waste vs. Population

Year	b factor	R^2	Result
2006	b<1 0.16	0.0076	Sub-linear, if x variable (Pop) increase by 1%, Y variable (E-waste) will increase by% 0.16
2007	b<1 0.41	0.0606	Sub-linear, if x variable (Pop) increase by 1%, Y variable (E-waste) will increase by% 0.41
2008	b<1 0.67	0.1747	Sub-linear, if x variable (Pop) increase by 1%, Y variable (E-waste) will increase by% 0.67
2009	b<1 0.85	0.2665	Sub-linear, if x variable (Pop) increase by 1%, Y variable (E-waste) will increase by% 0.85
2010	b<1 0.97	0.3393	Sub-linear, if x variable (Pop) increase by 1%, Y variable (E-waste) will increase by% 0.97

Source : (Faiaz & Soltan , 2013)

9.20   Global energy crisis due to Population Explosion

Please see the chapter global energy crisis

9.21   Population Explosion causes draining of wetlands

In the USA, the coastal area within 80km of the coast which comprises only 13% of the land area of the continental the USA covers half of the country's population (nearly 51%) (Rappaport & Sachs , 2003) as cited in (Lee, et al., 2006). Similarly, in Australia about 84% of the population lives within the coastal region(Australian Bureau of Statistics, 2002), for instance, the population in the city of Gold Coast in Queensland increased by 2,40,500 in the period between 1986 and 2003 (Australian Bureau of Statistics, 2002); (Office of Urban Management, 2004) as cited in (Lee, et al., 2006). According to Callaway & Zedler (Callaway & Zedler), increasing coastal population causes a decline in wetlands all over the world. It was stated in Dakki & El Hamzaoui(Dakki & El Hamzaoui, 1997) as cited in (Andy, Hamzaoui, Agbani, & Franchimont, 2002), over the past two decades rapid economic development and human population increase have caused accelerated wetland loss in Morocco.

9.22   Intensive farming due to population explosion

Please see the chapter Intensive farming

9.23   Urbanization-urban sprawl-settlements due to population explosion

Please see the chapter Urbanization-urban sprawl-settlements

9.24   Population explosion as a keystone environmental problem

The increasing population causes deforestation, which leads to the loss of valuable genes, water regulators, flood controllers, watersheds, protectors of inland and coastal fisheries, and climate stabilisers. This also leads to the destruction of mineral cycles and several food chains, which are essential to keep the environment balanced.

As mentioned by Paul Ehrlich in Population Explosion, I=PAT, which means I: - impact in the environment equals population multiplied by A: - affluence (the amount of energy and food supply the population consumes) multiplied by the amount of destructive T: - technology a country has, thus with the increasing population there are impacts on the environment.

More people need more space, more food from agriculture, fisheries, poultry and meat, more jobs, more vehicles, more energy, more water supply, more infrastructures such as apartments, shopping malls, factories, industries, more roads, railroads and highways, hospitals, schools, and playgrounds. This results in more pollution, more land degradation, more waste generation, more deforestation, more greenhouse gas emission and global warming, ozone depletion, more spreading of epidemics, more animal abuse and killing for meat, more acid rain and more chances for disasters such as radiation emission from nuclear power reactors, more chances for hazardous chemical discharge, oil spills, more excavation of soil and minerals cause more deadly landslides, increased terrorism and war.

In human history, the first revolution (Cultural Revolution) occurred 100,000 yrs. ago during the time of the Ice Age, when humans lived as a hunter-gatherer. They had more culturally expanded communities than earlier human forms. With the Food supply increases, there was a dramatic increase in population. By the end of the Ice Age, the human population was about 5 million.(The population explosion, 2016).The second revolution was around 8000 B.C., which is an agricultural revolution. Here humans were able to cultivate crops at the desired location, agriculture evolved. These agriculturists developed villages and towns; the population increased further. However, there were certain setbacks such as the Black Death (1346-1353) or the bubonic plague which killed around 75-200 million people in Europe. In the 1650s the world's population reached 500 million, then in 1760, the industrial revolution (third revolution) began. This event deeply changed the human lifestyle, as fossil fuel replaced wood. Improvements in the fields such as medicine, economy, and sanitation followed. By the year 1800, the hypothetical human population reached one billion. At the beginning of the 19th-century machines replaced human employees, this led to further improvement in the social status and standard of living in Europe and North America. In the year of 1900, the global population reached 1.6 billion and increased to 2 billion by 1927 (100% increase). From 1943 with the green revolution (fourth revolution) it further skyrocketed and during the 20[th]century, it increased steeply to 6 billion (400% increase in just 100 years). This exponential growth led to the high consumption of natural resources and man-made resources, which also brought about environmental problems such as deforestation, soil degradation and erosion, air water and land pollution, greenhouse gas emission, waste accumulation, and increased demand for freshwater. In addition, it was estimated that 0.01 and 0.1% of all species become extinct each year (if 0.01% is true: 200-2000 and if 0.1% is true: 10,000-100,000 species become extinct annually) ("How many species are we losing?", 2016). Furthermore, urban sprawl causes habitat destruction, invasive species, increased pollutants, and negative effects on human health such as spreading of pandemic (e.g. COVID 19 during 2020 in highly populated areas), obesity, stress, and hypertension.

The population explosion is the *pioneer or precursor and a keystone link*. We may find a solution to most of the environmental problems when the human population is reduced to that of the pre-industrial era. Today, the world's population is 7.7 billion, and it has been projected to rise to 10 billion by 2050(Harvey, 2019), or more accurately 9.1 billion by 2050 ("How to Food the world in 2050", n.d.). The increasing population causes overexploitation of natural resources, deforestation, urbanization and urban sprawl, solid waste and sewage, the establishment of dams, intensive farming, global energy crisis and burning of fossil fuels, plastic waste, e-waste, and animal slaughter and cruelty. When the human population is reduced, then natural resources may be sustained, and problems such as deforestation, urban sprawl, solid waste, dams, intensive farming, energy crisis and fossil fuel burning, plastic waste, e-waste generation, animal slaughtering, and cruelty to animals may all come to an end. Along with indirectly linked problems such as biodiversity loss, caused by intensive farming and deforestation may also be reduced to a great extent (Fig.9.2).

Evidence 1: Population explosion causes intensive farming

According to Harvey (Harvey, 2019),the author raised the question "Can we ditch intensive farming - and still feed the world?" In brief, global food production must increase by 50% in the next 30 years, to serve the growing population that is about to reach 10 billion by 2050. Harvey, further elaborated that "compare to 2010 an extra 7,400tn calories is required in 2050." Also, by that time (2050), the world would require a landmass twice the size of India for food production to sustain the increased population. But the intensive farming and its related components such as inorganic fertilisers, chemical pesticides, GMO's, deforestation for agriculture are expected to be reduced or avoided by that time (2050), and to be substituted by organic farming, agroforestry, urban farming, and permaculture systems that are relatively less productive.

Evidence 2: Population explosion causes urbanization-urban sprawl-settlements

According to the United Nations ("Department of Economic and Social Affairs", 2018), "68% of the world population projected to live in urban areas by 2050." It further elaborates that "today 55% of the world's population lives in urban areas, and the growing population tends to add another 2.5 billion people to urban areas by 2050."

Evidence 3: Population explosion causes water pollution & scarcity

According to "The Guardian"("The Guardian", 2018), the United Nations reported that "by 2050, 4.8 billion to 5.7 billion people will live in water-scarce areas at least for one month each year. And today, almost half of the world's population (3.6 billion) live in water-scarce areas. According to Malik, Yasar, Tabinda, & Abubakar (Malik, Yasar, Tabinda, & Abubakar, 2012), "about 78% of the population was extracting groundwater at the rate of 2-3 hours per a day, whereas, 4% and 2% population had the use of 4-5 hours and 6 or more hours respectively per a day."

Evidence 4: Population explosion causes overexploitation of natural resources

According to "UNEP" ("UNEP", 2017),"International Resource Panel Report said material resource use expected to reach nearly 90 billion tonnes in 2017, and may more than double from 2015 to 2050." Thus, overexploitation of natural resources is expected to double by 2050 due to the increasing population and its growing needs.

Evidence 5: Population explosion causes deforestation

According to "Department of Economic and Social Affairs" ("Department of Economic and Social Affairs", 2018), "the demand for wood alone is expected to triple to 10 billion cubic meters by 2050" However, "increasing population also increases the demand for agricultural production and conversion of forest to arable land to meet this demand in most of the tropical and low-income countries."

Evidence 6: Population explosion causes global energy crisis or fossil fuel combustion

According to "OECD report"("OECD report", 2011), "global energy demand is rapidly increasing, arising from population and economic growth, thus, energy demand growth is projected to rise by 90% in 2035. According to "Bloomberg" ("Bloomberg", 2018), "global electricity demand to increase 57% by 2050."

Population explosion also tends to increase poverty, food security, solid waste and sewage, animal slaughter and cruelty, plastic pollution, e-waste, and draining of wetlands. Population explosion is a precursor to almost every environmental issue. If the human population remained unchanged since the pre-industrial era, the world would not face much of the present man-made environmental problems.

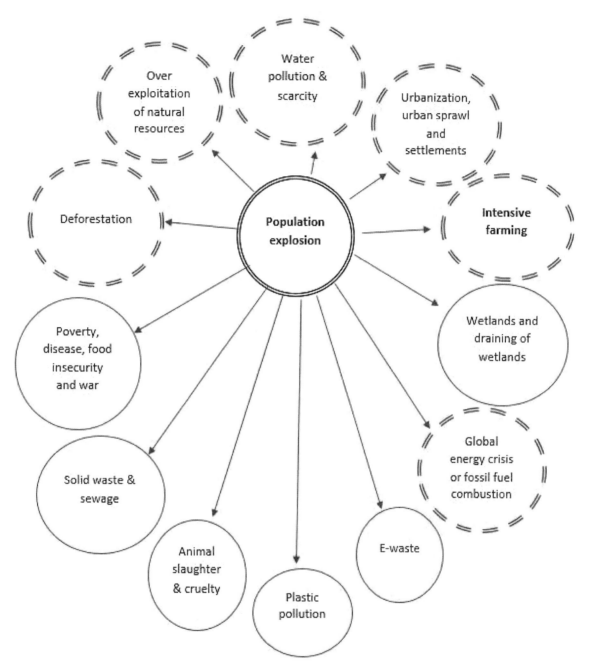

Figure 9.2 Population explosion as keystone environmental problem with the disappearance of intensive farming, deforestation, urbanization, water pollution-water scarcity, and overexploitation of natural resources on its mitigation (hypothetical diagram)

[In the figure black circle is the problem being examined, blue circles are cause man-made environmental problems, red circles are effect man-made environmental problems, double lined circles are keystone man-made environmental problems, and circles with dashed lines

247

(either single or double lined) are the man-made environmental problems that disappear when the problem being examined (black circle) is mitigated]

Increasing human population is a keystone environmental problem, where resulted environmental problems such as intensive farming, global energy crisis, urbanization, over-exploitation of natural resources, deforestation and water pollution-scarcity show almost complete dependency on it. Thus, efforts taken to reduce human population also mitigate most of the resulted environmental problems.

Regenerative vs. Sustainable vs. Conventional solutions

Measures taken to reduce increasing human population such as funding family planning, restricting child marriage by raising the legal age marriage as minimum 18, child tax, one child policies, sterilization such as vasectomy and tubal ligation are **greener** solutions because they are less harmful than conventional practices. In history, cruel killing techniques were used as **conventional** methods, such as Live mustering, shooting or killing, immunocontraception (alter immune system to fight against incoming gametes of opposite gender- this is currently not allowed in humans, but implemented to farm animals) and live mustering such as sending for military service, wars and biological weapons (man-made diseases). For instance, killing of Jews in concentration camps by Adolf Hitler during World War II is this kind of population reduction (figure 9.3).

Besides, solutions such as contraception, raising the status of women, spread of education (including women education through gender equality), increase awareness through sex education, raising the status of the women, promote late marriages, and self-control, decrease infant mortality, promote skilled migration and establish civilization on another planet e.g. Mars (- Elon Musk) are **sustainable** techniques (net zero or neutral) because according to the definition of sustainable development stated in the 1987 Brundtland commission report, "development that meets the needs of the present without compromising the ability of future generations to meet their needs" Thus, aforesaid solutions could be categorized as sustainable solutions. However, both greener solutions and sustainable solutions are often very expensive, this is due to their high energy requirements such as arranging awareness programmes, providing suitable incentives, issuing contraceptive devices free of charge, or at a least price requires immense labour and relatively higher money allocations.

Restorative solutions such as adoption (instead of spending money on making own child for childless parents through expensive technologies), and it is more beneficial than sustainable solution because they are more resilient than sustainable solutions, however,

248

human superiority over nature is a common characteristic feature of this type of solution. And the system also depicts relatively low energy expenditure and more systemic vitality. **Reconciliatory** solutions such as change in social outlook (childless couples are no longer disrespected by the society), social security (quality old age care for childless elders) and encouraging adults becoming celibate monks ascertain the recovery of the problem. Reconciliatory solutions for human population increase are less expensive due to low energy and high systemic vitality. It can also co-evolve (adapt) with nature. It also shows very high resilience to the changes in the environmental factors.

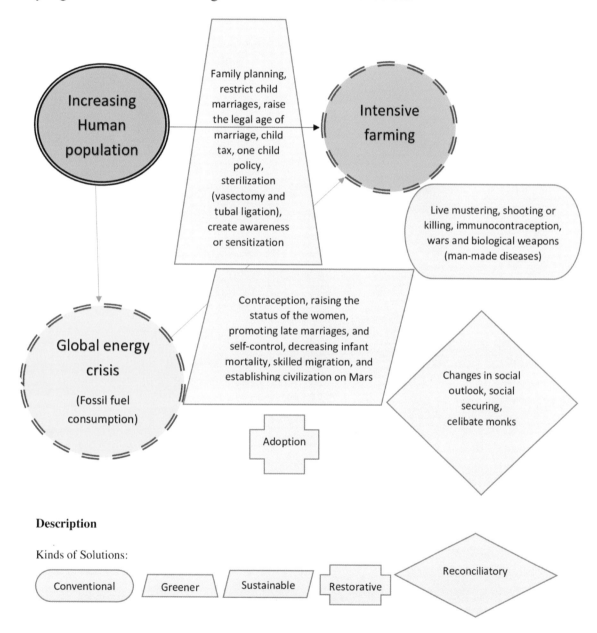

Figure 9.3 Solutions to increasing human population

Black circle: problem under concern, Blue circle: cause, Red circle: effect, Double lined circle: keystone environmental problem, Single lined circle: environmental problem, Dotted lined circle: problem to be mitigated when keystone environmental problem get solved, Black arrow: cause-effect link for which solutions are given, Blue arrow: cause-effect link

N.B.: - Each problem in the circles is connected to many other problems on the basis of cause-and-effect links, and they are not shown here.

10.   Path of Keystone Environmental Problems

10.1 Introduction

Unless keystone environmental problems are found it is not possible to establish a pathway of environmental crisis. However, in the scientific literature there were few attempts showing interconnected nature of environmental problems evolving from human population growth. After the industrial revolution and increase in quality of medication the human death rate began to fall while the birth rate and expected individual lifespan increased dramatically. More industries and employment opportunities were created, increasing energy demand was met by fossil fuels. Thus, environmental degradation proliferated into variety of environmental problems. These environmental problems can be classified into two categories such as global environmental issues (population explosion, global warming, ozone depletion, ocean acidification, biodiversity loss, etc.) and local environmental issues (groundwater pollution, water scarcity, air pollution, desertification, acid rain, eutrophication, agrochemicals, outbreak of pests and weeds, etc.).

10.2 History

In the past hardly research papers documented the path of major environmental problems based on their interconnected nature as cause and effect. For instance, according to the paper published by the Ministry of the Environment of Japan (2001) as mentioned in "eanet.asia" website, accessed in 2018 ("eanet.asia", n.d.), interconnected nature of several environmental problems such as overexploitation of natural resources, intensive farming, deforestation, energy crisis, urban sprawl, pollution (air/ freshwater, groundwater, and marine), hazardous wastes, ozone depletion, soil degradation, and acid rain was considered (figure10.1). However, this paper did not provide evidence for the links through examples, and increasing population, economic growth, and growing affluence were considered as *precursor links* (the link that is not resulting from any environmental problem but it is the origin or cause of all other environmental problems).

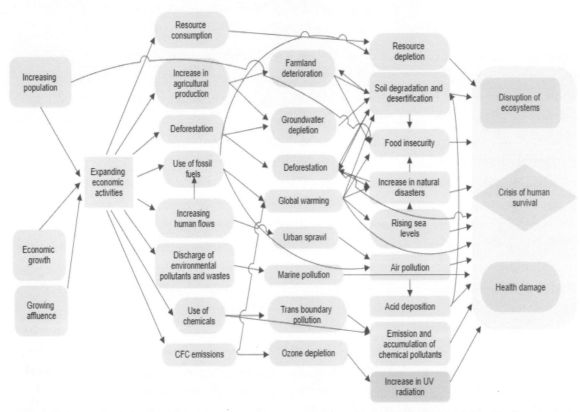

Figure 10.1 Path of Global Environmental Issues published by the Ministry of the Environment of Japan (2001)
Adapted from ("eanet.asia", n.d.)

10.3 Establishing the path of keystone environmental problems

It was also possible to identify the hypothetical path of the keystone environmental issues as given below (fig. 10.2).

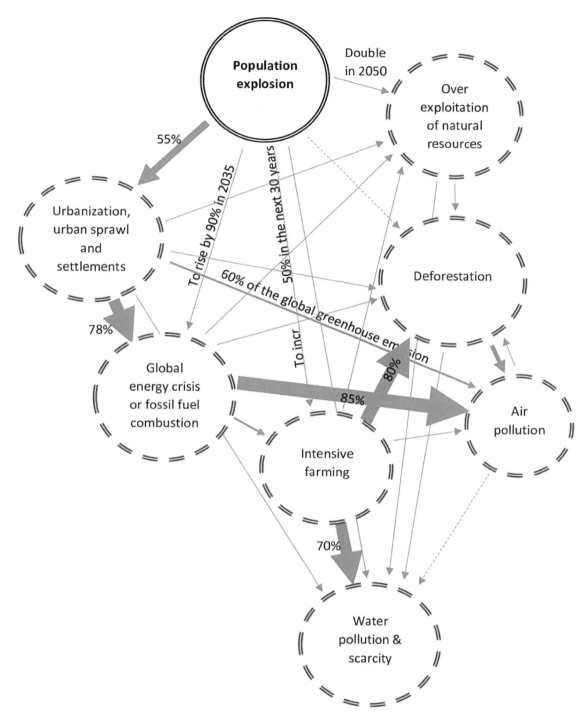

Figure 10.2 Path of the keystone man-made environmental issues (hypothetical diagram)

[In the figure black circle is the problem being examined, red circles are the effect man-made environmental problems, double lined circles are keystone man-made environmental problems, and circles with dashed lines are the man-made environmental problems that disappear when the problem being examined (black circle) is mitigated]

253

- According to the United Nations ("Department of Economic and Social Affairs", 2018), today **55%** of the world's population lives in urban areas.
- According to "UNEP"("UNEP", 2017), overexploitation of natural resources expected to **double by 2050** due to the increasing population and its growing needs.
- According to "OECD report"("OECD report", 2011), "global energy demand is rapidly increasing, arising from population and economic growth, thus, energy demand growth is projected to rise by **90%** in 2035.
- According to Harvey(Harvey, 2019), the author has raised the question that "Can we ditch intensive farming - and still feed the world?" In brief, global food production must increase by **50%** in the next 30 years.
- According to UN-Habitat, **60%** of the global greenhouse emission is from urban cities (Climate Action Summit, 2019)
- Agriculture is the direct driver for worldwide deforestation, **80%** of deforestation worldwide are due to agriculture or intensive farming (Agriculture is the direct driver for worldwide deforestation, 2012).
- According to FAO(FAO, 2011) as cited in (Water for Sustainable Food and Agriculture: A report produced for the G20 Presidency of Germany, 2017), agriculture accounts for **70%** of total freshwater withdrawals on average worldwide.
- According to "OECD report" ("OECD report", 2011), fossil fuel combustion accounted for **84%** of global greenhouse gas emissions in 2009.
- According to International Energy Agency (IEA) WEO-2016 Special Report Energy and Air Pollution(International Energy Agency (IEA) WEO-2016 Special Report Energy and Air Pollution, 2016) as cited in (Perera, 2018) "energy-related fossil fuel combustion in high and middle-income countries and biomass burning in low-income countries account for most of the global air pollution, generating **85%** of airborne respirable particulate pollution and almost all Sulphur dioxide and nitrogen oxide emissions to the atmosphere."

Above eight encircled man-made environmental issues are keystone links(hypothetically) and removing such links could bring many directly and indirectly linked environmental problems to an end. But human adaptability factors prevent such solutions in reality. Thus, instead of cutting links, shortcuts are established to solve the problem by regenerative means. However, this is not the case for all man-made environmental problems.

E.g. removing deforestation is not possible due to economic needs. And some government policies can influence severe deforestation (politics). Thus, deforestation still happening unabatedly even in Amazonian rain forests and Indonesian rain forests that are rich in biodiversity.

Certain man-made environmental problems can be solved by either sustainable or regenerative or by both ways. However, when handling keystone environmental issue, the systemic solutions and their possible projected outcome should be well studied prior to the implementation. Otherwise they would end up in a disaster.

e.g.

Sri Lanka banned importation and application of agrochemicals (intensive farming – a keystone issue) in May 2021, in a year later, in May 2022 the country faced severe economic crisis, social unrest and political instability.

10.4 Direction of the path of keystone environmental problems

According to the above given path of the keystone environmental problems, population explosion is the precursor. The major cause of population explosion is after the industrial revolution and discovery of modern medicine with vaccination and antibiotics a considerable fall in human death rate was occurred, which increased human life span and reduced child mortality dramatically. This is followed by urbanization such as emergence of cities, vehicular transportation, and increased quality of human lifestyle. Subsequently, intensive farming, over exploitation of natural resource and global energy crisis (led to fossil fuel consumption) resulted into severe deforestation. This situation had exacerbated water scarcity-water pollution and reduction in air quality due to air pollution.

Furthermore, unabated keystone environmental problems can emerge into either intranational or international environmental conflicts that may even leads to a military warfare. The following chapter discusses (with examples and flowcharts) that how the unabated keystone environmental problems emerge into environmental disputes or wars.

11. Supporting evidences for keystone environmental problems emerge into environmental conflicts

11.1. Introduction to Environmental conflict

Environmental conflicts occur for three main purposes

1) Over-consumption of renewable resources

2) Pollution or unfavourable change in the environment

3) Impoverishment of the space for living

According to Schwartz & Singh(Schwartz & Singh, 1999), Environmental conflict is a subset of environmental security (fig. 11.1), and was initially mentioned in an article titled "Redefining Security" written by Lester Brown of the World watch institute in 1977. It further justified that the security threats leading to military warfare could also cause by environmental problems that are derived from human population increase, resource depletion, and pollution.

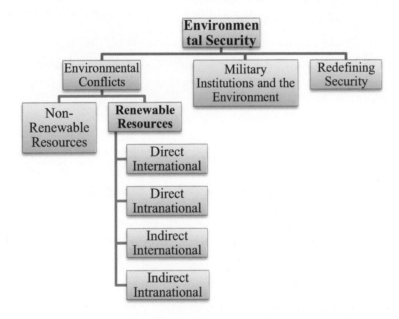

Figure 11.1 Environmental security and its related subdivisions
Source: (Schwartz & Singh, 1999)

In the past most of the conflicts and international warfare caused by resource scarcity, more precisely non-renewable resources such as oil and minerals. But today even depletion of renewable resources such as forests, fish stocks, crop land, clean air and potable water. This is because modern day conflicts also exacerbated by increasing human population

256

(keystone environmental issue), which directly influence resource consumption (keystone environmental issue). Even global environmental issues such as global warming that lead to draught and crop loss, or water scarcity and leads to mass migration could also cause environmental conflicts.

Keystone environmental problems can emerge into environmental conflicts (fig. 11.2).

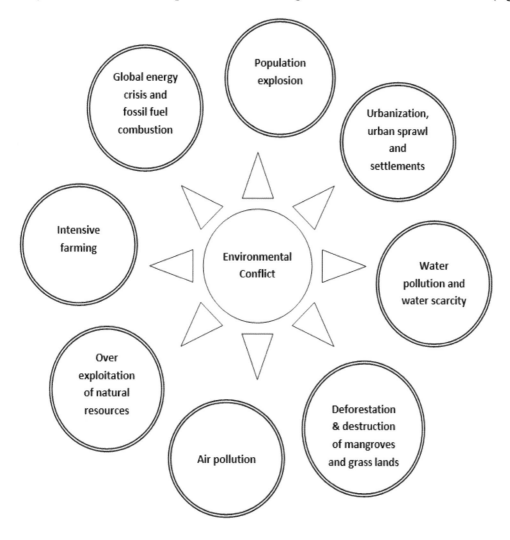

Figure 11.2 Keystone environmental problems emerge into environmental conflicts

a). Direct Environmental Conflict

Direct environmental conflicts are where there is an international competition for renewable resources such as water, crude oil, crop land, fish and forest, nations may even tend to justify it by military action in the name of economic preservation and national security this can even occur between states e.g. conflict for 'Cauvery' water resource between Tamil

Nadu and Kerala in India, Sudan and South Sudan for oil resources, and Egypt and Ethiopia for Nile water flow and etc. (Schwartz & Singh, 1999).

b). Indirect Environmental Conflict

Indirect environmental conflicts occur where factors such as soil erosion, agricultural contamination and water pollution create or elevate other social issues such as poverty, famine, ethnic cleavages, mass migration and uneven distribution of resources e.g. desertification and famine in East African countries such as Ethiopia, pollution of mine tailings in Papua, New Guinea, deforestation and soil erosion in Mexico, over fishing and water pollution of Kenya, pollution from oil exploration in Nigeria and etc. (Schwartz & Singh, 1999).

Both direct and indirect environmental conflicts could be further classified based on whether they occur within a country (intra) or between countries (inter) national territorial regions?

Direct intranational environmental conflicts

This implies direct conflict over access to natural resources within national boundaries. However, the clash may happen between different ethnic class or different states, or different level of people.

E.g. Cauvery River water dispute between Tamil Nadu and Karnataka states in India.

Direct international environmental conflicts

Population explosion is the keystone precursor for this conflict, which causes depletion of natural resources. Renewable resource such as cropland, fish, and forest may cause international competition, and may leads to conflict between countries.

E.g. in Northern Sudan, problems such as soil degradation, deforestation, and reduced rainfall caused decline in availability of arable land and decreased available fish stocks. This situation led to ethnic clashes since 1991. Thousands of civilians were killed due to these incidents. It has been revealed that environmental issues such as overfishing, water pollution, deforestation, and desertification were the direct causes for the clashes, impoverishment and migration of the Kenyan people.

Indirect intranational environmental conflict

Here, conflicts such as ethnic violence, urban crime, crisis between states occur within a country leads to migration or caused by migration into another's territory due to environmental causes such as competition for land and water resource, soil degradation, poverty, agrochemicals, etc.

Indirect international environmental conflict

Here, conflict between nations that occur when resource scarcity interacts with other economic and social factors. Competition for renewable resources such as deforestation, over fishing, soil degradation, water pollution, impacts of climate change, etc. may cause conflict between nations.

11.2. Direct Intranational environmental conflicts

11.2.1. Chauvery water dispute between Tamil Nadu and Karnataka (Indian States)
[Water scarcity, intensive farming and population explosion as keystone environmental problems]

Chauvery River flows through two South Indian states Karnataka (upstream) and Tamil Nadu (downstream) (figure 11.3). Chauvery dispute prevails over centuries. In British India, two agreements between Madras Presidency (now Tamil Nadu) and Mysore state (now Karnataka) were made on water sharing in 1872 and 1924. However, the latter lapsed in 1974. On 2nd June 1990 Indian government launched Cauvery Water Disputes Tribunal (CWDT). In 1991 an interim sharing order was passed by the CWDT. However, Karnataka refused to release more water as stipulated by the order. In 1993, Tamil Nadu Chief Minister Jayalalithaa demanded more water as stipulated by the interim order. In 1998, Chauvery River Authority was established to ascertain the implementation of the interim order of the CWDT. In 2002, Prime Minister Atal Bihari Vajpayee instructed Karnataka to release only 9000 cusecs of water to Tamil Nadu. Tamil Nadu warned that it will seek Supreme Court. In 2005, Karnataka refused to implement the distress-sharing formula. In 2007, CWDT stated that the 1872 and 1924 agreements are still valid. At present days the population has doubled in both states, even extent of irrigated areas and dams were increased. Thus, water demand also increased. At the same time deforestation close to catchment areas also reduced the water flow and caused frequent droughts. The Karnataka protested against the decision of the CWDT. In 2015 Jayalalithaa wrote to Prime Minister Narendra Modi and urged him to instruct Karnataka to release more water since that was a distress year. On 2nd September 2016 Supreme Court asked Karnataka to release 12,000 cusecs of water to Tamil Nadu modifying its earlier order of 15,000 cusecs. Then the violence erupted. Natives of Tamil Nadu living in Karnataka were attacked, and vehicles registered in Tamil Nadu were set ablaze. About 30 buses were set ablaze. On the other side in Tamil Nadu vehicles from Karnataka were set ablaze (fig. 11.4). Adapted from (Ganesan & Venkatesh, 2016)

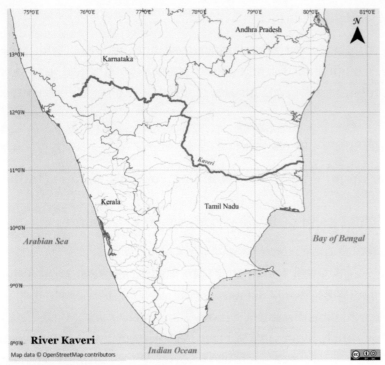

Figure 11.3 River Chauvery (Kaveri)
   Source: (Coder, n.d.) License: CC-by-SA 3.0

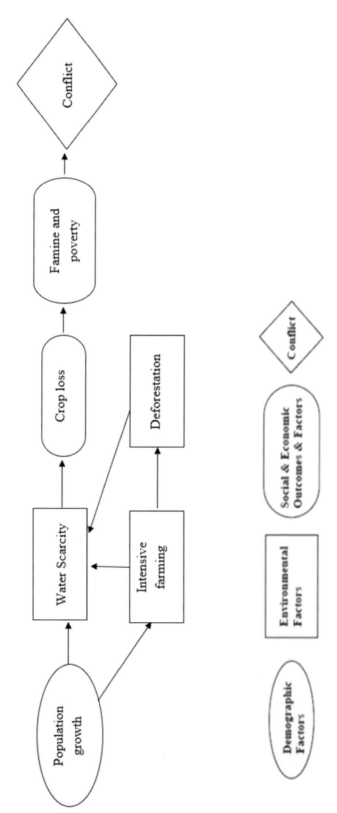

Figure 11.4 Flowchart on Chauvery River dispute

261

11.3. Direct International Environmental Conflicts

11.3.1. Environmental conflict on over exploitation of Fish stocks in Palk Strait among fishermen of India and Sri Lanka.

[Overexploitation of natural resources and population explosion as keystone environmental problems]

Poaching of fish stock beyond the borders of India and Sri Lanka by the fishermen of both countries by violating international maritime boundaries (IMBL) becomes a major international direct environmental conflict between both nations. It has been reported Indian fishermen are steeling US$ 750 million annually from Sri Lankan coastal waters. Bilateral agreements of 1974&76 are being violated. Heavy use of trawlers which are not permitted to fish on coastal seas and the use of internationally banned bottom sea net by Indian poachers is a major threat to the coastal resources of north Sri Lanka. Trawlers catch fish flocks unselectively, catch may include several non-targeted species and juvenile stages of fish in unsustainable manner, thus it is a major threat to the live hood of fishing communities in the North Sri Lanka as well as threat to the coastal biodiversity. Arresting and imprisonment of fishermen by coastal guards of both countries continues.

It has been complained that Indian fishermen are using illegal methods of fishing which is banned in Sri Lanka as well as internationally (e.g., bottom trawling). Use of deep see trawlers are not suitable in the Palk strait as it is a shallow and consisting highly valuable coral reef structures, as per 1993 Marine fishing regulation act of India, trawlers are permitted beyond three nautical miles from the shores but they often violate the act due to high catch in the region. More impressively unlike Sri Lankan vessels those Indian trawlers are provided with GPS tracking systems and they clearly know their location in the sea (beyond the boarder or not). Trawler fishing is an unselective way of fishing, it destroys the coral reefs which are vital for the biodiversity in the region and it also catches juvenile forms of fish and untargeted organisms such as endangered sea turtles. Sri Lankan fishermen do have multiday boats and they are not destructive as trawler fishery. And Sri Lanka has completely banned bottom trawling since 2017 by the amendment to Section 28A of the Fisheries and Aquatic Resources Act No 02 of 1996. It has been noticed that Indian trawlers are arriving from Nagapattinam, Thanjavur, Pudukottai and Ramanathapuram and they violate the IMBL and poach in the Sri Lankan territorial waters such as Delft, Pesalai, Iranathivu and up to Pulmoddai at the East coast of Sri Lanka (fig. 11.5)(Waduge, 2014).

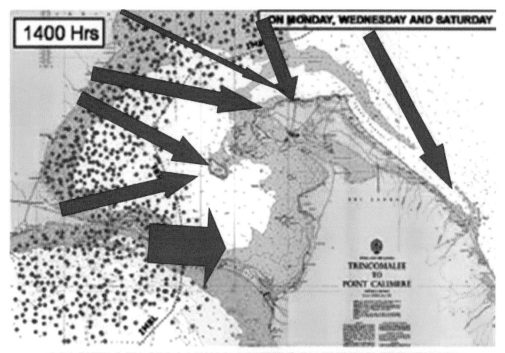

Figure 11.5 Poaching in Sri Lankan waters by Indian fishermen
Source:https://www.sundaytimes.lk/110227/News/nws_17.html

In 2021, Sri Lankan Ministry of Fisheries with the assistance of Navy has inaugurated a splendid move to sink abandoned deteriorating buses in the northern sea floor, which may create artificial coral like structures to create habitats and breeding grounds for juveniles and fishes, respectively (fig. 11.6). However, it has overseen by the India-based local public media ('You Tubers') as a threat to the Indian fishing bottom trawlers trespassing maritime borders into Sri Lanka. As a consequence, Indian fishermen encroached into Sri Lankan water and destroyed the fishing nets of North Sri Lankan fishermen in the sea, which causes loss of several million rupees, and a Northern Sri Lankan fisherman believed to be killed (missing) by angry Indian fishermen who trespassed their waters for poaching. While, Sri Lankan coast guards keep seizing their boats that trespass the maritime boundary (fig. 11.7).

Figure 11.6 Corroding busses drowned into sea by Sri Lanka
Source: ("dailythanthi.com", 2021)

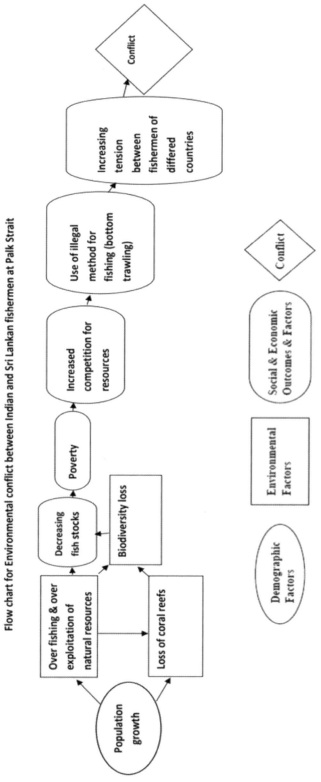

Figure 11.7 Flowchart for Environmental conflict on Poaching in Sri Lankan waters by Indian fishermen

11.3.2. Environmental Conflict in Northeast India and Bangladesh due to flooding (natural disaster) caused by climate change led to migration.

In Bangladesh, deforestation and encroachment have increased flooding incidents and resource depletion. Millions of Bengalis have migrated to states of Assam and Tripura in Northeast India. This situation destabilizes political strength and threatened indigenous culture, and increased competition over natural resources. In the period from 1979 to 1985 ethnic riots occurred resulted in the death of about 4000 civilians (fig. 11.8).

Figure 11.8 One third of Bangladesh under water by flooding
Source: https://pixabay.com/photos/bangladesh-flood-helpless-people-5939912/

Under cc (free for commercial use)

(Flowchart is given in the chapter 3: indirect intranational environmental conflicts)

Similarly, in Pakistan, environmental problems such as increasing human population, soil erosion, deforestation, and water pollution and scarcity, shortage for arable land affected the rural population and led to periodic riots between several groups.

Source: (Schwartz & Singh, 1999)

11.3.3. West bank water crisis between Israel and Palestine

In spring 1951, shooting incidents and Israeli air raid at Al-Hima were recorded; in 1953 also another shooting incident occurred, in 1955 Israel hit Arab villages and killed 50 civilians. Armed insurgencies were recorded during the years 1962, 1964, 1965, 1966, and 1967. After the 1967 six-day war Israel obligated Palestinians to get permission prior to any development related to water consumption such as drilling new wells. 40% of the Israel's water supply comes from Palestinian territory mainly the aquifers in the west bank(Lowi, 1993). While 36 new wells were built in Jewish settlement in the period

266

between 1967 and 1989(Lowi, 1993), however, nowadays more than 50% its water come from desalinization (fig. 11.9).

In 1990s, Jordan, Palestine, and Israel were exhausted with development idea, which would either end up in conflict or compromise.

Source: ("old united nations university website", n.d.)

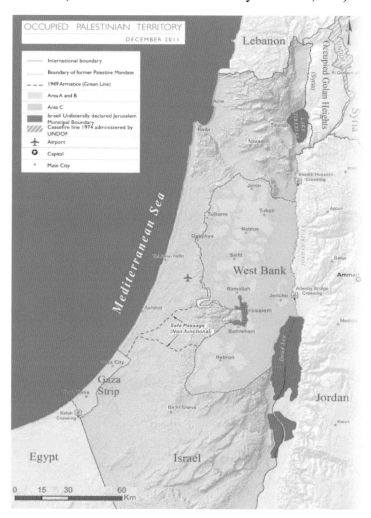

Figure 11.9 West bank water crisis
Source:
https://upload.wikimedia.org/wikipedia/commons/e/ea/Occupied_Palestinian_Territories.j
pg

Wickey-nl *(occupied Palestinian territory: Overview Map*, as of December 2011. Published by United Nations Office for the Coordination of Humanitarian Affairs, 25 January 2012).

(Flowchart is given in the chapter 4: indirect international environmental conflicts)

11.3.4. Russia's invasion into Ukraine in 2022

[Global energy crisis, water scarcity and population explosion as keystone environmental problems]

After the separation of Ukraine from Soviet Union, Russia had to pay for Ukraine for transferring its natural gas exports to Europe via the pipelines belongs to Ukrainian soil. In addition, Ukraine poses over 1 trillion cubic meters of natural gas resources, however, this was 5.4 trillion cubic meters before Crimea was annexed by the Russian federation (fig. 11.10 and 11.11). Since 80% of Ukraine's gas resource occupied in Crimea and the importance of Crimea's geographical location were the believed causes for the Russia's interest in Crimea. As the consequence Ukraine cut the water supply to Crimea by blocking the North Crimean canal that brings water from the Dnieper River. Due to this Agriculture in Crimea dwindled down. Since 85% of the water supply was declined, Crimean people migrated to other regions. In addition, to overcome this crisis Ukraine expressed its interest to join with NATO alliance. This tragedy is also could be considered as one of the reasons for the full-scale Russian invasion into Ukraine from 24th of February 2022, though Vladimir Putin, stated that the nuclear and intercontinental ballistic missile capabilities of Ukraine with the support of the west as the direct cause for the war.

Figure 11.10 North Crimean canal and Crimea
Source:
https://commons.wikimedia.org/wiki/File:Possible_routes_of_alleged_Russian_invasion_
of_Ukraine_(January_2022).png
Under the license CC0 1.0

Flow chart for Environmental conflict between Russia and Ukraine

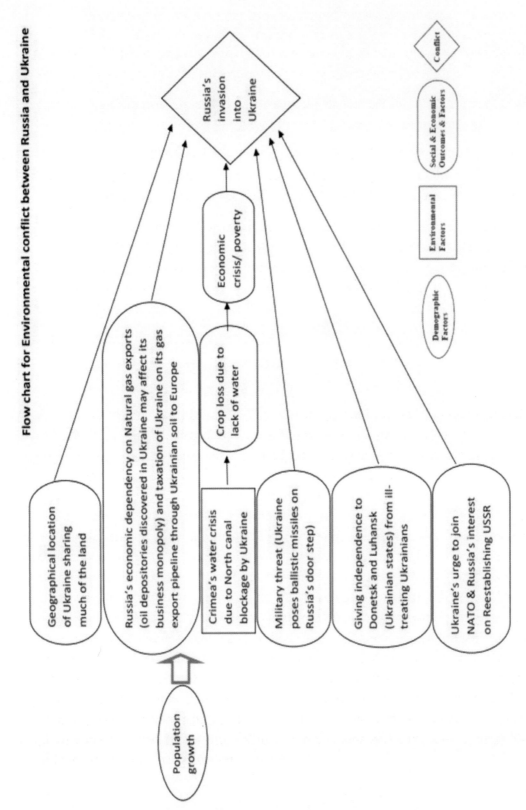

Figure 11.11 Flowchart for Environmental conflict between Russia and Ukraine

11.3.5. Alto Cenepa war
[Intensive farming, deforestation and population explosion as keystone environmental problems]

In 1995 clash between South American nations Peru and Ecuador occurred due to the border demarcation along the headwaters of Cenepa River, in the remote outpost. In November 1994, Peruvian border patrols encountered Ecuadorian outposts in areas claimed by Peru. This has then become a military conflict at the Tiwinza outpost. In late February both sides signed the Montevideo Declaration, which led to ceasefire. However, negotiation took more than four years and came to effect by May 1999. Ecuador agreed to cancel its claim to the areas at headwater of Cnepa River, while Peru delivered one square mile of its territory at Tiwinza out post. Both sides claimed victory (fig. 11.12 and 11.13).Adapted from ('techwar', n.d.).

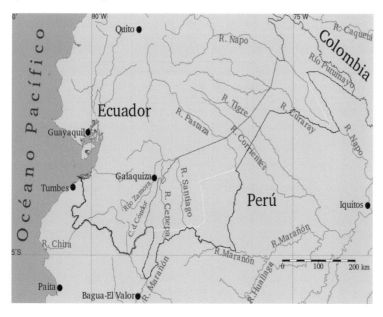

Figure 11.12 Map of Ecuador and Peru
   Source: https://commons.wikimedia.org/wiki/File:Tratado_Garc%C3%ADa-Herrera.png

271

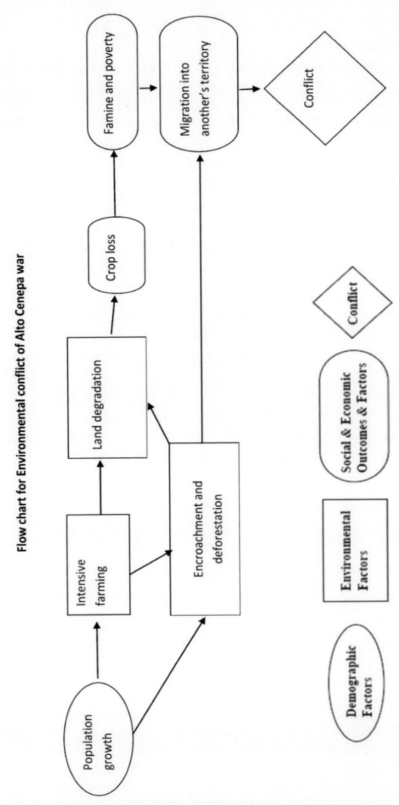

Figure 11.13 Flowchart for Environmental conflict of Alto Cenepa war

272

11.3.6. Establishing Dam to mitigate energy crisis in Ethiopia led to water scarcity in Egypt

[Global energy crisis, water scarcity and population explosion as keystone environmental problems]

In 2011 Ethiopia made a decision to build Grand Ethiopian Renaissance Dam (GERD) to meet its hydropower electricity needs, which is expected to be the largest hydropower plant in Africa, bigger than greater London and cover 1700 sq km. Nile River flows in Africa from South to North, in the North downstream Egypt fears the GERD would reduce the water availability to Egypt. Egypt relies on Nile River for 90% of its water supply. According to its own estimates, if Ethiopia builds the dam in 10 years it will cut the Egypt's water supply by 14% and destroy 18% of its farmland, and if Ethiopia builds the dam in 7 years it will cut 22% of Egypt's water supply would be lost and destroy one-third of its farmland, and five-year window would destroy half of the Egypt's farmland. Thus, Egypt worked against to the GERD. According to Ethiopian source, Egypt sent rebels to neighbouring Eritrea to sabotage the dam, and also promotes another Nile sharing country Sudan to send its troops to its border. Thus, the issue has become three-way dispute among Egypt, Ethiopia and Sudan (fig. 11.14 and 11.15). However, today both of these nations engaged in talks, but the questions such as possibilities of drought in Egypt remain unanswered.

Adapted from ("What's behind the Egypt-Ethiopia Nile dispute? | Start Here", 2020)

Figure 11.14 Location map of Grand Ethiopian Renaissance Dam
Source:
https://upload.wikimedia.org/wikipedia/commons/5/51/Renaissance_Reservoir.jpg

274

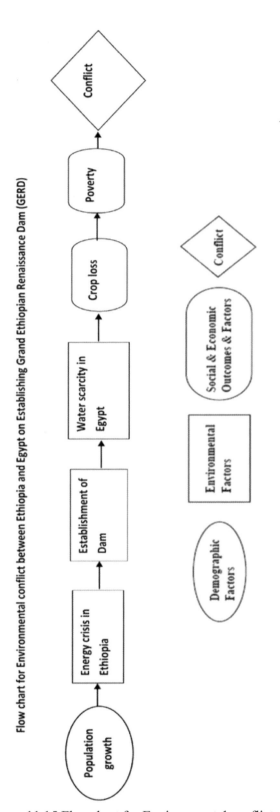

Flow chart for Environmental conflict between Ethiopia and Egypt on Establishing Grand Ethiopian Renaissance Dam (GERD)

Figure 11.15 Flowchart for Environmental conflict on Establishing Grand Ethiopian Renaissance Dam

275

11.4.1.   Population explosion causes poverty, deforestation, land degradation (erosion) led to conflict in Philippines
[Intensive farming, deforestation and population explosion as keystone environmental problems]

In Philippines in the period of 1970's and 80's environmental problems such as population explosion, deforestation, and soil erosion have reduced the agriculture productivity of the land. The average amount of arable land per rural inhabitant has declined to less than one acre, and it was predicted to fall to 0.6 acres per capita by the year 2000. Only 3% of the land owners controlled one-quarter of the country, while 60% of the rural families starve for land (fig. 11.16 and 11.17).

Land scarcity due to increasing rural population also leads to deforestation, and soil erosion. Rural community has been forced to migrate to ecologically fragile upland. About 70% of the Filipinos depend on agriculture and fishing for their livelihood. Chronic poverty turned Filipinos to join NPA's anti-government movement. Adapted from (Schwartz & Singh, 1999)

Figure 11.16 Army of Philippines resisting violence
Source: https://upload.wikimedia.org/wikipedia/commons/5/53/Philippine_Army_AIFV.jpeg

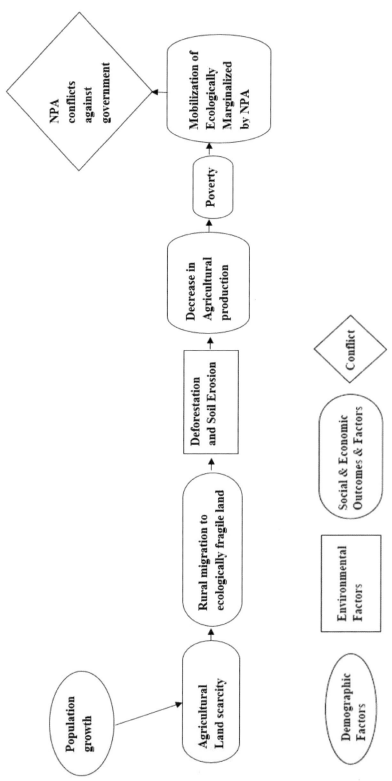

Figure 11.17 Flowchart of Environmental conflict for Philippines
Source: (Schwartz & Singh, 1999)

277

11.4.2. Impacts of Climate change (non-manmade) such as drought and pest outbreak, and impacts of population explosion causes land degradation and famine led to conflict for land resources in Ethiopia
[**Non manmade or naturally caused environmental problems cannot be considered for keystone environmental problem, except population explosion**]

In 1980's, in Ethiopia, drought condition due to (non-anthropogenic) climate change and famine due to increasing population and resulted land degradation caused migration of afar pastoralists into settled agriculture lands, which led to clashes between immigrant pastoralists and agriculturists. At the same time pest outbreak (could be an impact of climate change and intensive farming- monoculture) also affected the settled agriculturists and aggravated the competition for available land (fig. 11.18 and 11.19). Adapted from (Semait, 1989) as cited in (Schwartz & Singh, 1999)

Figure 11.18 Starvation used as weapon of war in Ethiopia

Source:

https://commons.wikimedia.org/wiki/File:Malnourished_children,_weakened_by_hunger. jpg

Credit: DFID - UK Department for International Development

Used under CC by 2.0

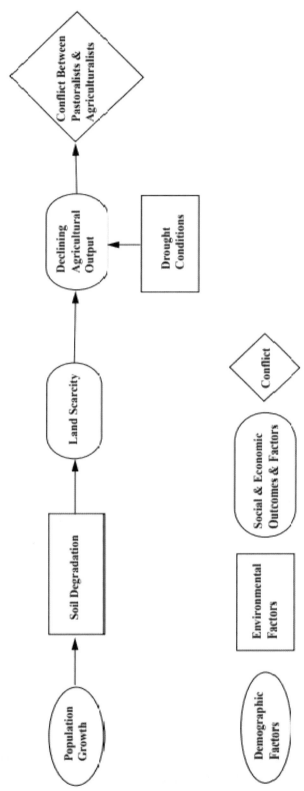

Figure 11.19 Flowchart of Environmental conflict for Ethiopia
      Source: Source: (Schwartz & Singh, 1999)

11.4.3. Deforestation, land degradation, intensive farming, water scarcity, overexploitation of natural resources and energy crisis caused by population explosion led to environmental conflict in Mexico

[Deforestation, intensive farming, water scarcity, overexploitation of natural resources, global energy crisis and population explosion as keystone environmental problems]

In Chiapas, Mexico the wealthier social class has access to the most of the fertile land, while indigenes (indigenous people) and campesinos (Spanish speaking subsistence farmers) have been provided a little fertile land. However, the 1917 Mexican constitution focused on redistribution of land to ecologically marginalized peasants, but indigenes and campesinos felt that the Partido Revolutionary Institution (PRI) was purposely avoiding this idea as part of PRI's 1992 economic reform policies. This resulted in weakened Mexican government and highly dissatisfied peasantry, whom also affected by cropland loss due to deforestation and land degradation (fig. 12.20 and 12.21).

In addition, issues such as water scarcity and energy crisis (electricity) also affected the region. In the period between 1974 and 1986 the Lacandon Rain Forest was declined at the rate of 7.7% per year and 42% was overtaken by secondary forest. It has been estimated in the period between 1974 and 1986 about 20 to 50% of the high land was affected by soil erosion. This is accompanied by 5% of coffee plantation, which was degraded by heavy water logging. Soil erosion was mainly aggravated by intense rainfall, winds, deforestation and intensive farming (unsustainable farming), and subsequent famine and poverty on the indigenes and campesinos resulted from ecological marginalization led to a rebel movement by Ejercito Zapatista de Leberacion Nacional (EZIN). Adapted from (Schwartz & Singh, 1999)

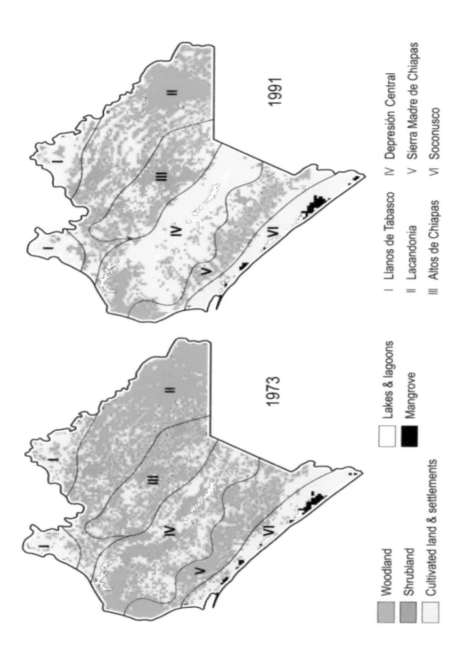

Figure 11.20 Land use in Chiapas, between 1973 and 1991 shows deforestation
  Source: Evaluation of Landsat data by Ignacio March, ECOSUR, San Cristóbal de las Casas

As cited in (Richter, 2000).Used under CC BY 2.0

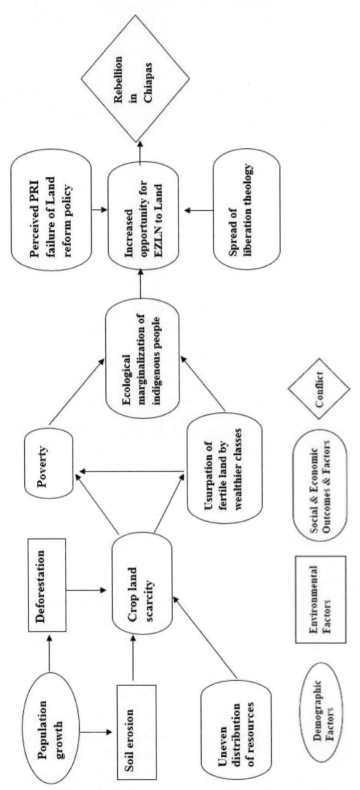

Figure 11.21 Flowchart for Environmental conflict for Chiapas, Mexico
Source: (Schwartz & Singh, 1999)

282

11.4.4. Population explosion in Northeast India due to intense immigration of Bengalis affected by deforestation, resource depletion, loss of wetlands and flooding resulted by land degradation causes environmental conflict.

[Deforestation, overexploitation of natural resources and population explosion as keystone environmental problems]

In Bangladesh deforestation and intense human encroachment adjacent to river banks resulted in flooding events and depletion of natural resources. Lacks of natural resources and intense flooding have caused millions of Bengalis to migrate to Assam and Tripura in Northeast India. However, this situation affected the political stability and became a threat to indigenous culture. In addition, increased competition over resources led to ethnic clashes. As Bengali migrants are Muslims and indigenous people are Hindus, in the period between 1979 and 1985 ethnic rioting caused death of more than 4000 people in Assam and Tripura of Northeast India (fig. 11.22 and 11.23).

In 1988 Bangladesh experienced a massive flooding event, which affected 1.6 million tons of rice production. Wetlands are converted to agriculture lands, and road development (urbanization) made low-lying areas more vulnerable to flooding. Deforestation in the Himalayas (upstream) also exacerbated flooding. Adapted from (Schwartz & Singh, 1999)

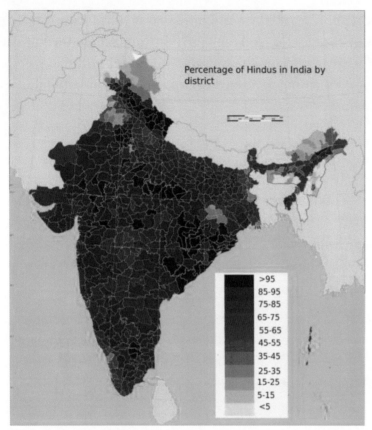

Percentage of Hindus in India by district

>95
85-95
75-85
65-75
55-65
45-55
35-45
25-35
15-25
5-15
<5

Figure 11.22 Map shows less Hindu population in Northeast India due to intense immigration of Muslim Bengalis

Source:https://commons.wikimedia.org/wiki/File:India_Hindu_district_map_2011.png

Credit: 'Superbeniamin'   Used under CC BY-SA 4.0

Flow Chart of Environmental Conflict for India (Northeast) Case Study

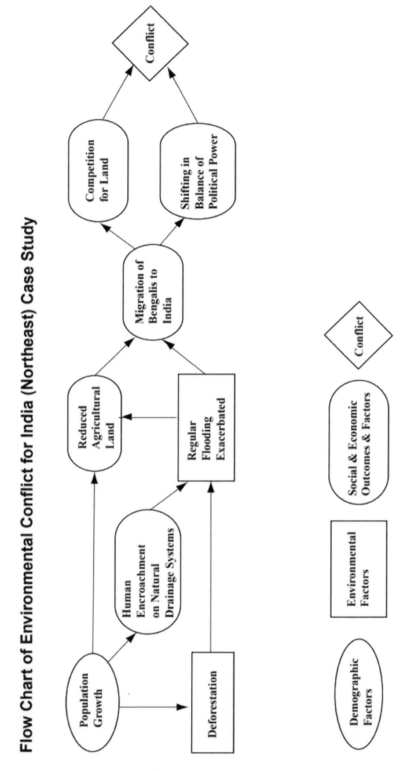

Figure 11.23 Flowchart of Environmental conflict for Northeast India
Source: (Schwartz & Singh, 1999) Credit: Peje suizo

11.4.5. Population explosion caused reduced land availability, and land degradation eventually led to loss of crop production and poverty causes environmental conflict in Peru.

[Population explosion as a keystone environmental problem]

In Peru's southern highlands (Ayacucho region) during 1980's population explosion reduced the land availability for agriculture, which is 0.2 ha. per capita. This problem was further aggravated by land degradation and subsequent loss in agriculture production led to economic crisis in the Southern highland peasantry mainly in the period between 1970's and 1980's. Failure in the implementation of agrarian reforms established under the military government from 1968 to 1980 initiated clashes between affected people, unemployed graduates also joined the protest led by Sendero Luminoso ('Shining path'), which then identified as a terrorist organization took tens of thousands of lives (fig. 11.24 and 11.25). Adapted from (McClintock & Cynthia, 1989) as cited in (Schwartz & Singh, 1999).

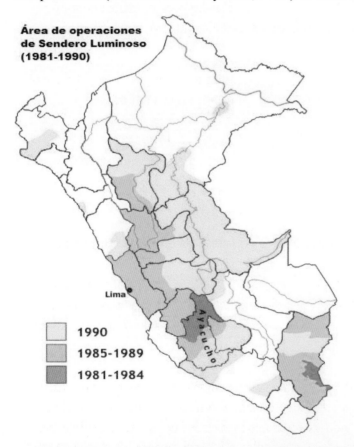

Figure 11.24 Land area operated by Sendero Luminoso (shining path)
Source:
https://commons.wikimedia.org/wiki/File:Area_de_operaciones_de_Sendero_Luminoso_(1981-1990).png

286

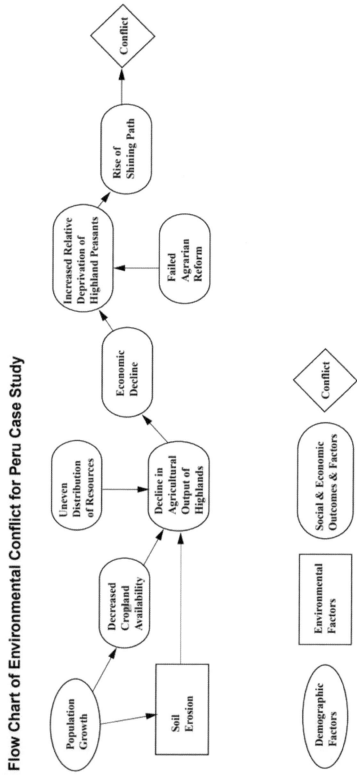

Figure 11.25 Flowchart of Environmental conflict for Peru
Source: (Schwartz & Singh, 1999)

287

11.4.6. Water pollution and scarcity, deforestation and land degradation caused by population explosion led to environmental conflicts in Pakistan. [Water pollution and scarcity, deforestation and population explosion as keystone environmental problems]

In Pakistan, population explosion accompanied by (non-manmade) climate change-drought resulted in water scarcity and water pollution, deforestation and soil degradation.

The major causes of water pollution are industrial and domestic wastewater effluents, heavy silting along with prolonged drought condition led to scarcity for potable water.

Intensive farming (increased demand for crop land) and the energy crisis (fuel wood consumption) led to reduced forest cover from 14.2% to 5.2% of Pakistan's total land area. Impacts of deforestation associated with land degradation due to loss of organic matter, soil salinization, water logging, and flooding made Pakistani soil infertile. Subsequent loss of agriculture production and famine led to clashes between social or ethnic classes mainly in urban regions such as Karachi (fig. 11.26 and 11.27). Adapted from (Schwartz & Singh, 1999)

Figure 11.26 Karachi rioting aftermath

Source: https://commons.wikimedia.org/wiki/File:Karachi_rioting_aftermath.jpg

Credit: Waheed M. Zuberi

Flow Chart of Environmental Conflict for Pakistan Case Study

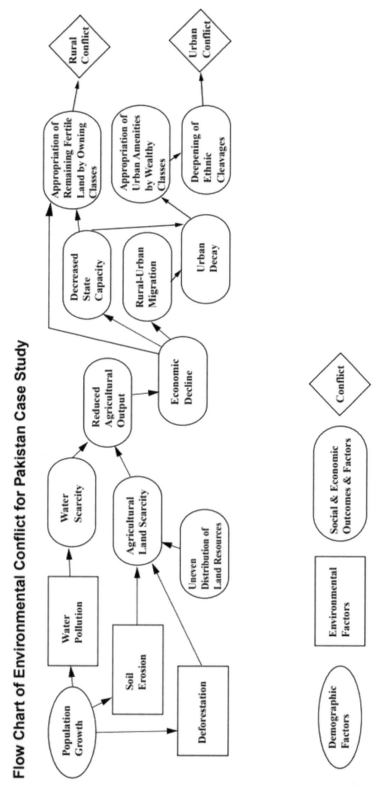

Figure 11.27 Flowchart of Environmental conflict for Pakistan
    Source: (Schwartz & Singh, 1999)

289

11.4.7. Desertification (land degradation) and deforestation due to intensive farming resulted from population explosion in North Sudan causes environmental conflict between North and South Sudan
[Intensive farming, deforestation and population explosion as keystone environmental problems]

From 1966 to 1972 and in 1983 a devastating civil war was occurred between North Sudan and South Sudan. After the independence of Sudan in 1956 large scale mechanized (intensive) farming was practiced in Northern Sudan. By 1980's this situation led to land degradation and desertification in the Northern Sudan. All forest area expected to be denuded by 2003 due to deforestation and energy crisis (fuel wood) caused by increased population in North Sudan. However, land degradation also exacerbated by impacts of drought by (non-manmade) climate change, and overgrazing. The Jallaba (wealthier Arab Sudanese) people of the North then migrated to South Sudan in search of arable land. Since 1970s Jallaba had begun several schemes related to oil, water and land resources in Southern Sudan. Then the intense completion between ecologically marginalized Northern Sudan immigrant and South Sudanese cause clashes. Wealthier and politically stronger (Jallaba) people have formed Sudan People's Liberation Army (SPLA), and the war intensified (fig. 11.28 and 11.29). Adapted from (Schwartz & Singh, 1999)

Figure 11.28 Map of North and South Sudan
Source: https://commons.wikimedia.org/wiki/File:South_Sudan_Sudan_Locator-
cropped.png   Used under CC0 1.0

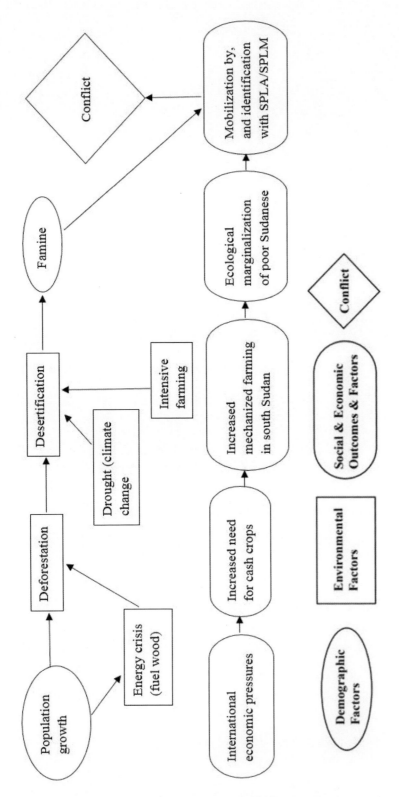

Figure 11.29 Flowchart of Environmental conflict for Sudan
Source: (Schwartz & Singh, 1999)

292

11.4.8. Over fishing (resource depletion), eutrophication, water pollution, deforestation and desertification caused environmental conflict between Kenyan tribes

[Overexploitation of natural resources, deforestation, water pollution, intensive farming and population explosion as keystone environmental problems]

Lake Victoria is the third largest fresh water lake in the world found in Kenya. The lake has been over exploited by over fishing and degraded by water pollution, where toxic chemicals flow from seven Kenyan rivers feed the lake. Increased eutrophication due to the massive influx of nitrogen, phosphorous, and sulphur caused death zones due to deoxygenized regions created by algal blooms resulted in fish deaths.

In the period between 1970 and 1990 Kenya lost 11,450 ha. of forests. Deforestation result into soil degradation and desertification. Silting caused by soil erosion also pollutes the nearby lakes such as Lake Jipe, Bogoria, and Turkana.

Impacts of intensive farming practices such as pollution by agrochemicals also exacerbated desertification and land degradation. About 483,860 km^2 or 83% of total land of Kenya was decertified. This led to reduced food production and economic crisis. Thus, agriculturist (Kikuyu people) has been migrating in search of fertile land since 1960's. Kikuyu agriculturists occupied Rift valley, where the Kalenjin and other pastoralists reside. Clashes occurred in 1991 and 1992 between Kalenjin warriors and members of pastoralist tribes such as Maasai and the Kikuyu agriculturists (fig. 11.30, 11.31 and 11.32).

Migration had caused clashes in 1993 where 1500 people killed. 1994 clashed were more wide spread to other parts of Kenya. In addition to Kikuyu people, Kalenjin warriors and Maasai tribes also targeted other tribes, such as Luo, Luhya, Kisii, Kamba, Meru and Teso. Adapted from (Schwartz & Singh, 1999)

Figure 11.30 Kikuyu agriculturists
Source:
https://commons.wikimedia.org/wiki/File:Traditional_Kikuyu_men_and_women_dancing
.jpg

Figure 11.31 Maasai pastoralists
Source: https://commons.wikimedia.org/wiki/File:Maasai_Tribe_Kenya.jpg

Flow Chart of Environmental Conflict for Kenya Case Study

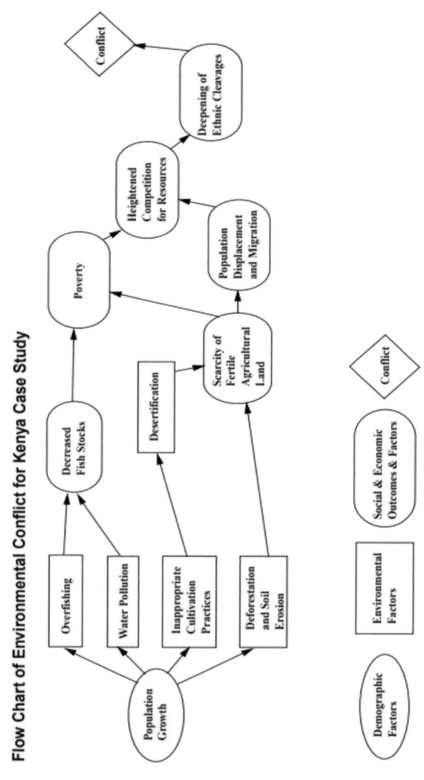

Figure 11.32 Flowchart of Environmental conflict for Kenya
Source: (Schwartz & Singh, 1999)

295

11.5. Indirect International Environmental Conflicts

11.5.1. Deforestation, over exploitation of natural resources and land degradation caused by population explosion led to environmental conflict between El Salvador and Honduras.

[Over exploitation of natural resources, deforestation and population explosion as keystone environmental problems]

1969 invasion of El Salvador into Honduras led to a 100-day war, which killed thousands of civilians and converted over 100 thousand people into homeless and jobless refugees. It has been revealed that the cause for the war is population explosion and resulted competition over resources, which forced marginal people in El Salvador to migrate into Honduras in search of resources.

Deforestation in El Salvador caused the depletion of entire virgin forest cover in the region. Intensive farming (over irrigation) also affected the top soil and resulted in land degradation (fig. 11.33 and 11.34). Arrival of Salvadoran immigrant exacerbated competition for resources in Honduras. This resulted in the economic crisis among small scale farmers of Honduras. Dispute between Honduras farmers and the immigrant of El Salvador led to war. Adapted from (Schwartz & Singh, 1999)

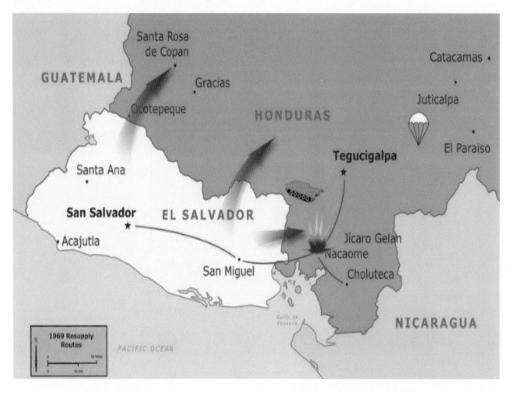

Figure 11.33 El Salvador's invasion into Honduras 1969
Source: (Briscoe, 2007)

296

Flow Chart of Environmental Conflict for El Salvador - Honduras Case Study

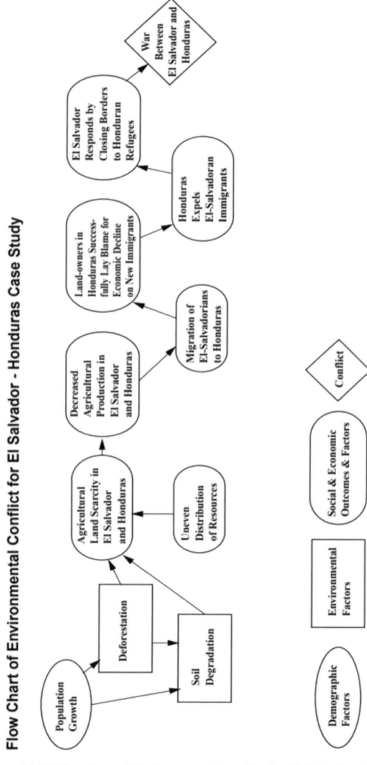

Figure 11.34 Flowchart of Environmental conflict for El Salvador- Honduras
   Source: (Schwartz & Singh, 1999)

11.5.2.   Desertification due to over grazing, resource depletion, famine, and water scarcity (drought) pioneered by population explosion in Northern Somalia led to migration into eastern Ethiopia, which caused environmental conflict

[Over exploitation of natural resources, deforestation, water scarcity and population explosion as keystone environmental problems]

1977-78 war between Somalia and Ethiopia was initiated from clashes between Ishaq and Ogaden pastoral groups. In northern Somalia high demand for meat exports to Middle East in 1950s, 60s and 70s lead to overcrowding of cattle and intense grazing degrade the land, accompanied by water scarcity (Markakis, 1989) and drought led to famine in the region. Thus, Ishaq people of Northern Somalia periodically migrated to east Ethiopian Haud region in search of resources (fig. 11.35 and 11.36). The resistance against immigrant Ishaq pastoral group by the Ogaden led to war between Somalia and Ethiopia in 1977. Adapted from(Markakis, 1989) as cited in(Schwartz & Singh, 1999).

Figure 11.35 Map shows Haud and Ogaden territories

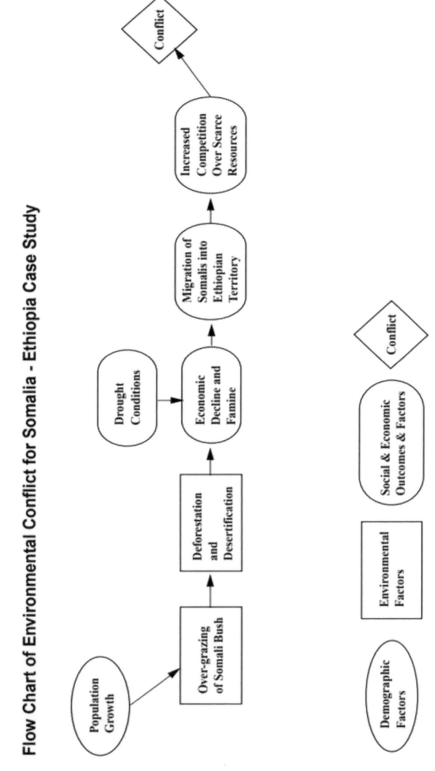

Figure 11.36 Flowchart of Environmental conflict for Somalia-Ethiopia
Source: (Schwartz & Singh, 1999)

11.5.3. Water scarcity pioneered by population explosion led to environmental conflict between Israel and Palestine (West Bank)
[Water scarcity and pollution, over exploitation of natural resources and population explosion as keystone environmental problems]

In 1950s Jordan and United Nations Relief and Work Agency (UNRWA) for Palestine Refugees were working on irrigation scheme for the benefit of Jordan's agriculture and resettlement of Palestinian refugees. And they have decided to divert Yarmouk River into Lake Tiberias and to construct irrigation canals on both side of the Jordan valley. The project was expecting to irrigate 43,500 ha in Jordan and 6000 ha in Syria. In addition, a hydroelectric power plant also generates annually 28,300 kWh of electricity for bother nations. It was believed Bunger plan would settle 0ver 100 thousand people. However, in 1953 just before the implementation of the plan Israel protested for its riparian rights to the Yarmouk River in the Bunger plan, even though Israel had only 10 km of land on the Yarmouk.

In 1967 Israel went to war on Arab nations because Arabs tried to divert the Jordan River head waters that feed Israel(Cooley, 1984). At that time the west bank aquifers provided 25-40% of Israel's water(Starr, 1991); (Falkenmark, 1989) as cited in (Schwartz & Singh, 1999). Dispute between Israel and Arab nations began in 1987 lasted till 1992. Due to the increased water demands government of Israel restricted the Palestinians on drilling wells, while allow the same to Jewish west bank settlers without any restrictions. However, Palestinians also suffer from salinization of aquifers due to Mediterranean Sea water intrusion (fig. 11.37 and 11.38).

Adapted from (Schwartz & Singh, 1999)

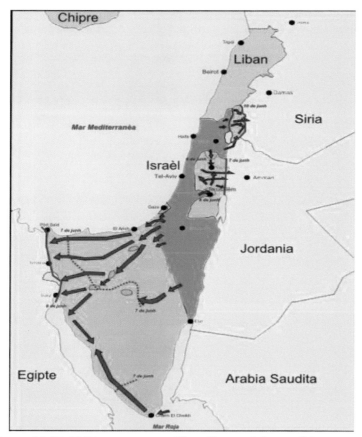

Figure 11.37 1967 movement of Israeli armed forces (blue arrow) and newly captured areas by Israel (light blue)

Source:

https://commons.wikimedia.org/wiki/File:Gu%C3%A8rra_dei_Si%C3%A8is_Jorns.png

Credit: Nicolas Eynaud

301

Flow Chart of Environmental Conflict for Israel - Palestine (West Bank) Case Study

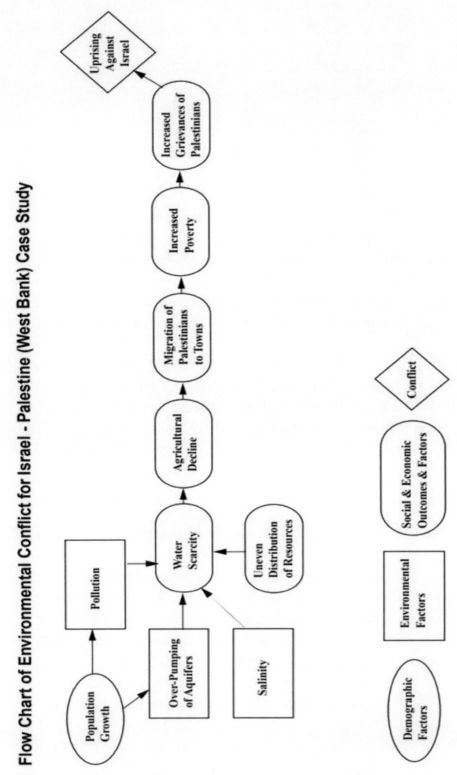

Figure 11.38 Flowchart of Environmental conflict for Israel- Palestine
Source: (Schwartz & Singh, 1999)

11.5.4. Population explosion resulted into intensive farming led to land degradation, depletion of resources and water scarcity, and the migration of Moors of Mauritania into Senegal led to environmental conflict.

[Intensive farming, over exploitation of natural resources, water scarcity and population explosion as keystone environmental problems]

In the regions Mauritania and Senegal, increasing population caused intensive farming and intensive farming led to land degradation, resource depletion, famine, and water scarcity. This is also accompanied by persistent drought (caused by climate change). To overcome this crisis both Black African residing in Senegal River and Moors of Northern Mauritania decided to build series of dams along Senegal River. After the establishment of dams, Northern Mauritanian Moors have migrated to Southern Senegal in the mid 1980's; the land was previously administered by black Africans of Senegal (fig. 11.39 and 11.40). This situation resulted into clashes between Moors and black Africans. During 1989 riots in Senegal killed 35 Moors and over 17,000 shops owned by Moors were looted or destroyed, similarly, riots in Mauritania killed over 200 black Africans. However, in 1992 diplomatic ties were restored between both ethnic communities.

Adapted from (Schwartz & Singh, 1999)

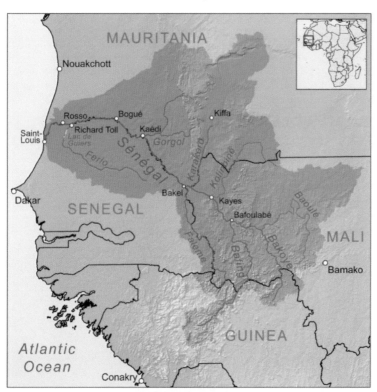

Figure 11.39 Map of Senegal River basin
Source: https://upload.wikimedia.org/wikipedia/commons/7/7a/Senegalrivermap.png
Credit: KmusserUsed under CC BY-SA 3.0

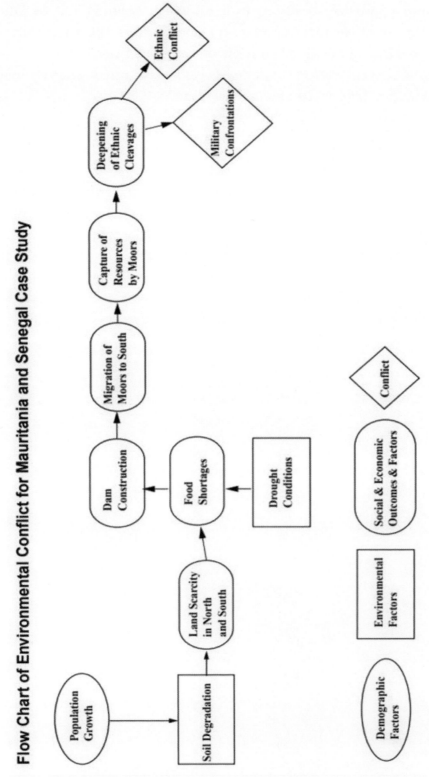

Figure 11.40 Flowchart of Environmental conflict for Mauritania and Senegal
    Source: (Schwartz & Singh, 1999)

304

11.5.5. **Water pollution-water scarcity due to salt water intrusion and agrochemicals affected agriculture and caused famine and diseases including infant mortality in the Gaza**

[**Urbanization and urban sprawl, water pollution and water scarcity, overexploitation of natural resources, intensive farming and population explosion as keystone environmental problems**]

The Palestinian Authority (PA) chaired by Palestinian Liberation Organization (PLO) headed by Yasser Arafat, who faced political opposition from Islamic militants such as Hamas. Here, both PA and Hamas were engaged in war against Israel.

It has been revealed environmental factors such as water scarcity and water pollution caused by salt water intrusion, agrochemicals and industrial effluents led to diseases the elevated child mortality. Even though Palestinian water requirement as high as annually 100 to 140 cubic meters, the available consumable fresh water is only 65 cubic meters per year. Salt water intrusion of aquifers from Mediterranean further degraded the water quality. Farmers were insisted to cultivate salt tolerant crops, which subsequently resulted in food shortage and severe economic crisis. By using this circumstance Yasser Arafat's political opponent Hamas increased its popularity gained more support to legitimize its suicide raids on Israel (fig. 11.41 and 11.42).

Adapted from (Schwartz & Singh, 1999)

Figure 11.41 Water crisis of west bank Gaza
Source:
https://commons.wikimedia.org/wiki/File:Water_supply_in_West_Bank_and_Gaza_February_2014_2water_photoblog.jpg
Credit: Muhammad Sabah, B'TselemUsed under CC BY 4.0

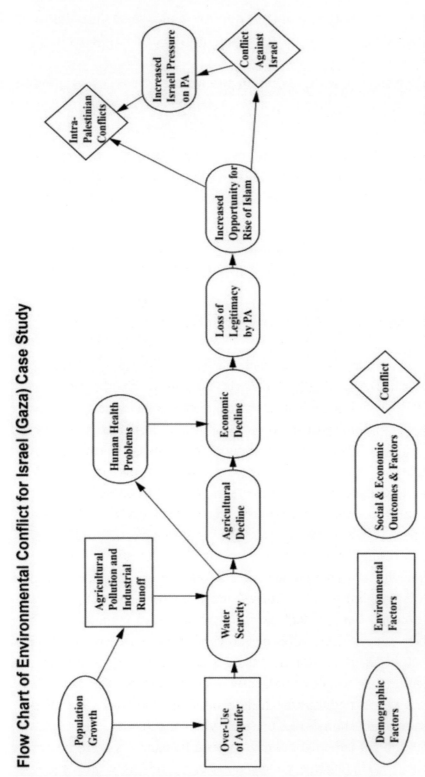

Figure 11.42 Flowchart of Environmental conflict for Israel (Gaza)
Source: (Schwartz & Singh, 1999)

306

11.5.6. Emissions of the transboundary air pollutants from the USA cause acid deposition in Canada
[Urbanization and urban sprawl, air pollution and population explosion as keystone environmental problems]

According to (Munton, 1997), in the 1980s acid rain in Canadian states was caused primarily by transboundary air pollutants (SO_x and NO_x) from the United States (fig 11.43 and 11.44). Each year Smelters, industrial boilers, and coal power plants in the US emit tonnes of air pollutants into the atmosphere. These pollutants are carried by the air current and precipitated as acid rain in the Canadian States. Both nations adopted national acid rain controls by 1990. In 1991, US-Canada air quality agreement was signed, which led to a significant reduction in acid deposition in Canada. In 1995, the establishment of cap-and-trade programmes in the United States reduced SO_2 emissions by 32% from the 1990 levels ("United States- Canada Air quality agreement", 2015).

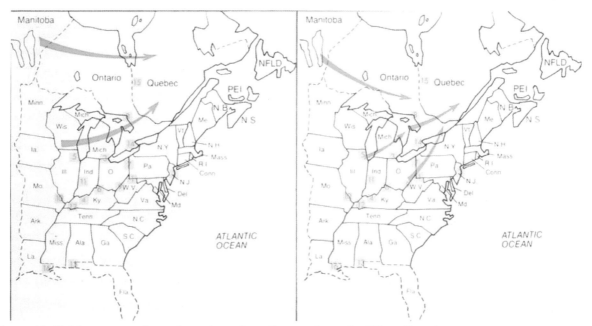

Figure 11.43 Movement of transboundary air pollutants from the US to Canada
Source: https://www.flickr.com/photos/internetarchivebookimages/20539276245

Credit: Ontario Ministry of Environment, License: Public domain

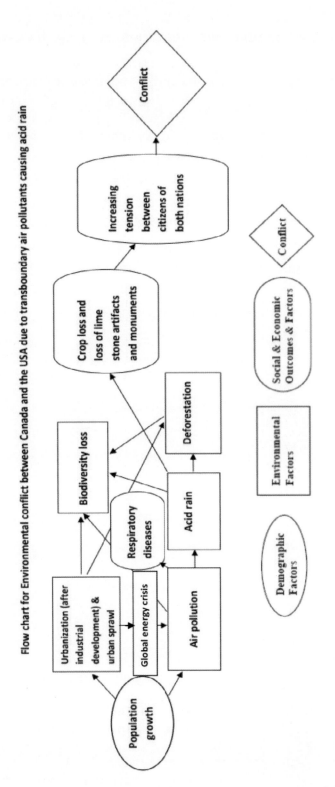

Figure 11.44 Flowchart for Environmental conflict between Canada and the USA due to transboundary air pollutants causing acid rain

It has been found primary environmental problems are the causative factors of every environmental conflict regardless of whether it is a keystone environmental problem or not. For instance, air pollution (by SO_x and NO_x) is the primary (initial) and keystone environmental problem of 1980s transboundary air pollution crisis between the USA and Canada. Whereas, acid rain, deforestation (by loss of chlorophyll) and biodiversity loss are secondary, tertiary and quaternary environmental issues respectively. When mitigating a primary environmental issue if it results into disappearance of secondary and subsequent environmental problems, then that mitigated problem is a keystone environmental problem. However, keystone environmental problems also result from non-keystone environmental problems in the chain of cause-effect relationship, e.g. Keystone air pollution causes a non-keystone acid rain problem, and acid rain causes loss of chlorophyll in forest trees, thus causing deforestation. However, similar to air pollution (primary problem) deforestation (tertiary problem) is also a known keystone environmental problem (where mitigating deforestation can reduce biodiversity loss and soil erosion). Similarly, in the case of the 1995 Alto Cenepa war, intensive farming is the primary and keystone environmental problem resulting in agrochemicals (secondary), water pollution (tertiary), eutrophication (quaternary), and biodiversity loss (quinary). When the keystone environmental problem gets mitigated the entire resulting environmental problems get abated. In the above scenario, water pollution is placed as a tertiary environmental issue, however, water pollution is a known keystone issue because when water pollution is mitigated the resulting eutrophication can be completely abated. However, in the same scenario eutrophication is not a keystone environmental problem because if eutrophication is mitigated the resulting biodiversity loss cannot be mitigated for sure. This is because biodiversity loss can occur due to various other causes instead. For instance, an industrial runoff with hazardous chemical pollutants can cause the same, even introduction of an exotic predator or competitor species can also result in the loss of certain species leading to biodiversity loss. Thus, there is a clear difference between a keystone environmental problem and a non-keystone environmental problem regardless of whether it is a primary environmental problem (initiative) or placed somewhere in the middle of the chain (secondary, tertiary, etc.).

The occurrences of more adverse results from environmental problems resonate together with social, cultural, political, and economic factors and exacerbate the chances of igniting an environmental conflict or war. The following table (table 11.1) depicts the role of keystone environmental problems as primary environmental problems (primary cause from where crisis originates), secondary, tertiary, quaternary, etc. environmental problems in igniting an environmental conflict.

Table 11.1 Occurrences of keystone environmental problems on igniting global environmental conflicts or warfare

Type of environmental conflict (International or intranational)	Keystone environmental problems / Examples of environmental problems	Population explosion (growth)	Water pollution - scarcity- salination	Intensive farming	Deforestation	Over-exploitation of natural resources	Global energy crisis	Urbanization-urban sprawl-settlements
Direct Intra	Chauvery River dispute	Yes	Yes	Yes	Yes	No	No	No
Direct Inter	Strait among fishermen of India and Sri Lanka	Yes	No	No	No	Yes	No	No
Direct Inter	Russia's invasion of Ukraine in 2022	Yes	Yes	No	No	No	Yes	No
Direct Inter	Alto Cenepa war	Yes	No	Yes	Yes	No	No	No
Direct Inter	Grand Ethiopian Renaissance Dam crisis	Yes	Yes	No	No	No	Yes	No
Indirect Intra	Philippines conflict	Yes	No	No	Yes	Yes	No	No
Indirect Intra	Ethiopian conflict	Yes	Yes	No	No	Yes	No	No
Indirect Intra	Mexican conflict	Yes	No	No	Yes	Yes	No	No
Indirect Intra	Bengalis immigrat conflict in North India	Yes	No	No	Yes	Yes	No	No
Indirect Intra	Peru's rnvironmental conflict	Yes	No	Yes	Yes	Yes	No	No
Indirect Intra	Pakistan's conflict	Yes	Yes	No	Yes	Yes	No	Yes
Indirect Intra	North Sudan and South Sudan	Yes	No	Yes	Yes	No	Yes	No
Indirect Inter	El Salvador and Honduras	Yes	No	Yes	Yes	Yes	No	No
Indirect Inter	Somalia and Ethiopia	Yes	Yes	Yes	Yes	Yes	No	No
Indirect Inter	Israel and Palestine (West Bank)	Yes	Yes	Yes	No	Yes	Yes	Yes
Indirect Inter	Mauritania and Senegal 1989	Yes	Yes	Yes	No	Yes	No	No
Indirect Inter	Gaza conflict	Yes	Yes	Yes	No	Yes	No	No
Indirect Inter	USA and Canada 1980s (acid rain)	Yes	No	No	Yes	No	Yes	Yes

In general, all kinds of environmental problems can ignite a conflict situation, and can be at any position (primary secondary, tertiary, etc.) on igniting an environmental dispute.

And, keystone environmental problems are unique due to their ability to conquer the occurrence of other dependent environmental problems. This is because dependent environmental issues completely depend on the keystone environmental problem alone without having any other causative environmental problem. Thus, when keystone problem gets mitigated all other dependent issues also get vanished. Keystone environmental problem can occur at any position (primary, secondary, tertiary, etc.) in the web of environmental issues. However, when a keystone environmental problem gets mitigated the entire links (environmental issues) following it also get collapsed or abated along with it. It has been found global environmental conflicts and warfare ignited by labyrinth (combination) of keystone environmental problems depicted in table 11.1 and figure 11.45. Thus, it has been revealed that environmental conflicts having several keystone environmental problem roots act together with social, cultural, political, and economic factors on igniting a conflict or warfare.

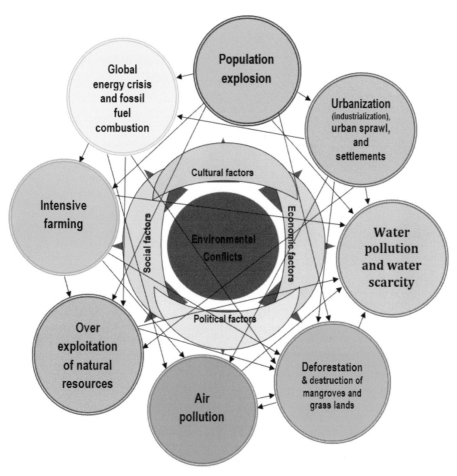

Figure 11.45 Labyrinth of Keystone environmental problems that ignites environmental conflicts in varying combination

11.7 Summery

Study found labyrinth of keystone environmental problems together with socioeconomic factors play a vital role in ignition of environmental conflicts. Keystone environmental problems can be found at any position (as primary cause, secondary, tertiary, etc.) on the emergence of environmental problems igniting conflicts. It has been evident that resolving keystone environmental problems could also bring other linked (dependent) non-keystone environmental problems to a halt. However, study revealed labyrinth of keystone environmental problems resonates together with social, cultural, political, and economic factors ignite environmental conflict or warfare. Thus, unless root keystone links are identified and get mitigated, it is not possible to terminate the labyrinth of keystone environmental problems that ignites environmental conflicts and wars.

References

1. *"123HelpMe.com"*. (2016, 02 08). Retrieved 2016, from http://www.123helpme.com/view.asp?id=19868

2. *"Air pollution and food production"*. (n.d.). Retrieved 9 21, 2018, from UNECE.

3. *"Air Pollution and Forest Decline Is There a Link?"*. (1990). U.S. Department of Agriculture Forest Service. Retrieved 10 23, 2018, from https://naldc.nal.usda.gov/download/CAT30948427/PDF

4. *"awe.gov.au"*. (2016). Retrieved 03 18, 2022, from https://www.awe.gov.au/sites/default/files/documents/factsheet-wetlands-water-quality.pdf

5. *"Bloomberg"*. (2018, 9 4). Retrieved 11 5, 2019, from "about.bnef.com": https://about.bnef.com/blog/global-electricity-demand-increase-57-2050/

6. *"buzzle.com"*. (2016). Retrieved 02 2016, from http://www.buzzle.com/articles/what-does-zero-population-growth-zpg-mean.html

7. *"Carnegie Mellon University"*. (2003). Retrieved 06 12, 2014, from http://environ.andrew.cmu.edu/m3/s6/12appendix1.shtml.

8. *"Causes of global warming"*. (n.d.). (WWF) Retrieved 10 17, 2018, from http://www.wwf.org.au/what-we-do/climate/causes-of-global-warming#gs.11ZElug

9. *"cgge.aag.org"*. (2011). Retrieved 02 2016, from http://cgge.aag.org/PopulationandNaturalResources1e/CF_PopNatRes_Jan10/CF_PopNatRes_Jan1019.html

10. *citizen.org*. (2023). (Public Citizen Inc. and Public Citizen Foundation) Retrieved 03 10, 2023, from https://www.citizen.org/article/nuclear-power-is-not-clean-or-green/

11. "Climate Central. Highest Levels in 800,000 Years". (n.d.). Retrieved 9 27, 2017, from http://www.climatecentral.org/gallery/graphics/highest-levels-in-800000-years

12. "CoffeeWithMarkets". (2013, 05 30). Retrieved 08 01, 2022, from https://upload.wikimedia.org/wikipedia/commons/7/7c/Annual_Changes_In_Global_Forest_Cover_With_Sub-Regional_Trends.png

13. *"commons.wikimedia.org"*. (2011, 03 16). (D. Globe, Producer) Retrieved 07 24, 2022, from https://commons.wikimedia.org/wiki/File:Fukushima_I_by_Digital_Globe.jpg

14. *"Conserve Energy Future"*. (n.d.). Retrieved 9 16, 2018, from https://www.conserve-energy-future.com/effects-of-oil-spills.php

15. *"dailythanthi.com"*. (2021, 06 13). Retrieved 06 14, 2021, from https://www.dailythanthi.com/News/State/2021/06/13073828/In-the-sea-area-of-Kachchativu-Old-buses-Government.vpf

16. *"darksky.org"*. (2016, 6 10). (Internaitonal Dark-Sky Association) Retrieved 11 11, 2019, from https://www.darksky.org/80-of-world-population-lives-under-skyglow-new-study-finds/

17. *"Department of Economic and Social Affairs"*. (2018, 5 16). Retrieved 5 11, 2019, from www.un.org: https://www.un.org/development/desa/en/news/population/2018-revision-of-world-urbanization-prospects.html

18. *"Department of Economic and Social Affairs"*. (2018, 2 20). Retrieved from www.un.org: https://www.un.org/development/desa/en/news/forest/halting-deforestation-for-sdgs.html

19. *"disasterium.com"*. (2013). Retrieved 12 07, 2014, from http://www.disasterium.com/10-worst-man-made-disasters-of-all-time/

20. " Destructive fishing practices". (2015). Retrieved 03 30, 2015, from http://wwf.panda.org/about_our_earth/blue_planet/problems/problems_fishing/destructive_fishing/

21. *"Earth eclipse"*. (n.d.). Retrieved 11 18, 2018, from https://www.eartheclipse.com/pollution/various-causes-of-plastic-pollution.html

22. *"ec.princeton.edu"*. (2015). Retrieved 02 2016, from http://ec.princeton.edu/info/ecp.html

23. *"Education Global Methane Inventory"*. (2010). (NASA GISS Institute on global climate and planet) Retrieved 5 5, 2015, from http://icp.giss.nasa.gov/education/methane/intro/cycle.html

24. *"eea.europa.eu"*. (n.d.). Retrieved 12 07, 2014, from http://www.eea.europa.eu/highlights/sahara-dust-sea-spray-.

25. Elton, C. (2023). Retrieved 04 20, 2023, from https://www.euronews.com/green/2023/04/05/really-encouraging-plastic-bag-bans-work-say-campaigners-where-is-europe-lagging-behind

26. *"en.unesco.org"*. (2013). Retrieved 01 2016, from http://en.unesco.org/gem-report/sites/gem-report/files/girls-factsheet-en.pdf

27. *"en.unesco.org"*. (2013). Retrieved 02 2016, from http://en.unesco.org/gem-report/sites/gem-report/files/girls-factsheet-en.pdf

28. *"energy.gov"*. (2013, 8 14). (o. o. electricity, Producer) Retrieved 11 11, 2019, from https://www.energy.gov/oe/articles/10-years-after-2003-northeast-blackout

29. *"Environmental History Resource Guide for South Africa"*. (n.d.). Retrieved from https://sites.google.com/site/southafricarobertson/poverty/poverty#_ftn1

30. "epa.gov" (2022) Retrieved 03 10, 2023, from https://www.epa.gov/gmi/importance-methane

31. *"eWaste Guide"*. (n.d.). Retrieved from http://www.ewaste.in

32. *"extwprlegs1.fao.org"*. (2017). Retrieved 06 14, 2021, from ttp://extwprlegs1.fao.org/docs/pdf/sri171859.pdf

33. *"FAO"*. (n.d.). Retrieved 11 5, 2019, from "How to Food the world in 2050": http://www.fao.org/fileadmin/templates/wsfs/docs/expert_paper/How_to_Feed_the_World_in_2050.pdf

34. *"faostat data"*. (2014). Retrieved 11 7, 2018, from https://top5ofanything.com/index.php?h=d4d1ef5e

35. *"foe.co.uk"*. (2009). (Sustainable Europe Research Institute (SERI) Austria and Global 2000) Retrieved 02 13, 2016, from https://www.foe.co.uk/sites/default/files/downloads/overconsumption.pdf

36. *"footprintnetwork.org"*. (2016). Retrieved 05 01, 2014, from http://www.footprintnetwork.org/en/index.php/GFN/page/footprint_basics_overview/

37. *"giornalettismo.com"*. (n.d.). Retrieved 07 10, 2022, from http://www.giornalettismo.com/archives/908317/niente-ferma-la-deforestazione/deforestation/.

38. *"greateratlantic.fisheries.noaa.gov"*. (2014). Retrieved 03 30, 2015, from http://www.greateratlantic.fisheries.noaa.gov/sfd/RecFishing/RecreationalFishingHabitat.pdf

39. *"Greenpeace"*. (2016, 7 1). Retrieved 9 3, 2018, from https://www.greenpeace.org/archive-international/en/campaigns/climate-change/coal/Coal-mining-impacts/

40. *"Greenpeace"*. (n.d.). Retrieved 9 3, 2018, from https://www.greenpeace.org/usa/arctic/issues/oil-drilling/

41. *"Greenpeace"*. (n.d.). Retrieved 9 4, 2018, from http://www.greenpeace.org/eastasia/campaigns/toxics/problems/e-waste/guiyu/

42. *"guttmacher.org"*. (2014, 09 17). Retrieved 01 2016, from https://www.guttmacher.org/media/nr/2014/09/17/sfp-sedgh-up.html

43. *"guttmacher.org"*. (2015). Retrieved 02 2016, from http://www.guttmacher.org/pubs/fb_contraceptive_serv.html

44. *"healthypeople.gov"*. (2016). Retrieved 02 2016, from
    https://www.healthypeople.gov/2020/topics-objectives/topic/family-planning#three

45. *"Helpsavenature"*. (2018, 3 5). Retrieved 10 22, 2018, from https://helpsavenature.com/how-
    is-deforestation-related-to-population-growth

46. *"Helpsavenature"*. (2018, 2 19). Retrieved 7 1, 2018, from helpsavenature.com:
    https://helpsavenature.com/facts-about-water-pollution

47. *"hindustantimes"*. (2018, 5 27). Retrieved 8 1, 2018, from hindustantimes.com:
    https://www.hindustantimes.com/environment/at-least-10-species-in-the-ganga-face-
    extinction-say-ministry-reports/story-ecpjjZPoeiMZofK6oRexEL.html

48. *"How many species are we losing?"*. (2016). Retrieved 2016, from www.panda.org:
    http://wwf.panda.org/about_our_earth/biodiversity/biodiversity/

49. "humansociety.org"(n.d.). "An HSUS Report: The Impact of Industrialized Animal
    Agriculture on World Hunger". The Human Society of the United States. Retrieved 11 5,
    2018, from https://www.humanesociety.org/sites/default/files/docs/hsus-report-
    industrialized-animal-agriculture-world-hunger.pdf

50. *"iipdigital.usembassy.gov"*. (2012). Retrieved 12 07, 2014, from
    http://iipdigital.usembassy.gov/st/english/gallery/2012/02/201202171105.html#axzz3L8Z72
    Nfs.

51. "Jannah Firdaus Mediapro Art & Story" (2022) Retrieved 04 24, 2023, from
    https://medium.com/@xenovandestra/best-wild-elephant-elephantus-ferox-repellent-plants-
    flowers-from-nature-english-version-a34aa745f2d9

52. "Keekeesocean: E Waste in India". (2012). Youtube. Retrieved 2014, from
    http://www.youtube.com/watch?v=sFfaYc_pIx8

53. "KNOPS". (2017, 12 18). *The 50 noisiest cities*. Retrieved 8 21, 2018, from
    https://knops.co/noise-pollution-50-noisiest-cities/

54. *"marshall.edu"*. (n.d.). Retrieved 02 2016, from
    https://www.marshall.edu/wcenter/emergency-contraception-and-birth-control/types-of-birth-
    control/

55. *"Minnesota Department of Health"*. (n.d.). Retrieved 12 06, 2014, from
    http://www.health.state.mn.us/divs/eh/indoorair/voc/.

56. *"Noise Solutions"*. (2015, 6 10). Retrieved 8 21, 2018, from "Noise and urbanization":
    https://www.noisesolutions.com/noise-and-urbanization/

57. *"nsf.gov"*. (n.d.). Retrieved 12 06, 2014, from
    http://www.nsf.gov/news/news_summ.jsp?cntn_id=110580.

58. *"ocean.si.edu"*. (n.d.). Retrieved 11 12, 2018, from https://ocean.si.edu/ocean-
    life/invertebrates/ocean-acidification

59. *"oceanconservance.org"*. (n.d.). Retrieved 11 16, 2018, from
    https://oceanconservancy.org/trash-free-seas/plastics-in-the-ocean/

60. *"oceanservice.noaa.gov"*. (2014). (NOAA) Retrieved 03 30, 2015, from
    http://oceanservice.noaa.gov/facts/lionfish.html

61. *"old united nations university website"*. (n.d.). Retrieved 03 20, 2022, from
    https://archive.unu.edu/unupress/unupbooks/80858e/80858E0n.htm

62. *"onegreenplanet.org"*. (n.d.). Retrieved from
    http://www.onegreenplanet.org/animalsandnature/this-is-how-animal-agriculture-causes-
    deforestation

63. *"Overconsumption? Our Use of the World's Natural Resources"*. (2009). (SERI and Global
    2000) Retrieved 02 13, 2016, from Sustainable Europe Research Institute (SERI), Austria
    and GLOBAL 2000 (Friends of the Earth Austria):
    https://www.foe.co.uk/sites/default/files/downloads/overconsumption.pdf

64. UNEP (2005). *"Persistance organic pollutants: national implementation plan for 2005-
    2020"*. Riga. Retrieved 9 25, 2018, from UNEP-POPS-NIP-Latvia-1.English.pdf

65. *"peta.org"*. (n.d.). Retrieved 11 7, 2018, from http://www.peta.org/issues/animals-used-for-
    food/factory-farming/cows/

66. *"pork checkoff"*. (n.d.). Retrieved 11 7, 2018, from https://www.pork.org/facts/stats/u-s-pork-
    exports/top-10-pork-producing-countries/

67. *"rainforest resque.org"*. (n.d.). Retrieved 8 27, 2018, from https://www.rainforest-
    rescue.org/petitions/1121/keep-loggers-and-the-palm-oil-industry-out-of-the-peruvian-
    amazon

68. *"Rainforestinfo"*. (n.d.). Retrieved 11 21, 2014, from
    http://www.rainforestinfo.org.au/background/causes.htm

69. *"rainforestinfo.org.au"*. (n.d.). Retrieved 11 21, 2014, from The causes of rainforest
    destruction: http://www.rainforestinfo.org.au/background/causes.htm

70. *"Rainforest-rescue"*. (2017). Retrieved 8 27, 2018, from https://www.rainforest-
    rescue.org/topics/palm-oil

71. *"Research paper"*. (n.d.). Retrieved 9 16, 2018, from https://research-paper.essayempire.com/examples/history/oil-spills-research-paper/

72. *"Seeing the forest for the trees"*. (n.d.). Retrieved 10 22, 2018, from populationconnection.org: https://www.populationconnection.org/article/seeing-forest-trees-population-growth-deforestation/

73. *"Silvicultural systems"*. (n.d.). Retrieved 07 10, 2022, from http://www.daviesand.com/Choices/Silvicultural_Systems/

74. *"Silviculture methods"*. (n.d.). Retrieved 11 22, 2014, from http://www.state.tn.us/agriculture/publications/forestry/silviculture.pdf

75. "Landfill Gast to Energy" (2009). *"Survey on the Current Status of Municipal Solid Waste Management in Indian Cities and the Potentialof Landfill Gas to Energy Projects in India.*

76. *"Sustainablog.org"*. (2001). Retrieved 11 22, 2014, from http://sustainablog.org/2011/07/reforestation-projects/.

77. *"The Beef Industry and Deforestation"*. (2016, 8 8). Retrieved 10 22, 2018, from "rainforest partnership.org": https://rainforestpartnership.org/the-beef-industry-and-deforestation/

78. *"The Guardian"*. (2018). Retrieved 11 5, 2019, from www.theguardian.com: https://www.theguardian.com/environment/2018/mar/19/water-shortages-could-affect-5bn-people-by-2050-un-report-warns

79. *"The Merig"*. (2014). Retrieved 8 28, 2018, from https://sites.psu.edu/troymerig/2014/03/27/deforestation/

80. *"The Ozone hole"*. (n.d.). Retrieved 4 2, 2015, from The ozine hole history: http://www.theozonehole.com/ozoneholehistory.htm

81. *"Timeforchange.org"*. (n.d.). Retrieved 5 1, 2016, from Time for change: http://timeforchange.org/what-is-a-carbon-footprint-definition

82. *"Total Reduced Sulphur compounds"*. (2010). Retrieved 12 06, 2014, from "airqualityontario.com": http://www.airqualityontario.com/science/pollutants/trs.php.

83. *"toxipedia.org"*. (2011). Retrieved 10 26, 2014, from http://toxipedia.org

84. *"ukessays.com"*. (2016). Retrieved 02 2016, from http://www.ukessays.com/essays/environmental-sciences/human-population-growth-and-its-effect-environmental-sciences-essay.php

85. *"un.org"*. (2015). Retrieved 04 2016, from
   http://www.un.org/en/development/desa/population/publications/pdf/family/trendsContracept
   iveUse2015Report.pdf

86. *"UN.org"*. (2018, 05 16). Retrieved 10 30, 2020, from
   https://www.un.org/development/desa/en/news/population/2018-revision-of-world-
   urbanization-prospects.html

87. *"unfccc.int"*. (2018, 10 01). Retrieved 03 18, 2022, from https://unfccc.int/news/wetlands-
   disappearing-three-times-faster-than-forests

88. *"unpopulation.org"*. (2013). Retrieved 02 2016, from unpopulation.org

89. *"Unsustainable fishing"*. (2015). Retrieved 03 30, 2015, from
   http://wwf.panda.org/about_our_earth/blue_planet/problems/problems_fishing/

90. *"Vietnam News"*. (2016, 2 15). Retrieved 8 31, 2018, from
   https://vietnamnews.vn/environment/282321/environment-ministry-worried-for-mineral-
   overexploitation-in-delta.html#1A8fLsH16vwTFJcG.97

91. IIASA (2016). *"Water Futures and Solutions: Asia 2050"*. International Institute for Applied
   Systems Analysis.

92. *"waterencyclopedia.com"*. (n.d.). Retrieved 03 30, 2015, from
   http://www.waterencyclopedia.com/Oc-Po/Oil-Spills-Impact-on-the-Ocean.html

93. *"wgo.int"*. (2016). Retrieved 01 2016, from
   http://www.who.int/reproductivehealth/topics/unsafe_abortion/magnitude/en/

94. *"What's behind the Egypt-Ethiopia Nile dispute? | Start Here"*. (2020, 01 26). Retrieved 03
   20, 2022, from https://www.youtube.com/watch?v=JdizU0arrJ0

95. *"What's Driving Deforestation?"*. (n.d.). Retrieved 10 22, 2018, from "union of concerned
   scientists": https://www.ucsusa.org/global-warming/stop-deforestation/whats-driving-
   deforestation#.W81V3XszaM8

96. *"whichcountry"*. (n.d.). Retrieved 11 7, 2018, from https://www.whichcountry.co/top-
   chicken-producers-in-the-world/

97. Wijesekera, D.T.S., Amarasinghe, M.C.S.T., Dassanaike, P.N., De Silva, T.H.H.,
   Kuruwitaarachchi, N. (2021) Modern solution for human elephant conflict. 2nd International
   Conference for Emerging Technology, INCET 2021, art. no. 9456214.

98. *"World Energy Needs and Nuclear Power"*. (2018, 9). Retrieved 9 17, 2018, from
   http://www.world-nuclear.org/information-library/current-and-future-generation/world-
   energy-needs-and-nuclear-power.aspx

99. *"WWF Global"*. (2017). Retrieved 8 28, 2018, from wwf.panda.org: http://wwf.panda.org/our_work/forests/deforestation_causes/forest_conversion/

100. *"WWF Global"*. (2017). Retrieved 8 28, 2018, from http://wwf.panda.org/our_work/oceans/problems/destructive_fishing/

101. *"WWF"*. (n.d.). Retrieved 9 19, 2018, from WWF Global: http://wwf.panda.org/our_work/water/intro/threats/

102. *"wwf.panda.org"*. (2015). Retrieved 03 30, 2015, from http://wwf.panda.org/about_our_earth/blue_planet/problems/problems_fishing/

103. *"wwf.panda.org"*. (2016). Retrieved 01 2016, from http://wwf.panda.org/about_our_earth/biodiversity/biodiversity/

104. *"www.newhealthadvisor.com"*. (2014). Retrieved 02 2016, from http://www.newhealthadvisor.com/How-to-Avoid-Pregnancy.html

105. *"www.niwa.co.nz"*. (2009). Retrieved 03 30, 2015, from https://www.niwa.co.nz/coasts-and-oceans/research-projects/effects-of-ocean-acidification-on-plankton-in-new-zealand-waters).

106. *"www.worldwildlife.org"*. (n.d.). Retrieved 10 30, 2020, from https://www.worldwildlife.org/threats/water-scarcity

107. US DH&HS (2005). *11th Report on Carcinogens.* US Public Health Service, U.S. Department of Health and Human Services . USA: National Toxicology Program.

108. " news.sciencemag.org " (2002). Retrieved 12 06, 2014, from http://news.sciencemag.org/2002/11/forest-fires-kick-greenhouse-gas.

109. UN (2014). (U. N. Change, Producer, & United Nations) Retrieved 12 07, 2014, from http://unfccc.int/kyoto_protocol/items/3145.php

110. UNenvironment(2017, 12 3). Retrieved 11 5, 2019, from www.unenvironment.org: https://www.unenvironment.org/news-and-stories/press-release/resource-use-expected-double-2050-better-natural-resource-use

111. UNICEF (2016). "Clear the Air for Children". UNICEF. Retrieved 10 6, 2017, from www.unicef.org/publications/index_92957.html

112. AbdManaf, L., Samah, M., & MohdZukki, N. (2009, 11). Municipal solid waste management in Malaysia: Practices and challenges. *Waste Management, 29*(11), 2902-2906. doi:https://doi.org/10.1016/j.wasman.2008.07.015

113. Acuto, M. (2020, 04 24). COVID-19: Lessons for an Urban(izing) World. *One Earth, 2*(4), 317-319. Retrieved 10 26, 2020, from https://www.ncbi.nlm.nih.gov/pmc/articles/PMC7159854/

114. Adu, P. (2017, 02 24). Understanding Qualitative Content Analysis. USA. Retrieved 10 23, 2020, from https://www.slideshare.net/kontorphilip/qualitative-content-analysis-for-systematic-reviews

115. Agamuthu, P. (2009). Challenges and opportunities in Agro-waste management: An Asian perspective. *Inaugural meeting of First Regional 3R Forum in Asia.* Tokyo, Japan.

116. US DH&HS (1999). *Agency for Toxic Substances and Disease Registry.* Mamaroneck Dialysis Clinic, Health Consultation. U.S. Department of Health and Human Services.

117. WURC (2012). *Agriculture is the direct driver for worldwide deforestation.* Wageningen University and Research Centre. Retrieved 11 3, 2019, from https://www.sciencedaily.com/releases/2012/09/120925091608.htm

118. WHO (2016). *Air Pollution, Climate and Health.* Department of Public Health and Environment. Switzerland: WHO. Retrieved 9 21, 2018, from http://www.who.int/sustainable-development/AirPollution_Climate_Health_Factsheet.pdf

119. WHO (2005). *Air Quality Guidelines Global Update 2005.* Geneva, Switzerland: World Health Organization.

120. Al-Amin, M. (2014). "Domestic Energy Crisis and Deforestation Challenges in Nigeria". *Journal of Environment and Earth Science, 4*(2). Retrieved from https://www.iiste.org/Journals/index.php/JEES/article/view/10740

121. Al-Amin, M. (2014). Domestic Energy Crisis and Deforestation Challenges in Nigeria. *Journal of Environment and Earth Science, 4*(2). Retrieved 9 3, 2018, from https://pdfs.semanticscholar.org/c445/6f273a29abea0e12406f2e22e0e0ffd90e8f.pdf

122. Alberts, E. (2018, 9 13). *This Is One Big Reason North Carolina Isn't Ready For The Hurricane.* Retrieved 10 15, 2018, from thedodo.com: https://www.thedodo.com/on-the-farm/hurricane-florence-hog-farm-waste-pools

123. Alemayehu, T. (2001). The Impact of Uncontrolled Waste Disposal on Surface Water Quality in Addis Abbaba, Ethiopia. *Ethiopian Journal of Science, 24*, 93-104. Retrieved 9 4, 2018, from http://dx.doi.org/10.4314/sinet.v24i1.18177

124. Allen, C., Macalady, A., Chenchouni, H., Bachelet, D., McDowell, N., Vennetier, M., . . . Cobb, N. (2010, 2 5). A global overview of drought and heat-induced tree mortality reveals emerging climate change risks for forests. *Forest Ecology and Management, 259*(4), 600-684. doi:https://doi.org/10.1016/j.foreco.2009.09.001

125. Allsopp, M, Santillo, D, Johnston, P., & Stringer, R. (1999, 8). The Tip of the Iceberg: State of knowledge of persistent organic pollutants in Europe and the Arctic. *Greenpeace.*

126. Allsopp, M., Erry, B., Stringer, R., Johnston, P., & Santillo, D. (2000, 3). Recipe for Disaster: A review of persistent organic pollutants in food. *Greenpeace.*

127. Al-Suhaimy , U. (2013, 7 2). *Saudi Arabia: the desalination nation.* Retrieved 8 17, 2015, from http://www.aawsat.net/2013/07/article55308131

128. WHO (2016). *Ambient Air Pollution: A Global Assessment of Exposure and Burden of Disease.* World Health Organization. Retrieved 9 7, 2017, from http://who.int/phe/publications/air-pollution-global-assessment/en/

129. Amini, N., & Crescenzi, C. (2003). Feasibility of an on-line restricted access material/liquid chromatography/tandem mass spectrometry method in the rapid and sensitive determination of organophosphorus triesters in human blood plasma. *Journal of Chromatography B , 795*(2), 245-256.

130. Andy, J., Hamzaoui, M., Agbani, M., & Franchimont, J. (2002). The conservation status of Moroccan wetlands with particular reference to waterbirds and to changes since 1978. *Biological Conservation, 104*, 71–82. Retrieved 9 19, 2018

131. Anup, S. (2015). *Climate Change and Global Warming Introduction.* Retrieved 5 5, 2015

132. *arctic sea ice.* (2015). Retrieved 5 5, 2015, from http://climate.nasa.gov/vital-signs/arctic-sea-ice/

133. Ashraf, M., Kahlown, M., & Ashfaq, A. (2007). Impact of small dams on agriculture and groundwater development: A case study from Pakistan. *Agricultural water management, 92*(1-2), 90-98. Retrieved from https://doi.org/10.1016/j.agwat.2007.05.007

134. Atkins, W. (n.d.). *Sciences and Issues Water Encyclopedia.* Retrieved 9 15, 2018, from http://www.waterencyclopedia.com/Ge-Hy/Hydroelectric-Power.html

135. Aubell, H., & Mensah, H. (2007). *Natural Resource Exploitation, Environment and Poverty; Linkages and Impact on Rural Households in Asutifi District in Ghana.* university of Agder, Faculty of Economics and Social Sciences. AURA. Retrieved from https://brage.bibsys.no/xmlui/handle/11250/135131

136. Auclair, A., Martin, H., & Walker, S. (1990). A case study of forest decline in Western Canada and the adjacent United States. *Water, Air, and Soil Pollution, 53*(1-2), 13–31. Retrieved 10 24, 2018, from https://link.springer.com/article/10.1007/BF00154989

137. Babiker, A. (1982). Urbanization and desertification in the Sudan with special reference to Khartoum. *GeoJournal, 6*(1), 69–76. doi:https://doi.org/10.1007/BF00446596

138. Bai, Z., Dent, D., Wu, Y., & Jong, R. (2013). Land Degradation and Ecosystem Services. In R. Lal, K. Lorenz, R. Hüttl, B. Schneider, & J. Braun, *Ecosystem Services and Carbon Sequestration in the Biosphere.* Springer Science & Business Media Dordrecht. doi:10.1007/978-94-007-6455-2_15

139. Bankole, O. (2013, June). Urban Environmental Graphics: Impact, problems and visual pollution of signs nd billboards in Nigerian cirties. *International Journal of Education and Research, 1*(6). Retrieved 8 23, 2018, from http://www.ijern.com/journal/June-2013/36.pdf

140. Barbosa, A. (2008, 5 14). Deforestation: damage from dams adds to emissions. *nature, 453*, 280. doi:https://doi.org/10.1038/453280b

141. Baroni, L., Cenci , L., Tettamanti , M., & Berati , M. (2007). Evaluating the environmental impact of various dietary patterns combined with different food production systems. *European Journal of Clinical Nutrition, 61*, 279-86.

142. Bauer, S., Tsigaridis, K., & Miller, R. (2016, 05 16). Significant atmospheric aerosol pollution caused by world food cultivation. *Geophysical Research Letters, 43*(10). doi:https://doi.org/10.1002/2016GL068354

143. Baum, G., Januar, H., Ferse, S., & Kunzmann, A. (2015, 9 17). Local and Regional Impacts of Pollution on Coral Reefs along the Thousand Islands North of the Megacity Jakarta, Indonesia. (N. U. Singapore, Ed.) *Olos One, 10*(9). doi:https://doi.org/10.1371/journal.pone.0138271

144. Beary , H. (n.d.). *Bangalore faces e-waste hazards.* Retrieved from http://www.news.bbc.co.uk/1/hi/world/south_asia/4222521.stm

145. Bekele, H. (2005). Urbanization and Urban Sprawl. Stockholm: Department of Infrastructure Section of Building and Real Estate Economics Kungliga Tekniska Högskolan. Retrieved 03 21, 2022

146. Bengtsson, J., Ahnstrom, J., & Weibull, A.-C. (2005, 4). The effects of organic agriculture on biodiversity and abundance: a meta-analysis. *Journal of Applied Ecology, 42*(2), 261-269. Retrieved 11 22, 2018, from https://besjournals.onlinelibrary.wiley.com/doi/full/10.1111/j.1365-2664.2005.01005.x

147. Berger, L., & Green, B. (n.d.). *outreach.* Retrieved 8 28, 2018, from https://outreach.stakeholderforum.org/index.php/previous-editions/cop-19/191-cop19-day-4-forests-and-agriculture/11565-industrial-animal-agriculture-and-deforestation-acknowledging-industrial-livestock-production-as-a-driver-of-forest-loss

148. Bhattacharyya, R., Ghosh, B., Mishra, P., Mandal, B., Rao, C., Sarkar, D., . . . Franzluebbers, A. (2015). Soil Degradation in India: Challenges and Potential Solutions. *Sustainability, 7*, 3528-3570. doi:10.3390/su7043528

149. Binns, J., Illgner, P., & Nel, E. (2001, 08). Water shortage, deforestation and development: South Africa's working for water programme. *Land Degradation and Development, 12*(04), 341-355. doi:https://doi.org/10.1002/ldr.455

150. Birdsall , N. (1980). Population growth and poverty in the developing world. *Population Bulletin, 35*(5), 1-48. Retrieved 11 2, 2018, from https://www.ncbi.nlm.nih.gov/pubmed/12262264

151. Black, E., & Buesseler , K. (2014). Spatial variability and the fate of cesium in coastal sediments near Fukushima, Japan. *Biogeosciences, 11*, 5123–5137.

152. Blair , R. (2001). Birds and butterflies along urban gradients in two ecoregionsof the U.S. In J. Lockwood, & M. McKinney, *Biotic Ho-mogenization.* (pp. 33–56). Norwell (MA): Kluwer.

153. Bose, R., Sundar, S., & Nesamani, K. (2000). *Clearing the air: better vehicles, better fuels.* New Delhi: Tata Energy Research Institute (TERI).

154. Bradshaw, C. (2012, 3 1). Little left to lose: deforestation and forest degradation in Australia since European colonization. *Journal of Plant Ecology, 5*(1), 109–120. Retrieved 10 25, 2018, from https://doi.org/10.1093/jpe/rtr038

155. Brecher, R. (2003). *"hazmatmag.com"*. Retrieved 12 06, 2014, from http://www.hazmatmag.com/features/peroxyacetyl-nitrate-pan.

156. Bridgeman, L. (2020, 05 15). *sentientmedia.org.* Retrieved 10 30, 2020, from https://sentientmedia.org/intensive-agriculture/

157. Brien, S., Emahalala, E., Beard, V., & Rakotondrainy, R. (2003, 9 2). Decline of the Madagascar radiated tortoise Geochelone radiata due to overexploitation. *Cambridge Core, 37*(3), 338-343. doi:https://doi.org/10.1017/S0030605303000590

158. Brigden, K., Iryna , L., & Santillo , D. (2008, 8 10). Chemical contamination at e-waste recycling and disposal sites in Accra and Korforidua, Ghana,. *Greenpeace Toxic Tech.*

159. Briscoe, C. (2007). THE 1969 EL SALVADOR–HONDURAS WAR. *Veritas, 3*(1). Retrieved 04 05, 2022, from https://arsof-history.org/articles/v3n1_paraiso_sb_war.html

160. Britannica, E. o. (2019, 03 25). *eutrophication. Encyclopedia Britannica.* Retrieved 09 23, 2022, from https://www.britannica.com/science/eutrophication

161. Brovkin, V., Sitch, S., Von Bloh, W., Claussen, M., Bauer , E., & Cramer, W. (2004, 8). Role of land cover changes for atmospheric CO2 increase and climate change during the last 150 years. *Global Change Bioloogy, 10*(8), 1253-1266. Retrieved 11 13, 2018, from https://doi.org/10.1111/j.1365-2486.2004.00812.x

162. Buesseler, K., & al., e. (2012). Fukushima-derived radionuclides in the ocean and biota off Japan. *Proc Natl Acad Sci USA, 109*(16), 5984–5988.

163. Bünemann, E., Schwenke, G., & Zwieten, L. (2006). Impact of agricultural inputs on soil organisms – a review. *Soil Res., 44*, 379-406.

164. Butler , R. (2007, 4 9). *Could global deforestation fight climate change?* Retrieved 10 16, 2018, from Mongabay: https://news.mongabay.com/2007/04/could-global-deforestation-fight-climate-change/

165. Butler, R. (2012, 7 27). *"Mongabay"*. Retrieved from https://rainforests.mongabay.com/0813b.htm

166. Butler, R. (2013, 11 15). *mongobay.com*. Retrieved from https://news.mongabay.com/2013/11/malaysia-has-the-worlds-highest-deforestation-rate-reveals-google-forest-map/

167. Cadmium. (1992). *Environmental Health Criteria , 135*.

168. Cadmium. (1992). *Environmental Health Criteria , 135*.

169. Callaway, J., & Zedler, J. (n.d.). Restoration of urban salt marshes: lessons from southern California. *Urban Ecosys, 7*, 107–24.

170. Canfield, R., Henderson, C., Cory-Slechta, D., Cox, C., Jusko, T., & Lanphear, B. (2003). Intellectual impairment in children with blood lead concentrations below 10 mu g per deciliter. *New England Journal of Medicine, 348*(16), 1517-1526.

171. Cannon , J. (2018, 3 12). *mongobay.com*. Retrieved 8 27, 2018, from https://news.mongabay.com/2018/03/oil-palm-rubber-could-trigger-storm-of-deforestation-in-the-congo-basin/

172. Carrington, D. (2018, 5 21). *The Guardian.com*. Retrieved 11 6, 2018, from https://www.theguardian.com/environment/2018/may/21/human-race-just-001-of-all-life-but-has-destroyed-over-80-of-wild-mammals-study

173. Chakravarty, S., Ghosh, S., Suresh, C., Dey, A., & Shukla, G. (2012). Deforestation: Causes, Effects and Control Strategies. In A. Dr. Clement, *Global Perspectives on Sustainable Forest Management* (pp. 16-17). China: InTech. Retrieved 10 23, 2018, from http://www.intechopen.com/books/globalperspectives-on-sustainable-forest-management/deforestation-causes-effects-and-control-strategies

174. Chamier, J., Schachtschneider, K., le Maitre, D., Ashton, P., & van Wilgen, B. (2012). Impacts of invasive alien plants on water quality, with particular emphasis on South Africa. *Water SA, 38*(02). doi:http://dx.doi.org/10.4314/wsa.v38i2.19 AJOL African Journals Online

175. Chan, K. (2001). An overview of some tillage impacts on earthworm population abundance and diversity — implications for functioning in soils. *Soil Till. Res.*(57), 179-191.

176. Chandra, G. (2008, 05 23). Nature limits filarial transmission. *Parasites and vectors.* doi:10.1186/1756-3305-1-13

177. Chandrajith , R., Seneviratna , S., & Wickramaarachchi , K. (2010). Natural radionuclides and trace elements in rice field soils in relation to fertilizer application: study of a Chronic Kidney Disease of unknown etiology area in Sri Lanka. *Environ Earth Sci, 60*, 193–201.

178. Charles , F., Blake, R., & Lee, D. (1995). Livestock, Deforestation, and Policy Making: Intensification of Cattle Production Systems in Central America Revisited. *Journal of Dairy Science, 78*(3), 719–734. Retrieved 8 28, 2018, from https://www.journalofdairyscience.org/article/S0022-0302(95)76684-X/abstract

179. Chartier, L., Zimmermann, A., & Ladle, R. (2011, 10). Habitat loss and human–elephant conflict in Assam, India: does a critical threshold exist? *Oryx, 45*(4), 528-533. Retrieved 10 23, 2018, from https://doi.org/10.1017/S0030605311000044

180. Chasant, M. (2018, 12 26). Retrieved 08 02, 2022, from https://commons.wikimedia.org/wiki/File:Agbogbloshie_Ghana.jpg

181. Chellaney , B. (2012). Asia's worsening water crisis. *Survival, 54*, 143–56.

182. Chen, J. (2007, 01 16). Rapid urbanization in China: A real challenge to soil protection and food security. *CATENA, 69*(01), 1-15. doi:https://doi.org/10.1016/j.catena.2006.04.019

183. Chindah, A., Braide, S., Amakiri, J., & Onokurhefe, J. (2007). Effect of crude oil on the development of mangrove (Rhizophora mangle L.) seedlings from Niger. *Revista UDO Agrícola, 7*(1), 181-194. Retrieved 03 22, 2019, from http://www.bioline.org.br/pdf?cg07019

184. Chris , C. (1992). *Tropical Rain Forests.* New York: Routledge.

185. Chris , C. (1992). *Tropical Rain Forests.* New York: Rutledge.

186. Clark, G., & Malamud, P. (Eds.). (n.d.). *Biodiversity of Wetlands.* Retrieved 7 31, 2018, from www.tropicalforestnetwork.com: http://www.tropicalforestnetwork.com/wetlands.html

187. Claudia, R. (2010). *Evaluating the Effects of Colonialism on Deforestation in Madagascar: A Social and Environmental History.* Retrieved 11 21, 2014, from https://etd.ohiolink.edu/ap/0?0:APPLICATION_PROCESS%3DDOWNLOAD_ETD_SUB_DOC_ACCNUM:::F1501_ID:oberlin1277525774%2Cinline%2F

188. UN (2019). *Climate Action Summit.* United Natioins. Retrieved 10 21, 2019, from https://www.un.org/en/climatechange/cities-pollution.shtml

189. IPCC.ch (2007). *Climate Change 2007: Working group III, Mitigation of Climate change, Chapter 09.* Retrieved 11 22, 2014, from https://www.ipcc.ch/pdf/assessment-report/ar4/wg3/ar4-wg3-chapter9.pdf.

190. Coder, N. (n.d.). *"en.wikipedia.org".* Retrieved 07 22, 2022, from https://en.wikipedia.org/wiki/Kaveri#/media/File:River_Cauvery_EN.png

191. Colchester , & Lohmann . (1993). *The struggle for Land and the Fate of the Forest.* London: Zed books.

192. Colchester , M. (2010). Land acquisition, human rights violations and indigenous peoples on the palm oil frontier. *Forest Peoples Programme and International Land Coalition.* Moreton-in Mash UK.

193. Colchester, M., & Lohmann, L. (1993). *The Struggle for land and the fate of the forests.* Penang, Malaysia :: Zed Books.

194. Conelly, W., & Chaiken, M. (2000, 3). Intensive Farming, Agro-Diversity, and Food Security under Conditions of Extreme Population Pressure in Western Kenya. *Human Ecology, 28*(1), 19-51. Retrieved 11 23, 2018, from https://www.jstor.org/stable/4603343

195. FAF (2016). *Contamination of air by pesticides.* French Agency for Food, Environmental and Occupational Health & Safety. Retrieved from https://www.anses.fr/en/content/contamination-air-pesticides

196. Cook, J., Nuccitell, D., Green, S., Richardson, M., Winkler, B., Painting, R., . . . Skuce, A. (2013, 5 15). Quantifying the consensus on anthropogenic global warming in the scientific literature. *Environmental research letters, 8,* 024024 (7pp). doi:10.1088/1748-9326/8/2/024024

197. Cooke, C. (2016, 6 28). *civileats.* Retrieved 70 9, 2018, from https://civileats.com/2016/06/28/north-carolinas-cafos-produce-15000-olympic-size-pools-worth-of-waste/

198. Cooley, J. (1984). The war over water. *Foreign Policy, 54,* 13-26.

199. Corcoran, P., Belontz , S., Ryan, K., & Helm, P. (2018). Microplastics in riverine sediments and the factors affecting their accumulation. *sixth international marine debris conference, Plastic pollution in fresh water environment of the world.* California, USA. Retrieved 9 4, 2018, from http://internationalmarinedebrisconference.org/index.php/plastic-debris-pollution-in-freshwater-environments-of-the-world/

200. NETL (2015). *Cost and Performance Baseline for Fossil Energy Plants.* Albany: National Energy Technology Laboratory.

201. Council, W. E. (2013). *World Energy Resources 2013 Survey: Summary.* London, UK: World Energy Council.

202. Cramer, W., Bondeau, A., Schaphoff, S., Lucht, W., Smith, B., & Sitch, S. (2004, 3 29). Tropical forests and the global carbon cycle: impacts of atmospheric carbon dioxide, climate change and rate of deforestation. *Philosophical transactions of the Royal Society B, biological sciences.* doi:10.1098/rstb.2003.1428

203. Cristina Ilea, R. (2009). Intensive Livestock Farming: Global Trends, Increased Environmental Concerns, and Ethical Solutions. *J Agric Environ Ethics, 22*(2), 153–167. doi:10.1007/s10806-008-9136-3

204. Cronan, C., & Schofield, C. (1979). Aluminium leaching response to acid precipitation: effects on high elevation watersheds in the north east. *Science, 204*, 304-306.

205. Crutzen, P., Aselmann, I., & Seiler, W. (1986). Methane Production by Domestic Animals, Wild Ruminants, Other Herbivorous Fauna, and Humans. *Tellus B 38B, 3-4*, 271 - 284. doi:10.1111/j.1600-0889.1986.tb00193.x

206. Dagoumas, A., & Kitsios, F. (2014, 10). Assessing the impact of the economic crisis on energy poverty in Greece. *Sustainable Cities and Society, 13*, 267-278. Retrieved 02 04, 2019, from https://www.sciencedirect.com/science/article/pii/S2210670714000201

207. Dai, L. (2014). Tackling Diffuse Water Pollution from Agriculture in China:. *Utrecht Law Review, 10*(2). Retrieved 9 6, 2018, from https://www.utrechtlawreview.org/

208. Dakki, M., & El Hamzaoui, M. (1997). *Rapport National sur les Zones Humides (Maroc; MedWet report).* Rabat: Administration des Eaux et Forêts et de la Conservation des Sols.

209. Dalton, J. (2018, 3 3). *www.independent.co.uk.* Retrieved 8 5, 2018, from https://www.independent.co.uk/news/uk/home-news/wildlife-extinct-revolutionise-food-farming-species-declines-wiped-out-a8233511.html

210. Das, B., Bhave, P., Sapkota, A., & Byanju, R. (2018, 9). Estimating emissions from open burning of municipal solid waste in municipalities of Nepal. *Waste Management, 79*, 481-490. doi:https://doi.org/10.1016/j.wasman.2018.08.013

211. Dateline. (2011). Youtube. Retrieved 2014, from http://www.youtube.com/watch?v=dd_ZttK3PuM

212. Davis, J., & Froend, R. (1999). Loss and degradation of wetlands in southwestern Australia: underlying causes, consequences and solutions. *Wetlands Ecology and Management, 7*, 13–23. Retrieved 9 18, 2018, from https://link.springer.com/article/10.1023/A:1008400404021

213. Deiters, T. (n.d.). *Farmer suicides India.* Retrieved 07 01, 2021, from Tom Deiters [YouTube channel] You Tube: https://www.youtube.com/watch?v=yGA7HDTkivI

214. Demir, M., Dindaroğlu, T., & Yılmaz, S. (2014, 3 10). Effects of forest areas on air quality; Aras Basin and its environment. *J Environ Health Sci Eng., 12*, 60. doi:10.1186/2052-336X-12-60

215. Denison, J. (Producer). (2014). *Top 10 largest oil spills in history* [Motion Picture]. Retrieved from https://www.youtube.com/watch?v=PU06GuQ7svA

216. Derraik, J. (2002, 9). The pollution of the marine environment by plastic debris: a review. *Marine Pollution Bulletin, 44*(9), 842-852. doi:https://doi.org/10.1016/S0025-326X(02)00220-5

217. Dhruvanarayan, V., & Ram, B. (1983). Estimation of soil erosion in India. *J. Irrig. Drain. Eng., 109*, 419–434.

218. Dickson, W. (1978). Some effects of the acidification of Swedish lakes. *Verhandlungen der International Vereinigung fiur Theoretische und Angewandte Limnologie, 20*, 851-856.

219. Dien , B., & Vong , V. (2006). Analysis of pesticide compound residues in some water sources in the province of Gia Lai and DakLak. *Vietnam Food Administrator.*

220. Donarreiskoffer, & casito. (2005). Retrieved 08 02, 2022, from https://commons.wikimedia.org/wiki/File:World_population_evolution.png

221. Dowd, M. (n.d.). *How Nuclear Bombs Affect the Environment.* Retrieved 9 25, 2018, from seattlepi.com: https://education.seattlepi.com/nuclear-bombs-affect-environment-6173.html

222. UM (2004). *Draft South East Queen-sland Regional Plan.* Bribane: Office of Urban Management, Queensland government.

223. ASA (1998). *Dredging Impact Study. A report submitted by Ade Sobande and Associates (ASA) to Shell Petroleum Development Company of Nigeria (SPDC).* Warri.

224. Durotoye, B. (1998). The value of Geoenvironmental Assessment in Development and Protection of New Urban areas in Nigeria. *University of Ibadan Journal of Current Issues in Nigeria Environment, 10*, 51-60.

225. Ecobichon, D., Davies, J., Doull, J., Ehrich, M., Joy, R., McMillan, D., . . . Tilson, H. (1990). Neurotoxic effects of pesticides. In C. Wilkinson, & S. Baker, *The Effect of Pesticides on Human Health* (pp. 131–199). Princeton, NJ: Princeton Scientific Publishing.

226. Efbrazil. (2020, 03 16). Retrieved 08 01, 2022, from https://upload.wikimedia.org/wikipedia/commons/4/46/CO2_Emissions_by_Source_Since_1880.svg

227. Ehrlich, & Ehrlich. (2008, 08 04). *"e360.yale.edu".* Retrieved 02 11, 2016, from http://e360.yale.edu/feature/too_many_people_too_much_consumption/2041/

228. Ehrlich, P., & Ehrlich, A. (1990). *The population explosion*. New York: Simon and Schuster.

229. Ehrlich, P., & Ehrlich, A. (2008, 8 4). *Too Many People, Too Much Consumption*. Retrieved 9 17, 2018, from Yale Environment 360: http://e360.yale.edu/feature/too_many_people_too_much_consumption/2041/

230. EIA—International Energy Outlook 2017. (2017). Retrieved 9 27, 2017, from www.eia.gov/outlooks/ieo/

231. Elinder, C., & Jarup, L. (1996). Cadmium exposure and health risks: recent findings. *Ambio, 25*(5), 370-373.

232. Elinder, C., & Jarup, L. (1996). Cadmium exposure and health risks: recent findings. *Ambio, 25*(5), 370-373.

233. Elizabeth, L. (2015, 4 5). *MPR news*. Retrieved 9 19, 2018, from https://www.mprnews.org/story/2015/04/05/land-conversion

234. Elliott, J., & Frickel, S. (2013). The Historical Nature of Cities: A Study of Urbanization and Hazardous Waste Accumulation. *American Sociological Review, 78*(4), 521–543. doi:10.1177/0003122413493285

235. IEA (2016). *Emissions from Fuel Combustion: Key CO_2 Emissions Trends*. Retrieved 10 6, 2017, from https://www.iea.org/publications/freepublications/publication/co2-emissions-fromfuel-combustion---2016-edition---excerpt---key-trends.html

236. Emmanuel, O. (2017). *Effects of Deforestation on Land Degradation*. (A. W. Oluwole, Ed.) LAP LAMBERT Academic Publishing.

237. *en.wikipedia.org*. (n.d.). Retrieved 03 30, 2015, from http://en.wikipedia.org/wiki/Overfishing

238. Energy-Related CO2 Emissions from Natural Gas Surpass Coal as Fuel Use Patterns Change. (n.d.). Retrieved 10 2, 2017, from www.eia.gov/todayinenergy/detail.php?id=27552#

239. Environmental challenges. (1997). In C. o. Committee on Research Opportunities and Priorities for EPA, *Building a Foundation for Sound Environmental Decisions*. National Academies Press. Retrieved from https://www.nap.edu/read/5756/chapter/3

240. Eo, S., Song, Y., Han, G., Hong, S., & Shim, W. (2018). Spatiotemporal Distribution and Characteristic of > 20 μm Microplastics and Annual Load on Nakdong River in South Korea. *Sixth International Marine Debris Conference, Plastic debris pollution in fresh water environment of the world*. Retrieved 9 4, 2018, from http://internationalmarinedebrisconference.org/index.php/plastic-debris-pollution-in-freshwater-environments-of-the-world/

241. Epstein, P., Ford, T., Puccia , C., & Possas , C. (1994). Marine Ecosystem Health. Implications for Public Health. *New York Academy of Sciences, 740*, 13–23.

242. EricaDeNicola, M., Aburizaiza, O., Siddique, A., Khwaja, H., & David , O. (2015). Climate Change and Water Scarcity: The Case of Saudi Arabia. *Annals of Global Health, 81*(3), 342-353. Retrieved 9 10, 2018, from https://doi.org/10.1016/j.aogh.2015.08.005

243. Eriksen, M., Lebreton, L., Carson, H., Thiel, M., Moore, C., Borerro, J., . . . Reisser, J. (2014, 12 10). Plastic Pollution in the World's Oceans: More than 5 Trillion Plastic Pieces Weighing over 250,000 Tons Afloat at Sea. *PLOS one, 9*(12). doi:https://doi.org/10.1371/journal.pone.0111913

244. Esetlili, M., Kurucu, Y., Turk, T., & Ozen, F. (2016, 7). Land degradation due to coastal urbanization. *Journal of environmental protection and ecology, 17*(2), 696-702. Retrieved from https://www.researchgate.net/publication/305473825_LAND_DEGRADATION_DUE_TO_COASTAL_URBANISATION

245. E-Waste: The next hazard wave. (2007). *Consumer Voice, 3*(6).

246. Ezaza, W. (1988). Geological factors influencing over exploitation and land degradation in the Usambara mountains of Northern Tanzania. *Mountain Research and Development, 8*(2), 157-163. Retrieved from https://www.jstor.org/stable/3673443?seq=1#page_scan_tab_contents

247. Fagariba, C., Song, S., & Soule, S. (2018). Livelihood Economic Activities Causing Deforestation in Northern Ghana: Evidence of Sissala West District. *Open Journal of Ecology, 8*, 57-74. Retrieved 10 22, 2018, from http://file.scirp.org/Html/5-1380883_82157.htm

248. Faiaz , N., & Soltan , H. (2013). *The Crisis of Increasing E-waste in European Countries.* (C. Yu-Sang, Ed.) Retrieved 11 19, 2018, from www.poplas.org/uploads/member_studies/7351/study/E-Waste

249. Falkenmark, M. (1989). Middle-East Hydropolitics: Water Scarcity and Conflicts in the Middle East. *Ambio, 18*(6), 350.

250. FAO. (2002). Small-Scale Palm oil processing in Africa. *FAO Agricultural Services Bulletin, 148*. Retrieved 9 13, 2018

251. FAO. (2002). *The state of food and agriculture.* Rome: FAO. Retrieved 8 27, 2018, from http://www.fao.org/docrep/004/y6000e/y6000e00.htm

252. FAO. (2005). *"Global Forest Resource Assessment 2005".* Forestry. Rome: FAO.

253. FAO. (2009). *FAOSTAT online statistical service.* Rome, Italy: Food and Agriculture Organization of the United Nations. Retrieved 9 13, 2018, from http://faostat.fao.org/

254. FAO. (2009). *'State of the world's forests'.* Washington DC: UN.

255. FAO. (2010). *Global Forest Resources Assessment 2010.* Rome, Italy: Food and Agriculture Organization of the United Nations.

256. FAO. (2014). *The State of World Fishereies and Aquaculture opportunities and challenges.* Rome: FAO. Retrieved 8 29, 2018, from http://www.fao.org/3/a-i3720e.pdf

257. FAO/LEAD. (2006). *Livestock's long shadow. Environmental issues and options.* Food and Agriculture Organization of the United Nations. Rome: Google scholar.

258. Fearnside, P. (2006). Tropical Deforestation and Global Warming. *Science, 312*, 1137. doi:10.1126/science.312.5777.1137c

259. Fearnside, P. (2017, 9 26). *How a Dam Building Boom Is Transforming the Brazilian Amazon.* Retrieved 10 8, 2018, from YaleEnvironment360: https://e360.yale.edu/features/how-a-dam-building-boom-is-transforming-the-brazilian-amazon

260. Feuerbacher, A., Luckmann, J., Boysen, O., Zikeli, S., & Grethe, H. (2018, 06 13). Is Bhutan destined for 100% organic? Assessing the economy-wide effects of a large-scale conversion policy. *Plos One, 13*(6). doi:https://doi.org/10.1371/journal.pone.0199025

261. Fiala , N. (2009, 2). How meat contributes to global warming. *Scientific American Magazine.* Retrieved 10 17, 2018, from http://www.environmentportal.in/files/Global%20warming.doc

262. Fick, J., Söderström, H., Lindberg, R., Phan, C., Tysklind, M., & Larsson, D. (2010, 1 6). Contamination of surface, ground, and drinking water from pharmaceutical production. *Environmental Toxicology and Chemistry.* doi:https://doi.org/10.1897/09-073.1

263. Finding Solutions Together. Proposal - The Energy Crisis and Climate Change. (2016). *Global Economic Symposium.* Retrieved 02 16, 2016, from http://www.global-economic-symposium.org/knowledgebase/the-global-environment/the-energy-crisis-and-climate-change/proposals/the-energy-crisis-and-climate-change

264. Fitzherbert , E., Struebig , M., Morel , A., Danielsen , F., Brühl , C., Donald , P., & Phalan , B. (2008). How will oil palm expansion affect biodiversity? *Trends in Ecology and Evolution, 23*(10), 539-545.

265. Fitzpatrick, T. (2008, 10 22). *"the Source".* Retrieved 8 27, 2018, from https://source.wustl.edu/2008/10/population-growth-drives-depletion-of-natural-resources/

266. Flannigan, M., & Van Wagner, C. (1991). Climate change and wildfire in Canada. *Canadian Journal of Forest Research, 21*(1), 66-72. doi:https://doi.org/10.1139/x91-010

267. Flannigan, M., Stocks, B., Turetsky, M., & Wotton, M. (2009). Impacts of climate change on fire activity and fire management in the circumboreal forest. *Global Change Biology, 15*(3), 549-560. doi:https://doi.org/10.1111/j.1365-2486.2008.01660.x

268. Fogarty , E. (2011). *Antarctica: Assessing and Protecting Australia's National Interests. Policy Brief.* Sydney: Lowy Institute for International Policy. Retrieved 9 17, 2018, from https://www.files.ethz.ch/isn/132284/Fogarty,%20Antarctica_web.pdf

269. Folke, C., Kautsky, N., & Troell, M. (1994). The Costs of Eutrophication from Salmon Farming: Implications for Policy. *Journal of Environmental iManagernmt, 40*, 173-182. Retrieved 10 31, 2018, from https://s3.amazonaws.com/academia.edu.documents/46870059/The_Costs_of_Eutrophication _from_Salmon_20160628-10275- 1s0vvcz.pdf?AWSAccessKeyId=AKIAIWOWYYGZ2Y53UL3A&Expires=1540964802&Si gnature=L9rfOnEoqRh8Ak4R1JB9gf%2BMgrk%3D&response-content-disposition=inli

270. Forys, E., & Allen, C. (2005). The Impacts of Sprawl on Biodiversity: The Ant Fauna of the Lower Florida Keys. *Ecology and Society, 10*(1). doi:10.5751/ES-01307-100125

271. Fox, M., Snyder, A., Vincent, J., & Raichle, M. (2007). Intrinsic fluctuations within cortical systems account for intertrial variability in human behavior. *Neuron, 56*.

272. Galloway, J., Townsend, A., Erisman, J., Bekunda, M., Cai, Z., Freney, J., . . . Sutton, M. (2008). Transformation of the nitrogen cycle: Recent trends, questions, and potential solutions. *Science, 320*(5878), 889– 892. doi:10.1126/science.1136674

273. Ganesan, R., & Venkatesh, S. (2016, 09 28). *"downtoearth.org.in".* Retrieved 07 22, 2022, from https://www.downtoearth.org.in/feature/war-zone-cauvery-55848

274. Gao, X., Schlosser, C., Fant, C., & Strzepek, K. (2018, 6 19). The impact of climate change policy on the risk of water stress in southern and eastern Asia. *Environmental Research Letters, 13*(6). Retrieved 9 10, 2018, from http://iopscience.iop.org/article/10.1088/1748- 9326/aaca9e#erlaaca9es2

275. Garty, J. (2001). Biomonitoring Atmospheric Heavy Metals with Lichens: Theory and Application. *Critical reviews in plant sciences, 20*(04), 309-371. doi:https://doi.org/10.1080/20013591099254

276. Gaworecki , M. (2016, 6 29). *mongabay.* Retrieved 7 30, 2018, from news.mongabay.com: https://news.mongabay.com/2016/06/forest-degradation-in-brazil-can-have-just-as-drastic- an-impact-on-biodiversity-as-deforestation/

277. Geist, H. (1999). Global assessment of deforestation related to tobacco farming. *Tobacco Control, 8*, 18–28. Retrieved 8 28, 2018, from https://pdfs.semanticscholar.org/1f29/b580312a724b7ac26a30267ea58f947a793c.pdf

278. Gerretsen, I. (2020, 12 8). 'bbc.com'. Retrieved 08 26, 2021, from https://www.bbc.com/future/article/20201204-climate-change-how-chemicals-in-your-fridge-warm-the-planet

279. Getter, C., Scott, G., & Michel , J. (1981). *The effects of oil spills in mangrove forest: a comparison of five oil spill sites in the Guld of Mexico and the Carribbean sea.* TROPICS (Tropical Research on Oil Pollution in Coastal Systems), Research Planning Institute, Inc. doi:10.7901/2169-3358-1981-1-535

280. Ghose , M., & Majee, S. (2001, 10). Air pollution caused by opencast mining and its abatement measures in India. *J Environ Manage., 63*(2), 193-202. Retrieved 11 9, 2018, from https://www.ncbi.nlm.nih.gov/pubmed/11721598

281. Gillett, N., Weaver , A., Zwiers, F., & Flannigan, M. (2004, 9 29). Detecting the effect of climate change on Canadian forest fires. *Geophysical Research Letters, 31*(18). doi:https://doi.org/10.1029/2004GL020876

282. Godfray, H., Beddington, J., Crute, I., Haddad, L., Lawrence, D., Muir, J., . . . Toulmin, C. (2010, 2 12). Food Security: The Challenge of Feeding 9 Billion People. *Science, 327*. Retrieved 8 28, 2018, from web.mit.edu: http://web.mit.edu/12.000/www/m2019/pdfs/Godfray_2010_Science.pdf

283. Golbaz, S., Farzadkia, M., Vanani, A., & Emamjomeh, M. (2017). Livestock slaughterhouses waste management in urban environment. *Int. J. Hum. Capital Urban Manage, 2*(2), 163-170. doi:10.22034/ijhcum.2017.02.02.008

284. Goswami, S., Das, M., & Guru, B. (2010). Environmental Degradation Due to Exploitation of Mineral Resources a Senario in Orissa. *The Bioscan, 2*, 295-304.

285. *Greenhouse Gas Emissions.* (n.d.). Retrieved 10 12, 2017, from https://www3.epa.gov/climatechange/ghgemissions/

286. GRID-Arendal. (2005, 10 4). *"grida.no"*. Retrieved 08 01, 2022, from www.grida.no/resources/7464

287. Grosberg, R., Vermeij, G., & Wainwright, P. (2012, 11 6). Biodiversity in water and on land. *Current Biology, 22*(21), R900- R903. doi:https://doi.org/10.1016/j.cub.2012.09.050

288. Grover, D. (2014). *"populationeducation.org"*. Retrieved 02 2016, from https://www.populationeducation.org/content/what-demographic-transition-model

289. Guenzi, , W., Ahlrichs, J., Chesters, G., Bloodworth, M., & Nash, R. (1974). *Pesticides in soil and water.* (C. Richard , Ed.)

290. Gunadasa, H. (2014). Practical Aspects on Air Pollution Control. *Training course on Air Quality, Noise & Vibration impacts in relation to environmental impact assessment.* Retrieved 07 10, 2022

291. Gunawardhana, A., & Herath, N. (2018). Analysis of causes, impacts and mitigation strategies for human-elephant conflict: A case study in Anuradhapura District of Sri Lanka. *Proceedings of the 4th International Research Symposium of Rajarata University of Sri Lanka investing in Biodiversity and Ecosystem Services 'Caring Nature- Creating Wealth' 17-18 October 2018.* Anuradhapura, Mihintale, Sri Lanka. Retrieved 10 24, 2018, from https://www.researchgate.net/publication/328359673_Analysis_of_causes_impacts_and_miti gation_strategies_for_human-elephant_conflict_A_case_study_in_Anuradhapura_District_of_Sri_Lanka

292. Gunnemyr, M. (2019, 4). Causing Global Warming. *Ethical Theory and Moral Practice, 22*(2), 399–424. doi:https://doi.org/10.1007/s10677-019-09990-w

293. Hallock-Muller, P. (2005, 08 09). *Mangrove Forest Decline and its Effect on Coral Reefs.* (L. Luckey-Bethany, Ed.) Retrieved 11 12, 2018, from https://secoora.org/mangrove_forest_decline/

294. Hamidi, S., Ewing, R., & Sabouri, S. (2020, 07). Longitudinal analyses of the relationship between development density and the COVID-19 morbidity and mortality rates: Early evidence from 1,165 metropolitan counties in the United States. *Health Place, 64*, 102378. doi:10.1016/j.healthplace.2020.102378

295. Harada, M. (2008, 9 25). Minamata Disease: Methylmercury Poisoning in Japan Caused by Environmental Pollution. *Critical Review in Toxicology, 25*(1), 1-24 .

296. Harvey, F. (2019, 01 28). *Can we ditch intensive farming - and still feed the world?* Retrieved 11 5, 2019, from www.theguardian.com/: https://www.theguardian.com/news/2019/jan/28/can-we-ditch-intensive-farming-and-still-feed-the-world

297. Health and Environmental Effects of Ultraviolet Radiation A Scientific Summary of Environmental Health Criteria 160 Ultraviolet Radiation. (1995). Retrieved 9 21, 2018, from http://www.who.int/uv/publications/UVEHeffects.pdf

298. Helfrich, L., Neves, R., Libey, G., & Newcomb, T. (n.d.). *Extension Specialists, Fisheries and Wildlife Sciences.* Virginia Tech.

299. Hettige, N., Weerasekara, K., & Azmy, S. (2012). Assessment of marine litter along selected beaches in the Western, Province of Sri Lanka. Retrieved 4 29, 2016

300. Hill, B. (n.d.). Retrieved 11 22, 2014, from
     http://www1.american.edu/ted/VIETWOOD.HTM.

301. Hinrichsen , D. (1988). Acid rain and forest decline. In E. Goldsmith, & N. Hildyard, *The Earth report: the essential guide to global ecological issues* (pp. 65-78). Los Angeles, California: Price Stern Sloan. Retrieved 10 23, 2018, from https://www.popline.org/node/378118

302. Hoffner, E. (2021, 03 31). *"mongabay.com"*. Retrieved 03 24, 2023, from https://news.mongabay.com/2021/03/in-brazil-palm-oil-is-being-grown-sustainably-via-agroforestry/

303. Hogan. (2014). *Deforestation*. Retrieved 11 21, 2014, from "eoearth.org": http://www.eoearth.org/view/article/151673

304. Hogue, J. (n.d.). Retrieved 08 02, 2022, from https://pixnio.com/objects/telephone-wires

305. Hollaway, L. C. (2023). Sustainable energy production: Key material requirements. In J. Bai, *Advanced Fiber-Reinforced Polymer(FRP) Composites for Structural Applications.* Woodhead Publishing Series in Civil and Structural Engineering.

306. Honkanen, T., & Helminen, H. (2000). Impacts of Fish Farming on Eutrophication: Comparisons among Different Characteristics of Ecosystem. *International Review of Hydro Biology*. Retrieved 10 31, 2018, from https://doi.org/10.1002/1522-2632(200011)85:5/6<673::AID-IROH673>3.0.CO;2-O

307. Hooda, P., Edwards, A., Anderson, H., & Miller, A. (2000, 4 24). A review of water quality concerns in livestock farming areas. *The Science of the Total Environment, 250*(1-3), 143-167. Retrieved 9 6, 2018, from https://www.sciencedirect.com/science/article/pii/S0048969700003739

308. Hooijer , A., Silvius , M., Wösten , H., & Page , S. (2006). *PEAT-CO2, assessment of CO2 emissions from drained peatlands in SE Asia.* Delft, The Netherlands: Delft Hydraulics.

309. Horvath , A., & Rachlew, E. (2016, 01). Nuclear power in the 21st century: Challenges and possibilities. *AMBIO, 45(Suppl 1)*, 38–49. doi:10.1007/s13280-015-0732-y

310. Hosier, R., & Kipondya, W. (1993, 5). Urban household energy use in Tanzania: Prices, substitutes and poverty. *Energy Policy, 21*(5), 454-473. Retrieved 02 04, 2019, from https://www.sciencedirect.com/science/article/pii/030142159390035E

311. WHO (2016). *Household Air Pollution and Health.* World Health Organization. Retrieved 10 12, 2017, from http://www.who.int/mediacentre/factsheets/fs292/en/

312. Huang , J., Nkrumah , P., Anim , D., & Mensah , E. (2014). E-waste disposal effects on the aquatic environment: Accra, Ghana. *Rev Environ Contam Toxicol., 229*, 19-34. doi:10.1007/978-3-319-03777-6_2

313. Huang, C., Li, X.-Y., Shi, L.-J., & Jiang, X.-L. (2018, 11 18). Patterns of human-wildlife conflict and compensation practices around Daxueshan Nature Reserve, China. *Zoological Research, 39*(6), 406–412. doi:10.24272/j.issn.2095-8137.2018.056

314. Hubbard , R., Newton , G., & Hill , G. (2004). Water quality and the grazing animal. *J Anim Sci., 82*, E255-263. Retrieved 10 37, 2018, from https://www.ncbi.nlm.nih.gov/pubmed/15471806

315. Huber, K. (2008, 07). *"www.c2es.org"*. Retrieved 07 17, 2022, from https://www.c2es.org/document/decarbonizing-u-s-agriculture-forestry-and-land-use/

316. Hydropower and deforestation: An unexpected linkage or an obvious one? (2014). *Forest Asia summit*. Jakarta. Retrieved 10 8, 2018, from http://www.cifor.org/forestsasia/hydropower-deforestation-unexpected-linkage-obvious-one/

317. IARC Monographs programme on the evaluation of carcinogenic risks to humans: Some Organic Solvents, Resin Monomers and Related Compounds. (1989). *Pigments and Occupational Exposures in Paint Manufacture and Painting, 47*, 291–306.

318. WEO (2016). *International Energy Agency (IEA) WEO-2016 Special Report Energy and Air Pollution*. Paris, France: International Energy Agency.

319. Imevbore, V. (2001). Managing environmental impacts- the case study of the Niger Delta in Nigeria . International management conference on developing sustainable environmental strategy for commercial success in the upstream oil and gas sector. London: Global Business Network Ltd.

320. International Energy Agency. (2018, 3 22). Retrieved 9 17, 2018, from Global energy demand grew by 2.1% in 2017, and carbon emissions rose for the first time since 2014: https://www.iea.org/newsroom/news/2018/march/global-energy-demand-grew-by-21-in-2017-and-carbon-emissions-rose-for-the-firs.html

321. Iram, A., Rasool, L., Shahzad, F., & Saeed, Y. (2012). Impact of Urban Sprawl on Public Health: An Analysis of Lahore - Pakistan. *World Applied Sciences Journal, 20*(1), 80-86. doi:10.5829/idosi.wasj.2012.20.01.2806

322. Jambeck, J., Geyer, R., Wilcox, C., Siegler, T., Perryman, M., Andrady, A., . . . Law, K. (2015, 2 13). Plastic waste inputs from land into the ocean. *Science, 347*(6223). Retrieved 11 16, 2018, from http://wedocs.unep.org/bitstream/handle/20.500.11822/17969/Plastic_waste_inputs_from_land_into_the_ocean.pdf?sequence=1&isAllowed=y

323. Jang, Y., Ranatunga, R., Mok, J., Kim, K., Hong, S., Choi, Y., & Gunasekara, A. (2018, 03). Composition and abundance of marine debris stranded on the beaches of Sri Lanka: Results from the first island-wide survey. *Marine Pollution Bulletin, 128*, 126-131. Retrieved 11 8, 2020, from
https://www.sciencedirect.com/science/article/abs/pii/S0025326X18300213?via%3Dihub

324. Jean-Christophe, B. (2012, 04 25). Retrieved from
https://commons.wikimedia.org/wiki/File:NYC_-_Times_Square.JPG

325. Jha , S., & Bawa , K. (2006). Population growth, human development, and deforestation in biodiversity hotspots. *Conserv. Biol., 20*(3), 906-12. Retrieved 10 22, 2018, from
https://www.ncbi.nlm.nih.gov/pubmed/16909582

326. Jimoh, O., Ayodeji, M., & Mohammed, B. (2003). Effects of agrochemicals on surface waters and groundwaters in the Tunga-Kawo (Nigeria) irrigation scheme. *Hydrological Sciences Journal, 48*(6), 1013-1023. doi:10.1623/hysj.48.6.1013.51426

327. John, C. (2010). *10 Indicators of a Human Fingerprint on Climate Change, Skeptical Science.* Retrieved from http://www.skepticalscience.com/news.php?n=292

328. Johnston , R. (2001). Synanthropic birds of North America. In J. Marzluff , R. Bowman , & R. Donnelly , *Avian Ecology in an Urban-izing World* (pp. 49-67). Norwell (MA): Kluwer.

329. Jonas, H., Abram, N., & Ancrenaz, M. (2017). *Addressing the impact of large-scale oil palm plantations on orangutan conservation in Borneo.* International Institute for Environment and Development (UK). Retrieved 06 19, 2019, from
https://pubs.iied.org/pdfs/12605IIED.pdf

330. Jonsson, M., Bergstro, A., Blomqvist, M., & Drakare, S. (2001). Allochthonous organic carbon and phytoplankton/bacterioplankton production relationships in lakes. *Ecology, 81*, 3250–3255.

331. Josephson, A. L., Ricker-Gilbert, J., & Florax, R. J. (2014, 10). How does population density influence agricultural intensification and productivity? Evidence from Ethiopia. *Food Policy, 48*, 142-152. Retrieved 11 23, 2018, from https://doi.org/10.1016/j.foodpol.2014.03.004

332. Kaimovitz , D. (1996). *https://www.cifor.org/.* Retrieved 8 28, 2018, from
http://www.cifor.org/publications/pdf_files/SPubs/SP-LStock-n.pdf

333. Kaplan, M. (2014). Retrieved 7 12, 2014, from http://www.anapsid.org/pyrethroids.html.

334. Kartika, E., & Koopmans, F. (2013). *Human-tiger conflict: An overview of incidents, causes and resolution.* Retrieved 10 24, 2018, from
https://www.researchgate.net/publication/301285543_Human-tiger_conflict_An_overview_of_incidents_causes_and_resolution

338

335. Kasuya, M., Teranishi, H., Aoshima, K., Katoh, T., Horiguchi, H., Morikawa, Y., . . . Iwata, K. (1992, 6 1). Water Pollution by Cadmium and the Onset of Itai-itai Disease. *Water Sci Technol, 25*(11), 149-156. Retrieved 9 10, 2018, from https://doi.org/10.2166/wst.1992.0286

336. Kaur, S., & Sharma, S. (2016). Agrarian crisis – over exploitation of natural resources. *International Journal of Advanced Education and Research, 1*(7), 63-65.

337. Keledjian, A., Brogan, G., Lowell, B., Warrenchuk, J., Enticknap, B., Shester, G., . . . Cano-Stocco, D. (2014). *Oceana.* Retrieved 8 29, 2018, from Oceana.org: http://oceana.org/sites/default/files/reports/Bycatch_Report_FINAL.pdf

338. Kemp, D. (2004). *Exploring Environmental Issues an integrated appro.*

339. Kessler, R. (2013, 10 1). The Minamata Convention on Mercury: A First Step toward Protecting Future Generations. *Environmental Health Perspectives, 121*(10), A304–a309. doi:10.1289/ehp.121-A304

340. Khan, A., Arshad, S., & Mohsin, M. (2014). Population Growth and Its Impact on Urban Expansion: A Case Study of Bahawalpur, Pakistan. *Universal Journal of Geoscience, 2*(8), 229-241. doi:10.13189/ujg.2014.020801

341. Khan, R., Israili, S., Ahmad, H., & Mohan, A. (2005, 9). Heavy Metal Pollution Assessment in Surface Water Bodies and its Suitability for Irrigation around the Neyevli Lignite Mines and Associated Industrial Complex, Tamil Nadu, India. *Mine Water and the Environment, 24*(3), 155–161. Retrieved 11 8, 2018, from https://link.springer.com/article/10.1007/s10230-005-0087-x

342. Kibirige, J. (1997). Population growth, poverty and health. *Social Science & Medicine, 45*(2), 247-259. doi:https://doi.org/10.1016/S0277-9536(96)00341-3

343. Kim, B., Ikeda, T., Park, H., Kim, H., Hyun, M., Kano, K., . . . Tatsumi, H. (1999). Electrochemical activity of an Fe(III)-reducing bacterium, Shewanella putrefaciens IR-1, in the presence of alternative electron acceptors. *Biotechnol. Tech. , 13*, 475–478.

344. Kimpel, R. (2006, 03 25). Retrieved 08 02, 2022, from https://www.flickr.com/photos/rkimpeljr/209687857/

345. King, G., Mieszkowski, M., Jason, T., & Rainham, D. (2012). Noise Levels Associated with Urban Land Use. *J Urban Health, 89*(6), 1017–1030. doi:10.1007/s11524-012-9721-7

346. Knobbe, E. (2018). *Center for biological diversity.* Retrieved 10 15, 2018, from https://www.biologicaldiversity.org/news/press_releases/2018/factory-farms-03-07-2018.php

347. Konstantinou, I., Hela, D., & Albanis, T. (2006). The status of pesticide pollution in surface waters (rivers and lakes) of Greece. Part I. Review on occurrence and levels. *Environmental*

Pollution, 141(3), 555-570. Retrieved 9 3, 2018, from
https://doi.org/10.1016/j.envpol.2005.07.024

348. Kovacic, Z., & Salazar, O. (2017). The lose-lose predicament of deforestation through subsistencefarming: Unpacking agricultural expansion in the Ecuadorian Amazon. *Journal of Rural Studies, 51*, 106. Retrieved 10 24, 2018, from https://www.researchgate.net/publication/313606466_The_lose-lose_predicament_of_deforestation_through_subsistence_farming_Unpacking_agricultural_expansion_in_the_Ecuadorian_Amazon

349. Krzyzanowski , M., Kuna-Dibbert , B., & Schneider, J. (2005). *Health Effects of Transport Related Air pollution.* WHO.

350. Kumari, K., Kumar, S., Vineel, R., Khare, A., & Kumar, R. (2017, 7). Emission from Open Burning of Municipal Solid Waste in India. *Environmental Technology.* doi:10.1080/09593330.2017.1351489

351. Kyba, C. C., Kuester, T., Miguel, A. S., Baugh, K., Jechow, A., & al., e. (2017). Artificially lit surface of Earth at night increasing in radiance and extent. *Science Advances, 3*(11). doi:10.1126/sciadv.1701528

352. Kyba, C., Ruhtz, T., Fischer, J., & Hölker, F. (2011, 12 17). Lunar skylight polarization signal polluted by urban lighting. *Journal of Geographical Research.* doi:https://doi.org/10.1029/2011JD016698

353. Ladan, S. (2016). Harnessing small scale dams for improving agricultural productivity in Northern Nigeria: case study of Mashi earh dam Katsina state. *Nigeria's Economic development Conference At: Federal University Dutsin ma Katsina State Nigeria.* Katsina State, Nigeria. Retrieved 10 4, 2018, from https://www.researchgate.net/publication/309591806_HARNESSING_SMALL_SCALE_DAMS_FOR_IMPROVING_AGRICULTURAL_PRODUCTIVITY_IN_NORTHERN_NIGERIA_CASE_STUDY_OF_MASHI_EARTH_DAM_KATSINA_STATE

354. Laura, M. (2012, 7 16). *mmn.com.* Retrieved 9 16, 2018, from https://www.mnn.com/earth-matters/wilderness-resources/stories/the-13-largest-oil-spills-in-history

355. Lawrence, C. (1998). *Fisheries report: Final Report, FRDC Project 94/075: Enhancement of yabby production from Western Australian farm dams.* Fisheries Research Division, WA Marine Research Laboratories, Western Australia 6020. Retrieved 10 4, 2018, from http://www.frdc.com.au/Archived-Reports/FRDC%20Projects/1994-075-DLD.pdf

356. Lebreton, L., Joost van der Zwet, Damsteeg, J.-W., Slat, B., Andrady, A., & Reisser, J. (2017, 06 07). Retrieved from https://www.nature.com/articles/ncomms15611

357. Lebreton, L., van der Zwet, J., Damsteeg, J.-W., Slat, B., Andrady, A., & Reisser, J. (2017, 6 7). River plastic emissions to the world's oceans. *Nature Communications, 8.* Retrieved 11 14, 2018, from https://www.nature.com/articles/ncomms15611

358. Lee, S., Dunn, R., Young, R., Welsh, D., Connolly, R., Dale, P., . . . Teasdale, P. (2006, 3). Impact of urbanization on coastal wetland structure and function. *Austral Ecology, 31*(2). doi:10.1111/j.1442-9993.2006.01581.x

359. Legler , J., & Brouwer , A. (2003). Are brominated flame retardants endocrine disruptors? *Environment International, 29*, 879-885.

360. Lewis, D. (1973, 10). Causation. *The Journal of Philosophy, 70*(17), 556-567. doi:10.2307/2025310

361. FAO (2006b). *Livestock a major threat to environment.* Food and Agriculture Organization of the United Nations (FAO). Retrieved from http://www.fao.org/newsroom/en/news/2006/1000448/index.html

362. FAO (n.d.). *Livestock policy brief 3.* FAO, Livestock Information, Sector Analysis and Policy Branch, Animal Production and Health Division. FAO. Retrieved 10 25, 2018, from http://www.fao.org/3/a-a0262e.pdf

363. FAO (2006a). *Livestock's long shadow: Environmental issues and options.* Food and Agriculture Organization of the United Nations (FAO). Retrieved from http://www.fao.org/docrep/010/a0701e/a0701e00.htm

364. Llacuna , S., Gorriz , A., Durfort , M., & Nadal , J. (1993, 1 24). Effects of air pollution on passerine birds and small mammals. *Arch Environ Contam Toxicol., 24*(1), 59-66. Retrieved 12 31, 2018, from https://www.ncbi.nlm.nih.gov/pubmed/8466292

365. Loehr, R. (1978). Hazardous Solid Waste from Agriculture. *Environmental Health Perspectives, 27*, 261-273. doi:10.2307/3428887

366. Loew, T. (2016, 12 7). Fukushima radiation has reached U.S. shores. *Statesman Journal.* Retrieved 9 6, 2018, from https://www.statesmanjournal.com/story/tech/science/environment/2016/12/07/fukushima-radiation-has-reached-us-shores/95045692/

367. Lowi, M. (1993). Bridging the Divide: Transboundary Resource Disputes and the Case of West Bank Water. *International Security, 18*(01), 113-138. Retrieved 04 03, 2022

368. Lu, C., Zhang, L., Zhong, Y., Ren, W., Tobias, M., Mu, Z., . . . Xue, B. (2015). An overview of e-waste management in China. *Journal of Material Cycles and Waste Management, 17*(01), 1–12. doi:10.1007/s10163-014-0256-8

369. Luo, K., Hu, X., He, Q., Wu, Z., Cheng, H., Hu, Z., & Mazumder, A. (2018, 4 15). Impacts of rapid urbanization on the water quality and macroinvertebrate communities of streams: A case study in Liangjiang New Area, China. (D. Barcelo, Ed.) *Science of the Total Environment, 621*, 1601-1614. Retrieved from https://www.sciencedirect.com/science/article/pii/S0048969717327729

370. Luoma, J. R. (2012). *China's Reforestation Programs: Big Success or Just an Illusion?* Retrieved 11 22, 2014, from http://e360.yale.edu/feature/chinas_reforestation_programs_big_success_or_just_an_illusion/2484/.

371. Lynton, W., & Kenneth, W. (1985). Screening Models for Estimating Toxic Air Pollution Near a Hazardous Waste Landfill. *Journal of Air pollution control association, 35*(11). doi:https://doi.org/10.1080/00022470.1985.10466023

372. Ma. (2005, 4 1). Differential sensitivity of three cyanobacterial and five green algal species to organotins and pyrethroids pesticides. *Sci Total Environ., 341*(1-3), 109-17. Retrieved 03 15, 2015, from http://www.ncbi.nlm.nih.gov/pubmed/15833245

373. Malik, A., Yasar, A., Tabinda, A., & Abubakar, M. (2012). Water-Borne Diseases, Cost of Illness and Willingness to Pay for Diseases Interventions in Rural Communities of Developing Countries. *Iran J Public Health, 41*(6), 39–49. Retrieved 11 13, 2019, from https://www.ncbi.nlm.nih.gov/pmc/articles/PMC3469006/

374. Maltby , E. (1986). *Waterlogged wealth.* London : Earthscan.

375. Maltby , E., & Immirzi , P. (1993). Carbon dynamics in peatlands and other wetland soils. Regional and global perspectives. *Chemosphere, 27*, 999–1023. Retrieved 9 19, 2018

376. Malthus, & Boserup. (2012). *"coolgeography.co.uk".* Retrieved 02 2016, from http://www.coolgeography.co.uk/A-level/AQA/Year%2012/Population/Population%20&%20resources/Population%20&%20resources.htm

377. Mandal, F. B. (2010, 11 6). *Interconnected Environmental Problems.* Retrieved 12 27, 2018, from http://ezinearticles.com: http://ezinearticles.com/?Interconnected-Environmental-Problems&id=5337231

378. Mangave, H. (2004). *A study of Elephant population and its habitats in the northern West Bengal, North East India.* M. Sc. Thesis, Bharathidasan University, Unpubl.

379. Mao, D., Wang, Z., Wu, J., Wu, B., Zeng, Y., Song, K., . . . Luo, L. (2018, 3 23). China's wetlands loss to urban expansion. *Wiley online library.* Retrieved from https://doi.org/10.1002/ldr.2939

380. Mapulanga, A., & Naito, H. (2019, 04 23). Effect of deforestation on access to clean drinking water. *PNAS, 116*(17), 8249-8254. doi:https://doi.org/10.1073/pnas.1814970116

381. UNEP (2009). *Marine litter: a global challenge.* Retrieved 11 14, 2018, from https://wedocs.unep.org/handle/20.500.11822/2428

382. Mark, P., Wakeford, R., Bouville, A., & Simon, S. (2016, 4 5). Measurement of Fukushima-related radioactive contamination in aquatic species. *PNAS, 113*(14), 3720-3721. Retrieved 9 5, 2018, from http://www.pnas.org/content/113/14/3720

383. Markakis, J. (1989). The Ishaq-Ogaden Dispute. In A. H. Ornäs, & M. M. Salih, *Ecology and Politics* (p. 158).

384. Marques, R., Silva, A., Rodrigues, L., & Coelho, G. (2012, 12). Impacts of urban solid waste disposal on the quality of surface water in three cities of Minas Gerais - Brazil. *Ciênc. agrotec., 36*(6). Retrieved 9 3, 2018, from http://dx.doi.org/10.1590/S1413-70542012000600010

385. Marten, G. (2005). *"ecotippingpoints".* Retrieved 11 22, 2014, from http://www.ecotippingpoints.org/our-stories/indepth/japan-community-forest-management-silviculture.html.

386. Martin, V. (2010). *"autolife".* Retrieved from http://www.autolife.umd.umich.edu/Environment/E_Overview/E_Overview4.htm.

387. *Massive Greenhouse Gases May Be Released As Destruction, Drying Of World Wetlands Worsen.* (2008, 7 21). Retrieved 9 17, 2018, from ScienceDaily: www.sciencedaily.com/releases/2008/07/080720150209.htm

388. Mathur, N., Bhatnagar, P., Nagar, P., & Bijarnia, M. (2005, 5). Mutagenicity assessment of effluents from textile/dye industries of Sanganer, Jaipur (India): a case study. *Ecotoxicology and Environmental safety, 61*(1), 105-113. Retrieved 9 5, 2018, from https://www.sciencedirect.com/science/article/pii/S0147651304001307

389. Maysonet, C. (2011, 12 26). *Water pollution due to solid wastes.* Retrieved from https://enciclopediapr.org/en/encyclopedia/water-pollution-due-to-solid-wastes/

390. McCarthy, J. (2017, 11 2). *Global Citizen.* Retrieved from https://www.globalcitizen.org/en/content/6-natural-resources-exploited-on-earth/

391. McClintock, & Cynthia. (1989). Peru's Sendero Luminoso Rebellion: Origins and Trajectory . In *Power and Popular Protest: Latin American Social Movements.* Berkley, California: University of California Press.

392. McGee, K., Doukas, M., Kessler, R., & Gerlach, T. (1997). Retrieved 12 06, 2014, from http://pubs.usgs.gov/of/1997/of97-262/of97-262.html.

393. Mckinney, M. (2002). Urbanization, Biodiversity, and Conservation. *BioScience*, 883-890. doi:10.1641/0006-3568(2002)052[0883:UBAC]2.0.CO;2

394. Mcmanus, J., Rodolfo , B., & Cleto , L. (1997). Effects of Some Destructive Fishing Methods on Coral Cover and Potential Rates of Recovery. *Environmental Management, 21*(1), 69–78. Retrieved 8 28, 2018, from file:///C:/Users/siva/Desktop/s002679900006.pdf

395. McMichael, A. (2003). *Climate change and human health. Risk and responses.* Geneva: WHO.

396. Mcnally, A., Verdin, K., Harrison, L., Getirana, A., Jacob, J., Shukla, S., . . . Verdin, J. (2019). Acute Water-Scarcity Monitoring for Africa. *Water, 11*(10), 1968. doi:10.3390/w11101968

397. Mega, E. (2017, 11 17). Retrieved 8 28, 2018, from Scientific American: https://www.scientificamerican.com/article/amazon-gold-rush-continues-to-destroy-peru-rsquo-s-rain-forest/

398. Mekonnen , M., & Hoekstra , A. (2016). Four billion people facing severe water scarcity. *Sci Adv., 2*, e1500323.

399. Metcalf, & Eddy. (1995). *Wastewater Engineering Treatment, Disposal and Reuse.* New York: McGraw-Hill.

400. Metha, P. (2015). *"economicsdiscussion.net"*. Retrieved 02 2016, from http://www.economicsdiscussion.net/essays/measures-to-control-population-of-india/2249

401. Michalopoulos, C., Tzamtzis, N., & Liodakis, S. (2016, 2). Groundwater Contamination Due to Activities of an Intensive Hog Farming Operation Located on a Geologic Fault in East Mediterranean: A Study on COD, BOD5 and Microbial Load. *Bulletin of Environmental Contamination and Toxicology, 96*(2), 229–234. Retrieved 11 6, 2018

402. Mitchell , D. (2011). *Biofuels in Africa: Opportunities, Prospects and Challenges.* Washington DC: The World Bank.

403. Miteva , D., Loucks , C., & Pattanayak , S. (2015, 07 01). Social and Environmental Impacts of Forest Management Certification in Indonesia. *PLoS One, 10*(07). doi:10.1371/journal.pone.0129675. eCollection 2015.

404. Mohammed, I., & Butswat, I. (2005). Trend of Vegetation Decline in the Adjoining Forest of Yankari Game Reserve, Bauchi State. *International Journal of Environmental Issue., 3*(2), 120-121.

405. Mohankumar, S., & Kottaiveeran, K. (2011). *International Journal of Pharmaceutical & Biological Archives , 2*(6), 1621-1626.

406. Mohiuddin, K., Ogawa, Y., Zakir, H., Otomo, K., & Shikazono, N. (2011). Heavy metals contamination in water and sediments of an urban river in a developing country. *Int. J. Environ. Sci. Tech., 8*(4), 723-736. Retrieved 9 5, 2018, from https://link.springer.com/article/10.1007/BF03326257

407. Moiwo, J., Yang, Y., Li, H., Han, S., & Yang, Y. (2010, 10 15). Impact of water resource exploitation on the hydrology and water storage in Baiyangdian Lake. *Hydrological Process, 24*(21), 3026-3039. doi:https://doi.org/10.1002/hyp.7716

408. Moore, M., Gould, P., & Keary, B. (2003). Global urbanization and impact on health. *International Journal of Hygiene and Environmental Health, 206*(4-5), 269.

409. Morisset, V., Ahluwalia, J., Nagy, I., & Urban, L. (2001). Possible mechanisms of cannabinoid-induced antinociception in the spinal cord. *Eur J Pharmacol, 429*, 93–100.

410. Mujeeb, W. (2017, 7 23). *universityacademia.com*. Retrieved 9 15, 2018, from http://universityacademia.com/kalabagh-dam-energy-crisis/

411. Muneera, M., & Kaleel, M. (2016). Emerging challenges of urbanization: a case study of Kalmunai municipal area in Ampara district. *World Scientific News, 59*, 35-51. Retrieved from http://www.worldscientificnews.com/wp-content/uploads/2016/06/WSN-59-2016-35-51-2.pdf

412. Munton, D. (1997). Acid Rain and Transboundary Air Quality in Canadian-American Relations. *American Review of Canadian Studies, 27*(03), 327-358. Retrieved 07 30, 2022, from https://doi.org/10.1080/02722019709481554

413. Muthukuda Arachchi, K. (2012). *Air Quality*. [ppt.], Central Enviornmental Authority, Environmental Pollution Control Division, Battaramulla, Sri Lanka.

414. Myhre, G., Shindell, D., Bréon, F., Collins, W., Fuglestvedt, J., Huang, J., . . . al., e. (2013). Anthropogenic and Natural Radiative Forcing. In *Climate Change 2013: The Physical Science Basis. Contribution of Working Group I to the Fifth Assessment Report of the Intergovernmental Panel on Climate Change.* Cambridge, UK; New York, NY, USA: Intergovernmental Panel on Climate Change.

415. "www.humansociety.org" (n.d.). Retrieved 10 9, 2018, from: http://www.humanesociety.org/assets/pdfs/legislation/gafs_manure.pdf

416. "eanet.asia" (n.d.). Retrieved 7 11, 2018, from: http://www.eanet.asia/product/e_learning/page1_2.html

417. Nabuurs, G. J., Masera, O., Andrasko, K., Benitez-Ponce, P., Boer, R., Dutschke, M., . . . al., e. (2007). *Forestry.In Climate Change 2007: Mitigation. Contribution of Working Group III*

to the Fourth Assessment Report of the Intergovernmental Panel on Climate Change. Cambridge and NY: Cambridge University Press.

418. *NASA Global Climate change.* (n.d.). Retrieved 2018, from https://climate.nasa.gov/vital-signs/ice-sheets/

419. Nascimento, M., Rocha, G., & Andrade, J. (2017, 5 23). Pesticides in fine airborne particles: from a green analysis method to atmospheric characterization and risk assessment. *Sci Rep., 7*(2267). doi:10.1038/s41598-017-02518-1

420. Nasution, M., Afriani, A., & Erwinsyah. (2014). Indonesian Palm Oil Industry in Supporting Energy Securities in Indonesia. *International Conference on Economics, Energy, Environment and Agricultural Sciences.* Kuala Lumpur, Malaysia: PAK publishing group.

421. NBSS&LUP. (2004). *National Bureau of Soil Survey & Land Use Planning Soil Map (1:1 Million scale).* Nagpur, India.

422. Nicholson, C., Blake , R., & Lee, D. (1995). Livestock, Deforestation, and Policy Making: Intensification of Cattle Production Systems in Central America (Revisited). *Journal of Dairy Science, 78*(3), 719–734.

423. *Nitrous oxide emission.* (2015). Retrieved 5 5, 2015, from http://epa.gov/climatechange/ghgemissions/gases/n2o.html

424. Nixon, A., & Curran, T. (1998, 9 30). *publications.gc.ca.* (Parliamentary Research Branch) Retrieved 10 15, 2019, from http://publications.gc.ca/Collection-R/LoPBdP/CIR/7937-e.htm#ISSUE

425. Noaa's Greenhouse Gas Index Up 40 Percent Since 1990. (2017). Retrieved 10 4, 2017, from http://www.noaa.gov/news/noaa-s-greenhouse-gas-index-up-40-percent-since-1990

426. Norén, A. (2016, 9 12). Don't heat me up. Retrieved 8 15, 2018, from https://blog.nus.edu.sg/dontheatmeup/2016/09/12/causes-of-thermal-water-pollution-deforestation-and-soil-erosion/

427. Norton , T. (1996). Conserving biological diversity in Australia's temperate eucalypt forests. *For Ecol Manage, 85*, 21-33.

428. NRC. (1996). *Aerosol Radiative Forcing and Climate Change.* National Research Council. Washington, D.C.: National Academy Press.

429. Nuccitelli, D. (2013, 5 16). Survey finds 97% of climate science papers agree warming is man-made. *The Guardian.* Retrieved 9 27, 2018, from The Guardian: https://www.theguardian.com/environment/climate-consensus-97-per-cent/2013/may/16/climate-change-scienceofclimatechange

430. Obi, F., Ugwuishiwu, B., & Nwakaire, J. (2016, 10). Agriculturalwaste concept, generation, utilization and management. *Nigerian Journal of Technology (NIJOTECH), 35*(4), 957–964. doi:https://www.ajol.info/index.php/njt/article/view/145135

431. Ocean Acidification Summary for Policymakers. (2013). *Third Symposium on the Ocean in a High-CO2 World.* Stockholm, Sweden: International Geosphere-Biosphere Programme. Retrieved 1 2018

432. Odihi, J. (1993). *Deforestation in Afforestation in NE semi-arid zone of Nigeria: policy contradiction or government propaganda?*

433. OECD (2011). *OECD Green growth studies: Energy.* Retrieved 11 5, 2019, from https://www.oecd.org/greengrowth/greening-energy/49157219.pdf

434. Oghenerobor, B., Gladys, O., & Tomilola, D. (2014). Heavy Metal Pollutants in Wastewater Effluents: Sources, Effects and Remediation. *Advances in Bioscience and Bioengineering, 2*(4), 37-43.

435. Oh, E., Edgar, G., Kirkpatrick, J., Stuart-Smith, R., & Barrett, N. (2015). Broad-scale impacts of salmon farms on temperate macroalgal assemblages on rocky reefs. *Marine Pollution Bulletin, 98*(1-2), 201-209. Retrieved 10 31, 2018, from https://www.sciencedirect.com/science/article/pii/S0025326X15004166?via%3Dihub

436. Ohimain, E. (2003). Environmental Impacts of oil mining activities in the Niger Delta Mangrove Ecosystem. *8th International Congress on Mine Water & the Environment.* Johannesburg: South Africa. Retrieved 9 17, 2018, from https://www.imwa.info/docs/imwa_2003/imwa_2003_503-517.pdf

437. Oki, T., & Kanae, S. (2006). Global hydrological cycles and world water resources. *Science, 313*, 1068–72.

438. Olivier, J., Janssens-Maenhout, G., Muntean, M., & Jeroen, P. (2013). *Trends in global CO2 emissions: 2013 Report.* PBL Netherlands Environmental Assessment Agency.

439. Oloruntoba, E., Ademola, R., Sridhar, M., Agbola, S., Omokhodion, F., Ana, G., & Alabi, T. (2012). Urban environmental noise pollution and perceived health effects in Ibadan, Nigeria. *African Journal Biomedical Research, 15*(2), 77-84. Retrieved 8 21, 2018, from https://www.researchgate.net/publication/286761717_Urban_environmental_noise_pollution _and_perceived_health_effects_in_Ibadan_Nigeria

440. Ong, J. (1995). The ecology of mangrove conservation and management. *Hydrobiologia, 295*, 343–351.

441. Ong, J. (2003). Plants of the Merbok mangrove, Kedah, Malaysia and the urgent need for their conservation. *Folia Malaysiana, 4*, 1-18.

442. Ophardt, C. (2003). *Acid Rain Effects on Forests.* Retrieved from http://chemistry.elmhurst.edu/vchembook/196forests.html

443. Oppenlander, R. (2014, 11 26). *comfortablyunaware.com.* Retrieved 8 30, 2018, from http://comfortablyunaware.com/blog/freshwater-depletion-realities-of-choice/

444. orano.group. (n.d.). (Orano) Retrieved 03 10, 2023, from https://www.orano.group/en/unpacking-nuclear/7-good-reasons-for-turning-to-nuclear-power-to-combat-global-warming

445. Osman , K. (2014). *Soil degradation, conservation and remediation.* Springer .

446. Otegbeye, G. (2003). Development of Apisilviculture for poverty alleviation: A Case Study of Katsina State of Nigeria. *A paper presented at Annual Conference ofNigeria Statistical Association*, (pp. 48-53).

447. Owens, B. (2019, 08 13). *"The Narwhal Logo".* Retrieved from "thenarwhal.ca": https://thenarwhal.ca/acid-rain-not-over-yet-tiny-shrimp/

448. Oyeniyi, N. (2000). Improved Small Scale Irrigation and Agricultural Changes in Kano. In J. Falola, K. Ahmed, M. Liman, & A. Maiwada, *Issues in Land Administration and Development in Northern Nigeria.* Department of Geography Bayero University Kano.

449. *Ozone Depletion.* (2015). (Sunny Levin institute) Retrieved 4 3, 2015, from Globalization 101: http://www.globalization101.org/ozone-depletion/

450. Palatinus, A., Centa, M., Viršek, M., & Peterlin, M. (2018). Analysis of microplastic pollution in Slovenian watercourses and lakes. *Sixth International Marine Debris Conference, Plastic pollution in fresh water environment of the world.* Retrieved 9 4, 2018, from http://internationalmarinedebrisconference.org/index.php/plastic-debris-pollution-in-freshwater-environments-of-the-world/

451. Pansuk, J., Junpen, A., & Garivait, S. (2018, 7 20). Assessment of Air Pollution from Household SolidWaste Open Burning in Thailand. *Sustainabi;ity.* Retrieved 10 11, 2018, from https://www.researchgate.net/publication/326550627_Assessment_of_Air_Pollution_from_Household_Solid_Waste_Open_Burning_in_Thailand

452. Parry, M., Canziani, O., Palutikof, J., & van der Linden, P. (2007). *Impacts, Adaptation and Vulnerability. Contribution of Working Group II to the Fourth Assessment Report of the Intergovernmental Panel on Climate Change.* Cambridge, UK: Cambridge University Press.

453. Parry, M., Canziani, O., Palutikof, J., Linden, P., & Hanson, C. (2007). *Impacts, Adaptation and Vulnerability. Contribution of Working Group II to the Fourth Assessment Report of the Intergovernmental Panel on Climate Change.* Cambridge, UK: Campridge university press.

454. Partanen, A., Dunne, E., Bergman, T., Laakso, A., Kokkola, H., Ovadnevaite, J., . . . Korhonen, H. (2014). Global modelling of direct and indirect effects of sea spray aerosol using a source function encapsulating wave state. *Atmos. Chem. Phys., 14*, 11731–11752.

455. Pathak, H., & Pathak, D. (2012, 6 22). Eutrophication: Impact of Excess Nutrient Status in Lake Water Ecosystem. *J Environ Anal Toxicol, 2*, 148. doi:10.4172/2161-0525.1000148

456. Pathak, V., & Kushwaha, B. (2013, 2). Study of air pollution at municipal solid waste dumping Site Satna. *Indian Journal of Environmental Protection, 33*(2), 159-164. Retrieved 10 11, 2018

457. Patric, J. K. (2014). Retrieved 12 07, 2014, from http://news.discovery.com/earth/weather-extreme-events/sahara-desert-dust-blows-across-atlantic-to-americas-140707.htm.

458. Paul , H. (1993). *The Third Revolution.* England: Clays, St. Ives.

459. Pearce, F. (2017, 6 24). Billion-dollar dams are making water shortages, not solving them. *New Scientiest.* Retrieved 10 7, 2018, from https://www.newscientist.com/article/2134785-billion-dollar-dams-are-making-water-shortages-not-solving-them/

460. Pearson, E., & Frangipane, E. (1973). Marine pollution and marine waste disposal. *Proceedings of second international congress San Remo.* Pergamm on press. Retrieved from https://books.google.lk/books?id=DRbLBAAAQBAJ&pg=PA211&lpg=PA211&dq=surfactant+pollutants+on+marine+fish&source=bl&ots=LjydilUua2&sig=UTXzpaq5w-2kJ-TYjRxM2Skpo7Q&hl=ta&sa=X&ei=5cwYVeWFHpC1uAT46oDIDg&ved=0CDYQ6AEwBA#v=onepage&q=surfactant%20pollutants%20on

461. Pendergrast, N. (2015). Live Animal Export, Humane Slaughter and Media Hegemony. *Animal Studies, 4*(1), 99-125. Retrieved 8 29, 2018, from https://pdfs.semanticscholar.org/6e62/965b18d5864b3c690b15aaff5a677e471756.pdf

462. Perera, F. (2018). Pollution from Fossil-Fuel Combustion is the Leading Environmental Threat to Global Pediatric Health and Equity: Solutions Exist. *International Journal of Environmental Research and Public Health, 15*(1), 16. doi:10.3390/ijerph15010016

463. Perera, F. (2018, 1). Pollution from Fossil-Fuel Combustion is the Leading Environmental Threat to Global Pediatric Health and Equity: Solutions Exist. *Int J Environ Res Public Health., 15*(1), 16. doi:10.3390/ijerph15010016

464. Perrier de la Bâthie. (1921). *La Végétation Malgache Marseille: Musée Colonial.*

465. USEPA (2007). *Pesticides.* USEPA. Retrieved 6 8, 2014, from http://www.epa.gov/opp00001/pestsales/07pestsales/usage2007.ht

466. Peterson, & Tilling. (2000). Retrieved 2022, from https://d32ogoqmya1dw8.cloudfront.net/files/getsi/teaching_materials/volcanic_hazards/unit_2_prereading_day_2-_lava_diver.pdf

467. Pieterse , A., & Murphy , K. (1990). The Ecology and Management of Nuisance Aquatic Vegetation. In *Aquatic Weeds.* New York.: Oxford University Press.

468. Pimentel, D., Cooperstein, S., Randell, H., Filiberto, D., Sorrentino, S., Kaye, B., . . . Weinstein, C. (2007). Ecology of Increasing Diseases: Population Growth and Environmental Degradation. *Hum Ecol., 35*, 653–668. doi:10.1007/s10745-007-9128-3

469. Pinto, V. (2008). E-waste hazard: The impending challenge. *Indian J Occup Environ Med., 12*(2), 65–70. doi:10.4103/0019-5278.43263

470. Pires, N., Muniz, D., Kisaka, T., Simplicio, N., Bortoluzzi, L., Lima, J., & Oliveira-Filho, E. (2015, 9). Impacts of the Urbanization Process on Water Quality of Brazilian Savanna Rivers: The Case of Preto River in Formosa, Goiás State, Brazil. (M. Scholz, Ed.) *Int J Environ Res Public Health, 12*(9), 10671–10686. doi:10.3390/ijerph120910671

471. EC (2011). *Plastic Waste: Ecological and Human Health Impacts.* Science for Environment Policy Newsw Service. Director General of Envirnment Policy, European Commission. Retrieved 12 06, 2014, from http://ec.europa.eu/environment/integration/research/newsalert/pdf/IR1_en.pdf.

472. Platt, J. R. (2014, 2 24). *Scientific American.* Retrieved from https://blogs.scientificamerican.com/extinction-countdown/crisis-in-madagascar-90-percent-of-lemur-species-are-threatened-with-extinction/

473. Pletcher, K. (2016). *"www.britannica.com".* Retrieved 02 2016, from http://www.britannica.com/topic/one-child-policy

474. Polidoro, B., Carpenter, K., Collins, L., Duke, N., Ellison, A., Ellison, J., & al., e. (2010). The Loss of Species: Mangrove Extinction Risk and Geographic Areas of Global Concern. *PLoS ONE, 5*(4), e10095. Retrieved from https://doi.org/10.1371/journal.pone.0010095

475. Polunin. (1994). *Population and Global Security.* Cambridge University Press(Ed.).

476. Poole, G., & Berman, C. (2001). An ecological perspective on in-stream temperature: Natural heat dynamics and mechanisms of human-caused thermal degradation. *Environmental management, 27*(6), 787-802.

477. Pottinger, L. (2009). *How Dams Affect Water Supply.* Retrieved from International Rivers: https://www.internationalrivers.org/resources/how-dams-affect-water-supply-1727

478. Prado, G., & Ribeiro, H. (2011, 7). Grassification of the Amazon region and meat consumption: what is behind? *Saude soc., 20*(3). doi:http://dx.doi.org/10.1590/S0104-12902011000300017

479. US EIA (2014). *Primary Energy Consumption by Source and Sector.* Washington, DC, USA: U.S. Energy Information Administration.

480. Qin, B., Zhu, G., Gao, G., Zhang, Y., Li, W., Paerl, H., & Carmichael, W. (2010, 1). A Drinking Water Crisis in Lake Taihu, China: Linkage to Climatic Variability and Lake Management. *Environmental Management, 45*(1), 105–112. Retrieved 9 10, 2018, from https://link.springer.com/article/10.1007/s00267-009-9393-6

481. Rabalais, N., Turner, R., Díaz, R., & Justić, D. (2009). Global change and eutrophication of coastal waters. *ICES Journal of Marine Science, 66*, 1528–1537. Retrieved 9 10, 2018, from https://academic.oup.com/icesjms/article/66/7/1528/656749

482. Rain, D., Long, J., & Ratcliffe, M. (2007). Measuring Population Pressure on the Landscape: Comparative GIS Studies in China, India, and the United States. *Population and Environment, 28*(6), 321-336. Retrieved 03 21, 2022, from https://www.jstor.org/stable/27504004

483. Ramachandra , T., & Saira Varghese , K. (2004). Environmentally sound option for e-waste management. *Envis Journal of Human Settlements.* Retrieved 12 2013, from http://www.ces.iisc.ernet.in/energy/paper/ewaste/ewaste.html#5.

484. Rappaport, J., & Sachs , J. (2003). The United States as a coastal nation. *J. Econ. Growth, 8*, 5–46.

485. Raposo, M., Pinto-Gomes, C., & Nunes, L. (2020). Intensive Agricultural Practices as Enhancers of the Dispersion of Invasive Species: Notification of the Observation of a Case with Robinia pseudoacacia L. in Alentejo (Southern Portugal). *Research in Ecology, 2*(3), 42-49. doi:https://doi.org/10.30564/re.v2i3.2399

486. Ray, T. (2004a). Theory, selection and design of air pollution control equipment. *Air pollution Control in Industries, 1.*

487. Ray, T. (2004b). Application of air pollution control equipment. *Air pollution Control in Industries, 2.*

488. Repetto, R., & Holmes, T. (1983). The Role of Population in Resource Depletion in Developing Countries. *Population and Development Review, 9*(4), 609. doi:10.2307/1973542

489. (2000). *Resolving Environmental Conflicts in communities.* U.S. EPA.

490. Richards, P., & VanWey, L. (2015, 7 20). Where Deforestation Leads to Urbanization: How Resource Extraction is Leading to Urban Growth in the Brazilian Amazon. *Ann Assoc Am Geogr., 105*(4), 806–823. doi:10.1080/00045608.2015.1052337

491. Richter, M. (2000). The Ecological Crisis in Chiapas: A Case Study from Central America. *Mountain Research and Development, 20*(4), 332-339. Retrieved 04 05, 2022, from https://doi.org/10.1659/0276-4741(2000)020[0332:TECICA]2.0.CO;220

492. Ricke, K., Orr, J., Schneider, K., & Caldeira, K. (2013). Risks to coral reefs from ocean carbonate chemistry changes in recent earth system model projections. *Environmental Research Letters, 8*. doi:10.1088/1748-9326/8/3/034003

493. Rinkesh. (2016). *"what is the Energy Crisis? Conserve-energy-future.com "*. Retrieved 02 2016, from http://www.conserve-energy-future.com/causes-and-solutions-to-the-global-energy-crisis.php

494. Ritchie, H., & Roser, M. (2018). *"Plastic Pollution"*. Retrieved 11 16, 2018, from "our world in data": https://ourworldindata.org/plastic-pollution#global-plastic-production

495. Ritchie, H., & Roser, M. (2021). *Our World in Data*. Retrieved 07 10, 2022, from https://ourworldindata.org/forests-and-deforestation

496. Robbins, R. (2000). *The Political Economy of Twinkies: An Inquiry into the Real Cost of Things*. Retrieved 2005, from http://faculty.plattsburgh.edu/richard.robbins/political_economy_of_twinkies.

497. Robock, A., & Toon, O. (2012). Self-Assured Destruction: The Climate Impacts of Nuclear War. *68*(5), 66–74.

498. Ron Brecher. (2003). *Peroxyacetyl Nitrate (PAN)*. Retrieved 12 7, 2014, from http://www.hazmatmag.com/features/peroxyacetyl-nitrate-pan

499. Rosero-Bixby, L., & Palloni, A. (1998, 11). Population and Deforestation in Costa Rica. *Population and Environment, 20*(2), 149–185. Retrieved 10 22, 2018, from https://link.springer.com/article/10.1023/A:1023319327838

500. RSPO . (2011). Promoting the Growth and use of sustainable palm oil. *Roundtable on Sustainable Palm Oil*. Zurich.

501. Ruddiman, W. (2001). *Earth's Climate: Past and Future*. New York: W.H. Freeman & Sons.

502. Ruis, B. (n.d.). *Global Conservations Related to Forests...* Forestry Department, FAO Corporative Document Repository, Netherlands. Retrieved 11 25, 2014, from http://www.fao.org/docrep/003/y1237e/y1237e03.htm.

503. Ryder, G. (2017). *The United Nations world water development report.* Fontenoy, 75352 Paris 07 SP, France: United Nations Educational, Scientific and Cultural Organization. Retrieved 10 22, 2019, from https://unesdoc.unesco.org/ark:/48223/pf0000247153

504. Saad, A., Shariff, N., & Gairola, S. (2011, october). Nature and causes of land degradation and desertification in Libya: Need for sustainable land management. *African Journal of Biotechnology, 10*(63), 13680-13687. doi:10.5897/AJB11.1235

505. Saenger, P., Hegerl, E., & Davie, J. (1983). Global status of mangrove ecosystems. *The Environmentalist, 3.*

506. Saikawa, E., Prinn, R., Dlugokencky, E., Ishijima, K., Dutton, G., Hall, B., & Langenfelds, R. (2014). Global and regional emissions estimates for N2O. *Atmos. Chem. Phys., 14*, 4617–4641.

507. Salm, R. (1981). *Coastal resources in Sri Lanka, India and Pakistan: Description, use and management.* USA: U.S. Fish and Wildlife Service, International Affairs Office.

508. Salwa , M., Sara , A., Samia , H., Abdalla , E., Manal , Y., Samia , A., & Hala , E. (2016, 4 16). Heavy Metals Contaminants in Water and Fish from Four Different Sources in Sudan. *Journal of Infectious Diseases & Therapy, 4*, 275. doi:10.4172/2332-0877.1000275

509. Sanderfoot, O., & Holloway, T. (2017, 8 11). Air pollution impacts on avian species via inhalation exposure and associated outcomes. *Environmental Research Letters, 12*(8). Retrieved 12 31, 2018, from http://iopscience.iop.org/article/10.1088/1748-9326/aa8051/meta

510. Sattiraju, N. (2017, 3 21). *Yourstory.* Retrieved 8 30, 2018, from https://yourstory.com/2017/03/ignored-side-cauvery-debate/

511. Schneider, J. (2014). *Factory Farms, Fouled Waters: How Industrial Livestock Operations Pollute.* Environment Illinois research and Education Centre. Retrieved 9 6, 2018, from https://environmentillinois.org/sites/environment/files/reports/IL_FactoryFarms_web%20version.pdf

512. Schuyt, K. (2005). Economic consequences of wetland degradation for local populations in Africa. *Ecological Economics, 53* , 177 – 190. Retrieved from https://tarwi.lamolina.edu.pe/~corihuela/metodologia/lectura2_Schuyt(2005).pdf

513. Schwartz, D., & Singh, A. (1999). *Environmental Conditions, Resources, and Conflicts: An Introductory Overview and Data Collection.* UNEP.

514. *scientific american.* (2018). (SCIENTIFIC AMERICAN, A DIVISION OF SPRINGER NATURE AMERICA, INC) Retrieved 7 30, 2018, from scientificamerican.com: https://www.scientificamerican.com/article/deforestation-and-orangutans/

515. Semait, B. W. (1989). Ecology and politics: environmental stress and security in Africa. (p. 43). Scandinavian Institute of African Studies.

516. Seyam, I., Hoekstra, A., Ngabirano, G., & Savenije , H. (2001). The value of freshwater wetlands in the Zambezi Basin. *Proceedings of the AWRA/IWLRIUniversity of Dundee International Specialty Conference.* Dundee, UK.

517. Sharma, D. (2016). Impact of dams on river water quality. *International Journal of Current Advanced Research, 4.* Retrieved 10 6, 2018, from http://journalijcar.org/issues/impact-dams-river-water-quality

518. Sharma, S. (2008). Influence of Sea Water Ingress: A Case Study from East Coast Aquifer in India. *20th Salt Water Intrusion Meeting*, (pp. 250-253). Naples, Florida, USA. Retrieved 11 25, 2018, from http://swim-site.nl/pdf/swim20/file269-272.pdf

519. Shen, T. (1981). Control Techniques for Gas Emissions from Hazardous Waste Landfills. *Journal of the Air Pollution Control Association, 31*(2), 132-135. doi:10.1080/00022470.1981.10465200

520. Shine, K., Derwent, R., Wuebbles, D., & Morcrette, J. (2001). *Radiative Forcing of Climate.* IPCC. Retrieved 5 5, 2015, from https://www.ipcc.ch/ipccreports/far/wg_I/ipcc_far_wg_I_chapter_02.pdf

521. Singal, S. (2005). *Noise Pollution and Control Strategy.* Oxford, UK.: Alpha Science International Ltd.

522. Singh, A., & Agrawal, M. (2008). Acid rain and its ecological consequences. *Journal of Environmental Biology, 29*(1), 15-24. Retrieved 07 19, 2019, from https://pdfs.semanticscholar.org/e8f3/fa4f3badf2fa98e0a434266aaa3d7c796f98.pdf

523. Singh, A., & Narayanan, K. (2015). Agriculture intensification,population growth and cropland expansion: evidence frompost-Green Revolution Andhra Pradesh. *Forum for Global Knowledge Sharing.*

524. Singh, K. (1993). The 1990 tropical forest resources assessment. *Unasylva, 44*(174), 10-19.

525. Singh, R., Prasad, A., Chauhan, S., & Singh, S. (2015, 12). Impact of growing urbanization and air pollution on the regional climate over India. *INTERNATIONAL ASSOCIATION FOR URBAN CLIMATE*(14). Retrieved from http://home.iitk.ac.in/~ramesh/publications_pdf/Pages%205-11%20from%20IAUC014.pdf

526. Sivakumar, S. (2013, 6). Reclamation of Land and Improve Water Productivity of Jaffna Peninsula of Northern Sri Lanka by Improving the Water Quality of the Lagoons. *RJSITM, 2*(8). Retrieved 8 29, 2018, from https://www.researchgate.net/publication/247160827_Reclamation_of_Land_and_Improve_

Water_Productivity_of_Jaffna_Peninsula_of_Northern_Sri_Lanka_by_Improving_the_Wate
r_Quality_of_the_Lagoons

527. Sivaramanan, S., & Kotagama, S. (2018). Characterization, classification and abundance of
beah waste in selected locations of the coastal belt of Colombo district. *4th international
conferance of Marine Environmental Protection Authority* . Colombo, Sri Lanka: MEPA.

528. Sivaramanan, S., & Kotagama, S. W. (2022). Investigation into the Interconnected Nature of
Environmental Problems and Identifying Keystone Environmental Problems. *Current
Scientia (Vidyodaya journal of Science), 25* (02), 81-104.

529. Smith, P., Martino, D., Cai, Z., Gwary, D., & Janzen, H. (2007). Agriculture. In B. Metz, O.
Davidson, P. Bosch, R. Dave, & L. Meyer, *Climate Change 2007: Mitigation. Contribution
of Working Group III to the Fourth Assessment Report of the Intergovernmental Panel on
Climate Change.* Cambridge, United Kingdom and New York, NY, USA. : Cambridge
University Press.

530. Song, J., Webb, A., Parmenter, B., Allen, D., & McDonald-Buller, E. (2008). The Impacts of
Urbanization on Emissions and Air Quality: Comparison of Four Visions of Austin, Texas.
Environ. Sci. Technol., 42(19), 7294–7300. doi:10.1021/es800645j

531. Sonoda, H. (2007). *Kukule Ganga Hydroelectric Power Project.* jica. Retrieved 7 26, 2018,
from
https://www.jica.go.jp/english/our_work/evaluation/oda_loan/post/2008/pdf/e_project07_full
.pdf

532. Sonter, L., Herrera, D., Barrett, D., Galford, G., Moran, C., & Soares.Filho, B. (2017, 10 18).
Mining drives extensive deforestation in the Brazilian Amazon. *Nature Communications, 8.*
Retrieved 11 9, 2018, from https://www.nature.com/articles/s41467-017-00557-w

533. Souza Mazza, V., Gama Madruga, L., Ávila, L., Perlin, A., Machado, E., & Duarte, T. (2014,
9). Management of solid wastes on farms in the State of Rio Grande do Sul, Brazil. *Revista
em Agronegocio e Meio Ambiente, 7*(3), 683-706. Retrieved 10 9, 2018, from
https://www.researchgate.net/publication/287608174_Management_of_solid_wastes_on_far
ms_in_the_State_of_Rio_Grande_do_Sul_Brazil

534. Sowers, J., Vengosh, A., & Weinthal, E. (2011). Climate change, water resources, and the
politics of adaptation in the Middle East and North Africa. *Climate change, 104*, 599-627.

535. Stapleton, R. (2016). *Visual Pollution*. Retrieved 11 2, 2018, from
http://www.pollutionissues.com/Ve-Z/Visual-Pollution.html

536. Starr, J. R. (1991). Water Wars. *Foreign Policy, 82*, 24.

537. Sukumar, R., Baskaran, N., Dharmrajan, G., Roy, M., Suresh, H., & Narendran, K. (2003). *Study of the elephants in Buxa Tiger Reserve and adjoining areas in northern West Bengal and preparation of Conservation Action Plan.* Bangalore: Center for Ecological Sciences, Indian Institute of Science.

538. Swan, S., Main, K., Liu, F., Stewart, S., Kruse, R., Calafat, A., . . . Teague, J. (2005). Decrease in anogenital distance among male infants with prenatal phthalate exposure. *Environmental Health Perspectives, 113*(8), 1056-1061.

539. Taft, H. (2015). Water Scarcity. In *Food, Energy, and Water.* doi:10.1016/B978-0-12-800211-7.00016-8

540. TAMS/USAID. (1980). *Environmental Assessment of Accelerated Mahaweli Development Programme.* New York, USA.

541. Tang , F., Lenzen, M., & McBrat, A. (2021). Risk of pesticide pollution at the global scale. *Nature Geoscience.* doi:DOI: 10.1038/s41561-021-00712-5

542. Tardiff, R. (1992). *Methods to Assess Adverse Effects of Pesticides on Non-target Organisms, scope-49.* Scientific Group on Methodologies for the Safety Evaluation of Chemicals, International Council of Scientific Unions.

543. *'techwar'.* (n.d.). Retrieved 04 03, 2022, from https://teachwar.wordpress.com/resources/war-justifications-archive/alto-cenepa-war-1995/

544. *The History of Sri Lanka Coffee.* (n.d.). Retrieved 11 2014, from "www.srilankacoffee.com": http://srilankacoffee.com/history1.html

545. FAO (2011). *The state of the world's land and water resources for food and agriculture (SOLAW): managing systems at risk.* Rome and Earthscan, London: Food and agriculture organization of the United Nations. Retrieved from http://www.fao.org/docrep/017/i1688e/i1688e.pdf

546. Thiruchelvam, S., & Pathmarajah, S. (n.d.). *An Economic Analysis of Salinity Problems in the Mahaweli River System H Irrigation Scheme in Sri Lanka.* Retrieved from http://www.tropicalclimate.org/~mahaweli/RiverBasinMahaweli/projectinfo/reports/mahawelisalinityreport.htm

547. Thuyet , D., Luong-Van, J., & Austin, C. (2012). Impact of Shrimp Farm Effluent on Water Quality in Coastal Areas of the World Heritage-Listed Ha Long Bay. *American Journal of Environmental Sciences, 8*(2), 104-116. Retrieved 9 6, 2018, from http://thescipub.com/pdf/10.3844/ajessp.2012.104.116

548. Tian, H., Gao, J., Lu, L., Zhao, D., Cheng, K., & Qiu, P. (2012). Temporal Trends and Spatial Variation Characteristics of Hazardous Air Pollutant Emission Inventory from

Municipal Solid Waste Incineration in China. *Environ. Sci. Technol., 46*(18), 10364–10371. doi:10.1021/es302343s

549. WB (2010). *Tiger at The Top.* World Bank. Retrieved 8 22, 2012, from http://www.tigersummit.ru/eng/index

550. Timothy , P., Sarah, W., & Sandra, B. (2006). Guide book for the formulation of afforestation and reforestation projects under the clean development mechanism. *International Tropical Timber Organization, Technical Series, 25.*

551. Tiseo, I. (2020). *statista.com.* Retrieved 10 14, 2020, from https://www.statista.com/statistics/501303/volume-of-sulfur-dioxide-emissions-us/

552. Tovilla-Hernandez , C., Espino de la Lanza, G., & Orihuela-Belmonte , D. (2001). Impact of logging on a mangrove swamp in South Mexico: cost/benefit analysis. *Rev Biol Trop, 49,* 571–580.

553. Towers, L. (2015, 9 14). *The Fish Site.* Retrieved 8 29, 2018, from thefishsite.com: https://thefishsite.com/articles/state-of-the-global-market-for-shark-products

554. Towhid, O. (2014). *Soil degradation, conservation and remediation.* Springer .

555. US PHS (2007). *Toxicological Profile for lead.* United States Public Health Service. USA: Agency for Toxic Substances and Disease Registry.

556. U.S.EPA. (1996). *Strategic Plan for the Office of Research and Development.* U.S. Environmental Protection Agency.

557. *UNEP.* (2008, 4 24). Retrieved 9 21, 2018, from http://new.unep.org/Documents.Multilingual/Default.Print.asp?DocumentID=531&ArticleID=5775&l=en

558. UNEP. (2011, 12). *UNEP Global Environmental Alert Service (GEAS).* Retrieved 9 13, 2018, from https://na.unep.net/geas/archive/pdfs/Dec_11_Palm_Plantations.pdf

559. US EPA (2015). *United States—Canada Emissions Cap and Trading Feasibility Study.* US EPA and Trans boundary air issues branch Environment Canada. Retrieved 07 30, 2022, from https://www.epa.gov/sites/default/files/2015-07/documents/emissions_cap_and_trading_feasibility_study.pdf

560. Vale, M., & Houston. (n.d.). *Deforestation and Its Extreme Effect on Global Warming.* Retrieved 10 16, 2018, from Scientific American: https://www.scientificamerican.com/article/deforestation-and-global-warming/

561. Van Birgelen, A. (1998). Hexachlorobenzene as a possible major contributor to the dioxin activity of human milk. *Environ. Health Persp., 106*(11), 683-688.

562. Verhoeven, J., & Setter, T. (2010, 1). Agricultural use of wetlands: opportunities and limitations. *Ann Bot., 105* (1), 155–163. doi: 10.1093/aob/mcp172

563. Verma, R., Vinoda, K., Papireddy, M., & Gowda, A. (2016). Toxic Pollutants from Plastic Waste- A Review. *Procedia Environmental Sciences, 35*, 701-708. Retrieved 03 25, 2019, from https://www.researchgate.net/publication/305892272_Toxic_Pollutants_from_Plastic_Waste-_A_Review

564. Vieira, J., Morales-Hojas, R., Santos , R., & Vieira, C. (2007).

565. Vij, D. (2012). Urbanization and solid waste management in India: Present practices and future challenges. *Procedia - Social and Behavioral Sciences, 37*, 437 – 447. Retrieved 8 25, 2018, from https://www.researchgate.net/publication/257715582_Urbanization_and_Solid_Waste_Management_in_India_Present_Practices_and_Future_Challenges

566. Vosti, S., Braz, E., Carpentier, C., d'Oliveira, M., & Witcover, J. (2003). Rights tofrest products, deforestation and smallholder income: evidence from theWestern Brazilian Amazon. *World Dev., 31*, 1889-1901. doi:https://doi.org/10.1016/j.worlddev.2003.06.001

567. Waduge, S. (2014, 06 12). *"lankaweb.com"*. Retrieved 06 14, 2021, from http://www.lankaweb.com/news/ite ms/2014/06/12/indo-lanka-fishing- dispute-time-for-solutions/

568. Wakeford , R. (2011). And now, Fukushima. *J Radiol Prot, 31*(2), 167–176.

569. Waldman, S. (2017, 7 19). *The U.S. Is Not Ready to Clean Up an Arctic Oil Spill*. Retrieved 9 17, 2018, from Scientific American: https://www.scientificamerican.com/article/the-u-s-is-not-ready-to-clean-up-an-arctic-oil-spill/

570. Waldman, S. (2018, 10 31). *E&E News conservation*. Retrieved 11 3, 2019, from https://www.scientificamerican.com: https://www.scientificamerican.com/article/human-pressures-have-shrunk-wildlife-populations-by-60-percent/

571. Wargo, J. (2009). *Green Intelligence: Creating Environments That Protect Human Health*.

572. FAO (n.d.). *Water at a Glance: the relationship between water, agriculture, food security and poverty*. Rome: Food and Agriculture Organization. Retrieved from http://www.fao.org/nr/water/docs/wataraglance.pdf

573. FAO (2017). *Water for Sustainable Food and Agriculture: A report produced for the G20 Presidency of Germany*. Rome: Food and Agriculture Organization of the United Nations. Retrieved 11 3, 2019, from http://www.fao.org/3/a-i7959e.pdf

574. Wahl, D. C. (2016). Designing Regenerative Cultures invites us to co-create thriving communities. In D. C. Wahl, Designing Regenerative Cultures. UK: Triarchy Press. Retrieved 01 21, 2019

575. Watson, M. (n.d.). *"markswatson.com"*. Retrieved 01 2016, from http://www.markswatson.com/popcontrol.htm

576. Watts, J. (2017, 09 12). Retrieved 07 01, 2021, from "theguardian.com": https://www.theguardian.com/environment/2017/sep/12/third-of-earths-soil-acutely-degraded-due-to-agriculture-study

577. IEA (2016). *Weo-2016 Special Report Energy and Air Pollution.* Paris, France: International Energy Agency (IEA). Retrieved 9 14, 2018, from https://www.iea.org/publications/freepublications/publication/WorldEnergyOutlookSpecialReport2016EnergyandAirPollution.pdf

578. WHO (2006). *WHO Air quality guidelines for particulate matter, ozone, nitrogen dioxide and sulfur dioxide.* WHO.

579. WHO (2014). *Who Indoor Air Quality Guidelines: Household Fuel Combustion.* Geneva, Switzerland: World Health Organization.

580. Wickramasinghe, L., Harris, S., Jones , G., & Jennings, N. (2004, 10). Abundance and Species Richness of Nocturnal Insects on Organic and Conventional Farms: Effects of Agricultural Intensification on Bat Foraging. *Conservation Biology, 18*(5), 1283-1292. Retrieved 11 22, 2018, from https://onlinelibrary.wiley.com/doi/abs/10.1111/j.1523-1739.2004.00152.x

581. Wijesekera, D., Amarasinghe, M., Dassanaike, P., De Silva, T., & Kuruwitaarachchi, N. (2021). Modern Solution for Human Elephant Conflict. *2021 2nd International Conference for Emerging Technology (INCET).* doi:http://dx.doi.org/10.1109/INCET51464.2021.9456214

582. Winemiller, K. O., McIntyre, P. B., Castello, L., Fluet-Chouinard, E., Giarrizzo, T., Nam, S., . . . al., e. (2016, 8 1). Balancing hydropower and biodiversity in the Amazon, Congo, and Mekong. *Science, 351*(6269), pp. 128-129. doi:10.1126/science.aac7082

583. Wondyfraw, M. (2014). Mechanisms and Effects of Acid Rain on Environment. *J Earth Sci Clim Change, 5*(6), 204. doi:10.4172/2157-7617.1000204

584. Wong, C., Li, X., Zhang, G., Qi, S., & Peng, X. (2003, February). Atmospheric deposition of heavy metals in the Pearl River Delta, China. *Atmospheric Environment, 37*(06), 767-776. doi:https://doi.org/10.1016/S1352-2310(02)00929-9

585. Woodward , L. (2016, 2 11). Intensive, corporate agriculture is increasing poverty in Africa. *Ecologist.* Retrieved 11 5, 2018, from https://theecologist.org/2016/feb/11/intensive-corporate-agriculture-increasing-poverty-africa

586. WWF. (2011). *Palm oil: environmental impacts.* World Wildlife Fund.

587. *wwf.panda.org.* (2015). Retrieved 02 04, 2015, from http://wwf.panda.org/about_our_earth/blue_planet/problems/problems_fishing/destructive_fi shing/

588. *wwf.panda.org.* (2015). Retrieved 03 30, 2015, from http://wwf.panda.org/about_our_earth/blue_planet/problems/problems_fishing/fisheries_man agement/

589. Xue-li, C., Ya-lin, C., & Bu-li, C. (2007). Urbanization progress influence upon regional desertification process in semi-arid zone. Retrieved 9 12, 2018, from http://en.cnki.com.cn/Article_en/CJFDTOTAL-GHDL200703000.htm

590. ABS (2002). *Year Book Australia 2002: 2002 Population Distribution.* Canberra: Australian Bureau of Statistics.

591. Yibing Lu, & Hiroaki Yagoh. (2007). *Comparison of Air Pollution and Acid Deposition between Two Mega-Cities.* Retrieved 9 25, 2018, from https://www.eanet.asia/wp-content/uploads/2019/03/Report_5.pdf

592. Yonemoto, K., Gellin , G., & Epstein, W. (1983). Reduction in eumelanin by activation of glutathione reductase and gamma glutamyl transpeptidase after exposure to a depigmenting chemical. *Biochem. Pharmacol., 32,* 1379-82.

593. Yoshida , N., & Kanda , J. (2012). Geochemistry. Tracking the Fukushima radionuclides. *Science, 336*(6085), 1115–1116.

594. Zarfl, C., & et al. (2015). *Aquat. Sci., 77,* 161.

595. Zhang, D., Tan, S., & Gersberg, R. (2010, 8). Municipal solid waste management in China: Status, problems and challenges. *Journal of Environmental Management, 91*(8), 1623-1633. doi:https://doi.org/10.1016/j.jenvman.2010.03.012

596. Zhang, J., & Smith, K. (2003, 12). Indoor air pollution: a global health concern. *British Medical Bulletin, 68*(1), 209–225. Retrieved from https://doi.org/10.1093/bmb/ldg029

597. Zhang, Z., Zimmermann, N., Stenke, A., Li, X., Hodson, E., Zhu, G., . . . Poulter, B. (2017, 9 5). Emerging role of wetland methane emissions in driving 21st century climate change. (W. Lucht, Ed.) *PNAS, 114*(36), 9647-9652. Retrieved 9 20, 2018, from http://www.pnas.org/content/114/36/9647#abstract-2

Appendix

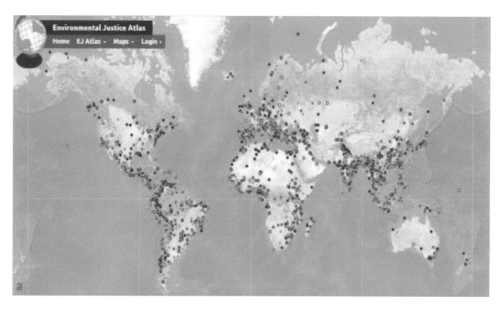

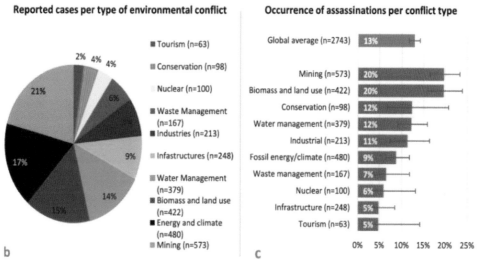

Figure 0.1 Environmental conflicts registered in the EJAtlas and occurrence of assassinations of environmental defenders across conflict types (n = 2743).

a: Geographical coverage of environmental conflicts reviewed here (each dot represents one case). b: Types of conflicts and coverage (pie colours corresponds to the colour of the cases shown in the map). c: Occurrence of assassinations of environmental defenders per conflict type. Error bars are 95% CIs.

Source:(Scheidel, et al., 2020); License: CC- by 1.0

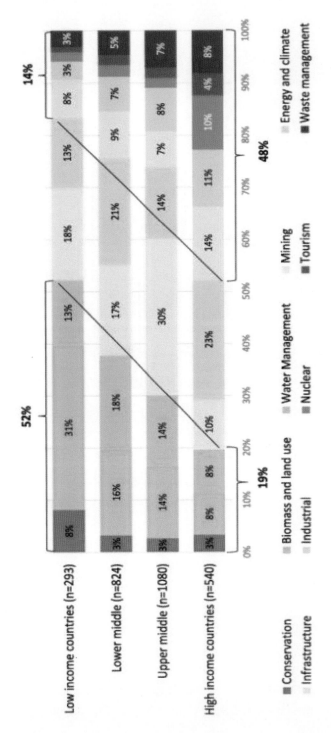

Figure 0.2 Occurrence of types of environmental conflicts across world income regions (n = 2737)

Source:(Scheidel, et al., 2020); License: CC by 1.0

b

c